A Voice of Thunder

A Voice of

Thunder

The Civil War Letters of
George E. Stephens

Edited by Donald Yacovone

University of Illinois Press   *Urbana and Chicago*

This book is printed on acid-free paper.

Library of Congress Cataloging-in-Publication Data
Stephens, George E.
    A voice of thunder : the Civil War letters of George E. Stephens / edited by
Donald Yacovone.
       p.   cm. — (Blacks in the New World)
    Includes bibliographical references and index.
    ISBN 0-252-02245-9 (cloth : alk. paper)
    1. Stephens, George E. 2. United States—History—Civil War, 1861–1865—
Personal narratives. 3. United States. Army. Massachusetts Infantry Regiment,
54th (1863–1865) 4. United States—History—Civil War, 1861–1865—Participa-
tion, Afro-American. 5. United States—History—Civil War, 1861–1865—
Journalists. 6. Afro-Americans—Massachusetts—Biography. 7. Afro-American
journalists—Massachusetts—Biography. I. Yacovone, Donald.
II. Title. III. Series.
E513.5 54th.S74   1997
973.7'415—dc20   95-50194
                                                            CIP

For my father,

Alfred F. Yacovone,

and my wife,

Cory Burke Yacovone

Heaven, as with a voice of thunder,
calls on you to arise from the dust.
—Henry Highland Garnet, "To the Slaves
of the United States of America," 1843

Contents

Maps and Illustrations

Preface

George E. Stephens was the most important black correspondent of the Civil War. A Philadelphia cabinetmaker and abolitionist leader, he chronicled the African-American quest for freedom during the early years of the war and in 1863 became the voice of the famed Fifty-fourth Massachusetts Regiment. His letters, written between 1859 and 1864, thundered against slavery and racism and give us the most penetrating portrait of the black Civil War experience that we are ever likely to find.

Stephens wrote for the *Weekly Anglo-African*, "the mouth-piece of the proscribed American throughout the Northern States." The dominant black newspaper of the 1860s, the *Anglo-African* spoke for and to African Americans. It proclaimed their opposition to slavery, advanced their demands for equality, and documented their lives. During the Civil War, it became the black soldier's paper. "We consider it," one trooper declared, "the most efficient exponent of our ideas, and defender of our rights now in circulation." At the war's end, former slaves in Richmond, Virginia, sent contributions north for the paper's support, and even white reformers such as Lydia Maria Child proudly declared that "I would not do without it."[1]

Reporting for the *Anglo-African* from southern Maryland and eastern Virginia in 1861 and 1862, Stephens detailed the Army of the Potomac's initial encounter with slavery. He recorded the heroism of fugitive slaves and the brutality Union troops inflicted on them. His letters, sometimes reprinted by white newspapers, demolished the Southern myth of the contented slave and proslavery Northern propaganda that blacks could not survive in freedom. Through Stephens, Northern readers obtained a true picture of slavery and its impact on the war.

As a recruiter for the Fifty-fourth Massachusetts Regiment, the first African-American regiment raised in the North, Stephens rallied

Northern blacks to the Union. Although many refused to fight for a "flag which has never meant freedom to them," Stephens insisted that the Emancipation Proclamation—whatever its shortcomings—had made the Union cause and the battle against slavery one.[2] Few could deny the magnitude of the Fifty-fourth's role in the war or in affirming equality. The fate of all African Americans, he held, rested on the regiment's success.

As a noncommissioned officer in the Fifty-fourth, Stephens crafted a gripping account of the momentous 18 July 1863 assault on Battery Wagner, near Charleston, South Carolina. Although the attack failed, the bravery Stephens and his comrades displayed discredited white accusations that blacks could not be effective soldiers. It also cleared the way for the recruitment of almost 180,000 black troops and a Union victory.

Having proven that blacks could be soldiers, Stephens and the Fifty-fourth then battled for the pay of soldiers. Although the War Department originally promised equal pay to black troops, it provided only about half the money given to whites. Stephens recorded the regiment's fierce, eighteen-month battle against this injustice. Endangering themselves and jeopardizing their families, the men of the Fifty-fourth and other black regiments in the Department of the South protested, refusing all pay rather than submit to the government's demeaning offer. The opposition, led by Stephens and his regiment, compelled the federal government to grant equal pay and asserted black claims to full citizenship.

No other work so vividly captures the black soldiers' experience in the war or their principled stand for equal rights. No other collection of documents gives us so personal a view of what it meant to be black in nineteenth-century America.

*   *   *

This book's beginning chapters recount Stephens's life in mid-nineteenth-century Philadelphia, his emergence as a leader of the city's black elite, and his role in the black abolitionist movement. I have tried to show how he reflected African-American sentiment during the epoch of the Civil War and the ways he helped shape the black response to the greatest crisis in American history. These chapters fill in the gaps of Stephens's life not covered by his *Anglo-African* correspondence, add new detail to the dramatic story of the Fifty-fourth

Massachusetts Regiment, and describe Stephens's work as a teacher in Reconstruction Virginia.

Stephens's forty-four *Anglo-African* letters form the heart of the book and represent all his published correspondence from surviving issues of the newspaper. Although daily events shaped the content of his letters, the course of the war gave them structure. Based on common themes or related incidents, the letters fell roughly into seven groups. I have gathered them into separate chapters, each prefaced with a brief introduction that sets the letters' context with greater specificity than in the book's biographical chapters. The document annotation provides a more precise level of information and brings, I hope, greater clarity to Stephens's writing.

In editorial method, I have relied on the guidelines set by the *Black Abolitionist Papers*. My overriding concern has been to remain true to Stephens's letters as they originally appeared. I have kept most nineteenth-century conventions, believing that preserving Stephens's inconsistencies provides a truer sense of his writing and the practices of the era's journalists. In the biographical chapters I quote original documents as written and avoid using the intrusive [*sic*]. With Stephens's *Anglo-African* letters, I have silently corrected the few misspellings or misprints that occurred to avoid confusion and because the original manuscripts do not survive for verification. Most errors surfaced in the rendering of proper names, probably because Stephens had no way to verify correct spellings, or when the *Anglo-African*'s editor transcribed his handwriting. All other editorial changes appear in brackets. I have supplied identifying notes for the individuals, events, battles, quotations, and obscure references Stephens mentioned. I regret the few that got away. My guiding principle has been to annotate everything that would bring greater understanding to the documents without a discouraging amount of tangential information. I also thought that something unfamiliar to me or not in standard reference works deserved an explanatory note. Common sense seemed a reliable guide.

For the reader's convenience, individual letter dates appear at the beginning of each document. Publication date in the *Anglo-African* is located at the end of each letter. I have used the terms *black* and *African American* interchangeably, both to reflect current usage and for the sake of style. In the document annotation, I have given the most attention to African-American subjects. Given the relative paucity of published sources concerning blacks in the Civil War, and the mountainous material available for whites, this seemed only right.

Composing this book sometimes seemed like a group effort, and I have had the good fortune to benefit from the assistance of many individuals and institutions. Without the rich resources and generosity of the Massachusetts Historical Society, this book could not have been written. I cannot sufficiently thank the society's director, Louis L. Tucker, for permitting me to take leave of my duties for an entire year, or my colleagues in the Publications Department, Conrad Wright, Edward Hanson, and Kate Viens, who bore additional burdens caused by my absence. I also owe a profound debt of gratitude to the American Philosophical Society and the American Council of Learned Societies; both provided timely and much-appreciated grants that allowed me to do basic research. The National Endowment for the Humanities awarded me a Travel to Collections Grant and a year-long fellowship to complete my research and write. I considered the endowment's award to be a high honor that came with the deep responsibility to produce good work. Without the NEH, much American history would be lost.

My first expedition to the National Archives left me dazed and bewildered. Its dizzying mass of documents relating to the Civil War proved overwhelming. Michael Meier in the Military Reference Branch saved me from complete despair, navigated me through the labyrinthine corridors, and taught me the secret codes that would produce documents. I thank Michael Knapp and the assistant branch chief, Charlotte Palmer Seely, who cut through the red tape and enabled me to see regimental records that I feared would be inaccessible. The entire staff at the National Archives was helpful and courteous. Rarely have I encountered more knowledgeable or cordial professionals since I began writing history.

I want to thank the host of archivists and librarians who helped me piece together Stephens's life. I am especially grateful to Melanie Wisner at Harvard's Houghton Library, who tracked down the microfilm copy of the *Weekly Anglo-African* for the 1863 to 1865 period. The Houghton owns the only extant copies of these years of the *Anglo-African.* The Library of Congress has the most complete run for 1859 through 1862, although it lacks many issues for 1861 and 1862. Stephens's letters reflect the incomparable quality of the paper and show how central it is to reconstructing African-American history during the Civil War. Christine F. Hughes at the Naval Research Center of the Department of the Navy and Patricia G. Bennett at the Charleston Library Society set me straight on Thomas B. Huger and the USS *Walker.* Gail M. Pietrzyk and Jane G. Bryan at the University of Pennsylvania's library and archives and Walter D. Stock at the Free Library of Philadelphia proved especially helpful in running down information on Benjamin C. Tilghman; Phil Lapsansky at the Library Company of Philadelphia helped me comprehend Stephen's Philadelphia during the 1850s; and Francis P. O'Neill at the Maryland Historical Society went beyond the call of duty in digging out information on Maryland legislators. I also want to acknowledge the assistance of Mary Ellen Chijioke at Swarthmore's Friends Historical Library, William R. Erwin, Jr., at Duke, Esme E. Bhan of the Moorland-Spingarn Research Center, Gould P. Colman, Cornell University, Ken Fones-Wolf, West Virginia University, and Marjorie Hill-Devine and staff at the Winthrop, Massachusetts, Public Library. I am especially appreciative of the assistance provided by Beverly Shank at the Medford, Massachusetts, Public Library, who graciously endured my relentless interlibrary loan requests. My colleagues in the M.H.S.'s library lightened my load considerably, and I want to thank Librarian Peter Drummey and his capable staff: Brenda Lawson, Virginia Smith, Chris Steele, Jennifer Tolpa, Catherine Craven, Mary Fabiszewski, Anne Bentley, James Harrison, and Joice Himawan, who I can't thank enough for drawing the maps for this book. Roger A. Davidson, Jr., a graduate student at Howard University, briefly served as a research assistant and dug up some invaluable information. Special thanks is reserved for Philip and Betty Emilio, who generously opened their home and made me feel like a member of the family. They gave me a more personal introduction to "Uncle Luis" and allowed me to see their astonishing family collection. Holding the key to Darien, Georgia's jail became a kind of epiphany.

I owe a deep debt to the series editors, August Meier and John H. Bracey, and to Mary Giles, who copyedited the manuscript. John's support helped make this book happen. Augie's exacting criticism transformed it; his legendary tenacity and dedication is astounding. I will never forget the day a letter—scrawling script across lined paper—arrived at the Historical Society. I nearly went into shock when

I discovered that Augie, laid up in a hospital bed, was responding to my last letter. To borrow from Blake, "wondrous the gods, more wondrous is the man."

I am pleased to acknowledge the help of C. Douglas Alves, Jr., director of the Calvert County Maryland Marine Museum and my friend for a quarter of a century, who answered queries and helped me appreciate southern Maryland. Edwin Redkey at SUNY, Purchase, and Julie Winch at UMass, Boston, read the biographical chapters. I am much indebted to Ed for sharing his research on the Fifty-fourth Massachusetts. Edwin Gittleman at UMass, Boston, helped clarify circumstances surrounding 28 May 1863. Joel Myerson, University of South Carolina, and Len Gougeon, University of Scranton, helped with an Emerson reference. Dennis Downey and Francis Bremer, both at Millersville University, are distinguished scholars, inspiring teachers, and even better friends. They helped this "p'or boy find his way home."

I first encountered George E. Stephens in 1986, when I began as assistant editor at the now-concluded Black Abolitionist Papers Project. My interpretation of the black role in the antislavery movement rests on volumes three through five of the *Black Abolitionist Papers.* My former colleagues C. Peter Ripley, Roy E. Finkenbine, and Michael F. Hembree taught me the craft of documentary editing. Pete also helped me to be critical of my work and introduced me to the mysteries of grant writing. The more time passes, the more I understand the value of his advice. Roy shared his encyclopedic knowledge of black history; he always could be relied on for the right answer. David Gordon, an unfailing friend, offered encouragement, read the manuscript, and helped with several references. Peter Burchard convinced me to get going on this book; he read two drafts and offered much needed help and sound judgment. Lately, a veritable army of researchers has been looking into the history of the Fifty-fourth, but Peter was on the parapets first.

As always, Ricky, Emily, Mary, and Doug are family, and I am lucky to have Dennis's and Traci's love. Frank cared enough to listen when I needed to talk. During my year of research and writing, Sarah and Lucy became better companions than they will ever know. My wife, Cory Burke Yacovone, helped with the proofing, read and reread the manuscript, and tolerated my moods. Her faith in this project has been a great comfort, although I saw her waver on Folly Island when the thermometer topped 104. Repaying her Southern kindness by casting our fate among cold Yankees was not quite what she had in mind. But, as the song says, there are "two cats in the yard and life used to be so hard, but now everything is easy because of you."

Notes

1. GES to Thomas Hamilton, 19 March 1860, *WAA*, 27 July 1861; "A Soldier of the 55th Mass. Vols." to Robert Hamilton, 15 January 1864, *WAA*, 30 January 1864; R. J. M. Blackett, ed., *Thomas Morris Chester, Black Civil War Correspondent: His Dispatches from the Virginia Front* (Baton Rouge: Louisiana State University Press, 1989), 327.

2. *WAA*, 4 May 1861; "Picket" to Henry Highland Garnet, 30 June 1864, *WAA*, 30 July 1864.

Abbreviations

BAP   C. Peter Ripley et al., eds. *The Black
                            Abolitionist Papers.* 5 vols. Chapel
                            Hill: University of North Carolina
                            Press, 1985–92.
BAPM   George Carter and C. Peter Ripley,
                            eds. *The Black Abolitionist Papers.*
                            Microfilm ed. 17 reels. New York:
                            Microfilming Corporation of Ameri-
                            ca, 1981–83; Ann Arbor: University
                            Microfilms International, 1984.
Bates, *History*   Samuel P. Bates. *History of Pennsyl-
                            vania Volunteers, 1861–5.* 5 vols.
                            Harrisburg: State of Pennsylvania,
                            1869–71.
Berlin, *The Black Military   Ira Berlin et al., eds. *Freedom:
    Experience*   A Documentary History of Emanci-
                            pation, 1861–1867,* series 2: *The
                            Black Military Experience.* Cam-
                            bridge: Cambridge University Press,
                            1982.
Berlin, *The Destruction   Ira Berlin et al., eds. *Freedom:
    of Slavery*   A Documentary History of Emanci-
                            pation, 1861–1867,* series 1: *The
                            Destruction of Slavery.* 3 vols.
                            Cambridge: Cambridge University
                            Press, 1985– .
BRFAL   Bureau of Refugees, Freedmen, and
                            Abandoned Lands.
DANB   Rayford W. Logan and Michael R.
                            Winston, eds. *Dictionary of Ameri-*

	can Negro Biography. New York: W. W. Norton, 1982.
Duncan, *Blue-Eyed Child of Fortune*	Russell Duncan, ed. *Blue-Eyed Child of Fortune: The Civil War Letters of Colonel Robert Gould Shaw.* Athens: University of Georgia Press, 1992.
Dyer, *Compendium*	Frederick H. Dyer. *A Compendium of the War of the Rebellion.* 3 vols. Des Moines, 1908. Reprint. Dayton: Morningside Bookshop, 1978.
Emilio, *A Brave Black Regiment*	Luis F. Emilio. *A Brave Black Regiment: History of the Fifty-fourth Regiment of Massachusetts Volunteer Infantry, 1863–1865.* 2d ed. Boston, 1894. Reprint. New York: Johnson Reprint, 1968.
HTIECW	Patricia Faust, ed. *Historical Times Illustrated Encyclopedia of the Civil War.* New York: Harper and Row, 1986.
LGC	Leon Gardiner Collection.
Massachusetts Soldiers, Sailors	*Massachusetts Soldiers, Sailors, and Marines in the Civil War.* 8 vols. Norwood: State of Massachusetts, 1931–35.
Nicolay and Hay, *Abraham Lincoln*	John G. Nicolay and John Hay. *Abraham Lincoln: A History.* 10 vols. New York: Century, 1890.
OR	*War of the Rebellion . . . Official Records of the Union and Confederate Armies.* 128 vols. Washington: Adjutant General's Office, 1880–1901.
ORN	*Official Record of the Union and Confederate Navies in the War of Rebellion.* 30 vols. Washington: Adjutant General's Office, 1894–1922.

RG	Record Group [National Archives].
USCT	United States Colored Troops.
WAA	*Weekly Anglo-African.* New York, 1859–65.
Warner, *Generals in Blue*	Ezra J. Warner. *Generals in Blue: Lives of the Union Commanders.* Baton Rouge: Louisiana State University Press, 1964.
Wearmouth, *Abstracts from the Port Tobacco Times*	Roberta J. Wearmouth, ed. *Abstracts from the Port Tobacco Times and Charles County* Advertiser, *1844–1875.* 3 vols. Bowie: Heritage Books, 1990–93.
WWWCW	Stewart Sifakis, ed. *Who Was Who in the Civil War.* New York: Facts on File, 1988.

Manuscript Repositories

HLHU	Houghton Library, Harvard University
HSP	Historical Society of Pennsylvania
MHS	Massachusetts Historical Society
MSA	Massachusetts State Archives
MSL	Massachusetts State Library
WVUL	West Virginia University Library

Part 1

The Life of George E. Stephens

Chapter 1

Getting at the "Throat of Treason and Slavery"

George E. Stephens never forgot the story of Nat Turner's rebellion. From "infancy up to my manhood," Stephens exclaimed, his father had stamped his "young mind and heart" with the horrors of Southern slavery and the history of America's bloodiest slave revolt. These riveting accounts bound him to those in chains and to the cause of black freedom. For Stephens, Nat Turner embodied black resistance to white oppression. The "thousand-fold crimes of this guilty nation against our race" burned in his heart and, like Nat Turner, he sought vengeance. "The fangs of the serpent of oppression has pierced my own bosom," Stephens confessed at the start of the Civil War, "until it swells with the hot blood of a revenge which nothing but the blood of a slaveholder can satiate."[1]

At the time of the Turner mayhem in August 1831, William and Mary Stephens, George's free, mixed-blood parents, lived in Northampton County on Virginia's eastern shore. Word of the bloody terror that whites launched to crush the revolt swept across Chesapeake Bay. To escape the spreading retribution, William Stephens and his family fled north to Pennsylvania. So many blacks traced the same route that fear-stricken whites deluged both houses of the Pennsylvania legislature with demands to halt the influx.[2]

Despite the hostile climate, the Stephens family settled in Philadelphia, and one year later, in 1832, George E. Stephens was born. His parents had one other child, Mary A. Stephens, who became a dressmaker, and raised Andrew F. Stevens, perhaps a nephew, who built a successful business and became a leader of the city's black community after the Civil War. By 1850 the Stephens family, unlike many of the city's twenty thousand or more blacks and masses of poor whites, had achieved an enviable level of education and stability.[3]

Given their race and class, the family had an unusually high level of literacy and, quite likely, both of Stephens's parents could read. During their first years in the city, the Stephens family boarded with other blacks—primarily with Susan Smith, a black laundress. After 1859, and for the rest of their lives, Stephens's parents lived in a sturdy brick house in an integrated portion of the city.[4]

William Stephens, a bootblack, waiter, and laborer, rose to become an influential member of Philadelphia's black community. Excluded from traditional avenues of power, education, and wealth, black leaders were usually ministers, craftsmen, or barbers, caterers, and hotel stewards. These occupations, however prosaic, possessed elite status among blacks because they represented the prospect of steady employment, brought capital into their communities, and, because of the services rendered to whites, gave blacks some influence. Such positions acquired additional prestige when combined with antislavery activism. Although records are scant, William Stephens clearly raised his status among blacks by assisting fugitives on the underground railroad and presiding over local antislavery meetings. He was also active in Philadelphia's First African Baptist Church and in 1853 became a licentiate, or lay preacher.[5]

Founded in 1809 by a former slave from Virginia, First Baptist attracted many black immigrants from the South. James Burrows, for instance, a former slave from Northampton, Virginia, preached in its pulpit from 1832 to 1846.[6] The congregation moved several times during the first half of the nineteenth century. Membership declined when the 1850 Fugitive Slave Law threatened the safety of both freeborn blacks and fugitive slaves. Over time, however, the church prospered, and by 1867 the congregation had erected a large brick building on Cherry Street. The Stephens family found First African's Southern parishioners and Burrows's connection to Northampton comforting, but the church's abolitionism attracted them even more. First African often opened its doors to antislavery meetings, and in 1859 it called James Underdue, a local black abolitionist, to the pulpit. During the Civil War, Underdue became chaplain of the Thirty-ninth United States Colored Troops (USCT). His military service embodied the congregation's antislavery spirit.[7]

Typical of nineteenth-century African Americans, George E. Stephens labored at several occupations. He worked as a sailor and an upholsterer, but by trade he was a cabinetmaker, an occupation that brought him elite status. Because most whites refused to hire blacks in the skilled trades, Stephens probably learned his trade from one of the nearly two dozen black cabinetmakers who labored in Philadelphia during the 1830s and 1840s. In the colonial era, white artisans, mariners, and manufacturers had employed slaves, but the pool of native black tradesmen remained small. Stephens more likely learned cabinetmaking from someone who had acquired his craft in slavery and, through manumission or escape, settled in the city. Samuel Harrison, for example, who lived in Philadelphia at the same time as Stephens and later became chaplain of the Fifty-fourth Massachusetts Regiment, learned shoemaking from a former South Carolina slave.[8]

Stephens obtained an extraordinary education for anyone in the nineteenth century, black or white. His letters reveal wide reading, energy, insight, and sharp analysis. He knew the Bible and Protestant history, nineteenth-century biographies, much popular literature, and more serious writers such as Coleridge and the Lake Poets. Unfortunately, Stephens did not record where he attended school. Although Philadelphia maintained a limited, segregated, public educational system and barred blacks from its secondary schools, several options remained open to a talented black student.[9]

Stephens probably attended First African's Sunday school or one of several primary schools founded by blacks beginning in 1804. The 1838 Quaker census revealed ten black-run city schools and fourteen other African-American schools taught by whites.[10] Quakers, benevolent societies, and the Pennsylvania Abolition Society (PAS) provided blacks with the most educational opportunities. The PAS began schooling black children in 1820 and opened another academy in 1832 designed to train black teachers. Quaker reformers like the family of Morris L. Hallowell, who would play a vital role in the history of the Fifty-fourth Massachusetts Regiment, supported black education. By one estimate, as many as 50 percent of the city's black children had obtained some education, despite official indifference and stony racism.[11]

The sting of racial prejudice, next to his father's stories of slavery, exerted the greatest influence upon Stephens. Philadelphia compiled one of the worst records of racial conflict in the North. "There is not perhaps anywhere to be found a city in which prejudice against color is more rampant," Frederick Douglass pronounced. Philadelphia "has its white schools and its colored schools, its white churches and its

colored churches, its white Christianity and its colored Christianity
... and the line is everywhere tightly drawn between them." One
black abolitionist complained in 1863 that in Philadelphia there "is
no more regard shown by the whites for the common and natural
rights of the colored population here than there is at Richmond."[12]

During the early days of the Republic, Philadelphia had enjoyed
racial peace. But by the 1820s, with a growing and increasingly successful black community and rising numbers of European immigrants
who competed with blacks for employment, racial harmony disintegrated. Historians have been quick to blame the white lower classes,
especially the Irish, for the precipitous decay. Yet the city's white elite
shared the repugnant racial values of the lower classes and may have
spawned them. As Robert Purvis, the city's most distinguished black
leader, bitterly lamented, the "press, church, magistrates, clergymen
and devils are against us."[13]

Vicious race riots plagued Philadelphia in the years before the Civil War. From 1834 to 1849, white mobs rampaged through black neigh-
borhoods, terrorizing residents, destroying property, or seeking to
drive the entire black population from the city. Inflamed by the annual August First celebration held in 1842 to commemorate the end
of West Indian slavery, mobs ran riot through the streets, hunting
blacks as if they were "noxious animals." They burned a black-owned
hall and church to obliterate signs of black achievement. Hundreds
of blacks fled the city for the woods and swamps of New Jersey.[14]

The "iron hand of prejudice," as the eloquent black abolitionist and
author William Wells Brown decried, kept most of black Philadelphia
in grinding poverty. Two-thirds were Southern-born and never rose
above the brutally harsh conditions they endured. "A. H. B.," a white
New York clergyman who surveyed Philadelphia's black population
in 1853, discovered that the very poorest rented rooms by the night,
largely from Irish landlords who hired their tenants to roam the streets
as rag and bone pickers. The poor of both races and sexes, A. H. B.
noted with irony, lived in "perfect equality," sometimes in the same
room, "crowded together without distinction," sharing "damp cellars,
leaky garrets, close and crowded rooms, filthy floors, beds full of ver-
min or no beds at all, sickening smells, the curses of the living, the
groans of the dying, [with] cold and hunger, delirium tremens, typhus
fever and consumption."[15]

A. H. B. also discovered a successful black Philadelphia. The black "respectable classes," like the Stephens family, appeared modestly successful, "industrious, [and] orderly." Generally, A. H. B. found city blacks better clothed and enjoying more favorable circumstances than their white counterparts in New England. But the upper third of black Philadelphia astonished him. "Never in my life," he confessed, had he "seen *gentlemen* of more elegant and unassuming manners than some colored men I have met." Their houses, although smaller than those owned by the same class of whites, tended to be better furnished and the relatively low rents and real estate prices encouraged black social development and the accumulation of wealth. Between 1837 and 1847 black personal savings increased dramatically, and the value of black-owned property increased by half. A. H. B. met two African-American families with more than $10,000 in personal wealth (not including real estate), two with between $5,000 and $10,000, and about 160 with more than $500.

Despite A. H. B.'s discoveries, few whites knew anything about the economic, cultural, and intellectual achievements of Stephens and the Philadelphia black elite.[16] As early as 1838, city blacks paid substantial taxes on real estate valued at between $500,000 and $600,000, and they possessed personal estate worth nearly $800,000. In 1863, the Philadelphia *Christian Recorder* reported that 75 percent of the city's native-born blacks were literate and 60 percent of the those between the ages of five and fifteen attended seventeen black-run schools. Furthermore, black private libraries possessed about twenty thousand volumes and black public libraries another four thousand. Blacks published two newspapers, owned nineteen churches, and established more than a hundred benevolent, literary, debating, temperance, reform, and antislavery societies. The Philadelphia black community, often characterized as steadily declining throughout the nineteenth century, overcame enormous hurtles to forge a vibrant and surprisingly prosperous society in the years before the Civil War.[17]

Philadelphia, Frederick Douglass proclaimed, "holds the destiny of our people." The black elite's wealth, education, and culture certainly made the city's black community one of the most important in the nation. Wealthy blacks such as James Forten, who had amassed a fortune of more than $100,000, and influential black families like the Purvises, William Stills, Jacob C. Whites, and George E. Stephenses guided the community. Not a clannish, monied power, the black elite was an open, heterogeneous group that rewarded talent, intelligence, and fortitude with group identity and access to important contacts in the white community. More important, it promoted black uplift and the determination to destroy slavery and racial prejudice.[18]

The black elite's tradition of antislavery activism stretched back to the eighteenth century and persisted long after the Civil War. Wealthy leaders such as James Forten or Robert Purvis allied with those of modest means to aid fugitive slaves, organize antislavery petition drives to the state and federal governments, desegregate the public transportation system, and oppose the hated American Colonization Society. Although little evidence survives concerning Stephens's early years, he became part of Philadelphia's black-led underground railroad system and in 1860 helped raise funds for the legal defense of those captured in the abortive rescue of the fugitive slave Moses Horner.[19]

Stephens also helped establish one of Philadelphia's most important black institutions. On 9 September 1853, he and sixteen associates founded the Banneker Institute, a literary society and library named to honor the African-American mathematician Benjamin Banneker. It gathered together many of the city's ablest young black men, several of whom had college degrees and one, Jesse Ewing Glasgow, Jr., who had attended the University of Edinburgh. The *Weekly Anglo-African* regularly reported the institute's activities and introduced Stephens to blacks throughout the North. One of the paper's correspondents pronounced Stephens "a promising young man, a ready and fluent writer . . . [who] possesses a vigorous intellect and an easy flow of ideas."[20]

Stephens gained his most important contacts and formed his closest friendships in the Banneker Institute circle. Parker T. Smith, abolitionist, journalist, and president of the institute, headed the *Anglo-African*'s Philadelphia Department, became his close ally, and probably brought Stephens to the paper's attention.[21] He also met William Still, the black director of the city's underground railroad; national black leaders such as Douglass and Brown; and such influential whites as the antislavery congressman William D. Kelley and Gen. Oliver O. Howard, who headed the Freedmen's Bureau.[22]

Serving in a variety of elective institute offices, Stephens helped set the institute's antislavery tone. He led debate on politics, antislavery strategy, and methods to achieve black social and political rights. At one of their first meetings members debated whether or not "the downfall of the Republic of the United States [would be] beneficial to the interest of the colored people." The institute petitioned the state legislature to gain black rights, and members reminded one another of their responsibilities to the oppressed. Jacob C. White, Jr., Stephens's closest friend, admonished fellow members to "untie the band of wickedness, that you undo the heavy burdens, and that you break every yoke" of the slaves.[23]

The institute sponsored antislavery celebrations, First of August rallies, and annual commemorations of the Emancipation Proclamation. Stephens, sometimes with his father's assistance, helped organize these events. He also delivered institute lectures on a broad range of subjects—love, morality, progress, religion, and literature—as well as slavery, colonization, and American politics. His orations were "listened to with interest and attention" and delivered with uncompromising firmness. He quickly earned a reputation for scorning the timid and condemning anyone who would kiss "the heel that would crush" them.[24]

At the 22 April 1858 meeting of the Banneker Institute, Stephens reviled Senator Stephen A. Douglas and the Kansas-Nebraska Act, which threatened to expand slavery into the territories. A delegation from the white, Philadelphia Congress of Literary Societies attended to scrutinized the institute's records for possible membership in the organization. Stephens's strident views, which one member of the examining committee protested, may have played a part in the congress's decision to reject the institute's request for membership. Notwithstanding Stephens's remarks, one thing barred approval: "prejudice against color."[25] This galling example of racial discrimination must have stung Stephens with special force. He had only recently returned from the most traumatic experience of his life, one that made his father's descriptions of slavery come to life.

*   ⋆   ⋆

Limited opportunities for black craftsmen had forced Stephens to abandon cabinetmaking. In November 1857, he turned to the sea and joined the crew of the USS *Walker*, an iron-hulled steamer assigned to the U.S. Coast Survey.[26] Stephens may have obtained his position through Thomas Bee Huger, a navy lieutenant temporarily serving on the *Walker* and scion of a distinguished Charleston, South Carolina, family. Huger, who resigned his commission and joined the Confederate navy during the Civil War, spent much of his time in Philadelphia and possibly received a recommendation to hire Stephens.[27]

For more than a century, ports such as Philadelphia had attracted large numbers of black mariners. In the first two decades of the nineteenth century, blacks held between 17 and 22 percent of Philadelphia's seafaring jobs. Steamers and merchant ships working out of Newport, Rhode Island, for example, almost always employed blacks, and half of some crews were African American. But by midcentury, fear of kidnapping and growing racial discrimination drove blacks out of the U.S. Navy and the maritime industry. Whether through good fortune, talent, or connections, in a period of declining opportunities for black sailors Stephens could count himself fortunate to have obtained his position on a government ship.[28]

Commanded by Benjamin F. Sands, the *Walker* navigated the eastern seaboard and the Gulf of Mexico, taking soundings and recording currents. The ship kept several carpenters on board, and Stephens probably bore responsibility for maintenance and obtaining supplies. In late November, the *Walker* left Philadelphia, hugging the coastline as it steamed south and arrived in Charleston on 2 December.[29] The next day, Huger ordered Stephens ashore to obtain supplies. Distracted by news of his wife's death, Huger knew better than to allow a free black sailor to leave his ship. The state's Negro Seamen's Act, adopted after the Denmark Vesey conspiracy in 1822, required that all free black sailors be remanded to jail while their ships remained in port. If the captain failed to pay the costs of incarceration, the luckless man would be sold into slavery.[30]

For the next two weeks, Stephens roamed Charleston's streets undisturbed. His father's paralyzing stories of slavery could not prepare him for what he saw. The city loomed as a "half-way house on the pathway of wrong to the region of the damned." "You sir," he wrote Jacob C. White, Jr., "have not perhaps been south of Masons and Dixons line, and Judge slavery therefore by the testimony you receive. You must witness it in all its loathsomeness. You must become a witness yourself." As he approached the docks one day from the *Walker*'s skiff, Stephens saw a coffle of two to three hundred emaciated, "half clad, filthy looking men women and children" standing mute and sorrowful as they braced for transportation to the rice plantations. Stephens walked up King Street to the city center, nervoused to little more than "the fag end of a series of pro-slavery administrations." Although Northern black opinion of Lincoln changed dramatically after the Civil War, in 1860 most believed that he embodied the "Godless will of a criminal nation."[38]

Stephens understood the depth of the nation's commitment to slavery. Its very character and economic life depended upon an unbounded drive for wealth, and, as he explained, "slavery is one of the main sources of her gain—war against slavery, is therefore hostility to everything American." Stephens doubted that even white antislavery leaders appreciated the enormity of the challenge they all faced.[39] During the late 1850s, such disillusionment led him into the black emigration movement. He contended that African Americans should work out their destiny elsewhere in the Western Hemisphere, free from American oppression. Stephens proudly heralded Haiti's revolutionary tradition and found the island nation's campaign to attract settlers appealing. Others, like the black activist John C. Bowers, approved all emigrationist schemes, even to Africa. "Our friends have even turned against us," Bowers lamented, and when "Gabriel blows his last trumpet, the negroes will still be in slavery, unless they emigrate."[40]

African emigration deeply divided blacks. For some, the African ventures of Martin R. Delany and Henry Highland Garnet offered escape from the effects of American slavery and racism. Stephens supported the spread of Western civilization into Africa and trusted that Africa's "mounts of wealth stored away in the virgin soil" eventually would rescue the continent from its presumed backwardness. One day, Stephens thought, Africa might even produce more cotton than the American South and drive slavery out of existence.[41]

But to Stephens, African emigration was indistinguishable from the American Colonization Society's hated program. "Any scheme that serves to alienate us from our native land, and more clearly rivets the fetters of the slave by removing his true friend and brethren, the free black," he declared, "should be scorned by us." Stephens maintained that "the disfranchised American looks with mistrust on any of the schemes advanced By their avowed friends. They have been duped and led into plans that have Brought no good and which have resulted disastrously [to] thousands of our fellow race."[42]

Stephens felt little kinship with Africans, far less affinity than New Englanders harbored for the English. He marked Africans a "Benighted race" and doubted that they had a civilization worthy of the name. Reared and educated by Northern middle-class standards, he laid claim to American identity and American citizenship; the Puritan founders and the Revolutionary Founding Fathers were his founders and his fathers. Crispus Attucks and other black patriots of the American Revolution, Stephens believed, had fought to establish the United States and sealed their American bonds with blood. He believed in the inevitable advance of civilization and democracy. The democratic movement that had begun with the American Revolution, Stephens felt, had simply not yet expanded to encompass black Americans. With time and sufficient effort, Stephens believed that all blacks would achieve equality. Thus, he avowed, black efforts should be confined to democratizing the Western Hemisphere and only then "look to the interests of our *African* brethren."[43]

*   *   *

"We want Nat Turner—not speeches; Denmark Vesey—not resolutions; John Brown—not meetings," cried the *Weekly Anglo-African* in April 1861.[44] For many blacks, the rebel attack on Fort Sumter had recast their fate. The war revived black hopes, curtailed Stephens's interest in emigration, and convinced many that slavery would be crushed along with the rebellion. Northern blacks immediately threw their support behind the national government and rushed to volunteer for military duty. Some in Boston promised a force of fifty thousand men, while companies of Philadelphia blacks openly drilled in preparation for service. The Banneker Institute advised its members to "be prepared [to] defend ourselves" and discussed taking up arms so that "our footprints [will] mark the hardened soil of oppression."[45]

On 20 April 1861, Alfred M. Green and Thomas Bowers, leading Philadelphia black abolitionists, announced the organization of two regiments of black troops. Forget past grievances, they asserted, and fight for "the love of country, of freedom, and of civil and religious toleration." Most assumed that the city's near unanimous repudiation of secession had welded interracial unity. They urged fellow blacks to fight, avowing that "peril and war blot out all distinctions of race and rank."[46]

But black hopes for unity against the slave power quickly vanished. Throughout the North, whites rebuffed black patriotism and advised them "to keep out of this; this is a white man's war." Blacks who rallied to Lincoln's call for volunteers heard countless times that "he doesn't mean you. Niggers ain't citizens."[47] Frances Ellen Watkins Harper, an abolitionist and the era's most famous black female poet, puzzled "at the blindness of the nation in refusing the negro's aid," men well "acquainted with both the enemy and the country, who might have, ere this, led their stumbling feet to victory."[48]

The government's rejection of their patriotism left most blacks outraged. The African Methodist Episcopal (AME) Church, the North's largest black denomination, advised its faithful that they had no business fighting for a government that persecuted them. Many doubted that any service they rendered would ever free them from racism.[49] Let "the government take care of itself," the *Anglo-African* advised, "and give our labors for the slave, and the slave alone." Summing up the sentiments of his brethren, Jacob C. White, Jr., concluded that the time to fight "has not yet come."[50]

Stephens took another view. At the outbreak of war, he became a cook and personal servant for Benjamin C. Tilghman, an officer in the Army of the Potomac's Twenty-sixth Pennsylvania Regiment. Tilghman, inventor, scientist, businessman, and lawyer, came from a wealthy Philadelphia family. The owner of a profitable steel business, he later went on to perfect the manufacturing of paper from wood fiber and invented sandblasting.[51] In 1862, Tilghman took command of the Twenty-sixth Pennsylvania, and in August 1863 he resigned to lead the Third USCT. For a white officer already in command of a regiment, this extraordinary move offered dramatic evidence of his antislavery convictions.[52]

Stephens, who was in Washington, D.C., during the First Battle of Bull Run, likely accompanied Tilghman and the Twenty-sixth's predecessor, Philadelphia's Washington Brigade, when it marched through Baltimore's rioting mobs on 19 April 1861 on its way to defend the Capital.[53] He remained with the Twenty-sixth until January 1863, taking time off for Banneker Institute speeches and visits home. Although he made little of it in his *Anglo-African* letters, Stephens used his position as Tilghman's cook and servant to "run off slaves from the plantations and farms all along from Port Tobacco [Maryland] down to Washington." The experience also gave him the opportunity to provide fellow blacks with their most reliable account of the war.[54]

Stephens's *Anglo-African* correspondence, copied without attribution by the white press, offered the paper's readers a personal view of combat, camp life, and the slaves' struggle for freedom.[55] He attacked proslavery propaganda depicting blacks as inherently lazy and shiftless and asserted that, when free, the former slaves worked harder and produced more than whites. They kept their meager homes neat and orderly and their families intact. Stephens documented the brutality that southern Maryland's white elite inflicted on its "property" and exposed the actions of Union soldiers who brutalized Southern blacks.

The sexual exploitation of slave women, an especially powerful indictment of the "peculiar institution," repulsed Stephens. The case of Mary Thomas, a slave who had fallen in love with a Union "contraband" worker and escaped her lecherous owner, personified slavery in one of its cruelest forms and black heroism at it greatest poignancy. After several failed escape attempts, Thomas was rescued by her lover and sympathetic Union soldiers who won her release by pummeling a slave catcher to within an inch of his life. "And why should she not triumph," Stephens exclaimed. "Did not she turn her back on slavery and ruin, while the path which she proposed to tread was illuminated with the bright hope of salvation, liberty, and love?"[56]

The first year of the war was the cruelest for fugitive slaves, and they quickly learned to fear Yankee soldiers "as little better than secessionists." Stephens found many Union troops "intemperate, brutal and ignorant, pregnant with negro hate, and strangers to every sentiment of honor and justice." Soldiers "from the cesspools of society" beat, kicked, or shot Southern blacks out of hate, rage, or for amusement. As one Yankee in the Fifth New York Regiment contended, "I think that the best way to settle the question of what to do with the darkies would be to shoot them."[57] They taunted female runaways for fun and stoned others for exercise. John Oliver, a black American Missionary Association teacher near Norfolk, Virginia, witnessed Yankees acting "more like wild animals than civilized beings. They took everything that they could lay their hands upon from the colored people and beat those that hade nothing for them to take." Other soldiers mistreated their black servants or, worst of all, kidnapped black children for sale to Confederates in Virginia.[58]

Although historians now axiomatically proclaim the influence slaves exerted on wartime federal policy, Stephens observed it firsthand. By flooding into Union lines, fugitive slaves deprived the Confederacy of their labor, made enforcement of the Fugitive Slave Law impossible, altered Union soldiers' attitudes toward slavery and the war, and helped force the North to adopt emancipation as a war aim. "I know what I am saying," Stephens asserted, "the eternal logic of facts tells me that the negro henceforth and forever, holds the balance of power in this country."[59]

The Union occupation of southern Maryland became a testing ground for federal policy. As Stephens revealed, the army could not enforce the Fugitive Slave Law and increasingly did not want to. He was outraged by the orders of Union generals permitting "loyal" slave-owners to retrieve their property from army camps, where so many fugitives sought refuge. At first, slave catchers found willing helpers among Union troops. But as time passed and Union soldiers witnessed the harsh realities of slave life, slaveowners and their minions were as likely to come away with a beating as a runaway.[60]

Stephens's letters forcefully depict the war's countervailing forces, as he expressed optimism over the eventual destruction of slavery and despair over the intractability of racial prejudice. He believed, with the *Anglo-African*, that "war is a swift educator" and the "slavehold-er's war against the Union is making abolitionists very fast." Much to Stephens's satisfaction, even Lincoln had difficulty compelling Union soldiers to retrieve runaway slaves. One trooper from the Tenth Massachusetts typified the transformation Stephens witnessed. Although he hated blacks, the soldier refused to "be instrumental in returning a slave to his master in any way shape or manner, I'll die first." Stephens confidently predicted that to defeat the South, the North would be compelled to expand the war and destroy slavery.[61]

As that Massachusetts soldier illustrated, the war may have changed opinions about slavery but it failed to transform the racial attitudes of Yankee troops. Stephens found that Northerners would rather suffer defeat and humiliation than call blacks brethren, "such is the rancour and persistency of their hatred for our race." At the disastrous battle of Fredericksburg in December 1862, Stephens witnessed black servants driven from shelter against Confederate shells at bayonet point by enraged white soldiers. "Let the damned nigger be killed—how dare they come here among white men," one snarled. No matter the circumstances, regardless of the peril, Stephens found that even in the flames of hell whites would "lisp and stammer curs-es on the race."[62]

In spite of widespread racial animosity and ambiguous Northern attitudes toward slavery, Lincoln saw that the Union could not be restored without emancipation. Battered by an intractable foe, suffering a distressing number of casualties, and needing more men, Lincoln determined to revolutionize the war. His September 1862 Preliminary Emancipation Proclamation, warning the South to give up the fight or loose their slaves, offered some blacks new hope. "A new era, a new dispensation of things is now upon us," the *Christian Recorder* exclaimed, "*to action, to action,* is the cry."[63]

Stephens remained skeptical. In August, Lincoln had stunned blacks by reviving the idea of colonization with his plan to settle freed slaves in Central America. Black leaders decried the move, and Frederick Douglass denounced Lincoln as "a genuine representative of American prejudice and Negro hatred." Stephens had good cause to doubt that the president would keep his promise to issue the final Emancipation Proclamation on 1 January 1863. "Oh! may the nation pause and reflect, and remember her pride, avarice and injustice," he proclaimed. Little in the war and even less in the nation's past offered evidence that Lincoln would act. Everything in American history pointed toward the infamous dictum of the 1857 Dred Scott decision that "black men have no rights that white men are bound to respect." If Lincoln kept his word, Stephens predicted that it would at least result in the "general arming of the freedmen." On that, he was absolutely correct.[64]

Stephens's wariness and suspicion regarding Lincoln's proclamation reflected Northern black opinion. Although jubilant at its adoption and thankful that the president remained true to his word, few hailed him as a savior. Constrained by wartime politics and Northern racial prejudice, Lincoln acted cautiously and, to most blacks, callously. "The colored people of the country rejoice in what Mr. Lincoln has done for them," William Wells Brown insisted, "but they all wish that Gen. Fremont had been in his place." They took Lincoln at his word that the proclamation was merely a war measure, and "*per se* no more humanitarian than a hundred pounder rifled cannon."[65] The hundreds of black rallies held to celebrate the proclamation gave God, not Lincoln, credit for the work—"God had made Abraham . . . His bell-ringer."[66] They censured the president for delaying it so long, not basing it on humanitarian principles, and for leaving the slaves of loyal masters still in chains. The proclamation, instead of a glorious testimony to principled action was, as one black paper regretted, brought forth "by timid and heaven-doubting mid-wives, and proved an incompetent and abominable abortion."[67]

By August 1864, Stephens had seen enough of Lincoln's proclamation and the North's unrelenting racism. He viewed the document as a strange "creature—an abortion wrung from the Executive womb by necessity." It "freed" slaves where Lincoln had no control—in the Confederacy—and ignored them where he did—in the border states. In the summer of 1864, some Union soldiers still enforced the Fugitive Slave Law, and slaveowners enjoyed rights denied to loyal blacks. These things proved to Stephens that the Emancipation Proclamation was a fraud, an "indice of a blind infatuation, and a fulmination of Executive folly and indecision."[68]

Nevertheless, Stephens recognized that the proclamation's call for black troops had transformed the war. Even the African emigrationist Henry Highland Garnet exclaimed that "We must fight! fight! fight!" The *Anglo-African*'s editor, Robert Hamilton, urged blacks to organize and enlist: "It is now or never; now if ever." The time had finally come for blacks to assert their power and recast the war into a battle against slavery and racial prejudice. "What better field to claim our rights than the field of battle?" Hamilton asked. "Where will prejudice be so speedily overcome?"[69]

Stephens had joined the Army of the Potomac to make his own war on slavery. But before 1 January 1863, the interests of Northern blacks and the federal government conflicted. A war to save "the Union as it was" meant defeat for African Americans. With the Emancipation Proclamation, however, Stephens could stand with the government and stand against slavery. To strike for the Union, as Frederick Douglass pronounced, "is to strike for the bondsmen." With uncommon clarity, Stephens and Douglass understood the opportunity Lincoln had given blacks. Now, as Douglass advised, they could "get at the throat of treason and slavery through the State of Massachusetts."[70]

Notes

1. GES to Robert Hamilton, 19 November 1861. Unless otherwise indicated, all Stephens letters cited are reproduced in this book.

2. 1830 U.S. Census; Carter G. Woodson, *Free Negro Heads of Families in the United States in 1830* (Washington: Association for the Study of Negro Life and History, 1925), 186; Julie Winch, *Philadelphia's Black Elite: Activ-*

ism, Accommodation, and the Struggle for Autonomy, 1787–1848 (Philadelphia: Temple University Press, 1988), 131–34.

3. Edward Needles, *Ten Years Progress; or, A Comparison of the State and Condition of the Colored People in the City and County of Philadelphia from 1837 to 1847* (Philadelphia: Merrihew and Thompson, 1849), 4–5; Pennsylvania Society for Promoting the Abolition of Slavery, *The Present State and Condition of the People of Color of the City of Philadelphia* (Philadelphia: PSAS, 1838), in *BAPM*, 2:317; Elizabeth M. Geffen, "Violence in Philadelphia in the 1840's and 1850's," *Pennsylvania History* 36 (October 1969): 384–89.

4. 1850 U.S. Census; Philadelphia city directories, 1846–1904; GES to Jacob C. White, Jr., 25 February 1859, Jacob C. White, Jr., Papers, LGC, HSP; *Education and Employment Statistics of the Colored People of Philadelphia* (1856), in Pennsylvania Abolition Society Papers, 2:6–7, HSP.

5. Paul J. Lammermeier, "The Urban Black Family of the Nineteenth Century: A Study of Black Family Structure in the Ohio Valley, 1850–1880," *Journal of Marriage and the Family* 35 (August 1973): 440–56; *WAA*, 1 October 1859, 21 April 1860; American Baptist Missionary Convention, *Annual Report and Minutes* (1853–69), information generously provided by Roy E. Finkenbine, Hampton University.

6. Mechal Sobel, *Trabelin' On: The Slave Journey to an Afro-Baptist Faith* (Westport: Greenwood Press, 1979), 271–72; Gary Nash, *Forging Freedom: The Formation of Philadelphia's Black Community, 1720–1840* (Cambridge: Harvard University Press, 1988), 201–2, 263.

7. Nash, *Forging Freedom*, 201–2; Edward D. Smith, *Climbing Jacob's Ladder: The Rise of Black Churches in Eastern American Cities, 1740–1877* (Washington: Smithsonian Institution Press, 1988), 47; Sobel, *Trabelin' On*, 271–72; Edwin S. Redkey, "Black Chaplains in the Union Army," *Civil War History* 33 (December 1987): 350; *WAA*, 5 May 1860.

8. "Census Facts Collected By Benjamin C. Bacon and Charles W. Gardner," (1838), Pennsylvania Abolition Society Papers, vol. 3, passim, HSP; *Present State and Condition of the People of Color*, in *BAPM*, 2:319; Nash, *Forging Freedom*, 11; Dennis Dickerson, "Reverend Samuel Harrison: A Nineteenth Century Black Clergyman," in *Black Apostles at Home and Abroad*, ed. David W. Wills and Richard Newman (Boston: G. K. Hall, 1982), 153–54.

9. GES to Jacob C. White, Jr., 25 February 1859, Jacob C. White, Jr., Papers, LGC, HSP; Harry C. Silcox, "Delay and Neglect: Negro Public Education in Antebellum Philadelphia, 1800–1860," *Pennsylvania Magazine of History and Biography* 97 (October 1973): 444–45, 449, 451–53.

10. Benjamin C. Bacon, *Statistics of the Colored People of Philadelphia*, 2d ed. (Philadelphia: Board of Education, 1859), 3–9; *Present State and Condition of the Free People of Color*, in *BAPM*, 2:329.

11. Roger Lane, *William Dorsey's Philadelphia and Ours: On the Past and Future of the Black City in America* (New York: Oxford University Press, 1991), 135; Russell F. Weigley, ed., *Philadelphia: A Three-Hundred-Year History* (New York: W. W. Norton, 1982), 224, 354; Silcox, "Delay and Neglect,"

453; Bacon, *Statistics of the Colored People*, 3–9; Clarkson Evening School Association, "Minute Book," 1859–61, Pennsylvania Abolition Society Papers, HSP; Edward Raymond Turner, *The Negro in Pennsylvania: Slavery-Servitude-Freedom, 1639–1861* (Washington: American Historical Association, 1911), 130–33; Esther Hayes to William Still, January 1858, LGC, HSP.

12. Douglass quoted in *Philadelphia*, ed. Weigley, 386; John Oliver to Robert Hamilton, 6 October 1863, *WAA*, 24 October 1863.

13. Nash, *Forging Freedom*, 223–26; John H. Johnson, untitled Banneker Institute lecture, Banneker Institute Papers, LGC, HSP; Purvis quoted in *Philadelphia*, ed. Weigley, 353–54.

14. Turner, *Negro in Pennsylvania*, 159–62; Geffen, "Violence in Philadelphia," 387–88.

15. Brown quoted in William Wells Brown, *The Negro in the American Rebellion: His Heroism and His Fidelity* (1880, reprint, Miami: Mnemosyne Publishing, 1969), 142; A. H. B. received the assistance of local black clergymen and Charles Reason, a black abolitionist leader and head of the city's Institute for Colored Youth. A.H.B. estimated the city's black population to be about 25,000, the highest figure ever cited for this period. The following summary is based on A.H.B.'s reports printed in the *Pennsylvania Freeman*, 27 January, 31 March, 7, 14 April 1853.

16. Nash, *Forging Freedom*, 134–36. For a revealing look at the antebellum Philadelphia black elite see Frank J. Webb, *The Garies and Their Friends* (1857, reprint New York: Arno Press, 1969).

17. *Present State and Condition of the People of Color*, in BAPM, 2:317; *Christian Recorder*, 15 August 1863; Nash, *Forging Freedom*, 6–7; *Present State and Condition of the People of Color*, in BAPM, 2:327–28; Winch, *Philadelphia's Black Elite*, 1–3. For the standard characterization of black Philadelphia's fortunes, see *Philadelphia: Work, Space, Family, and Group Experience in the Nineteenth Century*, ed. Theodore Hershberg (New York: Oxford University Press, 1981), especially 368–91, and Emma Lapsansky, "Friends, Wives, and Strivings: Networks and Community Values Among Nineteenth-Century Philadelphia Afroamerican Elites," *Pennsylvania Magazine of History and Biography* 108 (January 1984): 15–16.

18. Weigley, ed., *Philadelphia*, 352–53; Winch, *Philadelphia's Black Elite*, 3; Lapsansky, "Friends, Wives, and Strivings," 3–13.

19. Nash, *Forging Freedom*, 183–86, 189–90; BAP, 3:3–8, 37–40; *Autobiography of Dr. William Henry Johnson* (New York: Haskin House, 1970), 125–26; *WAA*, 7 April 1860.

20. Emma Jones Lapsansky, "'Discipline to the Mind': Philadelphia's Banneker Institute, 1854–1872," *Pennsylvania Magazine of History and Biography* 117 (January-April 1993): 83–102; *Autobiography of Dr. William Henry Johnson*, 130–31; "Obituary Resolutions," [1861?], Banneker Institute Papers, LGC, HSP; *The Press* [Philadelphia], 18 January 1861; *WAA*, 3 December 1859, 3 March 1860.

21. Lapsansky, "Discipline to the Mind," 93, 98; "Committee on Debate and Lectures," December 1857, Parker T. Smith to Jacob C. White, [Jr.], 22

June 1889, Banneker Institute Papers, LGC, HSP; *WAA*, 5 December 1863, 23 January 1864.

22. Banneker Institute "Minute Books," 1853–55, 1857–59, "Report of the Committee on Debates and Lectures," 13 February 1861, "Account Lists," 1866, 1867, undated, Banneker Institute Papers, LGC, HSP; *National Anti-Slavery Standard*, 23 December 1854, 6 January 1855.

23. "Rules of Committee on Debates and Lectures," May 1854, Jacob C. White, [Jr.?], lecture, n.d.; Banneker Institute "Minute Books," 1853–55, 1857–59, "Committee Report," 3 December 1857, "Catalogue of Book Purchases," 12 June 1861, Banneker Institute Papers, LGC, HSP.

24. Miscellaneous Handbills and Broadsides, "Minute Books," 1853–55, 1857–59, "Debates and Lectures," 1859–61, Banneker Institute Papers, LGC, HSP; "Report of the Joint Committee on West Indian Emancipation," 24 July 1855, in *BAP*M, 9:749; *WAA*, 19 November 1859, 6 February 1860.

25. "Debate Records," 1858; quotation from Jacob C. White, Jr., Davis D. Turner, and William H. Johnson to Banneker Institute, 21 May 1858, Banneker Institute Papers, LGC, HSP; *Autobiography of Dr. William Henry Johnson*, 131–32.

26. The following account of GES's experience on the *Walker* draws on his 8 January 1858 letter to Jacob C. White, Jr., and is reprinted in *BAP*, 4:371–76.

27. *National Cyclopedia of American Biography*, 63 vols. (New York: James T. White, 1898–), 5:13; Nicholas B. Wainwright, ed., *A Philadelphia Perspective: The Diary of Sidney George Fisher Covering the Years 1834–1871* (Philadelphia: Historical Society of Pennsylvania, 1967), 223; Thomas H. S. Hammersley, ed., *General Register of the United States Navy and Marine Corps, 1782–1882* (Washington: U.S. Government, 1882), 366; Alfred Huger to Thomas Bee Huger, 18 October 1856, Alfred Huger Papers, Duke University; Isaac Toucey to Lt. Thomas B. Huger, 29 September 1859, Correspondence of Alexander Dallas Bache, Superintendent of the Coast and Geodetic Survey, 1843–65, roll 205, no. 642, National Archives; Patricia G. Bennett, librarian, Charleston Library Society to Author, 18 July 1991.

28. W. Jeffrey Bolster, "'To Feel Like a Man': Black Seamen in the Northern States, 1800–1860," *Journal of American History* 76 (March 1990): 1174–77; Peter P. Hinks, "'Frequently Plunged into Slavery': Free Blacks and Kidnapping in Antebellum Boston," *Historical Journal of Massachusetts* 20 (Winter 1992): 24–25; Martha S. Putney, "Black Merchant Seamen of Newport, 1803–1865: A Case Study in Foreign Commerce," *Journal of Negro History* 57 (April 1972): 160, 166–68.

29. USS *Walker* Logbook, 1854–55, vol. 1, Records of the Coast and Geodetic Survey, RG 23, box 2223, National Archives; Benjamin Franklin Sands, *From Reefer to Rear-Admiral: Reminiscences and Journal Jottings of Nearly Half a Century of Naval Life* (New York: Frederick A. Stokes, 1899), 211–18; Christine F. Hughes to Author, 26 August 1991, Department of the Navy, Naval Historical Center.

30. *Charleston Mercury*, 7, 9 December 1857; Alfred Huger to Thomas Bee Huger, 6 November 1858, Alfred Huger Papers, Duke University; Philip M.

Hamer, "Great Britain, the United States, and the Negro Seamen's Acts, 1822–1848," *Journal of Southern History* 1 (February 1935): 3–28.

31. Marina Wikramanayake, *A World in Shadow: The Free Black in Antebellum South Carolina* (Columbia: University of South Carolina Press, 1973).

32. Michael P. Johnson and James L. Roark, eds., *No Chariot Let Down: Charleston's Free People of Color on the Eve of the Civil War* (Chapel Hill: University of North Carolina Press, 1984), 93–106, 127; Michael P. Johnson and James L. Roark, *Black Masters: A Free Family of Color in the Old South* (New York: W. W. Norton, 1984), 186–87, 190, 257.

33. GES to Jacob C. White, Jr., 18 February 1858, 25 February 1859, Jacob C. White, Jr., Papers, LGC, HSP; "Debate Records," 1858, "Minute Book," 1857–59, "Report," 14 March 1860, Banneker Institute Papers, LGC, HSP.

34. "Banneker" to Thomas Hamilton, 14 November 1859, *WAA*, 19 November 1859; *BAP*, 3:56–57.

35. *WAA*, 3, 10, 31 December 1859.

36. *WAA*, 4 July 1863; William Dusinberre, *Civil War Issues in Philadelphia, 1856–1865* (Philadelphia: University of Pennsylvania Press, 1965), 85–89.

37. "Banneker" to Thomas Hamilton, 30 January, 17 December 1860, *WAA*, 30 January, 17 December 1860.

38. *WAA*, 22 December 1860, 16 March 1861.

39. GES to Thomas Hamilton, 15 January 1861.

40. Winch, *Philadelphia's Black Elite*, 49–50, 57; *Christian Recorder*, 9 March 1861; *WAA*, 16 March 1861; Bowers quoted in "Banneker" to Thomas Hamilton, 22 January 1860, *WAA*, 28 January 1860.

41. GES to Jacob C. White, Jr., 25 February 1859, Jacob C. White, Jr., Papers, LGC, HSP.

42. GES to Thomas Hamilton, 14 November 1859.

43. Ibid.; GES to Jacob C. White, Jr., 25 February 1859, Jacob C. White, Jr., Papers, LGC, HSP.

44. *WAA*, 27 April 1861.

45. *Pine and Palm*, 31 August 1861; *WAA*, 4 May, 12 October 1861; "Memo," January 1861, "Annual Address of J. Wesley Simpson," 9 January 1861, Banneker Institute Papers, LGC, HSP.

46. Dusinberre, *Civil War Issues in Philadelphia*, 118, 154–55; *The Press* [Philadelphia], 15, 22 April 1861.

47. *WAA*, 27 April 1861; Edgar A. Toppin, "Humbly They Served: The Black Brigade in the Defense of Cincinnati," *Journal of Negro History* 48 (April 1963): 79; Peter H. Clark, *The Black Brigade of Cincinnati* (Cincinnati: n.p., 1864), 6, in *BAPM*, 15:158.

48. *Christian Recorder*, 27 September 1862, in *BAPM*, 14:511.

49. Clarence E. Walker, *Rock in a Weary Land: The African Methodist Episcopal Church during the Civil War and Reconstruction* (Baton Rouge: Louisiana State University Press, 1982), 32–34; Dusinberre, *Civil War Issues in Philadelphia*, 161–64; Parker T. Smith to Jacob C. White, Jr., 5 April 1862,

Jacob C. White, Jr., Papers, LGC, HSP; *Pine and Palm*, 25 May 1861; *WAA*, 14 September 1861.

50. *WAA*, 27 April 1861; William H. Parham to Jacob C. White, Jr., 12 October 1861, Jacob C. White, Jr., Papers, LGC, HSP.

51. *National Cyclopedia of American Biography*, 15:263–64; Philadelphia *Public Ledger*, 5 July 1901; Bates, *History*, 1:348–54, 373.

52. Tilghman's black soldiers believed that he embodied "justice, humanity, and firmness." Frank Hamilton Taylor, *Philadelphia in the Civil War, 1861–1865* (Philadelphia: City of Philadelphia, 1913), 189–90, 294; Richard H. L. Jewett to Eliza Nutting Jewett, 3 November 1863, Richard H. L. Jewett Papers, Boston Athenæum; Edwin S. Redkey, ed., *A Grand Army of Black Men: Letters from African-American Soldiers in the Union Army, 1861–1865* (New York: Cambridge University Press, 1992), 36.

53. GES to Robert Hamilton, 20 August 1864.

54. Miscellaneous handbills and broadsides, Banneker Institute Papers, LGC, HSP; GES to Luis F. Emilio, 27 December 1885, Philip and Betty Emilio Family Collection.

55. Some of his letters appeared in the *Brooklyn Star* and the Albany *Statesman. WAA*, 15 February 1862.

56. GES to Robert Hamilton, 17 October 1861, 2 March 1862.

57. GES to Robert Hamilton, 11 November 1861; Yankee from the Fifth New York quoted in Bell I. Wiley, "Billy Yank and the Black Folk," *Journal of Negro History* 36 (January 1951): 35.

58. Wiley, "Billy Yank and the Black Folk," 39–40; John Oliver quoted in Betty Mansfield, "That Fateful Class: Black Teachers of Virginia's Freedman, 1861–1882," Ph.D. diss., Catholic University of America, 1980, 138.

59. GES to Robert Hamilton, 20 January 1862.

60. Fred Shannon, "The Federal Government and the Negro Soldier, 1861–65," *Journal of Negro History* 11 (October 1926): 566; Benjamin Quarles, *The Negro in the Civil War* (1953, reprint, New York: Da Capo Press, 1989), 65–66, 69, 75, 76; Berlin, *The Destruction of Slavery*, 1:11–36.

61. GES to Robert Hamilton, 29 January 1862; *WAA*, 11 May 1861; Charles L. Wagandt, "The Army versus Maryland Slavery, 1862–1864," *Civil War History* 10 (June 1964): 141–43; soldier from the Tenth Massachusetts quoted in David W. Blight, "No Desperate Hero: Manhood and Freedom in a Union Soldier's Experience," in *Divided Houses: Gender and the Civil War*, ed. Catherine Clinton and Nina Silber (New York: Oxford University Press, 1992), 70.

62. GES to Robert Hamilton, 19 November, 6 December 1861, 13 February, 19 December 1862.

63. *Christian Recorder*, 4 October 1862.

64. GES to Robert Hamilton, 31 December 1862; *BAP*, 5:152.

65. Eric Foner, *Reconstruction: America's Unfinished Revolution, 1863–1877* (New York: Harper and Row, 1988), 7; *Liberator*, 3 June 1864, quoting Brown; *WAA*, 3 January 1863.

66. *WAA*, 10 January 1863.

67. *WAA*, 3, 17, 24 January 1863; the black paper quoted is *Pacific Appeal*, 7 March 1863.

68. GES to Robert Hamilton, 1 August 1864.

69. *WAA*, 17 January 1863.

70. *WAA*, 9 May 1863; Douglass quoted in Emilio, *A Brave Black Regiment*, 14.

Chapter 2

Liberty or Death: The Fifty-fourth Massachusetts Regiment

George Stephens insisted that the North could not win the war without African Americans: "Black Unionists will have to step in at last and settle the question." Massachusetts's Governor John A. Andrew agreed and, like Stephens, believed that recruitment of black troops also would guarantee the abolition of slavery and advance racial equality. At the beginning of 1863, Andrew organized the Fifty-fourth Regiment of Massachusetts Volunteer Infantry, the first black army unit raised in the North. Stephens promptly relinquished his position with Tilghman to join Andrew's regiment and the new war against slavery.

The idea of black soldiers affronted the racial pride of most whites, however. Democrats, who largely opposed the war and defended the South's right to own slaves, howled when a bill authorizing black troops reached the floor of Congress. "This is a government of white men," one legislator protested, "made by white men for white men, to be administered, protected, defended, and maintained by white men."[1]

Union soldiers recoiled at the thought of fighting alongside blacks. Many claimed that black recruitment represented nothing more than a hypocritical ploy by Northerners "to get rid of their 'niggers.'" The few African Americans who served in white units before 1863 did so at their peril. Regularly insulted and abused, they heard white soldiers threaten to kill any black who "would shoot a white man, even if he was a rebel."[2] When Union regiments of Louisiana blacks appeared on the battlefield early in 1863, some enraged whites fired on them. One haughty Connecticut Yankee jabbered that "a drove of hogs would do better brought down here for we could eat them and the niggers we can't." Only the South's frustrating ability to resist the Union onslaught—and staggering casualty lists—compelled the North to accept the idea of black soldiers. Even then, the acceptance was grudging, and the outcome was doubtful. [3]

In Boston, the seat of Northern abolitionism, bitter enemies of black recruitment lashed out at this "pestilent scheme." The conservative *Courier* insisted that the "truly patriotic and christian population of the North" rejected "an emancipation war." The Democratic and Catholic press feared "unspeakable crimes" by black soldiers or, like the Boston *Pilot* maintained that they "are not yet fit to lead. . . . *Twenty thousand negroes on the march would be smelled ten miles distant.*" Many Northerners, Governor Andrew quickly learned, maintained that the war continued not to save the Union, but "for the deliverance of black men, whom they do not much like."[4]

"Will the Blacks fight?" asked the North. Many doubted it. Yet friends of black rights pointed to the Haitian revolution as proof that blacks could fight zealously, and independent and semiofficial units already in the field offered convincing evidence of black bravery. In Kansas, Missouri, Georgia, South Carolina, and especially in Louisiana, regiments of former slaves displayed extraordinary heroism. Battles at Port Hudson and Milliken's Bend, Louisiana, refuted the notion that blacks could or would not fight. The exploits of the First South Carolina Volunteers, a regiment of former slaves commanded by the Massachusetts abolitionist and Unitarian clergyman Thomas Wentworth Higginson, filled the papers. Higginson, cognizant that his regiment was preparing the ground for those to come, published a series of letters from the front, praising his men for their valor under fire. They faced enemy infantry, cavalry, and artillery, Higginson assured doubters, and "in every instance, come off not only with unblemished honor, but with undisputed triumph."[5]

Ultimately, military necessity convinced whites to try the "experiment" of black recruitment. Soldiers and their families found persuasive the idea that blacks could stop a bullet as well as whites. As one Yankee remarked, "i would a little rather see a nigers head blowed of then a white mans." The Northern press turned arguments of racial inferiority upside down to justify the effort. Blacks, the Boston *Daily Advertiser* rationalized, accustomed to "obedience," "servility," and poverty, would not object to the rigors of military discipline or the privations of army life. Furthermore, the paper held, the "Negro has a ready ear for music, or for 'time' which every drill sergeant knows is the greatest requisite for accuracy in the manual." The black man's reputation for "good humor" also would prove an asset when the march became burdensome. As if trying to convince itself, the paper exclaimed that "no negro soldier can be so stupid as not to understand that his race had a peculiar interest in the issue of this war." Freedom and the vote, it argued, would be their reward for rescuing the Union.[6]

Confident that black bravery would overcome opposition, Governor Andrew won War Department approval on 26 January 1863 to organize the Fifty-fourth Massachusetts Regiment. Lewis Hayden, one of Boston's most influential black abolitionists and a confidant of Andrew, first suggested that the state raise a regiment of black troops. Andrew, a stout abolitionist, needed little encouragement, and on 9 February 1863 he named an advisory committee selected from some of the North's wealthiest families. Amos A. Lawrence, George Luther Stearns, William I. Bowditch, John Murray Forbes, Francis G. Shaw, a Massachusetts abolitionist transplanted to New York, Morris L. Hallowell of Philadelphia, and several others formed its core. They organized the regiment, equipped it, chose the officers to lead it, and conducted the campaign to fill it with the most able black men in the North.[7]

Andrew's advisors, resolute abolitionists, longed to defeat the South and destroy slavery. Determined and unsentimental, self-interest tempered their antislavery convictions. They intended to use "the *negro* for our salvation first and secondly for his own." Although committee members like Forbes and Lawrence had known blacks since their youthful days and recruited their former companions' children for the regiment, they retained odious racial opinions. Forbes, perhaps the most paternalistic of the group, said that military service would teach the black "to take care of himself, under protected rights." When he discussed the Fifty-fourth at Camp Meigs in Readville, just south of Boston, Forbes referred to the *"colored children* at camp Africa." Words like *nigger* or *darky* punctuated their cream-colored stationary. Although they aggressively asserted black rights, members followed up such endorsements with revulsion at the idea of "amalgamation." Stearns's wife described blacks as "children, all eye and ear." Because of their "tropical extraction," she asserted, they took great "delight in color" and should be uniformed as "Chasseurs d'Afrique," with red pants, blue jackets, and yellow turbans. "How splendid their dark skins would look in such a setting," especially with a matching regimental flag, Mary Stearns wrote to Governor Andrew. The recommendations might have been merely ludicrous if her abolitionist husband had not endorsed them as "cogent."[8]

Despite the committee's racial opinions, Andrew had chosen his advisors wisely. He had won over important members of the Beacon Hill aristocracy to the cause of black recruitment, and they dug deep into their purses for its support. The Forbeses, Shaws, and Lawrences wielded enormous power and influence. When they defended Andrew's plan, others listened and contributed. The state's antislavery community, with organizational and personal contacts throughout the Union, threw its weight behind the Fifty-fourth. Forbes, Sterns, and Lawrence each gave $1,000, and twenty others gave $500. Gerrit Smith, the great abolitionist from western New York, contributed $500 and advanced $200 more to Frederick Douglass, the regiment's most important black recruiter.[9]

The Fifty-fourth Massachusetts became the model for all future black regiments. Ultimately, the government organized about 150 regiments of black soldiers after the formation of the Fifty-fourth. It was, Andrew believed, "the most important corps to be organized during the whole war." If it failed, the entire effort to recruit blacks, and perhaps the Union cause itself, would be jeopardized. He meticulously sought information on how to organize the unit from such officers as Higginson and Edward Augustus Wild, a plucky soldier whose heroism at South Mountain had cost him an arm and who had recruited black troops in North Carolina. Higginson had bounding confidence in black soldiers and urged Andrew to reject any attempt by the War Department to assign the regiment to garrison duty: "Their place is with the advance."[10]

Andrew took particular care that the regiment's officers—all whites—opposed slavery and had complete "faith in the capacity of colored men for military service." Although other officers with uncompromising antislavery convictions eagerly sought command of the regiment, Andrew chose Robert Gould Shaw. An inspired choice, Shaw had considerable military experience—although only twenty-five—and his father played a pivotal role in creating the unit. Most important, his family connections made the regiment the personal treasure of the state's antislavery elite.[11]

Well-acquainted with the schemes of professed friends, blacks reacted cautiously to news of the regiment. When he began to organize the Fifty-fourth, Andrew met with the city's black leaders and asked them pointedly, "Will your people enlist in my regiment?" Everyone except his good friend Lewis Hayden said no. Andrew had sought War Department approval for commissioning black officers, but Secretary of War Edwin M. Stanton flatly turned the idea down. Although he left the door open for commissions sometime in the future, for now the Fifty-fourth's officers would all be white. Blacks protested that "our self respect demands that competent colored men shall be at least eligible to promotion." Individual blacks who wanted to join the Fifty-fourth wrote to the governor, demanding to know his position on commissions. Few hesitated to ask sharp questions concerning pay, bounties, state aid to families, treatment of prisoners, the relevance of the Supreme Court's Dred Scott decision, and black rights in general. Local black leaders urged their brethren to stay away from the unit.[12]

At first, distrust abounded. Henry Highland Garnet, who had heralded the Emancipation Proclamation as a triumph, doubted the North's sincerity. "I wish to know," he inquired, "what have black men to fight for in this war?" Others insisted that white racial attitudes would never change. "This is a *white* nation," one black activist bemoaned, "white men are the engineers over its . . . destiny; every dollar spent, every drop of blood shed and every life lost, was a *willing* sacrifice for the furtherance and perpetuity of a white nationality." Throughout the 1850s, blacks had sought an end to Massachusetts's "whites only" militia law. William Wells Brown demanded that the state abandon the offensive rule before recruiting blacks: "Equality first, guns afterward." Likely, Andrew promised to do just that, but when the Fifty-fourth left Massachusetts for glory in South Carolina, it violated state law. The legislature did not strike the word *white* from its militia statutes until 8 February 1864.[13]

Stephens, however, believed that military service represented the "speediest method which could be devised to eradicate that semblance of inferiority of our race, which cruel slavery has created." He placed his final hope for freedom on black recruitment. "It is the means—[the] only means by which the collective power of the negro race can be brought to bear on the civil and political affairs of the country." Blacks, convinced by leaders such as Stephens, soon agreed and backed Governor Andrew's plan for the Fifty-fourth Massachusetts. John S. Rock, the first black to gain the right to argue cases before the U.S. Supreme Court, initially opposed the regiment. Why, he questioned, should we "offer ourselves on the altar of our country" and suffer humiliating discrimination in the army? But Andrew's efforts to negotiate around the War Department's proscriptions and commission black chaplains and physicians convinced Rock and others that "the door to promotion" would not "be permanently closed against us."[14]

By March 1863, Frederick Douglass was calling upon Northern blacks to join the Fifty-fourth Massachusetts. "Men of Color, To Arms!" he cried. The time had come to "smite with death the power that would bury the Government and your liberty in the same hopeless grave." In the end, the idea of uniformed black men shooting slaveowners proved irresistible. As one black Pennsylvanian exclaimed, "They whipped my mother down South; they whipped my sister down South," and he was ready "to go down and whip them." The war offered blacks the opportunity to crush slavery and the nation's cruel racial stereotypes. "If we do not fight, we are traitors to our God, traitors to our country, traitors to our race, and traitors to ourselves." "Liberty or Death!" became the watchword.[15]

The Fifty-fourth Massachusetts had come to symbolize the black struggle for freedom. "Every black man and woman," the *Anglo-African* remarked, "feels a special interest in the success of this regiment." Its men came from virtually every black community in the North, not only from Massachusetts, which had too small a black population to fill the unit. Every soldier carried the aspirations of an entire people. They knew that the "eyes of the whole world" focused on them and that they must "prove ourselves men." Success on the battlefield might end slavery and racial injustice, Stephens reminded his brethren; failure meant disaster.[16]

Northern blacks now devoted themselves to the Fifty-fourth. Black sailors from the USS *Minnesota* contributed $50 for a national flag, exclaiming that those "who would be free, themselves must strike the blow." Women of the community and wives of enlisted men formed soldiers' relief societies to buy regimental flags and provide "those necessities" that the government did not supply.[17] Stephens, Frederick Douglass, William Wells Brown, Charles L. Remond, John S. Rock, Henry Highland Garnet, and scores of other men and women worked to raise the regiment. Nearly every black community formed its own recruitment committee. The old black antislavery and

Northern underground railroad network changed gears and shuttled men to Readville, Massachusetts, instead of to freedom in Canada. Stephen Meyers, head of the underground railroad station in Albany, New York, alone sent 110 men to Massachusetts. Even a sleepy Susquehanna River hamlet like Columbia, Pennsylvania, with a black population of five hundred, sent twenty-three men to Readville.[18]

Boston's famous African Meeting House and other black churches sponsored enlistment rallies. Governor Andrew, Wendell Phillips, and other abolitionists urged blacks to seize the moment. "One thing I know," Phillips exclaimed to one throng at the African Meeting House, "God has given the black race its first great historic chance for writing its name high in the history of the ages." William C. Nell, Boston's black abolitionist leader and the country's first black historian, organized the 1863 annual Crispus Attucks celebration to honor the Fifty-fourth. Blacks also felt a deep sense of gratitude to Andrew for his work. "Bless you, sir," one black women wrote the governor, and as a tribute to Andrew she named her newborn child after him.[19]

The enormous publicity surrounding creation of the Fifty-fourth brought out crackpots and scam artists who claimed to have legions of blacks waiting to join Andrew's regiment. One man from Ohio, looking for financial gain, promised the governor "plenty of patriotic darkies" for the unit. Black volunteers, however, faced real danger from racists, thugs, and street toughs. At the mustering office on Court Street in Boston, the regiment's recruitment officer had to smash a rogue in the face to stop him from kicking black enlistees. The army's official Boston recruiter glanced at a line of black volunteers and spit out "Jesus Christ" as he turned on his heels. On St. Patrick's Day in Buffalo, New York, rioters chased a group of black recruits through the streets. In Philadelphia, fear of violence forced some blacks to board trains secretly at night. White supporters even had to purchase recruits' train tickets, dreading that blacks bound for Massachusetts would provoke a mob.[20]

Philadelphia blacks braved the threats and responded to Massachusetts's call. The city's black leadership joined with white abolitionists in urging men to fill the regiment's ranks. At a 31 March 1863 rally, the Rev. Stephen Smith, one of the city's richest and most influential African Americans, praised the old Bay State as the "first to free the slaves, first to award citizenship to black men, first to give them schools, first to save Kansas for freedom, first to defend the capitol in the present war, first to send teachers to Port Royal slaves, and first to give black men a chance to fight for liberty."[21]

Stephens eagerly took up the work of recruitment. On 6 April 1863 he addressed one of Philadelphia's largest and most successful rallies. He urged men to immediately enlist: "We do not deserve the name of freemen," he declared, "if we disregard the teachings of the hour and fail to place in the balance against oppression, treason and tyranny, our interests, our arms, and our lives." Stephens spoke repeatedly to rallies at black churches to support the federal government's new war against the South. Join the Fifty-fourth, he proclaimed, and win "freedom and equal rights."[22]

Stephens held that the destiny of the Fifty-fourth Massachusetts Regiment would determine the fate of all African Americans. He reminded blacks that racial equality in the North and the slaves' freedom in the South depended upon what the regiment might do. If Northern blacks failed to support the Fifty-fourth, "We would be ranked with the most depraved and cowardly of men." With hope and urgency, he cautioned that "we have more to gain, if victorious, or more to lose, if defeated, than any other class of men." Blacks must see "the stern realities of the present hour" that "are here thundering at our very doors." The "sooner we awaken to their inexorable demands upon us," he implored, "the better for the race, the better for the country, the better for our families, and the better for ourselves."[23]

Stephens had visited the offices of the *Weekly Anglo-African* in New York City on 27 February 1863 and told Robert Hamilton, the paper's editor, that he would join the Fifty-fourth. After two months of recruiting, he made his way to Camp Meigs at Readville. The *Anglo-African* praised Stephens for setting the right example and assured its readers that the paper would continue publishing his popular correspondence, which had been appearing since 1859. Now, he would speak for the country's most important African-American regiment.[24]

According to his service records, Stephens stood five feet, six inches tall and had a light complexion. At thirty-one, he was about five years older than the average Union soldier. Although the majority of the Union army was between eighteen and forty-five, Civil War–era regiments tended to have more older troopers than their modern counterparts. Several men in the Fifty-fourth, for instance, were in their forties and fifties. Stephens's maturity and the experience he had gained with the Twenty-sixth Pennsylvania made him an ideal recruit. He received a promotion to sergeant in Company B only ten days after officially mustering on 30 April.[25]

Stephens had criticized the quality of soldiering and the military discipline he saw in the Army of the Potomac. He would find no grounds for complaint at Camp Meigs. Colonel Shaw maintained strict discipline and banned morally questionable amusements like card playing and drinking. "It is easier to form good habits in the beginning," he advised his fellow officers, "than to correct bad ones later." Each day reveille trumpeted precisely at 6 A.M.; close drills by squad were executed between 9 and noon and again from 1:30 to 5, followed by full dress parade. Shaw required the men to keep their clothes and gear neat and orderly, knapsacks arranged at the foot of bunks, and wool and india rubber blankets precisely folded and placed on beds. Whenever an officer entered enlisted men's quarters, a sergeant like Stephens barked the men to attention, and they instantly fell in and snapped a salute. Everyone felt the gravity of their mission and knew that they "must not fail."[26]

The new soldiers impressed the officers with their earnestness and the speed with which they learned army drills. By late March, Shaw believed that the Fifty-fourth would become "as good a regiment as any that has marched." He had not always manifested such enthusiasm. A few weeks earlier, the colonel bemoaned the quality of men. "They are not," he told his father, "of the best class of nigs." But Shaw had as much to learn—albeit on a different subject—as those he commanded. Although he continued to use language that would have deeply offended his men—had they heard it—their rapid progress greatly impressed him. "My heels are growing very fast," he advised Amos A. Lawrence, "for I am perfectly astonished at the general intelligence these darkeys display." As time passed, Shaw's racism ebbed, and he gained greater respect for the men he would fight with and die for.[27]

The regiment's appearance and conduct also impressed a steady stream of well-wishers and the curious who ventured to Readville. The usual plague of illnesses that visited army camps largely bypassed the regiment, and the number of desertions or those absent without leave remained below two dozen. The threat of encountering Irish policemen or a mob dissuaded the few who might have considered an unofficial "leave" in Boston. The rapid development of the regiment silenced the critics who earlier maintained that blacks could not become soldiers. Even the Boston *Courier* found little to feed its appetite for venom, and the Boston *Daily Advertiser* reported that "visitors have been surprised to find a remarkably fine body of men, with admirable drill and discipline, resolute and earnest; and have come away from the camp . . . with a strong confidence that it will do well."[28]

The regiment's determination and zeal, coupled with the officers' apparent lack of racial prejudice, swept Stephens along. He had the governor's word and assurances from his superior officers that the regiment would receive equal pay and equal treatment from the army. For the present, he could not be a line officer, but the appointment of a black surgeon and chaplain gave Stephens confidence that the color line eventually would be crossed. "The great pathway to honor and emolument," he informed his *Anglo-African* readers, "is opening wide to colored men."[29]

On 18 May, before two to three thousand friends of the regiment, including the state's antislavery leadership, Governor Andrew and his advisory committee presented the men with their regimental colors. A steady breeze tossed the flags under a cloudless sky. While Stephens eyed the Fifty-fourth's standard emblazoned with the words "Liberty, Loyalty, Unity," he heard the governor praise the regiment as "the desire of my own heart." No other Massachusetts regiment mattered as much to him. "My own personal honor, if I have any, is identified with yours," he proclaimed. "I stand or fall as a man and a magistrate with the rise or fall in history of the Fifty-Fourth Massachusetts regiment." When Andrew called Stephens and his fellow soldiers "citizens," the odious effects of the infamous Dred Scott decision seemed to vanish.[30]

There was still cause for concern. Governor Andrew and his staff intended to honor the Fifty-fourth on 28 May with a grand march through the streets of Boston before the regiment left for South Carolina and the war. With characteristic lack of confidence, Colonel Shaw insisted that the parade take place the same day the regiment shipped out to minimize the number of desertions and drunken rows. The governor and the regiment's supporters had other fears: a race riot. Andrew had dropped plans to march the regiment down Broadway in New York, a city well known for its incendiary racial tensions, when he heard rumors that the "mob element" intended to disrupt the ceremonies. The Fifty-fourth's officers received word that "the roughs in Boston proposed to attack us as we passed through" the city. Because recruits already had been assaulted, everyone took the warnings to heart. In New Bedford, where many men of Company C lived, enemies of the Fifty-fourth threatened to burn out the black community. At least twenty blacks armed themselves and patrolled the streets in anticipation of attack. One white abolitionist bought the chaplain of the Fifty-fifth Massachusetts Regiment (the state's second black unit, still forming at Readville) a revolver for his protection. Although Andrew believed that calm would rule, he took no chances and had "six rounds of ball cartridges" issued to the men, and the unit's rear guard marched with fixed bayonets.[31]

The Fifty-fourth arrived in Boston at 9 A.M. and formed at Park Square for its march through the city. Henry I. Bowditch, a member of Andrew's recruitment committee, waited nervously for what would happen next. An uncomfortable silence fell on the growing multitudes. Bowditch, risking a beating or the withering stares of angry Bostonians, removed his hat and swung out into the street. As he bellowed, "Three cheers for Col. Shaw," Shaw turned to see him. A tense moment passed, and then "three rousing cheers" erupted from the throng. For the rest of the day, glory, triumph, flowers, and handkerchiefs showered down on the men. Additional trains ran that morning to bring thousands of well-wishers into Boston. It was "Anniversary Week," and hundreds of abolitionists, reformers, and evangelicals had poured into the city for the yearly meeting of reform societies. Delegates to the New England Anti-Slavery Convention, the Educational Commission for Freedmen, the American Revival Associates, the Sabbath School Society, the Moral Reform Society, the Union Maternal Association, the Anti-Tobacco Society, and scores of others left their deliberations to join the adulation.[32]

Merchants suspended business for the day to join the men and women, black and white, who filled the streets and the windows of countless flag-draped buildings along the parade route. Governor Andrew, his entire military staff, the executive council, the state senate, Sen. Henry Wilson, the mayor, and city officials all stood on the steps of the State House to review the regiment. A drum corps of black children led the Fifty-fourth through the streets, accompanied by Patrick Gilmore's marching band playing the John Brown song. They passed the shuttered offices of the Boston *Pilot*, which had so recently scorned the very idea of black soldiers, and crossed over the spot where Crispus Attucks lost his life in the earlier cause for liberty. As the regiment paraded down Essex Street, they passed the home of Wendell Phillips, where William Lloyd Garrison stood on the balcony. As he overlooked the magnificent spectacle, one of his hands rested on a bust of John Brown.[33]

As Stephens and the regiment drilled on Boston Common and then resumed the march through the city, thousands of family members and friends broke into the ranks to kiss the men and distribute flowers. To the utter astonishment of George T. Downing, the wealthy Rhode Island black restauranteur, even Irish women waved their handkerchiefs in greeting. One black woman had traveled from Chicago to see her two sons off to war. Charged with emotion, she clasped their hands, kissed them, and left, tears streaming down her face. Strangers shook their hands, one officer recalled, and blessed them. Colonel Shaw's Uncle Howland strode to the front of the ranks to say farewell to his nephew, who leaned down from his horse to kiss him goodbye. The Quaker abolitionist, pacifist, and poet John Greenleaf Whittier turned out despite his distaste for the military. He saw in Shaw and his men "the very flower of grace and chivalry, he seemed to me beautiful and awful as an angel of God, come down to lead the hosts of freedom to victory." Amos A. Lawrence, who had played so central a role in organizing the regiment, stood on a window ledge on Franklin Street to view the procession. As he watched the men pass below, he prayed that they would "crush the rebellion, and . . . crush its cause with it: slavery. Would to God," he said, "I could fight these battles for these young men."[34]

The Fifty-fourth's enemies also made an appearance, but few noticed. The dyspeptics and dilettantes snarled in their diaries that the "Nigger Reg't left" or muttered that the regiment would run at the first sign of a fight. One malcontent who insulted the men found himself sprawled on the ground. More seriously, thugs beat Charles Remond Douglass, a son of Frederick Douglass, who had joined the regiment along with his brother Lewis but had been too ill to march. When the Fifty-fourth reached the wharf to board the *De Molay* for its journey south, street toughs tried to assault the rear of the column, but police intervened in time to save the thugs from several armed and angry black soldiers.[35]

The rush of men to the Fifty-fifth's recruiting office the next morning and the newspapers' radiant reports of the day more accurately reflected sentiment in the city. The Fifty-fourth's grand march, the

Boston *Evening Transcript* decreed, was "an event of momentous importance in the annals of the State and Union." One only had to recall that a few brief years earlier all the coercive powers of the state had united to return Anthony Burns, Thomas Sims, and others to bondage. "Now a thousand men of the same race march proudly through our avenues, to fight under the protection of the State and the Nation. . . . Glory enough for one day," William C. Nell, concluded, "'aye, indeed for a life-time.'"[36]

*   *   *

The *De Molay* steamed safely to South Carolina. Accustomed to long ocean voyages, Stephens likely weathered the trip without incident. Others in his regiment proved less seaworthy, and, only one day out, several succumbed to seasickness. The stench onboard overwhelmed many. A groom, taken along to care for the officers' horses, fell asleep on deck one night, rolled overboard, and drowned. Although only a few days passed before the ship docked at Hilton Head, South Carolina, some scuffling occurred among the men and the ship's crew. One man suffered a bayonet wound in the face, and a crew member was lashed to the rigging for stealing from a soldier. The sight of Hilton Head on 3 June and Beaufort the next day washed away the bitterness, however. As the regiment broke out in song, soldiers from other Massachusetts regiments already stationed in the Department of the South came to greet the ship, enthralled to see "a Boston vessel with a Massachusetts negro reg't on board come up to the dock of this most aristocratic old slave-holding city." Although several days passed before the ground stopped rolling beneath their feet, the men of the Fifty-fourth could hardly believe that they had finally arrived in the South to fight slavery.[37]

On 4 June the Fifty-fourth bivouacked on a plantation just outside Beaufort. The South Carolina Sea Islands, caressed by bright sunny skies, are blessed with warm, sandy soil, luxuriant evergreens, towering cypress trees, and expansive oaks draped with sweeping moss. Fig, palm, and orange trees, oleander as high as a house, and enchanting lilies with stems as thick as a man's thumb graced some of the most resplendent plantations of the South. The dove's early-morning coo and the mockingbird's fanciful songs kindled romance, while ominous alligators and six-foot-long turtles added to the wonderment. Insufferable fleas, blackflies, mosquitoes, fire ants, and other unseen abominations proved vexing but could not dampen the regiment's sense of awe or fierce determination.[38]

The Fifty-fourth remained in Beaufort for only a few days. On 10 June, Col. James Montgomery, the regiment's enigmatic brigade commander who led the Second South Carolina Volunteers, ordered the Fifty-fourth to board troop transports for a raid against Darien, Georgia. Quiet and mannerly, the Kentucky-born Montgomery retained an Old Testament-like sense of revenge from his days fighting pro-slavery forces in Kansas. Shaw and the men of the Fifty-fourth thought the attack would reap valuable military stores and cotton or free hundreds of slaves. Shaw was horrified, however, when Montgomery ordered the largely deserted town on the winding Altamaha River looted and burned. Shaw protested the orders and advised Governor Andrew that the action "disgusted me exceedingly," although he eventually softened his response to the destruction of Darien.

Stephens did not protest the raid at the time but later thought that such marauding would damage the Fifty-fourth's reputation. His company captured the regiment's first enemy flag, and nearly everyone came away with a memento of their first action. In the end, as the men returned to camp on St. Simon's Island and watched the glow of the flames that night, few mourned the destruction. "It may be the best way to treat those who for so many years have robbed so many thousands of their just dues," Lt. Richard Henry Lee Jewett wrote to his wife, "& made so many hearts suffer with anguish at their cruelty."[39]

The unit itched for a real fight against rebel troops. "Would it not be a proud thing if the colored troops should take a prominent part in the capture of Charleston?" one officer recorded in his diary. Shaw proudly watched his men perform like seasoned veterans. He still had not risen above Yankee paternalism though, and could not repress his sense of surprise that "negroes adapt themselves to all the discomforts & inconveniences of campaigning." He also doubted that the Fifty-fourth would perform adequately in battle. On 4 June he admitted to Thomas Wentworth Higginson that he considered placing the regiment "between two fires in case of need, and so cutting off their retreat."[40] The test for Shaw and the Fifty-fourth came soon enough.

On 11 July, in scorching heat and harassed by relentless sand flies and mosquitoes, the regiment landed on James Island, just south of Charleston harbor. On 15 July, Stephens's company along with two others manned the picket lines before the rebel earthworks. Stephens later recalled that the spirit of his men could hardly be contained. One soldier with a reputation as a "dare-devil" crawled out beyond the picket line to shoot at the rebels. "I thought it best," Stephens said, "not to report him." The next day, as Stephens spoke with Sgt. Peter Vogelsang, two or three shots drew their attention. When they looked up, nearly three hundred rebels came crashing toward them. Both ran to their posts as cannon shells and minnié balls filled the air. When Vogelsang and about eight men attempted to flee across a creek, rebels shot several of the men in the water. His position hopeless, Vogelsang turned and stood erect in response to a call for him to surrender. A rebel officer promptly shot him through the chest. Sgt. Joseph D. Wilson of Company H "swore he would not retreat & there died." Several men in Stephens's company also refused to give ground and, as Stephens wrote, fell facing the foe. A white soldier in the nearby Tenth Connecticut heard one rebel officer yell "take no prisoners." Some of the Fifty-fourth who could not be saved in the retreat were wounded and later found either bound and shot or bayonetted.[41]

Although surprised by the attack, the Fifty-fourth's stand delayed the rebels long enough for the Tenth Connecticut to escape encirclement and for Union gunboats to arrive and drive off the attackers. The regiment's heroism, Capt. Luis F. Emilio proudly reported, changed many "opinions in regard to Negro bravery." When the regiment arrived in the Department of the South, one officer recalled, it was "not counted worthy of the fellowship of white men." Even the commander of the Union naval forces blockading Charleston, Adm. Samuel F. Du Pont, had considered the unit an exercise in folly, "'Coal to Newcastle,' sure enough," he wrote to his wife.[42]

After the regiment's spirited defense on James Island, opinions changed. White units asked to be brigaded with the Fifty-fourth, and Gen. Alfred H. Terry, a divisional commander in the Department of the South, informed Shaw that he was "exceedingly pleased with the conduct of your regiment." Members of the Tenth Connecticut later visited the Fifty-fourth's camp to thank the men for saving their lives and express their desire to fight along side them. "I will take the gentleman of color everytime," one soldier remarked in the New York *Tribune*, "both because he *is* more of a gentleman, and a more loyal man."[43]

Union commanders allowed the regiment no time to lick its wounds. Relieved at 4 P.M. on the day of the battle, Stephens and the

Fifty-fourth marched all night, single-file, in pitch darkness and a driving rain, to Coles Island. Wet branches slapped their faces as the men struggled through brush and bog. One officer recalled that "I could not see a man 10 feet away & I could only keep my connection by holding on to the last man in the co. before me with one hand and seizing my orderly with the other." The next day, military transports took the regiment to Morris Island, where they briefly rested, ate, and received orders to move to the front.[44]

Although less barren today than in 1863, Morris Island still has all the appeal of a stark Pacific atoll. At the southern edge of Charleston harbor, the four-hundred-acre barrier island had served as Charleston's quarantined burial ground before the war and earned the prophetic name of Coffin Land. Beyond the wide sandy beaches lay low hills, salt marshes, and little else. Near the northern tip, stretching across the narrowest point on the island, sat Battery Wagner.

As part of the defensive network that ringed Charleston harbor, Wagner protected Fort Sumter's exposed southern wall. "Judicious in its location as it was formidable in its construction," Department of the South commander Quincy A. Gillmore remarked in one of the understatements of the war, Wagner commanded the northern half of Morris Island. Its sand and palmetto-log construction made it virtually impregnable to a frontal assault—"each portion of the work was a fort in itself"—and capable of withstanding thunderous cannon fire. At least twenty feet of sand covered its indestructible main bomb-proof, designed to shelter its 1,700–man garrison. Those who inspected the fortification after its evacuation thought that it could have absorbed the full fury of the Union cannons. "Altogether," one officer later remarked, "the general opinion is that it was madness to have assaulted this place on July 18th."[45]

The Union army's Department of the South, stretching along the sea coast from South Carolina to northern Florida, offered madness a congenial home. The department's major military operations, the seizure of Wagner, the invasion of Florida, and the siege of Charleston, proved disastrous or pointless. The War Department, the army, and the navy disagreed over strategy and tactics and fought over which branch of the service should take the lead in subduing the city. Their failure to better coordinate activities cost the lives of many Union soldiers. After withstanding nearly four years of Union blockades and sieges, rebels finally abandoned Charleston in February 1865. But they fled Sherman's massive army from the West, not Gillmore's command just five miles across the harbor.[46]

Worst of all, the Department of the South pursued a dubious goal. Although capturing the seat of secession early in the war would have boosted Northern morale and proved politically advantageous, the Lincoln administration never allocated sufficient resources for the task, finding, quite rightly, that the city had little military value and could be effectively neutralized by a blockade. Gillmore described his predicament succinctly in a 10 August 1863 letter to Lincoln's general-in-chief Henry W. Halleck. "General [P. G. T.] Beauregard has for the defense of Charleston twice as many men and more than five times as much artillery as I have . . . so long as it [the Union force] remains greatly inferior in numbers to that of the enemy," Gillmore complained, his army "must remain defensively upon these sea islands."[47]

Gillmore ultimately succeeded in tying down a Confederate force of about twenty thousand men, but the approximately eighteen thousand federal troops employed to accomplish that goal might have been put to better use elsewhere. In July 1863, the Philadelphia *Press* questioned the entire mission of the department. Charleston, it concluded, "has not been attacked by a great army, nor defended by one." Even former slaves in the Sea Islands understood that the Union army in the Department of the South would never gain much ground. One former slave advised the head of the Northern missionary and relief effort at Port Royal that "if you're as long beating Secesh everywhere as you have been in taking the town [Charleston], guess it'll take you some time!"[48]

Gillmore first attempted to take Battery Wagner with a daylight frontal assault on 11 July. Seven Union regiments ran headlong into Wagner's strongest walls. Withering cannon and rifle fire threw the survivors back across the sand. For the next several days Gillmore hammered out a strategy to take the fortress with the new U.S. Naval commander, Adm. John A. Dahlgren. Although they denied press reports that bitterness and rancor divided them and damaged military effectiveness, Gillmore and Dahlgren failed to get along. "Gillmore is an engineer," Dahlgren concluded, "but no general."[49]

Gillmore insisted on another frontal assault. This time he believed that a night assault preceded by a day-long artillery and naval barrage would leave Wagner's defenders so dazed or devastated that his attacking forces would enter the battery virtually unopposed. Rain delayed movement of the artillery on 17 July and held up the heavy bombardment until noon the next day, when broadsides from the navy's new gun platform, the USS *New Ironsides,* and five Monitors joined the barrage. By nightfall, nine thousand Union shells had screamed into Wagner in the heaviest bombardment of the war. A *Tribune* reporter who witnessed the shelling thought "no human being could live beneath so terrible a fire whether protected by bomb-proofs or not."[50]

Survive they did. Wagner's able commander Gen. William B. Taliaferro had arrived only one week earlier. Virginia born and Harvard educated, Taliaferro had been the U.S. Army's chief officer in Charles Town, Virginia, the day of John Brown's execution. At Wagner, he planned carefully, protected his cannon with sandbags, and drilled his men to rush to their fighting positions as soon as the bombardment lifted. Rebels also had broken the Union codes, and Taliaferro had intercepted enough messages to know what to expect. At sunset, as thunderstorms in the West replaced the thunder of federal artillery, rebel defenders found that they had lost only eight killed and twenty wounded. His men cleared Wagner's embrasures, doubled-loaded their cannon with grape and canister, and waited.[51]

Shaw had met with Gen. George Crockett Strong, Union field commander, on 2 July. With new confidence in his men, he asked Strong to include the Fifty-fourth in any fight involving his brigade "to give the black troops a chance to show what stuff they are made of." The Fifty-fourth's conduct had impressed Strong, and he wished to place it "where the most severe work was to be done and the highest honor to be won." Gen. Truman Seymour, ranking Union commander on the field, agreed, and the Fifty-fourth moved to the front and took cover in the sand to avoid rebel cannon fire.[52]

Stephens, on the far right wing of the first line, closest to the water's edge, recalled General Strong telling the men that a thousand soldiers waited just behind to support their charge. "Take that battery," he commanded, pointing at Wagner. He reminded the regiment that the whole world waited to hear of their efforts, of their success or failure. "Men," he asked, "are you ready to take that fort?" Each man exclaimed, "Yes!" Sgt. Robert J. Simmons, who would be captured in the attack and die in a rebel prison, turned to Stephens and said, "If anything be falls me don't forget to write my mother!" Despite Simmons's prophetic request, Stephens found the regiment surprisingly lighthearted "in the presence of danger." As he waited in the dimming light for word to attack, rebel cannon balls skipped across the sand. Few seemed concerned. "I guess da kinda specs we're comin," one man joked.[53]

Colonel Shaw paced up and down the line in the moments before nightfall. Stephens fixed his bayonet and heard, "Attention." Shaw, standing at the head of the formation, told the regiment to "prove yourselves men." As the order to move out hit their ears, "devious shrikes" from rebel cannon filled the air. The last words that many in the unit heard were to charge "at the double quick." Inside Wagner, Taliaferro's men saw only an indistinct mass of advancing columns soon lost in the darkness, smoke, and confusion. As Stephens recalled, the enemy "withheld their fire until we reached within fifty yards of the work, when jets of flame darted forth from every corner and embrasure." Not even the hell of Fredericksburg, he thought, matched the "terrific fire which blazed along the narrow approach to Wagner."[54]

Nothing went as planned. Rather than weak resistance, the regiment encountered the enemy at full strength. The Fifty-fourth had been told that federal artillery shells had filled the moat that lay in front of Wagner. Instead, they found a broad ditch filled with water. Temporarily stymied, the columns again advanced. "The bodies of our own men," one survivor recalled, served as "stepping stones in the water where we crossed." Shaw died on the parapets with his soldiers, toward the center of the work after staring down into a mass of glittering bayonets. Stephens and the remains of his column entered a portion of Wagner closest to the ocean but could advance no further. Rebels poured a continuously lethal fire into their ranks; the musketry "steadily grew hotter on our left," Stephens remembered. "We fired our rifles and fought as hard as we could," he explained to regimental historian Capt. Luis F. Emilio years later, but "the rebel fire grew hotter and fiercer." Musketry and cannon fire thinned his ranks, and "men all around me would fall and roll down the scarp into the ditch."[55]

Just as the rebel fire became hottest, a fresh Union battalion—probably the Forty-eighth and 100th New York Regiments—charged up from the moat toward Stephens's faltering position. Thinking that reinforcements had rescued him, Stephens was stunned to see the Union soldiers pour a volley into his position. "I was one of the men who shouted from where I stood 'Don't fire on us we are the Fifty-fourth.'" Perhaps at this moment a bullet or shell fragment shattered Stephens's gun, temporarily paralyzing his hands. Had the New Yorkers followed orders and charged with loaded but uncapped weapons they might have joined the Fifty-fourth's survivors and established a foothold that would have led to Wagner's capture. Instead, Union soldiers shot their own men, others surrendered, and a few—Stephens remembered only twelve to fifteen—slid back down the embankment to make their way to safety through "hissing bullets and bursting shells." When they reached Union lines, the horrified men found the rear guard drunk and shooting retreating soldiers, particularly blacks.[56]

"We had the advance of everything," Captain Emilio wrote to his parents after the fight; the regiment had "charged clear up to the fort; but it was no use." All the officers that entered Wagner with Stephens, except Emilio, lay dead or wounded. The supporting white troops had broken under the devastating rebel fire, and a third brigade failed to support the attack, leaving the Fifty-fourth stranded.[57] Those who had not escaped with Stephens and Emilio surrendered to an uncertain fate. Enraged rebels bayonetted many black troops, and only the presence of Confederate officers stopped the summary execution of others.[58] Confederate outrage at having to fight black soldiers knew few bounds. They refused to allow a truce, leaving Union wounded to their fate. Many of the wounded agonized through the night or drowned in the rising surf. Some survivors who had been hiding in the swamps and sand did not make their way back to camp until two days after the assault. The morning after the attack, Confederates stripped Shaw's body for souvenirs and buried him in a trench with his men. According to a Philadelphia *Inquirer* correspondent, one soldier who had been killed in the attack was later scalped and his ears severed. Months afterward, as the sea washed away a narrow sand ridge, the regiment discovered that the rebels had buried the Fifty-fourth's dead "face down-ward."[59]

The regiment's conduct initially came under harsh review because so many men returned without weapons. In the confusion, terror, and hand-to-hand combat, many soldiers had either lost their weapons or, like Stephens, had them shot out of their hands. The criticism quickly evaporated, though, when the full story of the assault became known. Many soldiers held Gillmore responsible for the slaughter. The general even admitted to Admiral Dahlgren that far too many men had been lost and the assault "ought not to have taken place." In 1886, however, when Emilio interviewed Gillmore, the retired general disclaimed all responsibility for the raid, saying that Seymour had been in charge and that he had not ordered it. In all, the battle cost 1,515 Union casualties. The Fifty-fourth, which sent six hundred men and twenty-three officers against Wagner, lost 272 in killed, wounded, and captured. Confederate defenders lost only 181 men.[60]

Sea Island blacks, who watched over the regiment, brought immense amounts of food to the Fifty-fourth's wounded recovering on St. Helena. Cartloads of melons and sweet potatoes poured into the hospitals for the relief of the men who, as one former slave put it, were "wounded for we." Another man walked seven miles to bring a "load of corn from our people for de sogers in the hospital."[61] Their concern also revealed enormous pride in what the Fifty-fourth had accomplished. Although its attack had failed, the regiment had won a far greater battle. Whatever the North thought of blacks, whites could no longer claim that black men could not be reliable soldiers. The Philadelphia *Press* spoke for most Northern papers when it proclaimed that the regiment's heroism at Wagner had settled the matter of black recruitment. "The employment of colored troops has ceased to be an experiment . . . we shall welcome the day when one hundred thousand of them are fighting for our flag." The Massachusetts Adjutant General's Office declared that all effective opposition to the use of black troops had ended, and "many of their fiercest enemies have become their fastest friends." Swelled with pride, it confidently predicted that "the time will come when they will be commanded by officers of their own color and race."[62]

The glory proved short-lived. The attack left the Fifty-fourth decimated and demoralized. Normal company activities such as morning reports and rosters proved impossible to collect, especially because so many officers lay dead or wounded. Although the regimental books listed 538 men "present for duty," only 350 actually reported on 1 August. Stephens's Company B had been decimated by the Wagner assault. It lost most of its officers, four out of five sergeants, and two of eight corporals. Although the company went into the battle with ninety-seven men, only seventy-six survived. A month after the engagement, sixty-one enlisted men possessed only twenty-six functioning rifles. Not until January 1864 did Stephens's company return to full strength. Morale sank further as the survivors reflected upon what had been lost. "The death of Colonel Shaw is a terrible blow to the regiment," the Fifty-fourth's surgeon reported to Governor Andrew. "The men had the greatest confidence and pride in him, in his judgment, prudence and watchfulness." Moreover, the loss of so many fine officers and men and the hardships of the weeks leading up to the assault had taken a toll. "They need time to rest," he told the governor.[63]

Although the Fifty-fourth desperately needed a respite, Union commanders immediately put it to work in the trenches in front of Wagner. For the sake of appearances, Stephens wrote that the regiment eagerly took up its new duties as fatigue workers, digging ditches. "I feel proud that we are thus honored with the post of danger," he informed readers of the *Anglo-African*. He felt nothing of the sort. From 19 July to 19 September, the regiment executed no military drills, obtained no further training, and did nothing but unload supplies and dig sap lines—ditches—toward Battery Wagner. As he informed William Still back in Philadelphia, the Fifty-fourth had become a group of "ditchers," not soldiers. "The spade and shovel is their only implement of warfare." The "Regiment," he advised Still, "is in a state of demoralization."[64]

Day and night, and under direct rebel fire, the Fifty-fourth and other black units were ordered to dig. While whites served as guards, blacks dug their way toward Wagner through the old quarantined graveyard and through fresher ones holding Union and Confederate dead. They performed herculean tasks, digging for eight to ten hours a day and so fast that observing rebel troops thought that the Yankees had invented some new ditch-digging machine. Unamused by the pace of the work, rebels within shouting distance taunted them or made the work more treacherous by firing cannon filled with glass, wire, and fragments of boiler plate.[65]

When not in the trenches, blacks received orders to dig wells for white troops. Although a few white units, especially the engineer corps, worked in the sap lines, black troops performed most of the hard labor. If there was "a ditch to dig, a gun to mount or a ship to unload," Col. Norwood P. Hallowell of the Fifty-fifth Massachusetts Regiment complained to Governor Andrew, a request was made for "*colored* soldiers." White troops pulled easy duty, and captured rebels did nothing, Hallowell charged, but lounge "around the beach having a very comfortable and jolly time." He warned Andrew that the treatment accorded to the state's blacks troops would cause trouble.

"The Colored soldiers put the . . . facts together, and ask their officers what it all means." The Fifty-fourth's soldiers knew all too well
what it meant and began sending anonymous letters to Andrew to
protest their treatment. "We suffer in Every Respect like we was Dogs
or cattle," one man bitterly complained.[66]

As if their ordeal was not painful enough, the crushing news of the
New York City draft riots reached the Fifty-fourth right after the Wagner assault. During the second week of July, white mobs vented their
opposition to the new federal draft by attacking city blacks. In an orgy
of hate, rioters beat and murdered scores of blacks and clashed with
police and federal troops. They destroyed black homes and burned the
Colored Orphan Asylum, screaming, "Kill the monkies, Roast the black
s--s of b-----s." Rioters dragged Abraham Franklin from his bed and beat
him to death in the street. Before his horror-stricken mother they
hanged Franklin's body from a lamp post, cut away his trousers at the
knees, hacked off pieces of flesh, and then set the corpse ablaze.[67]

"What cause or provocation have the New York rabble for disloyalty to their country, and for their bloody, atrocious assaults on my
countrymen?" Stephens asked. "Are we their enemies? Have we tyrannized over them? Have we maltreated them? Have we robbed them?
Are we alien enemies? Are we traitors?" he questioned. He reminded his readers that as the bloodthirsty mob beat and killed New York
blacks—including family members of Fifty-fourth soldiers—"we were
doing our utmost to sustain the honor of our country's flag, to perpetuate, if possible, those civil, social, and political liberties, they, who
so malignantly hate us, have so fully enjoyed." The regiment's disillusionment ran deep.[68]

Union commanders in the Department of the South heaped further
insult and humiliation on the Fifty-fourth. Because so many officers
had been killed or disabled in the Wagner attack, noncommissioned
officers such as Stephens effectively commanded their companies and
took the place of officers in formation. Col. Milton S. Littlefield, a
politically appointed officer with no military experience, temporarily led the regiment and refused to accept the sergeants' assumption
of officers' duties, ordering the sergeants back into the ranks. In any
other regiment, men who had proven themselves in battle would have
been rewarded with advancement. With so many vacancies in the
Fifty-fourth, Stephens and his fellow sergeants rightfully believed that
their heroism and proven leadership abilities would be rewarded with

a commission. Instead, inexperienced whites from other regiments without the antislavery convictions of the original officers received the promotions. Several openly opposed the idea of black officers. The "evidence teaches us," Stephens sadly informed William Still, "that col[ore]d. men have nothing to hope for here in the way of promotion." Disillusioned and incensed, he asked Still to help him transfer out of the regiment.[69]

Nothing ever came of Stephens's attempt, and he remained with the Fifty-fourth for the duration of the war. The Confederate evacuation of Wagner in the early morning of 7 September 1863 provided some relief. Sap lines had been completed up to Wagner's walls, and Gillmore planned to order yet another attack that morning. When men from the Fifty-fourth examined the improvements rebels had made to Wagner's defenses, they shuddered. Three-foot-long spikes protruded from the wall of the moat, and needle-sharp nails had been placed in boards at the bottom of the ditch. Land mines—"torpedoes"—one Union officer noted, were "as abundant as blueberries." "Providence," Emilio wrote home, had "interposed against more slaughter."[70]

There had been slaughter enough. As Stephens and his fellow soldiers inspected their long-sought-after prize, few could muster happiness or glee. Body parts littered the sands both in and out of the fortification, turning the area into a charnel house. Susie King Taylor, wife of a soldier in the Thirty-third USCT (First South Carolina Volunteers), served as an army nurse. When she visited Wagner she was sickened by the "fleshless heads and grinning jaws" that lined footpaths. One officer from the Fifty-fourth mourned the sands strewn with spent bullets, rusting iron, sticks, and bones. Almost "every yard of this desolate and barren sand," he sadly noted, had been enriched and made "sacred by the blood of someone's father son brother, or husband." Union casualties sustained in the attempt to capture Wagner, beginning on 10 July and concluding on 7 September 1863, totaled 2,318.[71]

Notes

1. GES to Robert Hamilton, 21 March 1862; Boston *Daily Advertiser,* 2 January 1863; Boston *Daily Courier,* 8 January 1863; Howard C. Westwood, *Black Troops, White Commanders, and Freedmen during the Civil War* (Carbondale: Southern Illinois University Press, 1992), 6–8; Randall Jimerson, *The*

Private Civil War: Popular Thought during the Sectional Conflict (Baton Rouge: Louisiana State University Press, 1988), 89–94; Leonard P. Curry, *Blueprint for Modern America: Nonmilitary Legislation of the First Civil War Congress* (Nashville: Vanderbilt University Press, 1968), 61–67; legislator's quotation from Forrest G. Wood, *Black Scare: The Racist Response to Emancipation and Reconstruction* (Berkeley: University of California Press, 1968), 43.

2. "Northern Negro Soldiers," New York *Atlas* clipping in Executive Department Letters, MSA; *WAA*, 11 April 1863.

3. Boston *Daily Courier*, 11 April 1863; John C. Ropes to John C. Gray, Jr., 7 February 1863, in John Chipman Gray and John Codman Ropes, *War Letters, 1862–1865* (Boston: Houghton, Mifflin, 1927), 78–82; Bell I. Wiley, "Billy Yank and the Black Folk," *Journal of Negro History* 36 (January 1951): 49–50; Frederick Douglass, *Life and Times of Frederick Douglass* (New York: Collier Books, 1962), 337; soldier's threat from Jimerson, *The Private Civil War*, 91–94.

4. Boston *Daily Courier*, 29 January, 4 February 1863; Boston *Post*, 23 February, 27 March 1863; *Pilot* in *Liberator*, 15 May 1863, emphasis in the original; John A. Andrew to William Lloyd Garrison, 7 April 1863, William Lloyd Garrison Papers, Boston Public Library.

5. Benjamin Quarles, *The Negro in the Civil War* (1953, reprint, New York: Da Capo Press, 1989), 111–18; Thomas Wentworth Higginson, *Army Life in a Black Regiment* (1890, reprint, Boston: Beacon Press, 1962); Boston *Daily Evening Traveller*, 11 February (Higginson's quotation), 13 February 1863. See also Boston *Daily Courier*, 21 February 1863; Charleston *Advertiser*, 4 April 1863; Boston *Post*, 21 April, 13 June 1863; Boston *Daily Advertiser*, 2 February 1863.

6. Jimerson, *The Private Civil War*, 96–110; Boston *Daily Advertiser*, 28 May 1863; unnamed Yankee quoted in Reid Mitchell, *Civil War Soldiers: Their Expectations and Their Experiences* (New York: Simon and Schuster, 1988), 195–96.

7. Frank Preston Stearns, *The Life and Public Services of George Luther Stearns* (Philadelphia: J. B. Lippincott, 1907), 286; George Washington Williams, *A History of the Negro Troops in the War of the Rebellion, 1861–65* (1888, reprint, New York: Bergman Publishers, 1968), 103; Richard P. Hallowell to Amos A. Lawrence, 12 February 1863, John A. Andrew to Amos A. Lawrence, 9 February 1863, "Draft Circular," January[?] 1863, Amos A. Lawrence Papers, MHS; John Murray Forbes to John Henry Clifford, 16 February 1863, John Henry Clifford Papers, MHS.

8. John Murray Forbes to John A. Andrew, 27 January 1863, John A. Andrew Papers, MHS; Amos A. Lawrence Diary, 19 February 1863, Elisa Green to Amos A. Lawrence, 17 August 1863, Amos A. Lawrence Papers, MHS; John Murray Forbes to Ednah Dow Cheney, 3 May 1863, Misc. Ms, Boston Public Library; Robert Gould Shaw to Sarah B. Shaw, 20 February 1863, Robert Gould Shaw Papers, HLHU; Samuel Gridly Howe to Louis Agassiz, 18 August 1863, Samuel G. Howe Papers, HLHU; John Murray Forbes to Robert Gould Shaw,

17 March 1863, Mary E. Stearns to John A. Andrew, 20 February 1863, and George L. Stearns to Andrew, 20 February 1863, Executive Department Letters, MSA.

9. "Circular," 13 February 1863, Misc. Bound Collection, 1838–1908, MHS; "Account Book," 1863, and Subscription Paper, 1863, Amos A. Lawrence Papers, MHS; Charles W. Slack to Edward W. Kinsley, "Wednesday," Edward W. Kinsley Papers, MHS; Emancipation League Records, Boston Public Library; Frederick Douglass to Gerrit Smith, 12 March 1863, Executive Department Letters, MSA; *Liberator*, 27 March, 20 November 1863; *Commonwealth*, 21 February 1863.

10. Dudley Taylor Cornish, *The Sable Arm: Negro Troops in the Union Army, 1861–1865* (New York: W. W. Norton, 1966), 288; John A. Andrew to Francis G. Shaw, 30 January 1863, in William Schouler, *Annual Report of the Adjutant General . . . 1863* (Boston: State of Massachusetts, 1864), 55–56; Thomas Wentworth Higginson to John A. Andrew, 19 January 1863, Executive Department letters, MSA; Richard Reid, "Raising the African Brigade: Early Black Recruitment in Civil War North Carolina," *North Carolina Historical Review* 70 (July 1993): 274–75.

11. Unidentified clipping, 10 April 1864, Fifty-fourth Regiment Papers, vol. 4, MHS; John Murray Forbes to John A. Andrew, 2 February 1863, John A. Andrew to Francis G. Shaw, 30 January 1863, John A. Andrew Papers, MHS; John Murray Forbes to John A. Andrew, 30 January 1863, typescript copy, Morris Hallowell to John Murray Forbes, 30 January 1863, Norwood Penrose Hallowell Papers, MHS; Robert Gould Shaw to John A. Andrew, 27 March 1863, Executive Department letters, MSA; Emilio, *A Brave Black Regiment*, 3–4.

12. Stearns, *Life and Public Services*, 286–87; Norwood P. Hallowell, "Lewis and Harriet Hayden," 28 December 1893, clipping in Norwood Penrose Hallowell Papers, MHS; George L. Stearns to John A. Andrew, 28 March 1863, Charles Henry Wesley to John A. Andrew, 10 February 1863, Mitchell S. Haynes to John A. Andrew, 27 March 1863, John A. Andrew to John Wilder, 23 May 1863, Thomas Wentworth Higginson to John A. Andrew, February-March[?] 1863, Executive Department Letters, MSA; Boston *Daily Evening Traveller*, 9 February 1863; Robert Gould Shaw to John A. Andrew, 8 April 1863, Robert Gould Shaw Papers, HLHU; John Whittier Messer Appleton to Luis F. Emilio, 19 March 1883, Fifty-fourth Regiment Papers, vol. 4, MHS; Berlin, *The Black Military Experience*, 304.

13. *WAA*, 14 February 1863; *General Statutes* (Boston: State of Massachusetts, 1861), 98; *Acts and Resolves Passed by the General Court of Massachusetts, 1864–65* (Boston: State of Massachusetts, 1865), 12; *Douglass' Monthly*, April, June 1863; *Pacific Appeal*, 16 May 1863; *Christian Recorder*, 1 August 1863; *Liberator*, 5 June 1863.

14. GES to William Still, 19 September 1863, LGC, HSP; John S. Rock to John A. Andrew, 24 February 1863, Executive Department Letters, MSA; John A. Andrew to Robert Gould Shaw, 14 May 1863, Misc. Bound Collection, 1838–1908, MHS; *WAA*, 4 April 1863; Edwin S. Redkey, "Black Chaplains in the Union Army," *Civil War History* 33 (December 1987): 331–32.

15. Douglass's address was widely reprinted in the Northern press, see New York *Tribune*, 5 March 1863, and *WAA*, 7 March 1863; *Liberator*, 12 June 1863; *WAA*, 14 February, 18 April 1863.

16. GES to Robert Hamilton, 2 April 1863; *WAA*, 4, 11, 18 April, 9, 16, 30 May 1863.

17. [William C. Nell], *Souvenir of the Massachusetts Fifty-fourth (Colored) Regiment* (n.p., n.d.); George T. Downing to John A. Andrew, 6 March 1863, George Homaness[?] to John A. Andrew, 19 August 1863, John Peck to Lewis Hayden, 21 February 1863, Executive Department Letters, MSA; Sarah H. Hunt to Dear Friend, March[?] 1863, Misc. Ms., Boston Public Library; *The Press* [Philadelphia], 11 March 1863.

18. Emilio, *A Brave Black Regiment*, 12; *Commonwealth*, 22 May 1863; *WAA*, 16 May 1863; "Hermit" to Robert Hamilton, 17 March 1863, *WAA*, 28 March 1863; Boston *Transcript*, 3 August 1887; H. P. Dunlap to John A. Andrew, 25 March 1863, Norwood P. Hallowell to Surgeon General Dale, 7 April 1863, Stephen Meyers to John A. Andrew, 19 March 1863, Executive Department Letters, MSA.

19. John Whittier Messer Appleton to Luis F. Emilio, 19 March 1883, Fifty-fourth Regiment Papers, vol. 4, MHS; Boston *Post*, 23 February 1863; Boston *Daily Courier*, 9 March 1863; Sarah D. Lopez to John A. Andrew, 20 February 1863, Executive Department Letters, MSA.

20. Frank W. Howe to John A. Andrew, 30 January 1863, Alonzo Manning to John A. Andrew, 9 May 1863, George L. Stearns to John A. Andrew, 28 March 1863, Executive Department Letters, MSA; John Whittier Messer Appleton, "Extracts from a Paper on Recruiting," misc. note, Fifty-fourth Regiment Papers, 1:13, MHS.

21. Frederick M. Binder, "Pennsylvania Negro Regiments in the Civil War," *Journal of Negro History* 37 (October 1952): 385–86; *WAA*, 11 April 1863; *Liberator*, 10 April 1863.

22. GES to Robert Hamilton, 2 April 1863; *WAA*, 18 April 1863; *Liberator*, 24 April 1863.

23. GES to Thomas Hamilton, 2 April, 3 October, 28 November 1863.

24. *WAA*, 7, 21 March, 9 May, 27 June, 22 August 1863.

25. Compiled service records, RG 94, National Archives; Descriptive rolls, Fifty-fourth Massachusetts Regiment, RG 94, National Archives; Bell Irvin Wiley, *The Life of Billy Yank: The Common Soldier of the Union* (Indianapolis: Bobbs-Merrill, 1952), 303.

26. Fifty-fourth Massachusetts Regiment Letterbooks, 5, 7, 17 March 1863, RG 94, National Archives; John Whittier Messer Appleton Letterbook, 25 April 1863, 3–4, John Whittier Messer Appleton Papers, WVUL.

27. "Recollections of Alfred S. Hartwell," typescript, n.d., Alfred S. Hartwell Papers, Hawaii State Archives; Robert Gould Shaw to Francis G. Shaw, 25 February 1863, Robert Gould Shaw to Sarah B. Shaw, 25 March 1863, Robert Gould Shaw Papers, HLHU; Robert Gould Shaw to Amos A. Lawrence, 25 March 1863, Amos A. Lawrence Papers, MHS; Undated note in bound volume, Norwood Penrose Hallowell Papers, MHS; Robert Gould Shaw to John A. Andrew, April 1863, Misc. Bound Collection, 1838–1908, MHS.

28. John Whittier Messer Appleton Letterbook, 25 April 1863, 4–5, John Messer Whittier Appleton Papers, WVUL; Robert Gould Shaw to Francis G. Shaw, 24 April 1863, Robert Gould Shaw Papers, HLHU; Fifty-fourth Massachusetts Company Books, RG 94, National Archives; John Benson case, Registry of Trials by General Courts Martial, RG 153, National Archives; Luis F. Emilio diary note, 17 May 1863, Fifty-fourth Regiment Papers, 1:75, MHS; Luis F. Emilio Diary, April-May 1863, Philip and Betty Emilio Family Collection; Boston *Daily Courier*, February-April 1863; Boston *Daily Advertiser*, 28 May 1863.

29. *WAA*, 2 May 1863; GES to Robert Hamilton, 1 May 1863.

30. *Commonwealth*, 22 May 1863.

31. Robert Gould Shaw to John A. Andrew, 14 May 1863, Executive Department Letters, MSA; G. W. Smalley to John A. Andrew, 19 May 1863, Ednah D. Cheney to John A. Andrew, 25 May 1863, John A. Andrew Papers, MHS; New York *Tribune*, 5 September 1863; John Whittier Messer Appleton Letterbook, n.d., 6–7, John Whittier Messer Appleton Papers, WVUL; Joseph Ricketson to Deborah Weston, 19 July 1863, Weston Papers, Boston Public Library; "Capt. Howard Recollections," February 1883, Fifty-fourth Regiment Papers, 1:81, MHS; Henry I. Bowditch, "Recollections," ms., Nathaniel Bowditch Memorial Collection, MHS.

32. Henry I. Bowditch, "Recollections," ms., Nathaniel Bowditch Memorial Collection, MHS; Boston *Daily Advertiser*, 29 May 1863; Charleston *Advertiser*, 30 May 1863.

33. Boston *Journal*, 28 May 1863; *WAA*, 6, 13 June 1863; Peter Burchard, *One Gallant Rush: Robert Gould Shaw and His Brave Black Regiment* (New York: St. Martin's Press, 1965), 1–3.

34. *WAA*, 6 June, 25 July 1863; Richard H. L. Jewett to Eliza Nutting Jewett, 2 June 1863, Richard H. L. Jewett Papers, Boston Athenæum; John Whittier Messer Appleton Letterbook, n.d., 7, John Whittier Messer Appleton Papers, WVUL; Henry I. Bowditch, "Recollections," ms., Nathaniel Bowditch Memorial Collection, MHS; Whittier quoted in Boston *Traveler*, 1 April 1890; Amos A. Lawrence Diary, [?] 1863, 321, MHS.

35. Frederic Cunningham Diary, 28 May 1863, MHS; Hermann Jackson Warner Diary, 28 May 1863, Hermann Jackson Warner Papers, 28:9106, MHS; *WAA*, 13 June 1863; Boston *Post*, 29 May 1863; Boston *Daily Courier*, 1 June 1863; John Murray Forbes to John A. Andrew, 22 July 1864, John A. Andrew Papers, MHS; John W. Blassingame et al., eds., *The Frederick Douglass Papers*, ser. 1: *Speeches, Debates and Interviews* (New Haven: Yale University Press, 1985), 3:586–87; Garth W. James, "Paper Read Before the Loyal Legion," Milwaukee *Sentinel*, 2 December 1888. Charles Remond Douglass did not accompany the Fifty-fourth to South Carolina but transferred to the Fifth Massachusetts Cavalry.

36. D. Sanford to Company E, 28 May 1863, Fifty-fourth Regiment Papers, vol. 4, MHS; Boston *Evening Transcript*, 28 May 1863; William C. Nell to Robert Hamilton, 2 June 1863, *WAA*, 13 June 1863.

37. Misc. notes and John Whittier Messer Appleton letter in *Commonwealth* (n.d.), Fifty-fourth Regiment Papers, 1:101, MHS; John Whittier Messer

Appleton Letterbook, 28 May 1863, 9, 11, John Whittier Messer Appleton Papers, WVUL; Edward W. Hooper to Robert William Hooper, 6 June 1863, Edward W. Hooper to Harry D. Chapin, 7 June 1863, Edward W. Hooper Papers, HLHU; Richard H. L. Jewett to Eliza Nutting Jewett, 4 June 1863, Richard H. L. Jewett Papers, Boston Athenæum; Emilio, *A Brave Black Regiment*, 35–37.

38. John Whittier Messer Appleton Letterbook, 4, 9 June 1863, 18–22, John Whittier Messer Appleton Papers, WVUL; Misc. notes, 9 June 1863, Fifty-fourth Regiment Papers, 1:111–13, MHS.

39. Robert Gould Shaw to John A. Andrew, 14 June, 2 July 1863, Executive Department Letters, MSA; Misc. notes, 10 June 1863, Fifty-fourth Regiment Papers, 1:116–17, MHS; Luis F. Emilio to Parents, 12 June 1863, Philip and Betty Emilio Family Collection; Richard H. L. Jewett to Eliza Nutting Jewett, 18 June 1863, Richard H. L. Jewett Papers, Boston Athenæum; Emilio, *A Brave Black Regiment*, 39–44.

40. John Whittier Messer Appleton diary notes, 26 June 1863, Robert Gould Shaw to John A. Andrew, 14 June 1863, Fifty-fourth Regiment Papers, 1:125, 130, MHS; Higginson, *Army Life in a Black Regiment*, 226.

41. John Whittier Messer Appleton to Wife, 7 June 1863, John Whittier Messer Appleton Letterbook, 17, John Whittier Messer Appleton Papers, WVUL; GES to Luis F. Emilio, 8 January 1886, Samuel Willard to Luis F. Emilio, 20 January 1884, Peter Vogelsang to Luis F. Emilio, n.d., Luis F. Emilio diary notes, 16 July 1863, Fifty-fourth Regiment Papers, 1:141–43, 145, 149, MHS; New York *Tribune*, 21 August 1863; GES to Robert Hamilton, 21 July 1863; Stephen R. Wise, *Gate of Hell: Campaign for Charleston Harbor, 1863* (Columbia: University of South Carolina Press, 1994), 89; Emilio, *A Brave Black Regiment*, 53–63. Vogelsang survived his wound and received an officer's commission at the war's end.

42. Luis F. Emilio to Father, 15[?] July 1863, in Philip and Betty Emilio Family Collection; Richard H. L. Jewett to Eliza Nutting Jewett, 17 July 1863, Richard H. L. Jewett Papers, Boston Athenæum; Samuel F. Du Pont to Sophia Du Pont, 5 June 1863, in *Samuel Francis Du Pont: A Selection from His Civil War Letters*, vol. 3: *The Repulse: 1863–1865*, ed. John D. Hayes (Ithaca: Cornell University Press for Eleutherian Mills Historical Library, 1969), 161.

43. Richard H. L. Jewett to Eliza Nutting Jewett, 17 July 1863, Richard H. L. Jewett Papers, Boston Athenæum; New York *Tribune*, 21 August 1863; Wise, *Gate of Hell*, 90.

44. Luis F. Emilio Diary, 15–17 July 1863, Philip and Betty Emilio Family Collection; John Whittier Messer Appleton, "That Night at Fort Wagner, by One Who Was There," *Putnam's Magazine*, Fifty-fourth Regiment Papers, 1:154, MHS.

45. *OR*, ser. 1, 28:14–15, 36, 279; Walter De Blois Briggs, ed., *Charles Edward Briggs: Civil War Surgeon in a Colored Regiment* (Berkeley: n.p., 1960), 102, 107–8; George Henry Gordon, *A War Diary of Events, 1863–1865* (Boston: J. R. Osgood, 1882), 214; Misc. notes, 12 September 1863, Fifty-fourth Regiment Papers, 1:250, MHS. Estimates of Wagner's garrison vary between

1,620 and 1,700; see Wise, *Gate of Hell*, 92, and William B. Taliaferro to George Pope, 2 February 1881, Fifty-fourth Regiment Papers, vol. 4, MHS.

46. Wise, *Gate of Hell*, sees the campaign to take Charleston Harbor in a more positive light. But see Rowena Reed, *Combined Operations in the Civil War* (Annapolis: United States Naval Institute Press, 1978), 41–42, 268–69, 278–79, 288–99.

47. Gordon, *A War Diary of Events*, 179–97, 212; Gillmore quotation from Alfred P. Rockwell, "The Operations against Charleston," in *Operations on the Atlantic Coast, 1861–1865, Virginia 1862, 1864, Vicksburg: Papers of the Military Historical Society of Massachusetts* (Boston: MHSM, 1912), 9:180.

48. *OR*, ser. 1, 28:56; *The Press* [Philadelphia], 31 July 1863; former slave's quotation from Edward L. Pierce, "The Freedman at Port Royal," *Atlantic Monthly* 12 (September 1863): 302.

49. William W. H. Davis, *History of the 104th Pennsylvania Regiment* (Philadelphia: Author, 1866), 246–47; Reed, *Combined Operations*, 305–7; Madeleine Vinton Dahlgren, *Memoir of John A. Dahlgren* (New York: Charles L. Webster, 1891), 391–95, 401–9, 423, quotation on 442.

50. *OR*, ser. 1, 28:76–77; Dahlgren, *Memoir of John A. Dahlgren*, 401–2; Wise, *Gate of Hell*, 93; Rockwell, "Operations against Charleston," 182; New York *Tribune*, 1 August 1863.

51. *OR*, ser. 1, 28:76–77; New York *Tribune*, 1 August 1863; Stephen B. Oates, *To Purge This Land with Blood: A Biography of John Brown* (New York: Harper and Row, 1970), 349; Wise, *Gate of Hell*, 84, 97; William B. Taliaferro to George Pope, 2 February 1881, Fifty-fourth Regiment Papers, vol. 4, MHS.

52. Robert Gould Shaw to John A. Andrew, 2 July 1863, Executive Department Letters, MSA; Edward L. Pierce to John A. Andrew, n.d., Fifty-fourth Regiment Papers, 1:161, MHS; Truman Seymour to John Pope, 3 February 1881, Fifty-fourth Regiment Papers, vol. 4, MHS.

53. Notes of a conversation with GES, 1884[?], GES to Luis F. Emilio, 27 December 1885, Fifty-fourth Regiment Papers, 1:165–66, MHS.

54. John Whittier Messer Appleton Letterbook, n.d., 57–61, John Whittier Messer Appleton Papers, WVUL; Appleton, "That Night at Fort Wagner," 1:166; William B. Taliaferro to George Pope, 2 February 1881, Fifty-fourth Regiment Papers, vol. 4, MHS; GES to Robert Hamilton, 21 July 1863; GES to Luis F. Emilio, 8 January 1886, Fifty-fourth Regiment Papers, 1:180–82, MHS.

55. Appleton, "That Night at Fort Wagner"; GES to Luis F. Emilio, 8 January 1886, Fifty-fourth Regiment Papers, 1:168–71, 180–82, MHS.

56. Ibid; Charles P. Lord to Sister, 20 July 1863, Charles P. Lord Papers, Duke University; GES to Robert Hamilton, 21 July 1863; "Declaration for Original Invalid Person," 2 August 1881, Statement by B. F. Pope, Assistant Surgeon, 28 March 1881[?], Stephens Pension File, RG 15, National Archives; Emilio, *A Brave Black Regiment*, 86; Henry F. W. Little, *The Seventh Regiment, New Hampshire Volunteers in the War of the Rebellion* (Concord: Ira C. Evans, 1896), 122–23; D. Eldredge, *The Third New Hampshire and All About It* (Boston: E. B. Stillings, 1893), 316.

57. Luis F. Emilio to Parents, 22 July 1863, Philip and Betty Emilio Family Collection; James W. Grace to Luis F. Emilio, 10 February 1894, Fifty-fourth Regiment Papers, vol. 4, MHS.

58. Howard C. Westwood, "Captive Black Union Soldiers in Charleston—What to Do?" *Civil War History* 28 (March 1982): 34; John Whittier Messer Appleton Letterbook, 7 February 1864, 159, John Whittier Messer Appleton Papers, WVUL; New York *Tribune*, 15 March[?] 1865, and misc. note, 13 September 1864, Fifty-fourth Regiment Papers, vol. 3, MHS; H. W. Littlefield interview with Daniel States, 17 January 1884, Fifty-fourth Regiment Papers, 1:209, MHS.

59. A. W. Muckenfuss to Luis F. Emilio, 22 April 1882, H.[?] Hendrick to Luis F. Emilio, 29 June 1882, H. R. Stoughton to Luis F. Emilio, 17 July 1882, Fifty-fourth Regiment Papers, vol. 4, MHS; Appleton, "That Night at Fort Wagner"; Dahlgren Diary, 19 October 1863, Fifty-fourth Regiment Papers, 1:191, 200, 419, MHS; *Inquirer* reported in William G. Hawkins, *Lunsford Lane; or, Another Helper from North Carolina* (1863, reprint, New York: Negro Universities Press, 1969), 240–41; Richard H. L. Jewett to Eliza Nutting Jewett, 5 January 1864, Richard H. L. Jewett Papers, Boston Athenæum; Luis F. Emilio Diary, 20 July 1863, Philip and Betty Emilio Family Collection; Fifty-fourth Massachusetts Regiment Letterbooks, 25 August 1863, RG 94, National Archives.

60. Edward N. Hallowell to Truman Seymour, 7 November 1863, Fifty-fourth Regiment Papers, 1:175–77, MHS, placed the regiment's losses at 256.

61. Edward W. Hooper to Robert William Hooper, 30 July 1863, Edward W. Hooper Papers, HLHU; Laura Matilda Towne, *Letters and Diary of Laura M. Towne* (New York: Negro Universities Press, 1969), 115–16; *Liberator*, 31 July 1863.

62. *The Press* [Philadelphia], 31 July 1863; Schouler, *Adjutant General's Report*, 62–63; Luis F. Emilio to Mother, 12 August 1863, Philip and Betty Emilio Family Collection; also see Boston *Post*, 1, 4, 17 August; Boston *Evening Transcript*, 4 August 1863; Charleston *Advertiser*, 20 June 1863; New York *Tribune*, 8 September 1865.

63. Fifty-fourth Massachusetts Regiment Letterbooks, Morning Reports, RG 94, National Archives; Lincoln R. Stone to John A. Andrew, 24 July 1863, in Schouler, *Adjutant General's Report*, 59–60.

64. GES to Robert Hamilton, 4 September 1863; Richard H. L. Jewett to Eliza Nutting Jewett, 23 July 1863, Richard H. L. Jewett Papers, Boston Athenæum; GES to William Still, 19 September 1863, LGC, HSP.

65. Luis F. Emilio to Mother, 12 August, 13 September 1863, Luis F. Emilio to Isa, 22 August 1863, Philip and Betty Emilio Family Collection; C. B. Parsons to Burt G. Wilder, 8 June 1914, Burt G. Wilder Papers, Cornell University; John Whittier Messer Appleton Letterbook, 13 November 1863, John Whittier Messer Appleton Papers, WVUL; Richard H. L. Jewett to Eliza Nutting Jewett, 14 October 1863, Richard H. L. Jewett Papers, Boston Athenæum; *OR* ser. 1, 28:279.

66. [Charles P. Bowditch], "War Letters of Charles P. Bowditch," *Proceedings of the Massachusetts Historical Society* 57 (May 1924): 446; Norwood P. Hallowell to John A. Andrew, 2 September 1863, Anonymous to John A. Andrew, 29 July 1863, Executive Department Letters, MSA.

67. Iver Bernstein, *The New York City Draft Riots: Their Significance for American Society and Politics in the Age of the Civil War* (New York: Oxford University Press, 1990); James H. Congdon to John A. Andrew, 20 August 1863, Executive Department letters, MSA; *WAA,* 25 July, 1 August 1863.

68. GES to Robert Hamilton, 7 August 1863.

69. GES to Robert Hamilton, 4 September 1863; GES to William Still, 19 September 1863, LGC, HSP.

70. [Bowditch], "War Letters," 441–42; Gordon, *A War Diary of Events,* 215, 220; Luis F. Emilio to Isa, 7 September 1863, Philip and Betty Emilio Family Collection.

71. Misc. Emilio notes, 12 September 1863, Fifty-fourth Regiment Papers, 1:251, MHS; Susie King Taylor, *Reminiscences of My Life in Camp with the 33d United States Colored Troops, Late 1st South Carolina Volunteers* (Boston: Author, 1902), 31; John Whittier Messer Appleton Letterbook, 13 November 1863, 101, John Whittier Messer Appleton Papers, WVUL; *OR,* ser. 1, 28:210.

Chapter 3

Equal Pay, Equal Rights, and the "Lincoln Despotism"

Stephens's 1862 prediction that the North could not win the war without "black Unionists" proved prophetic. The Fifty-fourth's valor on 18 July 1863 paved the way for the recruitment of 178,975 African-American soldiers and helped turn the tide toward a Union victory. The regiment's heroism, well-chronicled in art, literature, history, and film, extended beyond Battery Wagner. The Fifty-fourth waged an equally important battle against their own government's racist policies. Having fought to prove that blacks could be soldiers, the Fifty-fourth now had to fight for the pay of soldiers.

Although the Lincoln administration first promised equal pay, it belatedly determined that the Fifty-fourth and all other black troops had been enrolled under the July 1862 Militia Act, which mandated that blacks could be paid only $10 a month minus a $3 clothing allowance. Black troops, according to the act, could receive only $7 a month rather than the $13 a month accorded to whites. Thus, the highest-ranking black soldier received about half the pay of the lowest-ranking white. The government's discriminatory policy clearly fell hardest on black noncommissioned officers such as Stephens, who should have received between $17 and $21 a month.[1]

For eighteen months, the Fifty-fourth refused to accept any pay rather than submit to the federal government's demeaning offer. As Stephens and scores of other black soldiers made clear, they did not protest merely to gain more money. The issue was justice. "Because I am black," Stephens asserted, "they tamper with my rights."[2] The government not only had betrayed the men but also seemed determined to prevent blacks from grounding their claims for full citizenship on their military service. Unequal pay struck at the heart of black motivation to serve, undermined their claims to equality, and imperiled their hopes for the postwar world. Stephens found himself fighting one war against the slaveowning South and another against his own government's galling racism.

His *Anglo-African* letters chronicle his rage and the regiment's principled stand against federal policy. The government's refusal to grant equal pay, Stephens asserted, manifested an incessant and malignant racial prejudice that blacks had endured throughout American history. He denounced the "Lincoln despotism" for its intent to keep its foot on the necks of African Americans and compel them to accept a position of inferiority. "Thus free men were reduced to servitude," Stephens bitterly concluded. "No matter what services he might render—no matter how nobly he might acquit himself—he must carry with him the degradation of not being considered a man, but a thing."[3]

Some soldiers in other black regiments worried that Stephens's inflammatory denunciations might damage their quest for justice. "Let me say to those men," Stephens wrote, "we cannot be injured more. There is no insult—there is no cruelty—there is no wrong, which we have not suffered. Torture, massacre, mobs and slavery. Do you think that we will tamely submit like spaniels to every indignity?"[4] If anything, Stephens's *Anglo-African* correspondence understated the anger that brewed in the Fifty-fourth and other black regiments in the Department of the South. Few people ever realized how close the black troops came to full mutiny.

As early as March 1863, Colonel Shaw had warned Governor Andrew that the matter of pay had become a source of damaging irritation. Suspicious of their government's intent, the soldiers demanded their bounties. Shaw had hoped to head off a confrontation by requesting advance payment, which would, he informed the governor, "relieve the officers from constant fear of a row." Shortly after arriving in South Carolina, Shaw learned that the War Department had broken its promise and would only provide the pay given to noncombatant "contraband" laborers. He advised Andrew that the men would accept nothing less than full pay. The government's decision came at the same time that rumors swept through the regiment that its guns would be replaced with pikes and their official uniforms would be altered from regular issue. If not out to "altogether" annihilate black troops, the War Department gave Stephens every reason to suspect its motives.[5]

Almost to a man, the Fifty-fourth—including its officers—rejected the government's unjust offer. Sgt. Frederick Johnson, a Boston hairdresser in Company C, advised Governor Andrew that the men felt "they have been duped." He declared that if the regiment would not receive its full pay it should either be called back for home defense or discharged. Andrew responded to Johnson's letter, which the sergeant read to the unit's other noncommissioned officers, guaranteeing the state's support for the regiment. Johnson also had suggested that Andrew, to get an accurate view of black sentiment, should consult with black leaders in Boston—the Rev. Leonard A. Grimes, William C. Nell, or Lewis Hayden. Andrew not only spoke with them, especially Hayden, as Johnson suggested, but black leaders from across the North also contacted him. Ohio's John Mercer Langston urged the governor to fight the federal government's egregious policy. A broken promise on equal pay, Langston assured Andrew, made blacks doubt that justice would be forthcoming on all other issues.[6]

Parents, spouses, and champions of the Fifty-fourth sent protest letters to Andrew and his recruitment committee. Leonard A. Grimes's wife wrote to support Sergeant Johnson, a parishioner in her husband's church, pleading for equal pay. Such correspondence communicated the disillusionment and sense of "real sadness, and disappointment" that permeated the regiment. Committee members in particular felt deeply ashamed because they had promised enlistees the same pay and treatment as all other Union troops. "It is true," committee members admitted, "they *have been deceived*, they cannot even be permitted to die for their country on an equality with other soldiers, they have been made to feel that they still are only *niggars* not men."[7]

At noon on 30 September, the U.S. paymaster visited the Fifty-fourth and presented the government's offer of $7 a month. He explained that the law offered him no alternative and that the men might accept the pay under protest, which would still sustain their principle and relieve their families' suffering. Colonel Littlefield and a few other officers urged the men to accept the compromise. "The regiment to a man," one officer recorded in his journal, "refuses the insolent $10.00 or rather $7.00." Some officers expressed astonishment at the regiment's fierce determination to reject the offensive policy. Reflecting the growing level of racism among the unit's officers, they found the men's resolute stand "inconsistent with many traits of character that have been ascribed to their race."[8]

After the regiment refused the paymaster's proposal, Col. James Montgomery of the Second South Carolina Volunteers addressed the men. Montgomery, an early advocate of black recruitment and a fierce abolitionist, had the confidence of most black soldiers; his speech struck with the recoil of a three-hundred-pound Parrott gun. "You ought to be glad to pay for the privilege to fight, instead of squabbling about money," he exclaimed. He warned that their refusal to accept what the government offered amounted to mutiny, "and mutiny is punishable with death." Ignoring the regiment's enviable reputation, Montgomery declared that it still had not proven that blacks could fight as well as whites. He confessed, though, that black soldiers' "inherent" disadvantages left them with much to overcome. With words that enraged Stephens, Montgomery declared, "You are a race of slaves. A few years ago your fathers worshipped snakes and crocodiles in Africa." Stephens's indignation grew as he heard Montgomery announce to the assembled men, "Your features partake of a beastly character. Your features can be improved. Your beauty cannot recommend you. Your yellow faces are evidences of rascality. You should get rid of this bad blood. My advice to you is the lightest of you must marry the blackest women."[9]

Montgomery's outrageous remarks "fell with crushing effect on the regiment," Stephens wrote. Although everyone knew of the colonel's reputation for arbitrary justice and willingness to execute soldiers for infractions of the military code, no one suspected that he harbored such repulsive attitudes. The entire regiment, including officers, refused to acknowledge Montgomery and turned away when he appeared in camp. Stephens's *Anglo-African* correspondence unleashed the Fifty-fourth's indignation. We should be grateful for the privilege to fight? he asked in astonishment. "For what are we to be grateful? Here the white man has grown rich on our unpaid labor—has sold our children—insulted our wives—shut us out from the light of education, and even kept the Bible from us. . . . I think," Stephens thundered, "it a question of repentance on his part instead of gratitude on ours."[10]

When the paymaster returned on 31 October, the Fifty-fourth's new commander, Col. Edward N. Hallowell, Norwood P. Hallowell's brother, who had served under Shaw and had been severely wounded in the 18 July attack, supported the regiment's refusal to accept the $7 of-

fer. "My honor as a soldier & a gentleman, the honor of Massachusetts & the honor of the government of the United States," Hallowell
informed Andrew's military assistant Albert G. Browne, Jr., "was
pledged to the officers & men of the 54th that they should in all respects be treated as other soldiers of the U.S. Army." In the strongest
language he could muster, Hallowell urged the state to honor its
pledge to give the men equal pay. He also lobbied the governor's office,
the state's congressmen, and the regiment's recruitment committee
to gain the men their rights.[11]

On 12 December, Maj. James Sturgis and Edward W. Kinsley, Andrew's personal representatives, addressed the Fifty-fourth and presented the state's compromise measure. Although they assured the
men that Andrew was working to change federal policy, for the
present, the state legislature had adopted legislation to pay the men
the difference between black and white pay rates. Andrew supported
the regiment's stand but sought some way to defuse the crisis and end
the suffering caused by the government's infamous policy. The regiment met in separate groups, officers, noncommissioned officers, and
enlisted men to discuss the proposal. Stephens and his fellow sergeants met with Sturgis and Kinsley to advise them that although they
appreciated the state's generosity they could not accept the plan without compromising their principles. Most white officers supported
their decision, and Colonel Hallowell informed Andrew that nothing
short of full pay from the federal government would satisfy the regiment. Any distinction made between themselves and other federal
troops raised in Massachusetts, Hallowell notified Governor Andrew,
"would compromise their self respect." They would fight for the rest
of the war without any pay before they would submit to an act that
acknowledged "that because they have African blood in their veins,
they are less men."[12]

The crisis quickly spread beyond the confines of the Fifty-fourth
Massachusetts. Gen. Quincy A. Gillmore cautioned the army's general-in-chief Henry W. Halleck that "the pay of the white soldiers and
of the colored soldier should be the same. All distinctions calculated
to raise in the mind of the colored man a suspicion that he is regarded as an inferior being, should be scrupulously avoided." George L.
Stearns, who had assumed control over the federal government's black
recruitment campaign, resigned in protest over the War Department's
policy.[13]

Most officers in the Fifty-fifth Massachusetts Regiment also repudiated the government's action and for months refused to draw their own pay in protest. The Fifty-fifth assembled in tents or in the company "streets" at their camp on Folly Island, just south of Morris Island, to plan action. Nearly all determined to follow their sister regiment's lead and take nothing until given full pay. After one dress parade, the enlisted men assembled to hear Sgt. James Monroe Trotter, a Boston black leader, urge the men to stand firm on principle. They pledged "to die if necessary, for nothing, rather than take the pay and position of menials in the Union army."[14]

By the close of the year, morale in the Fifty-fourth had sunk to its lowest point. Away from his family, risking his life to save the Union, the average soldier felt betrayed and mocked by his own government. Despite repeated assurances from Andrew and other state political leaders that justice would be forthcoming, the men doubted it. Thoughts turned homeward. As one private in Company C wrote to his cousin, he did little but dream of home, "Where i could taste of your mince pie and chicken pies instead of eating salt junk and hard tack."[15]

Stephens became desperate. Other than the $50 bonus awarded to enlisted men upon joining the regiment, he had not received any pay since the Fifty-fourth arrived in South Carolina. Unable to send any money home, he applied for state aid. Stephens discovered, however, that because he was from Pennsylvania the state of Massachusetts considered him ineligible for assistance. He received a month's furlough in November, likely in deference to his personal ordeal, and returned home, probably to move his family into a less costly residence. City directories for the war years reveal that his family moved at least three times between 1860 and 1865.[16]

Stephens's family verged on destitution. Married sometime in 1857, Stephens supported his wife Susan, her three sons from a previous marriage, and her mother.[17] Norwood P. Hallowell, after resigning his command of the Fifty-fifth Massachusetts Regiment, returned to Philadelphia and called on the Stephens family. Although he reported no details, Hallowell advised Governor Andrew that Susan Stephens and her family suffered desperately. He had withdrawn $30 for them from the Massachusetts agent who provided such funds to the state's soldiers. Either through Hallowell's or Governor Andrew's intervention, Stephens's family received an additional $50 from a private city charitable fund and from the antislavery lawyer David

Brown. Although the cash undoubtedly relieved his family's immediate needs, the likelihood of a prolonged struggle over the question of equal pay made Stephens's determination to continue the protest a personally painful one.[18]

Stephens returned to his regiment at the end of December. For the month of January, the unit participated in minor skirmishes but primarily assisted in the siege of Charleston. On 1 January the Fifty-fourth and other black units in the Department of the South celebrated the Emancipation Proclamation. Three thousand freed slaves assembled at Camp Shaw on Morris Island to participate in the ceremonies and hear speeches by the noncommissioned officers. The speakers looked out upon a sea of proud upturned faces. They took advantage of the day to remind themselves, and the white officers who observed, that they had come to the South to end slavery and secure their rights. "We should not have it said," Sgt. William Gray asserted, "that knowing our rights we did not stand up for them."[19]

Morale temporarily improved. One sergeant in Company C formed a Masonic lodge on Morris Island, and several talented men in the regiment offered what one officer described as "grand Ethiopian entertainment," complete with "banjo, tambourine, & bones." Another soldier displayed his abilities on the violin, while others formed a glee club and conducted concerts in the officers' tents. Stephens recalled that camaraderie remained strong in the regiment and that the men assigned nicknames to anyone with an unusual appearance. They labeled one man "Sun" because of the "peculiar" shape of his head; another was "Snake" because he was slender and had an "ambling gait." They called the shorter men "Runts," another with oddly shaped feet earned the sobriquet of "Footsie," and still others earned names such as "Sleepy," "Stack," "Turtle," and "Duck" for reasons Stephens left to the imagination.[20]

New recruits returned the regiment to full strength, and new equipment replaced what had been lost in battle or worn out from incessant digging. On 27 January 1864, the Fifty-fourth's brigade received orders to embark for Hilton Head, South Carolina. The men, unaware of what awaited them, celebrated their release from fatigue duty.

General Gillmore assembled a force of eight thousand soldiers and sailors aboard thirty-five vessels to invade Jacksonville, Florida, for the third time in the war. On 5 February, Stephens boarded the steamer *Maple Leaf* and arrived at the mouth of the St. Johns River two days later. After braving turbulent seas, the armada steamed twenty miles up the St. Johns. The *Maple Leaf* arrived at Jacksonville's docks first, quickly followed by the remaining ships. After driving off a force of about fifty rebel cavalry, the soldiers secured the city. Little remained of the once active port, however. In two previous invasions—one by Higginson's black troops—Yankees had burned everything but private homes.[21]

With Charleston still in Confederate hands, Stephens may well have wondered why so large a force had been diverted to so inconsequential a place. Politics, not military strategy, sent the Fifty-fourth to Florida. Intent on returning the state to the Union in time for the fall elections, the Lincoln administration—especially Secretary of the Treasury Salmon P. Chase—convinced General Gillmore to launch the campaign.[22] Gillmore placed the thirty-nine-year-old Methodist minister's son and West Point graduate Gen. Truman Seymour in command of the expedition. A vain man who brought his wife and piano with him to Florida, Seymour earned a reputation for impulsive, if not reckless, action. His conduct in Florida cemented that assessment in the minds of his men and other Union commanders.[23]

Two days after landing in Florida, Seymour captured Baldwin, an important rail junction west of Jacksonville (map 1). The absence of resistance allowed Union troops to advance within three miles of Lake City by the morning of 11 February, but the sudden appearance of the enemy drove invading Union troops back to the safety of their Baldwin camp. Seymour notified General Gillmore that the presence of a large rebel force near Lake City made further progress inadvisable. "To be thwarted, defeated," he prophetically wrote, "will be a sad termination to a project, brilliant thus far." Seymour's staff warned that his command could not hold territory "toward the center of the state." For the present he remained at Baldwin. The Fifty-fourth took advantage of their penetration deep into rebel territory to free slaves. Although the officers had regular army routines on their minds, the men pressed them for permission to liberate local "property" and assist fugitives who entered the Fifty-fourth's camp. "It makes our mens eyes shine as they go by," one officer noted with approval.[24]

On 11 February, Seymour informed Gillmore that he might fortify Baldwin. A week later, he dropped this plan, broke camp, and moved west toward the Suwannee River, intending to take the state capital at Tallahassee. Predictably, Seymour violated orders not to undertake

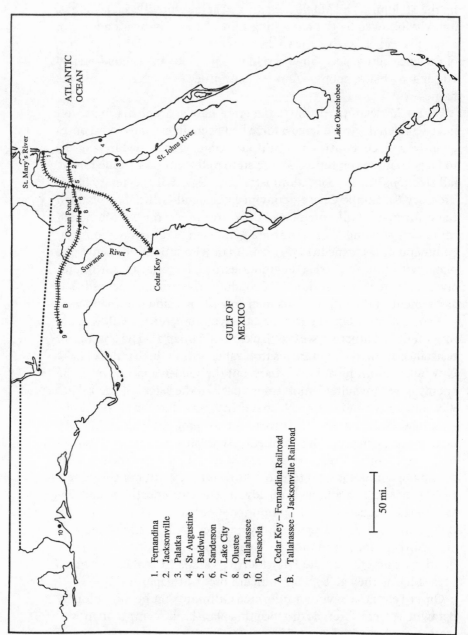

Map 1. North Florida and the Olustee Campaign

1. Fernandina
2. Jacksonville
3. Palatka
4. St. Augustine
5. Baldwin
6. Sanderson
7. Lake City
8. Olustee
9. Tallahassee
10. Pensacola

A. Cedar Key – Fernandina Railroad
B. Tallahassee – Jacksonville Railroad

ATLANTIC
OCEAN

GULF OF
MEXICO

St. Mary's River

Ocean Pond

Suwanee River

Cedar Key

St. Johns River

Lake Okeechobee

50 mi.

any action without Gillmore's approval, disregarded the advice of his own staff, and ignored repeated warnings that a rebel force as large as his own lay in wait for him at Olustee, east of Lake City. He waved off the dire concerns, declaring that he welcomed a fight "on relatively equal terms." When Gillmore learned of Seymour's startling decision, he sent Gen. John Turner to stop him. Thunderstorms delayed Turner for two days, allowing Seymour time to move.[25]

At 6 A.M. on 20 February, Seymour's command began its march from Baldwin to Barber's Station, twelve miles west. The damp, spongy ground put spring in the soldiers' step, and some men in the Fifty-fourth broke out in song, "We're bound for Tallahassee in the Morning," while others sang Stephen Foster's "Old Folks at Home." Towering long-leaf pine dominated the flat north Florida landscape, with sparse undergrowth of palmetto bush and wire grass. Both armies enjoyed a clear view of the field, and neither side possessed the element of surprise. Seymour's men, however, marched into a narrowing pocket, bounded on the south by swamps and the Tallahassee-Jacksonville rail line and on the north by Ocean Pond. As his force moved west they encountered a few locals who mocked the Union army's confidence and told them to expect a thrashing.[26]

The Confederate force of more than 5,200 men, ironically, included veterans of Battery Wagner. They had thrown up earthworks across the Jacksonville-Lake City road and sent out a surprisingly large number of skirmishers who made contact with Union forces between 2 and 3 P.M. Seymour never reached the rebel fortifications, and he sent his regiments into battle one at a time, enough to draw the enemy out of their position but too small a number to concentrate fire and inflict serious damage. Rebels cut his command to pieces. The raw Seventh New Hampshire broke under withering fire, leaving a gaping hole in Union lines and the Eighth USCT to bear the brunt of the rebel advance. The Eighth, although valiantly led, had no combat experience and stood exposed to murderous rebel fire. Out of 554 of its men, more than 300 were killed or wounded.[27]

Seymour's force suffered staggering losses. A steady stream of wounded flowed to the rear, where Montgomery's brigade, which again included the Fifty-fourth, had been held in reserve. About 4 P.M., the brigade received orders to move forward "at double quick." As Stephens and his fellow soldiers threw off coats and knapsacks, they cried "three cheers for the 54th and seven dollars a month!" For two miles they rushed passed the wounded, who shouted, "We're badly whipped," and "You'll get killed." Near the front lines, Seymour frantically galloped to the Fifty-fourth's commander, Edward N. Hallowell, exclaiming, "Colonel we have lost everything, and it all now depends on your regiment."[28]

Four hundred eighty enlisted men and fifteen officers of the Fifty-fourth Massachusetts rushed forward to halt the rebel drive and allow time for Seymour's army to withdraw. Stephens and his company stood at the center near Colonel Montgomery, who directed the fight from a stump. Stephens closely watched the man who had so grievously insulted the regiment a few months earlier direct Union fire and later admitted that Montgomery had led the men bravely. He also saw one man from his company, charged with zeal, rush beyond the line, fire his weapon, return to load, and then charge out to fire again. A rebel bullet through the head felled him. Lt. Col. Henry N. Hooper's groom seized a musket and shot a rebel captain charging their position. Confederate fire became intense, and half the color guard melted away.[29]

On the second discharge of their weapons, Stephens's company, in its excitement, fired their ramrods "at the Johnnies." Thinking fast, Stephens ordered his men to reload their weapons, jam the gun butts on the ground, cap their pieces, and fire. The tactic worked. He later recalled that none of his men used ramrods "after the firing became general." Their volleys became so rapid that one nearby white unit with new breech-loading rifles rang out, "Ha! You fellows have breech-loaders too!" Within a short time, the Fifty-fourth used up its entire supply of ammunition, about twenty thousand rounds. A fresh supply rushed to the front turned out to be the wrong caliber, and the men threw it into a mud hole. "Men we are whipped," Hooper shouted. "We are retreating horse, foot, and artillery!" He then ordered the Fifty-fourth to hold the line with bayonets and drilled the men in the manual of arms as they gradually worked their way to the rear. The maneuver, intermittently punctuated with cheers to deceive the enemy into believing that reinforcements had arrived, calmed the panicking men and forestalled a rebel charge that would have shattered the regiment.[30]

Eight miles from Jacksonville, the Fifty-fourth was ordered back three miles to drag in a crippled locomotive and cars loaded with supplies and wounded. By the time their ordeal ended, the men had marched about 120 miles in four and a half days. Half the regiment had worn out their boots and marched into Jacksonville barefoot. Many fell down stone dead with exhaustion and slept cradling their weapons, expecting a counterattack that never came. Unaccountably, the rebel force did not follow up its victory and allowed the federals to escape. The Department of the South, however, had sustained yet another devastating defeat, losing twice as many men as the enemy. In their haste to retreat, Union forces also abandoned most of their equipment and a large number of wounded black soldiers, many of whom rebels summarily executed.[31]

The Olustee disaster outraged the Fifty-fourth's supporters in Boston, who heaped blame for the defeat where it belonged, on General Seymour. He had neglected "even common military demands," the Boston *Evening Traveler* decried, "so that our forces fell into a trap." Racists blamed black troops for the rout. The Philadelphia *Ledger,* under the headline "Bad Conduct of a Negro Regiment," denounced black soldiers for breaking under fire and running away. In fact, as became quickly apparent, the African-American troops in Seymour's command, even the inexperienced Eighth USCT, acted with extraordinary heroism. The valor of the Fifty-fourth Massachusetts repudiated racist allegations of black cowardice. The regiment, one sergeant wrote to Edward Kinsley, "fought bravely, being the last to leave the Field." It saved the lives of many soldiers and prevented a defeat from becoming a crippling disaster for the Department of the South. As one eyewitness reported, *"Had it not been for the glorious Fifty-fourth Massachusetts, the whole brigade would have been captured or annihilated."*[32]

The Fifty-fourth remained in the Jacksonville area until returning to the familiar sands of Folly and Morris Islands on 17 April 1864. The regiment assigned Stephens and his company to Fort Green at the northern tip of Folly Island. He remained there for the rest of the year and did not participate in additional fighting on James Island or the Department of the South's next defeat in November at Honey Hill, South Carolina. Stephens received a break from guard duty during the summer, when he served as a reporter in a court-martial trial. He also may have received permission to visit his comrades stationed at Wagner, renamed Fort Strong, who stood watch over captured Confederate officers. Many soldiers roamed Morris Island, recalling their heroic charge of the previous year and those who had died at Battery

Wagner. "We made our name but at the cost of many gallant heroes," one officer lamented, "it was enough to burst our heart-strings."[33]

After the Olustee defeat, morale sank again in the Fifty-fourth. Dissention surged throughout the Department of the South over unequal pay and the War Department's refusal to commission blacks as officers. Executions in the Fifty-fifth Massachusetts Regiment and other black units in the department, intended to quell dissent, fueled strife and drove Stephens's comrades closer to the edge of mutiny.

In February, Charles Sumner, the powerful antislavery senator from Massachusetts, admitted that the prospects for legislation resolving the pay crisis seemed "doubtful." Although the state's influential politicians lobbied hard for equal pay, mulish opposition frustrated their efforts. Stephens became despondent. His own government treated him as a "thing and not a person," and the army executed black troops with unseemly swiftness if not outright illegality. "We are unprotected and there is no refuge—no appeal." Freedom became a false hope, and the nation, he mourned, remained determined "to maintain a line of demarkation between the white and black race, and to deny to the black equal rights and justice as enjoyed by the white." A year of service in the army, Stephens sadly concluded, "purged me of the major part of my patriotism."[34]

Black leaders back home, well aware of the Fifty-fourth's plight, shared Stephens's sense of despair. William Wells Brown attacked Lincoln. "We have an imbecile administration, and the most imbecile management that is possible to conceive of." Discouraged by the treatment of black soldiers, John S. Rock wondered what African Americans could expect once the war concluded and the government no longer needed their services. The resurgence of the racist Democratic party, the faltering war effort, and the federal government's timid reconstruction policies, especially in Louisiana, convinced many blacks that a Northern victory would not end oppression or even slavery. "The President of the United States," one black leader decried, had "pronounced a death-knell to our peaceful hopes."[35]

By January, Governor Andrew had received so many disturbing reports of conditions in the state's black regiments that he sent his advisor, the wealthy Boston merchant and Republican partisan Edward W. Kinsley, to investigate. Had he remained with the troops a few weeks longer, his report would have been explosive. Trust between the Fifty-fourth's men and their officers was crumbling. Although relations remained good in Stephens's company, dissention grew between black soldiers and officers who joined the regiment after 18 July 1863. The black troops, Stephens wrote in May, distrusted whites "whose antecedents or sentiments we know nothing of." One officer insulted Stephens when he "told me to my face that noncommissioned officers were not as good as they are in white regiments." Although the remaining original officers supported the regiment's demand for equal pay and commissions, the newer ones lacked antislavery zeal or, worse yet, were unabashed racists. When enlisted men in the Fifty-fourth petitioned their superiors to seek a commission for the regimental hospital steward Theodore Becker, three white officers protested. "They did not want a negro Doctor," an anonymous soldier reported to the *Christian Recorder*, "neither did they want negro officers." A few openly disparaged the men they commanded, declaring that "a negro stunk under their noses."[36]

Stephens became increasingly belligerent and intolerant of fellow soldiers who admonished him to keep silent before he destroyed the regiment's "glorious reputation." Official policy, not protests, threatened the black troops. "Our debasement is most complete," a soldier from the Fifty-fifth Massachusetts asserted in April. "No chances for promotion, no money for our families, and we [are] little better than an armed band of laborers with rusty muskets and bright spades." Contrary to orders, white officers in the Fifty-fifth ordered enlisted men to do degrading work as personal servants and cooks. Other officers in the Fifty-fifth, recently arrived in the South, openly boasted of their participation in the New York City draft riots. Before the end of the year, even the Fifty-fourth's abolitionist colonel, Edward N. Hallowell, had nearly given up on the Department of the South. "I'm disgusted with it," he wrote home, "& I wish I could get to the Army of the Potomac."[37]

Mutinous discontent in the Fifty-fourth began early in 1864. Anonymous letters appeared in Colonel Hallowell's tent before the Battle of Olustee, threatening that the men would refuse to fight if not immediately awarded equal pay. Word spread to the other black regiments in the department that the Fifty-fourth had gone into battle with provocative cries of "seven dollars a month." About half the regiment talked openly of refusing duty until given their full pay. Hallowell tried to quiet the growing unrest among the men by reading to them Sen. Henry Wilson's bill of 2 March 1864, which equal-

ized pay rates. Few were satisfied, especially as word filtered throughout the army that blacks in other regiments had stacked arms in response to the pay crisis and had been shot for it.[38]

The first and most notorious case of mutiny occurred on 29 February 1864, when Sgt. William Walker of the Third South Carolina
Volunteers (Twenty-first USCT) faced a firing squad for protesting
unequal pay. On 19 November 1863, Walker had ordered his company to stack arms in front of their colonel's tent. Warned that he would
be shot for mutiny if the protest continued, Walker refused to "do duty
any longer for seven dollars a month."[39]

The Walker case attracted enormous attention, stoking anger and
bitterness. Governor Andrew directed Senator Sumner to deliver a
letter of protest directly to President Lincoln. "The Government
which found no law to *pay* him except as *a nondescript or a contraband,*" Andrew fumed, "nevertheless found enough law to *shoot* him
as a *soldier.*" The army intended Walker's execution to show men
such as Stephens what they could expect if protests over pay continued. Although he did not encourage mutinous action in print,
Stephens rallied support from Northern blacks, their white antislavery allies, and fellow soldiers by defending black rights and voicing
the soldiers' discontent. The Fifty-fourth, Stephens contended, lived
"under a tyranny [as] inexorable as slavery itself."[40]

What Stephens did not say was how far conditions had deteriorated. When the regiment remained camped outside of Jacksonville in
April, discipline disintegrated. Capt. Luis F. Emilio, with unswerving
antislavery convictions, nevertheless worried that solidarity among
the men over the pay crisis was destroying the unit. On 12 April,
Colonel Hallowell assembled the regiment and informed them that
he planned to visit Washington to plead their case for equal pay. He
warned against insubordination and advised the men that he had given
Maj. John W. M. Appleton authority to shoot the first man who refused duty. The men grumbled after Hallowell dismissed them. When
Appleton returned to his tent he found an anonymous note declaring that, without equal pay, he had no right taking the regiment into
action. Carrying out Hallowell's orders, the note warned, would cost
him his life. Appleton reassembled the regiment and assured the men
of his commitment to their cause, but he warned that if ordered into
battle he would obey, threats to shoot him notwithstanding.[41]

Discontent erupted when the regiment left Florida on 17 April. Several soldiers on the troop transport *Cosmopolitan* planned to seize it and steam to New York, but they failed to persuade their comrades to join them. When the transport moored at Folly Island, the regiment's commanding officers waited on the dock in a driving rain for the men to disembark. The soldiers refused to leave and paced back and forth on deck, unsure of exactly what to do. Hallowell, who had not yet left for Washington, ordered Appleton to reboard and pull the men off. He grabbed one soldier by his pack and shoved him down the gangplank. Others followed, grumbling in the miserable weather, "Money or blood!" and, "Muster us out or pay us!"[42]

The immediate crisis passed, but anger boiled. The regiment had received no pay for more than a year. The men showed their tear-stained letters from home to sympathetic officers who felt both powerless and vexed by the politicians who stood in the way of legislation equalizing pay. One man in the Fifty-fourth who had lost his home in the 1851 Christiana, Pennsylvania, fugitive slave uprising, but had reestablished himself in Canada, was thrown back into destitution because of the pay strike. Sgt. Stephen A. Swails, who returned from Olustee with a bullet through the neck, received a letter informing him, inaccurately, that his family had been sent to the poor house. The news tore through the regiment. Other soldiers' families did lose their homes and learned that town officials had bound out their children for support. The government's refusal to uphold its promise to award black soldiers equal pay destroyed the regiment's will to fight and undermined its loyalty. One soldier in Company H wrote home that "we have not our Pay yet and I never think we will[.] Oh for shame on Such Equality[.] Such A Government as this dont suit me[.]"[43]

Conditions in the Fifty-fifth Massachusetts, with fewer antislavery officers, descended into mutiny. Desperate letters from home poured into the regiment. One poor woman begged her husband to send her just 50 cents. "Was it any wonder," one soldier wrote to the *Anglo-African*, "that the tears rolled in floods from that stout-hearted man's eyes?" Mutinous letters began appearing in the black press from anonymous soldiers in both regiments who could not endure the stress of the strike and the reprimands of their officers for complaining about pay. Col. Alfred S. Hartwell, new commander of Fifty-fifth, found that his soldiers refused orders to man picket lines. He assembled the men and informed each company commander, loud enough for all to hear, that anyone who refused orders would be court-martialed and shot. All but one complied. Hartwell ordered the protesting soldier bucked and gagged "until the doctor said that he could stand it no longer."[44]

Seventy-five men from the Fifty-fifth wrote to President Lincoln to demand equal pay. In clear language bordering on insubordination if not mutiny, the men demanded Lincoln's immediate action, which, if not forthcoming, would result in "more stringent measures" by the regiment. The Fifty-fifth would take no more insults from the federal government. For anyone who missed the point of the protests or doubted the soldiers' resolve, "Bay State" set them straight. Writing in the *Anglo-African*, he promised, "We, by God's help, will settle it for ourselves before this war is over, *and settle it right too, or die in the attempt.*"[45]

One man did die. Pvt. Wallace Baker, a twenty-year-old "farmer" from Hopkinsville, Tennessee, was, according to his fellow soldiers, awkward and quarrelsome. He felt especially recalcitrant in the afternoon of 1 May 1864, when Lt. Thomas F. Ellsworth ordered a company inspection at the Fifty-fifth's camp on Folly Island. Baker was the last man to assemble and fell in without his weapon and equipment. Given that he had all day to prepare, Ellsworth asked Baker why he was not ready. "I'm not going to hurry," he snapped.[46]

The confrontation quickly escalated. Baker refused to be silent and mocked the lieutenant, causing a roar of laughter in the ranks. Ellsworth then ordered Baker to his tent: "I won't do it, I'll be damned if I will." He than brayed his refusal to obey any "damned white officer." Ellsworth grabbed the private by the collar and shoved him toward his tent. Baker responded by knocking Ellsworth's hands away and striking him twice in the face. "You damned white officer," he shrieked, "do you think that you can strike me, and I not strike you back again? I will do it. I'm damned if I don't." Ellsworth drew his sword, but Baker seized it and struck the officer several more times. While the two men grappled, Ellsworth called out to the sergeants for help. No one budged. The company commander, Capt. John Gordon, rushed to assist, but the two men still struggled for the sword.

Ellsworth called for a guard to remove Baker, but the hundred or so men standing aside refused to move. Cpl. Henry Way—later court-martialed for his role in the affray—also refused Ellsworth's calls and told him that "if you or any other officer strikes me, I shall strike you back, and do my best to defend myself." Ellsworth and Gordon finally subdued Baker and confined him in the guardhouse.

Originally scheduled for 17 May, Baker's trial did not commence until 16 June. It moved swiftly although with procedural fairness. Lt. Col. Henry N. Hooper of the Fifty-fourth Massachusetts Regiment presided, and the trial records and regimental books make clear that the presiding officers searched for mitigating grounds to prevent the inevitable. There could be no denying, however, that Baker had committed mutiny and struck an officer; in the military code the penalty was death. They also knew that the crisis over unequal pay lay behind the confrontation. With discipline breaking down and no resolution of the pay issue in sight, the court ordered what military justice mandated. Baker was "to be shot to death with musketry."[47]

"It is by such stern and sad examples that the great arm of military law asserts it power," Colonel Hartwell wrote when he ordered Baker's execution on 18 June. The Fifty-fifth had come to South Carolina "in defence of the rights and civil and military equality of a race so long held in bondage." Baker, Hartwell explained, brought "reproach upon our regiment and cause." Every soldier on Folly Island assembled at 10:30 A.M. in the muggy and mosquito-choked air. Baker stood before his yawning grave "with unflinching courage," one enlisted man observed, denouncing his execution as an injustice. One of the Fifty-fifth's officers simply noted that Baker died "cursing to the last." Stephens witnessed the execution and remarked that Baker remained firm throughout, "And when he spoke no tremor could be detected in his voice." Three bullets to the head and four in his chest finally silenced Baker's protest.[48]

The commanders of the state's two black regiments deplored the execution. "For God's sake," Hartwell wrote to Andrew, "how long is the injustice of the government to be continued toward these men?" He wondered if the government intended to "goad them into mutiny and [then] quench the mutiny with blood?" The lieutenant colonel of the Fifty-fifth, Charles B. Fox, placed responsibility for Baker's death squarely on the federal government. The Massachusetts adjutant general agreed and blamed the government's mishandling of the pay crisis for the execution. If the army believed that it could shoot its way out of the controversy, subsequent events proved it wrong. Members of the regiment refused picket duty, and officers began to resign in disgust. Baker's company remained strife-torn, and at the end of June another soldier was court-martialed for clashing with an officer. Worse still, dissention splintered the Fifty-fourth Massachusetts.[49]

Stephens voiced the fury that swept through the Fifty-fourth over the pay crisis and Baker's execution: "Nearly eighteen months of service—of labor—of humiliation—of danger, and not one dollar." He denounced the government for reducing his wife to beggary. "What can wipe the wrong and insult this Lincoln despotism has put upon us?" he exclaimed "Suppose we had been white?" he asked. "Massachusetts would have inaugurated a rebellion in the East, and we would have been paid." He was determined speak out, "and nothing shall prevent me but double irons or a pistol-ball that shall take me out of the hell I am now suffering."[50]

Colonel Hallowell worried that he was losing control of his regiment. The "men [are] in a state of extreme dissatisfaction bordering on mutiny," he advised Governor Andrew. The pay crisis drove everyone to desperation, and, he wrote, the only way he could prevent anarchy was to shoot the regiment's troublemakers, "a catastrophe we should always deplore."[51] While Baker awaited his court-martial, the "catastrophe" Hallowell feared arrived. On 12 May, Lt. Robert R. Newell, who led Stephens's company, ordered six of his men to fall in. Each refused. Newell struck one with his sword and repeated his order. When the men still ignored his orders, Newell sent for his revolver. He repeated his command and when the soldiers balked, Newell shot one in the chest. The others scampered into line. Newell, with an easy-going reputation, turned "white as a sheet" and brought the man to the hospital. The incident shocked the company. If Newell would not hesitate to shoot them, the men thought, "what won't the others do?"[52]

A week later, Capt. Charles E. Tucker of Company H shot another man for disobeying orders. Then a detachment from Company A refused guard duty, and, as one officer noted, "great turmoil" roiled the regiment. Hallowell ordered his captains to get their pistols and commanded the men to fall in. Instead, the soldiers loitered in company streets and drew spectators from Company B, who pressed between the tents to witness the confrontation. When some of Stephens's men approached the officers, muskets in hand, Hallowell ordered his major to beat them back. Those who refused to move felt the butt end of a pistol against their skulls. Both Hallowell and Major Appleton turned to the protesting soldiers, pointed their revolvers at each man's head, and gave them a three count. "Do you refuse to go on guard? One, two." "No Sir!" came the reply. Hallowell passed down the line pointing his pistol at each head and asking the same question. All the men fell in, and the crisis passed.[53]

Hallowell, caught between his sympathy for his men and his duty as commanding officer, pleaded with Governor Andrew to force the War Department either to pay the men or muster the regiment out of service. He warned that several men had been shot in a "small mutiny," and without action a general mutiny would soon destroy the state's, if not the country's, most important black regiment.[54] Letters from Stephens and others in the regiment swamped the black press, renewing their demand for action and holding the state accountable for the crisis. "If we fight to maintain a Republican Government," another man in Company B insisted, "we want Republican privileges." The men maintained that they would no longer fight "for anything less than the white man fights for. . . . Give me my rights, the rights that this government owes me, the same rights that the white man has." More letters poured into Andrew's office, this time by men who attached their names to them, demanding full pay or their discharge.[55]

Officers from the Fifty-fourth and their antislavery allies at home, even the governor of Vermont and the Union League of New York, increased the pressure on Andrew to compel federal authorities to pay the men. Abolitionists and the state's politicians descended on Lincoln's attorney general and the secretary of war to lobby for equal pay. As late as 27 June, Attorney General Edward Bates still asserted that black and white pay rates could not be equalized because of the 1862 Militia Act.[56] Andrew filled with disgust. The federal government seemed intent on disgracing and degrading blacks, making them "in the eyes of all men 'only a nigger.'" Hot with impatience, he wrote to Charles Sumner, exclaiming that "I *demand* their rights as Massachusetts Volunteers according to the law." Near the end of May, he sent George S. Hale, president of Boston's common council, to ask President Lincoln to order full payment to the state's black regiments. Lincoln disclaimed any authority over the matter.[57]

Sumner lobbied other senators and congressmen who served on committees that oversaw military legislation. Most claimed that until Bates changed his ruling on the 1862 Militia Act nothing could be

done. "I lost no time in calling on the Sec. of War & the Atty Gen.,"
Sumner advised Governor Andrew, "& have pressed upon each the
duty of an early settlement of the case of the colored regts." But both
men resisted Sumner's efforts, and Bates refused to read any letters
from Andrew concerning black troops. Sumner had argued with Stanton so many times over the issue of equal pay that the secretary of
war "has lost his temper" and refused to meet with him again.[58]

To head off further mutiny, Andrew orchestrated an effort by friends
of the state's black regiments to assure the soldiers of his support. One
soldier's letter he received may have been especially worrisome. It
questioned Andrew's antislavery commitment and charged that "all
he cared for was to get them [black soldiers] into the service." Andrew
turned to Lewis Hayden for help. Hayden served as an unofficial liai-
son between Andrew and both the state's black regiments in South
Carolina. Because of his standing as a trusted black leader, Hayden's
assurances went far to quell unrest. He passed along copies of Andrew's correspondence with the War Department to the regiments to
prove the governor's fidelity and show how hard he labored in their
behalf. Other blacks, especially Boston's black women, staged fairs
to raise funds and collect goods for soldiers' families. White abolitionists and political leaders wrote to both regiments, professing their
complete support for equal pay and condemning the "criminal neglect
of the government to do justice to the colored troops." Edward W.
Kinsley contacted enlisted men in both regiments, pledging the state's
support and keeping them apprised of moves in Congress to equalize
pay. "All you Boys have to do is to *hold on*," he assured one sergeant
in the Fifty-fifth Massachusetts. "You will yet come out all right, and
get all that is due you both in money & honor."[59]

The pressure from antislavery congressmen and the black troops
in the field finally persuaded the government to act. In mid-June,
Congress adopted legislation authorizing equal pay retroactive to 1
January 1864. Unsatisfied with anything short of full reimbursement
from the beginning of enlistment, Andrew, Sumner, Wilson, and a
host of others pressed further. Finally, in July, Attorney General Bates
reversed his opinion and ruled that the 1862 Militia Act did not apply to black soldiers who had been free at the start of the war. This
meant that Stephens and most other blacks in the Massachusetts
units would receive equal pay from the first day of their service. But
the law excluded regiments such as the First South Carolina Volun-

teers and all soldiers who had been slaves at the start of the war, even though, as Sumner asserted, the 1862 Militia Act made "no distinction" between "free black & slave black in the military service."[60]

For Massachusetts's black regiments, Colonel Hallowell devised an ingenious "Quaker oath" that permitted soldiers to swear that before 19 April 1861 "no man had the right to demand unrequited labor of you, so help you God." By the end of August, most officers had employed Hallowell's handiwork, and with few exceptions the men complied. The South Carolina regiments, excluded from the law, continued their protest for another nine months until Congress agreed to full equal pay in March 1865.[61]

Between 28 September and 5 October, the Fifty-fourth and Fifty-fifth Massachusetts Regiments received their full pay. Jubilation swept through the Department of the South. Stephens, still stationed in lonely Fort Green, received his money on 29 September, one day after his regiment. Time after time soldiers exclaimed that they could "send money home at last to my wife, my child!" Dancing, singing, and shouts replaced the thunder of cannon throughout the day and into the night. "It was like the apparition of a man's self in a more perfect state," one officer remarked. Official celebrations on 10 October left the men in raptures. Equality had been won, and a black victory had been achieved. Not money but rights had been gained, proclaimed James Monroe Trotter in the Fifty-fifth Massachusetts. A "great principle of equal rights as men and soldiers had been decided in their favor." Stephens's personal ordeal had ended, but he played no role in organizing the celebrations. His thoughts drifted a few miles to the north and fixed on Charleston, where he had narrowly escaped enslavement nearly seven years earlier.[62]

*   *   *

At the beginning of February 1865, the Fifty-fourth went on the move. Ranging through James Island and looking west, they beheld evidence that General Sherman's victorious army approached. Pillars of black smoke filled the sky as the Yankees brought the war home to the South. "The saying is that when Sherman get[s] thro. South Carolina," Lieutenant Colonel Hooper remarked, "a crow can't fly across the country unless he carries rations." The Fifty-fourth adopted Sherman's tactics, seizing supplies and destroying Confederate property. With the eager encouragement of former slaves, the regiment put the torch to rice mills, barns, and plantation homes. Local blacks advised the tactic, the regiment reported, "to inspire their so-called masters whenever they had the opportunity." Colonel Hallowell explained to his sister that "we always leave the negro shanties, but the mansion houses are sure to go." Hallowell regretted the destruction. "It makes me sick to see such elegant furniture destroyed, but its South Carolina and it must be." The regiment did not share their commander's remorse. "The soldiers enjoy their work!!" Hallowell trumpeted. Moreover, the men took the time to instruct former slaves in "the use of firearms that they might better defend themselves."[63]

By 11 February, Charleston keenly felt the pressure of Sherman's approach. Much to the amusement of Union troops, the hated Charleston *Mercury* announced that because of "so much public and private inconvenience and suffering" it would suspend publication. A week later, on the night of 17 February, rebel forces began their evacuation of the city and gave the Yankees a stunning pyrotechnic display. They set three ironclads ablaze, and, when their magazines detonated, fiery sheets of metal rained down on the city, igniting scores of fires. Thousands of cotton bales and tons of rice lit the night, but nothing approached the volcanic eruption that resulted from the explosion of the Northeastern Railroad depot. Dense-packed with gunpowder and ammunition, the depot roared with a thunderous explosion that showered the city with debris and burned for three days. The following morning a *Tribune* reporter proclaimed what was on every Union soldier's mind: "Babylon has fallen."[64]

Stephens had not forgotten the offices of Charleston's slave dealers or the hundreds of worn and emaciated slaves he had seen waiting for transportation to the rice plantations and certain doom. That city, he wrote during the siege, "I would burn to ashes. Not one stone of its buildings would I leave upon another." When Stephens recalled all the brave men who had perished at Battery Wagner, he could think of only one thing: digging rebel graves beneath Charleston's "smoldering ruins."[65]

Stephens's company broke camp at Fort Green as soon as they heard that the rebels had evacuated Charleston. Once across Light House Inlet, they trekked over Morris Island and took rowboats to the city. Stephens recalled that his small group was "the first effective force to actually take possession of the modern Babylon." Later that day, the Twenty-first USCT, composed of former slaves, many of whom had been the property of Charleston masters, victoriously entered the city. Stephens observed that every building was shut up and not a white person could be seen. Blacks, however, filled the streets to welcome their liberators, "shouting welcomes & God blessings."[66]

Stephens quickly rejoined his regiment, which grandly entered the city on 25 February. The men crossed the Ashley River after a heavy fog lifted and, in the bright sunshine, marched up King Street, the same avenue Stephens had walked in 1857. City blacks gleefully thronged the streets to watch the parade, and even a few whites observed, unable to suppress their curiosity. A former slave rushed up to the regiment, exclaiming that he had waited "for you too long— *too* long!" One man in Company H reported that he "saw an old colored woman with a crutch—for she could not walk without one, having spent all her life in bondage—who, on seeing us, got so happy that she threw down her crutch and shouted that the year of jubilee had come."[67]

For the next week, Stephens served as provost guard in Charleston. "At every public building," James Redpath, the abolitionist reporter for the *Tribune,* observed black soldiers "halting citizens, ordering them back or examining their passes." The few whites who remained in the city were furious. The old order had evaporated. Blacks no longer offered the deference that the city's repressive black laws and racial etiquette required. Blacks, whether soldiers or former slaves, refused to give way on the sidewalks and even dared to approach a white man "and ask him for a light for their cigars!" Stephens, quite likely, presided at the gates of the Citadel, the military academy that had trained so many Confederate officers, and demanded passes from every white. The Fifty-fourth had been the first in the city, Garrison's *Liberator* reported, "and it is their privilege to guard it."[68]

Beginning on 14 March, Stephens and the Fifty-fourth roamed the coastal area and backcountry from Savannah, Georgia, to Georgetown, South Carolina. The slaves they encountered had stripped the homes of their former masters and "in plantation dress, laden with bundles and with a few small carts" followed the black regiment to freedom. They also provided the men with information about rebel troop strength and where their masters had buried their gold and silver. The Fifty-fifth Massachusetts, as it penetrated the interior, also received a joyous welcome from slaves. One woman shook the hand of nearly everyone in the regiment, while others shouted "Great God" and "Joy,

Joy, Joy." A mile-long train of wagons, carts and former slaves, some wearing stovepipe hats, others carrying jugs of molasses, buckets, or picture frames, trailed the unit as it sought out rebel resistance.[69]

The Fifty-fourth Massachusetts marched to the tune of "John Brown" as it attacked remaining rebels at Sumpterville, Camden, and Manchester Station. They destroyed bridges and locomotives, seven engines and fifty cars at Manchester. They skirmished with Confederates at Sumpterville on 9 April and fought their last engagement at Boykin's Mills, near Camden on 18 April 1865 (map 2). By the time word of the armistice reached the regiment, the Fifty-fourth had killed 160 Confederate soldiers while sustaining only twenty-five casualties. Furthermore, it had destroyed twenty-three locomotives, fifty-four cars, several bridges, smashed another million dollars of rolling stock, a machine shop, and burned a million dollars' worth of cotton. The regiment also had seized thousands of pounds of food stuffs, five hundred horses and mules, and, as Lieutenant Colonel Hooper proudly informed his wife, about six thousand slaves.[70]

The Fifty-fourth marched to Georgetown, South Carolina, on 21 April. It rained about noontime, and the unit made camp by 5:30 P.M. that evening on plantation grounds owned by John L. Manning, a former governor of the state. As the regiment ate dinner, word arrived that Confederate Gen. Joseph E. Johnston had agreed to surrender his forces to Sherman. Someone in the unit discovered Manning's wine cellar, and, as one officer recorded in his journal, all "had wine aplenty." A staff officer from General Beauregard informed the regiment that "the war had probably closed." Throughout the camp "guns were discharged and cheers without number [were] given for those who had sturdily stood by Freedom in her hour of need."[71]

The euphoria proved brief. Three days later, the Fifty-fourth learned of Lincoln's assassination. "We at first could not comprehend it," one officer wrote in shock, "it was too overwhelming, too lamentable, too distressing." The men felt that peace, which had been so real just moments before, "is *no more.*" Lieutenant Colonel Hooper believed that every man in the regiment wanted to reload his weapon and "exterminate the race that can do such things. Thus we all felt," he concluded. Few could imagine worse news than Lincoln's murder, but it came the next day when the Fifty-fourth learned that most of their fellow soldiers taken prisoner at Battery Wagner had either been killed or died in prison. Out of sixty or perhaps one hundred men presumed

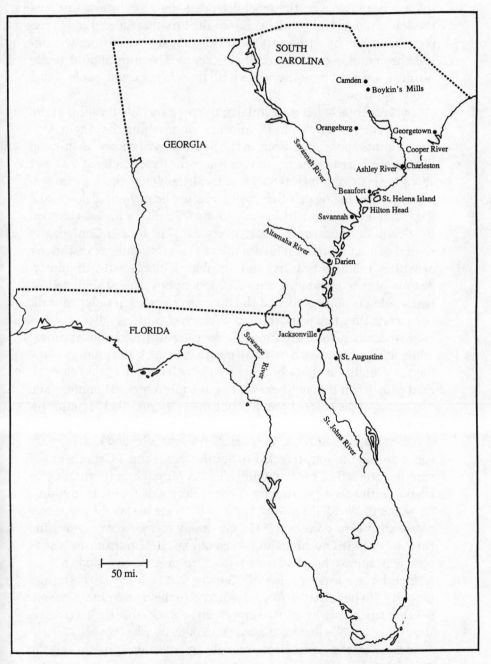

Map 2. The Fifty-fourth Massachusetts in the Department of the South

to have been taken by the rebel defenders, only seventeen survived the war. Colonel Hallowell expressed the fury that raced through the regiment when he wrote that the rebels "must be exterminated, unless they quickly get down on their knees." The army should "trifle no more, we must hunt them down till there is not a vestige of a Rebel left in the land."[72]

Southerners also felt vengeful. For them, peace only meant that the war had entered a new phase. Information reaching the *Anglo-African*'s editors about conditions in the South proved deeply disturbing. "If one-tenth part of the reports are true," the paper declared, "a most shocking state of things exist. From localities where there are no federal troops, come reports that . . . [blacks] are being hunted down like dogs, and dispatched without ceremony." Southern papers recorded the deaths of hundreds of blacks every day. The former Confederate capital at Richmond provided some of the most chilling testimony of whites robbing, beating, and murdering blacks with impunity. Astonishingly, occupying white Union troops abused their fellow black soldiers and compelled them to carry passes in order to walk the streets they had just captured. Worse yet, white soldiers cooperated with the planters to force blacks to return to the plantations, while others joined with ex-Confederates to attack and plunder black homes. Conditions became so chronically dangerous "that the colored people feel it is neither safe to go out or remain at home." The "situation of the colored people," one man reported, had become "intolerable."[73]

Albert Gallatin Browne, Sr., a Salem ship chandler and U.S. treasury agent during the war, traveled to South Carolina and Georgia in the summer and fall of 1865 and provided his Massachusetts antislavery friends with searing testimony of the suffering he found. If anything, he wrote to Wendell Phillips, the situation for blacks "is *positively worse* than before the war." He saw many former slaves "covering themselves with nothing but pieces of rags, held in front & rear as strangers approached." Whites refused to provide any food to their former slaves, and one planter told Browne that he would see his former property "in hell first" before he would give them anything. No wonder that when Browne advised one group of blacks that they were free, they replied, "Wee don no massa. Wees dont no what we bees."[74]

Enraged by the destruction wrought by invading Yankees and the humiliation of military defeat, whites turned their wrath on blacks.

"Their treatment of the negro is infamous," Browne wrote. "He is cruelly whipped and frequently shot down and the perpetrator often goes off with impunity." One child he met had stopped the contents of a double-barrelled shotgun. *"I counted fifty-seven* bird shot in his left side, mostly in the face & head," Browne wrote. Whites refused to abandon the institution of slavery and tried to shoot, beat, and whip blacks into submission. In Orangeburg, South Carolina, whites murdered former slaves who wandered off their plantations. "No man in the North who has not lived among these planters," a reporter from the *Tribune* asserted, "can understand what a brutal and vicious class of persons they are."[75]

Union troops made conditions worse for the ex-slaves by compelling them to sign labor contracts with their former masters. When they refused to fulfill the agreements, Yankees forced them back to the plantations at bayonet point. Where black troops served as the occupying force, local whites pressured Union commanders to withdraw them, and white regiments refused to serve alongside them. Two companies of the Fifty-fifth Massachusetts Regiment stationed at Orangeburg found their authority completely undercut by other Yankee units that refused to take orders from an officer in "a nigger regiment." Some former slaves at Orangeburg, perhaps assisted by men in the Fifty-fifth, armed themselves and openly drilled to intimidate their white oppressors. In another case near Barnwell, a group of armed blacks halted a party of white Union troops and destroyed the labor contracts they carried to area plantations. But successes proved rare, and the future remained uncertain.[76]

In Charleston, where Stephens and the Fifty-fourth returned to again serve as provost guard, conditions matched those at Richmond. "The war is not ended, as many fondly imagine," one Charleston correspondent informed the Boston *Transcript.* "It only changes form." Charles Macbeth, who had been mayor during Stephens's first encounter with the city and who wanted to enslave all free blacks, remained at the helm until October 1865. All along the coast, conditions deteriorated as former rebels and dispossessed landowners returned to claim their property. Most planters made no effort to hide their resentment of Yankee rule and pledged to reassert their control at the first opportunity. Even those who swore allegiance to the Union did so only to keep their property. Fear-stricken by Yankee rule and the presence of black Union troops, whites trembled in expectation of retribution. Dr. Benjamin Huger, father of Stephens's commander on the USS *Walker*, predicted that the city's history would be "written in blood."[77]

But whose blood? The first days of the Union occupation provided ominous warnings. Whites jeered the black soldiers who doused flames ignited by the departing rebel army. Rumors surged through Charleston that any blacks who demonstrated in support of the Union would pay for their actions once the troops departed. The Charleston *Courier*, now under federal control, downplayed reports from outlying areas that whites had gunned down black marchers. Blacks who streamed into the city looking for food, work, and safety exacerbated tensions and worried the Union commander, who pleaded with them to stay in the countryside. He reminded them that the federal government would provide only temporary relief and that they must work, "This is what freedom means, duty demands, and your government expects."[78]

Ignoring the threats and warnings, blacks seized homes abandoned by fleeing whites and flouted the old black codes with delight. Black school children paraded in the streets singing the "John Brown" song within earshot of John C. Calhoun's tomb. Led by Charleston's small but well-established free black elite, the former slaves began organizing soon after federal troops entered the city. On 29 March, they assembled in the Zion Presbyterian Church to thank Union forces and President Lincoln. A week earlier, between three and four thousand blacks had gathered for a mammoth emancipation celebration. The Twenty-first USCT joined with the city's black tradesmen and school children in a two-and-a-half-mile-long parade through the city. Fifty black butchers, carving knives upheld, marched beneath a banner depicting "a fat porker." Schoolboys held aloft a banner proclaiming what every black now felt, "We know no masters but ourselves." Representatives from black schools, churches, and fraternal associations joined 1,800 cheering and singing children and seven large blocs of firemen, carpenters, masons, wheelwrights, blacksmiths, painters, barbers, coachmen, and farmers. The marchers staged a mock slave sale followed by a hearse inscribed with the words "Slavery is Dead."[79]

By early summer, though, a virtual holocaust had descended on Charleston. Within a twenty-mile radius of the city, reported the Boston *Commonwealth*, the land was "fetid with the decaying bodies of colored men, who have been shot down when trying to escape their oppressors." In the city, Yankee soldiers declared war on the freed people. They attacked blacks on city streets or burst into their homes to rape and pillage. "Peaceable colored citizens have been kicked out of their homes, knocked down in the streets, bled with brickbats and bayonets, cut with knives, pounded and mauled in the places of business, by United States soldiers." As occurred elsewhere in the South, Union soldiers joined with former rebels and "the lords of Southern soil" to wreak vengeance on blacks.[80]

Union sailors and the 127th New York Regiment, largely raised by orthodox Protestant churches, proved the most vicious. One sailor who passed a black sitting on a doorstep struck him in the face out of blind rage. As he threatened to "kill the d— nigger," an officer from the Fifty-fourth happened by and arrested the sailor. On 18 June, soldiers from the New York unit clashed with men from the Thirty-fifth USCT, who had come to the defense of two black women harassed by whites. Tensions increased after the state's governor exclaimed on 3 July that "freedom will prove a curse instead of a blessing to the negro." Eighteen hundred Charleston blacks petitioned Governor Andrew for help in securing the vote and a military governor sympathetic to them. They also sought his assistance in removing the head of the Union garrison, who, as it turned out, also commanded the infamous 127th New York Regiment.[81]

In July 1865, the 165th New York Regiment (Duryea's Zouaves) teamed with former rebels and local whites to attack blacks systematically. After the Zouaves had driven the black vegetable vendors from the central market, local whites swept through to steal the produce. Night and day, mobs of Union soldiers and their rebel cohorts cruised the city in search of black victims. Outgunned if not outnumbered, blacks resorted to guerrilla warfare, lying in wait for a white soldier or a small group of Zouaves and pouncing on them with bricks and truncheons. Even black children organized for their own protection and instigated attacks on white troops.[82]

Unsatisfied with their campaign of terror against black citizens, both New York regiments attacked the Fifty-fourth. The confrontations sometimes resulted in pitched street battles, word of which military authorities attempted to suppress. Nevertheless, information about the clashes filtered out through journalists and such supporters of black troops as Albert G. Browne. During the second week of July, the Zouaves ambushed a detachment of the Fifty-fourth, leading to casualties on both sides. Browne believed that Gen. John Porter Hatch, who commanded the District of Charleston, hated black soldiers and encouraged arbitrary arrests of all blacks. A soldier from the Fifty-fourth who had been caught in a mass arrest witnessed white soldiers clubbing black prisoners and heard one of his captors declare, "We mean to hang all you damn niggers."[83]

Sgt. Charles Lenox of the Fifty-fourth informed Boston's William C. Nell that the New Yorkers planned to continue their attacks until Union commanders withdrew all black troops from the city. Officers from the Fifty-fourth in the provost guard ordered a curfew, hoping to quell the riots, but the battles continued day and night. By mid-July the outrages had so angered General Gillmore that he seized the Zouave's regimental colors and ordered the unit confined to Fort Strong (Battery Wagner). He instructed Strong's garrison to load its cannon with grape and aim them at the regiment. If the New Yorkers refused to give up their weapons, Gillmore instructed the garrison to fire. The Zouaves capitulated and were confined to the remains of Fort Sumter in Charleston Harbor.[84]

Despite Gillmore's action, other white regiments from New York and Pennsylvania continued the barbaric assaults. Local Union commanders condemned the violence, but their own men perpetrated the worse crimes, and the commanders themselves earned unenviable reputations as "trimmers" and close friends of former rebels.[85] Gillmore's chief of staff openly criticized the Fifty-fourth and refused to investigate the murder of blacks, believing that protection of city whites was his first priority. Other Union officers, who publicly claimed to support black rights, proved in private, as Browne discovered, "regular toads to the prominent Rebels, a pig headed martinet with no sympathy for the negro." He sadly concluded that "the negro is placed between the upper and neither mill stone and is ground to powder."[86]

Soldiers from the Fifty-fourth may have sought their own justice. Some carried sticks in violation of the provost marshall's orders as they searched the city for former rebels and their Yankee allies. One Charleston shopkeeper claimed that a squad of soldiers marched into his store, pointed a pistol at his chest, and walked out with cigars and money. Police reported other cases of assault and robbery by Fifty-fourth troops, but the increasing number of such reports may have been part of the campaign to compel the Union army to withdraw the unit. In September, after the regiment had returned home, local whites rioted against the Fifty-fifth Massachusetts. When they caught black soldiers on a drinking spree in the city, the mob screamed at police to "Kill the damn niggers!" The soldiers rushed for their muskets, but the whites had fled before the men returned. By the fall of 1865, both of Massachusetts's black regiments had been withdrawn, and whites temporarily succeeded in reinstituting the harsh black codes that brought a semblance of slavery back to the city.[87]

The Fifty-fourth had begun to collapse during the summer of 1865. When not battling local whites and other Union troops, the men drilled on the parade grounds of the Citadel to keep up sinking morale and occupy their time. The racism that Stephens found so vexing in several of his superior officers flourished under the trying conditions. Capt. Edward B. Emerson groused about the drills and the thousands of "tattered, dilapidated little darkies who throng our parade ground. This play soldier is abominable, we are all disgusted with it." What bothered Emerson and fellow officers far more was Colonel Hallowell's insistence on commissioning black officers.[88]

The Fifty-fourth had broken the color barrier in January 1865, when Sgt. Stephen A. Swails received his commission as a second lieutenant. Swails, the first African-American officer of a regular army combat regiment, won his shoulder straps after an acrimonious eleven-month campaign. Hallowell had recommended him for a commission after the Battle of Olustee, and Governor Andrew accepted the recommendation on 11 March 1864. But the Department of the South's commanders and the War Department rejected it because Swails "is believed to have African blood in him."[89]

Repeated protests and personal pleas from the governor's representative, who traveled to Washington to settle the question, only resulted in rude confrontations. Andrew felt great urgency in Swails's case, hoping to commission him quickly and dampen the deadly fire that burned over unequal pay in 1864. The army's repudiation of Swails's commission and three others in the Fifty-fifth Massachusetts further incited the mutinous conditions. "We want black commissioned officers," one soldier wrote the *Liberator*, "We want men whose hearts are truly loyal to the rights of man. . . . We want to demonstrate our ability to rule, as we have demonstrated our willingness to obey. In short we want simple justice."[90]

When the War Department grudgingly awarded Swails his commission in January 1865 the men had won an important battle. The *Anglo-African*, joyful over the victory, could not help but notice that the army had commissioned the lightest-skinned man in the regiment and rejected equally meritorious promotions to others. With the war over, the army began to relent and commissioned sergeants Peter Vogelsang and Frank M. Welch.[91] It drew the line, however, at Stephens. For much of the year, he had acted as a de facto lieutenant. He kept the company records, filled out reports, and even ordered the arrest of enlisted men absent without leave. Colonel Hallowell recognized Stephens's abilities and recommended him for promotion. Andrew approved the commission in July, but the army rejected it because of Stephens's race.[92]

The commissions Hallowell offered to Stephens and the other black soldiers infuriated several white officers. Capts. Edward B. Emerson and Watson Wilberforce Bridge nearly rebelled when Hallowell commissioned Stephens, Vogelsang, and Welch. "Things are going to the devil fast," Bridge moaned. Outraged, they threatened to resign and "do not propose to pass it [promotion of black enlisted men] by without notice." True to their word, both men quit in July right after Stephens's recommendation for promotion.[93]

Stephens made his last entry in the Fifty-fourth's company books on 20 August 1865. The regiment returned to Boston on 2 September to a welcome that rivaled its famous departure in 1863. Stephens assumed the position of a first lieutenant, despite the War Department's ruling, as the men marched triumphantly over Beacon Hill where Boston's black community turned out en masse to greet them. Led by the Shaw Guards, a black militia unit, the Fifty-fourth passed in review before Governor Andrew and his staff, retracing their steps of two years earlier. The *Anglo-African*'s Robert Hamilton met with Stephens before the celebration. He then proudly watched his former correspondent march with the other officers past the governor of Massachusetts, "black and white men, shoulder to shoulder." Hamilton confessed that he could hardly contain himself, his "joy was complete."[94]

Notes

1. Berlin, *The Black Military Experience*, 362–64.
2. GES to Robert Hamilton, 1 August 1864.
3. GES to Robert Hamilton, 7 August 1863.
4. GES to Robert Hamilton, 1 August 1864.
5. Robert Gould Shaw to John A. Andrew, 31 March 1863, 2 July 1863, Edward L. Pierce to John A. Andrew, 3 August 1863, Executive Department Letters, MSA.

6. Richard H. L. Jewett to Eliza Nutting Jewett, 9 August 1863, Richard H. L. Jewett Papers, Boston Athenæum; Sgt. Frederick Johnson to John A. Andrew, 10 August, 4 September 1863, John Mercer Langston to John A. Andrew, 28 June 1863, Executive Department Letters, MSA; Emilio, *A Brave Black Regiment*, 351. Andrew's response to Langston's letter appears in William Schouler, *Annual Report of the Adjutant General . . . 1863* (Boston: State of Massachusetts, 1864), 66–72.

7. Mrs. L. A. Grimes to John A. Andrew, n.d., Mary E. Clark to John A. Andrew, 15 November 1863, John Murray Forbes et al., to John A. Andrew, 11 November 1863, Executive Department Letters, MSA, emphasis in the original.

8. John Ritchie Journal, 27 September 1863, New York *Tribune*, 29 September 1863, Fifty-fourth Regiment Papers, 1:262, MHS; Luis F. Emilio Diary, 29, 30 September 1863, Philip and Betty Emilio Family Collection.

9. GES to Thomas Hamilton, 3 October 1863.

10. Ibid.

11. Luis F. Emilio diary notes, 31 October 1863, Fifth-fourth Regiment Papers, vol. 2, MHS; Edward N. Hallowell to Albert G. Browne, Jr., 2 August 1863, Executive Department Letters, MSA; Lt. Col. Henry Lee, Jr., to John A. Andrew, 18 September 1863, John A. Andrew Papers, MHS.

12. John A. Andrew to Quincy A. Gillmore, 3 December 1863, Edward W. Kinsley Papers, Duke University; John Whittier Messer Appleton Letterbook, 13 December 1863, John Whittier Messer Appleton Papers, WVUL; J. H. Stephenson to John A. Andrew, 20 November 1863, Edward N. Hallowell to John A. Andrew, 23 November 1863, Executive Department Letters, MSA; Luis F. Emilio Diary, 12 December 1863, Philip and Betty Emilio Family Collection.

13. *OR*, ser. 1, 28:127–28; George L. Stearns to John A. Andrew, 30 July 1863, Executive Department Letters, MSA; George Washington Williams, *A History of the Negro Troops in the War of the Rebellion, 1861–65* (New York, 1888, reprint, New York: Bergman Publishers, 1968), 120–24, 154–55.

14. Charles B. Fox, letter extracts, 14 August 1863, Charles B. Fox Papers, MHS; William H. Dupree and Charles L. Mitchell to Burt G. Wilder, 12 April 1909, Burt G. Wilder Papers, Cornell University.

15. John H. Johnson to Cousin, 31 December 1863, typescript copy, Brown Letters, American Antiquarian Society.

16. John A. Andrew Memo, 5 December 1863, Executive Department Letters, MSA; Stephens Pension File, RG 15, National Archives; Philadelphia city directories, 1860–65.

17. Perhaps from York, Pennsylvania, Susan A. Stephens had served on a committee of Philadelphia women to raise funds for the *Weekly Anglo-African*. Norwood P. Hallowell to John A. Andrew, 7 December 1863, Executive Department Letters, MSA; GES to Jacob C. White, Jr., 8 January 1858, *BAP*, 4:371–376; *WAA*, 11 March 1863.

18. Norwood P. Hallowell to John A. Andrew, 7 December 1863, H. Ware to Robert R. Corson, 5 December 1863, Executive Department Letters, MSA.

19. New York *Herald*, 19 January 1864; Peter Vogelsang interview, 24 May 1886, Fifty-fourth Regiment Papers, vol. 2, MHS; Luis F. Emilio Diary, 1 Jan-

uary 1864, Philip and Betty Emilio Family Collection; GES to Robert Hamilton, 5 January 1864.

20. Peter Vogelsang interview, 24 May 1886, 1:254, John Ritchie Journal, 22 December 1863, Fifty-fourth Regiment Papers, vol. 2, MHS; Luis F. Emilio to Isa, 22 December 1863, Luis F. Emilio Diary, 5 December 1863, GES to Luis F. Emilio, 27 December 1885, Philip and Betty Emilio Family Collection.

21. Emilio, *A Brave Black Regiment*, 147–49; David James Coles, "'A Fight, a Licking, and a Footrace': The 1864 Florida Campaign and the Battle of Olustee," M.A. thesis, Florida State University, 1985, 35–43; Julien Yonge, "The Occupation of Jacksonville, February 1864, and the Battle of Olustee; Letters of C. M. Duren, 54th Massachusetts Regiment, U.S.A.," *Florida Historical Quarterly* 32 (1954): 262.

22. Coles, "'A Fight, a Licking, and a Footrace,'" 5–7, 28–29; John Niven, *Salmon P. Chase: A Biography* (New York: Oxford University Press, 1995), 362; William W. H. Davis, *History of the 104th Pennsylvania Regiment* (Philadelphia: Author, 1866), 303.

23. Coles, "'A Fight, a Licking, and a Footrace,'" 74–75; John Whittier Messer Appleton Letterbook, 16 March 1864, 198, John Whittier Messer Appleton Papers, WVUL.

24. Coles, "'A Fight, a Licking, and a Footrace,'" 47–57; Misc. notes, 14 February 1864, Fifty-fourth Regiment Papers, vol. 2, MHS; John Whittier Messer Appleton Letter Book, 14 February 1864, John Whittier Messer Appleton Papers, WVUL.

25. Coles, "'A Fight, a Licking, and a Footrace,'" 54–57, 109–10; OR, ser. 1, 35:283, 285–86; Misc notes, 14 February 1864, Fifty-fourth Regiment Papers, vol. 2, MHS.

26. Coles, "'A Fight, a Licking, and a Footrace,'" 107–9, 117; Henry W. Littlefield, "A Paper on the Battle of Olustee. Feb. 20, 1864," 7 December 1886, Fifty-fourth Regiment Papers, vol. 4, MHS.

27. Coles, "'A Fight, a Licking, and a Footrace,'" 62–68, 95–96, 112–22.

28. Ibid., 128–32; Littlefield, "A Paper on the Battle of Olustee."

29. John Whittier Messer Appleton Letterbook, 20 February 1864, John Whittier Messer Appleton Papers, WVUL; Helmons interview, 22 January 1887, GES interview, 11 December 1883, GES to Luis F. Emilio, 8 January 1886, Fifty-fourth Regiment Papers, vol. 2, MHS; Charles W. Lenox to Luis F. Emilio, 16 September 1884, Fifty-fourth Regiment Papers, vol. 4, MHS.

30. GES to Luis F. Emilio, 8 January 1886, Helmons interview, 22 January 1887, Hooper interview, 12 October 1882, Fifty-fourth Regiment Papers, vol. 2, MHS; John Whittier Messer Appleton Letterbook, 20 February 1864, 176, John Whittier Messer Appleton Papers, WVUL; John Whittier Messer Appleton to William S. Appleton, 25 April 1899, Appleton Family Papers, box 11, MHS; OR, ser. 1, 35:315.

31. John Ritchie Journal, 22, 24, 25 February 1864, Luis F. Emilio diary notes, Fifty-fourth Regiment Papers, vol. 2, MHS; Coles, "'A Fight, a Licking, and a Footrace,'" 132–34, 146–51.

32. Boston *Daily Evening Traveler*, 29 February 1864; Charles W. Lenox to Edward W. Kinsley, 24 February 1864, Edward W. Kinsley Papers, Moorland-Spingarn Research Center, Howard University; Frederick M. Binder, "Pennsylvania Negro Regiments in the Civil War," *Journal of Negro History* 37 (October 1952): 407–9; *OR*, ser. 1, 35:288–90; eyewitness report from [Donald Yacovone], *We Fight for Freedom: Massachusetts, African Americans, and the Civil War* (Boston: Massachusetts Historical Society, 1993), 26, emphasis in original.

33. Edward N. Hallowell to John A. Andrew, 19 September 1864, Fifty-fourth Massachusetts Regiment Letterbooks, RG 94, National Archives; Robert R. Newell to Luis F. Emilio, 10 January 1865, GES to Luis F. Emilio, 14 June 1886, Fifty-fourth Regiment Papers, vol. 3, MHS; officer's quotation from Luis F. Emilio to Isa, 19 July 1864, Philip and Betty Emilio Family Collection.

34. Charles Sumner to Francis W. Bird, 22 February 1864, Charles Sumner Papers, HLHU; GES to Robert Hamilton, 6 March 1864.

35. *WAA*, 13, 27 August 1864; *BAP*, 3:65.

36. J. H. Stephenson to Dr. Le Baron Russell, 26 January 1864, Edward W. Kinsley Papers, Duke University; "Fort Green" to Editor, 21 August 1864, *Christian Recorder*, 24 September 1864; GES to Robert Hamilton, 26 May 1864.

37. "Picket" to Henry Highland Garnet, 30 June 1864, *WAA*, 30 July 1864; *WAA*, 30 April, 16, 30 July 1864; Fifty-fifth Massachusetts Regiment Orderly Books, RG 94, National Archives; Edward N. Hallowell to Aurora, 25 December 1864, Hallowell Papers, Haverford College.

38. *Liberator*, 8 April 1864; Charles B. Fox letter extracts, 28 April 1864, Charles B. Fox Papers, MHS; Edward N. Hallowell to Luis F. Emilio, [?] 1864, Fifty-fourth Regiment Papers, vol. 4, MHS; [Bowditch], "War Letters," 469; Howard C. Westwood, *Black Troops, White Commanders, and Freedmen during the Civil War* (Carbondale: Southern Illinois University Press, 1992), 142–66.

39. Howard C. Westwood, "The Cause and Consequence of a Union Black Soldier's Mutiny and Execution," *Civil War History* 31 (September 1985): 222–27.

40. Westwood, "The Cause and Consequence," 233, quoting Andrew; GES to Robert Hamilton, 6 March 1864, emphasis in the original.

41. John Whittier Messer Appleton Letterbook, 12 April 1864, 210, John Whittier Messer Appleton Papers, WVUL; Luis F. Emilio diary notes, 26 April 1864, Fifty-fourth Regiment Papers, vol. 2, MHS.

42. John Whittier Messer Appleton Letterbook, 18 April 1864, Fifty-fourth Regiment Papers, vol. 2, MHS.

43. Luis F. Emilio to Father, 29 April 1864, Philip and Betty Emilio Family Collection; Samuel Harrison to Robert Hamilton, 14 April 1864, *WAA*, 23 April 1864; *WAA*, 7 May 1864; Anonymous to John A. Andrew, 25 March 1864, Executive Department Letters, MSA; Thomas D. Freeman to William Freeman, 26 March 1864, Thomas D. Freeman to Martha, 25 April 1864, typescript copies, American Antiquarian Society.

44. An anonymous Sergeant to Elisha Weaver, 29 May 1864, *Christian Recorder*, 25 June 1864; Alfred S. Hartwell, "Recollections," ms., Alfred S. Hartwell Papers, Hawaii State Archives.

45. Berlin, *The Black Military Experience*, 398–402; "Bay State" [Fifty-fifth Mass.] to Robert Hamilton, 10 April 1864, *WAA*, 30 April 1864, emphasis in the original.

46. Fifty-fifth Massachusetts Regiment descriptive book, Company I, RG 94, National Archives. Details of this account are from the documentation in Baker's and Henry Way's court-martial trials, RG 153, National Archives.

47. Wallace Baker Court Martial, RG 153, National Archives; Fifty-fifth Massachusetts Regiment Orderly Books, Company I, RG 94, National Archives.

48. General Order No. 43, Alfred S. Hartwell, Fifty-fifth Massachusetts Regiment Orderly Books, RG 94, National Archives; George Thompson Garrison diary extracts, 19 June 1864, New York *Daily News*, 27 June 1864, Emilio Notes, Association of Officers of the Fifty-fifth Massachusetts Volunteer Infantry, box 1, MHS; "Picket" to Henry Highland Garnet, 30 June 1864, *WAA*, 30 July 1864; GES to Robert Hamilton, 18 June 1864.

49. Hartwell is quoted in his letter of 10 May 1864, Fifty-fourth Regiment Papers, 1:549, MHS; Charles B. Fox Diary, 18 June 1864, vol. 2, Charles B. Fox Papers, MHS; Thomas Appleton journal notes, 18 June 1864, George Thompson Garrison diary extracts, June 1864, Association of Officers of the Fifty-fifth Massachusetts Volunteer Infantry, box 1, MHS; Fifty-fifth Massachusetts Regiment Orderly Books, RG 94, National Archives; William Schouler, *Annual Report of the Adjutant General . . . 1865* (Boston: State of Massachusetts, 1866), 566.

50. GES to Robert Hamilton, 1 August 1864.

51. Norwood P. Hallowell to John A. Andrew, 17 May 1864, Executive Department Letters, MSA.

52. John Whittier Messer Appleton Letterbook, 12 May 1864, 223, John Whittier Messer Appleton Papers, WVUL; John Ritchie Journal, 12 May 1864, Fifty-fourth Regiment Papers, vol. 2, MHS; Richard H. L. Jewett, 14 May 1864, Richard H. L. Jewett Papers, Boston Athenæum.

53. John Whittier Messer Appleton Letterbook, 19 May 1864, 226–27, John Whittier Messer Appleton Papers, WVUL; John Whittier Messer Appleton Papers, 19 May 1864, John Ritchie Journal, 21 May 1864, Fifty-fourth Regiment Papers, vol. 2, MHS.

54. Edward N. Hallowell to John A. Andrew, 4 June 1864, Fifty-fourth Regiment Letterbooks, RG 94, National Archives; Edward N. Hallowell to H. Ware, 28 May 1864, Executive Department Letters, MSA.

55. J. H. Hall to Elisha Weaver, 3 August 1864, *Christian Recorder*, 27 August 1864; J. H. B. D. to Elisha Weaver, 24 May 1864, *Christian Recorder*, 11 June 1864; Isaac White to John A. Andrew, 31 July 1864, Executive Department Letters, MSA.

56. John Whittier Messer Appleton Letterbook, n.d., 281, John Whittier Messer Appleton Papers, WVUL; J. Gregory Smith to John A. Andrew, 25 April

1864, James Freeman Clarke to John A. Andrew, 27 June 1864, Union League of New York Petition, n.d., Executive Department Letters, MSA.

57. John A. Andrew to Edward W. Kinsley, 25 April 1864, newspaper clipping, Edward W. Kinsley Papers, Duke University; John A. Andrew to Charles Sumner, 16 February 1864, John A. Andrew to Abraham Lincoln, 27 May 1864, Executive Department Letters, MSA.

58. Charles Sumner to John A. Andrew, Sunday 1864, Charles Sumner to John A. Andrew, 18 June 1864, Executive Department Letters, MSA; Charles Sumner to Thomas Wentworth Higginson, 22 June 1864, in *The Selected Letters of Charles Sumner*, ed. Beverly Wilson Palmer, 2 vols. (Boston: Northeastern University Press, 1990), 2:245–46.

59. Lewis Hayden to Alfred S. Hartwell, 17 May 1864, Alfred S. Hartwell Papers, MSL; Albert G. Browne, Jr., to Luis F. Emilio, 26 April 1864, Philip and Betty Emilio Family Collection; Alexander Price to Ambrose E. Burnside, 2 November 1864, Edward W. Kinsley Papers, Duke University; Edward W. Kinsley to William Logan, 19 July, 10 August 1864, Edward W. Kinsley Papers, Letterbook, box 1, Moorland-Spingarn Research Center, Howard University; *Liberator*, 20 May 1864.

60. Berlin, *The Black Military Experience*, 367; Charles Sumner to John A. Andrew, Sunday 1864, Executive Department Letters, MSA.

61. John Ritchie Journal, 31 August 1864, Fifty-fourth Regiment Papers, vol. 3, MHS; Berlin, *The Black Military Experience*, 368.

62. New York *Tribune*, 17 November 1864; *WAA*, 3 December 1864; *Christian Recorder*, 12 November 1864; Luis F. Emilio diary notes, 29 September 1864, John Ritchie Journal, 5 October 1864, Fifty-fourth Regiment Papers, vol. 3, MHS; James Monroe Trotter to Edward W. Kinsley, 21 November 1864, Edward W. Kinsley Papers, Duke University.

63. Edward N. Hallowell to Sister, 17 February 1865, Hallowell Papers, Haverford College; Henry N. Hooper to [?], 3 February 1865, Schouler, *Adjutant General's Report*, 15 January–23 February 1865, Fifty-fourth Regiment Papers, vol. 3, MHS.

64. Charleston *Mercury*, 11 February 1865; New York *Tribune*, 22 February 1865; Charles Carlton Coffin, *The Boys of '61: or, Four Years of Fighting* (Boston: Estes and Lauriat, 1881), 465–66.

65. GES to Robert Hamilton, [September] 1863.

66. Fifty-fourth Massachusetts Regiment, Morning Reports, RG 94, National Archives; Schouler, *Adjutant General's Report*, 18 February 1865, GES to Luis F. Emilio, 14 January 1886, Fifty-fourth Regiment Papers, vol. 3, MHS; Coffin, *Boys of '61*, 467–68; Edward N. Hallowell to Capt. L. B. Perry, 11 June 1865, Fifty-fourth Massachusetts Regiment Letterbooks, RG 94, National Archives. There is some dispute over which Union regiment first entered Charleston. Both Stephens and the regimental books claim that Companies B and F were the first black units in the city on 18 June.

67. Luis F. Emilio diary notes, 27 February 1865, Fifty-fourth Regiment Papers, vol. 3, MHS; Walter De Blois Briggs, ed., *Charles Edward Briggs: Civil War Surgeon in a Colored Regiment* (Berkeley: n.p., 1960), 147–48; John

H. W. N. Collins to Elisha Weaver, 19 March 1865, in *A Grand Army of Black Men: Letters from African-American Soldiers in the Union Army, 1861–1865,* ed. Edwin S. Redkey (New York: Cambridge University Press, 1992), 78–79.

68. New York *Tribune,* 2 March 1865; *Liberator,* 10 March 1865.

69. Briggs, ed., *Charles Edward Briggs,* 149–50; Boston *Traveler,* 26 April 1865, and Schouler, *Adjutant General's Report,* 25 April 1865, in Fifty-fourth Regiment Papers, vol. 3, MHS; George Thompson Garrison diary notes, 20 February, 11, 12 April 1865, Association of Officers of the Fifty-fifth Massachusetts Volunteer Infantry, MHS.

70. Fifty-fourth Massachusetts Regiment Morning Reports, Letter Books, RG 94, National Archives; Lewis Reed Journal, 11 April 1865, Fifty-fourth Regiment Papers, vol. 3, MHS. Henry N. Hooper to Wife, 28 April 1865, Fifty-fourth Regiment Papers, vol. 3, MHS; Boston *Traveller,* 26 April 1865.

71. Lewis Reed Journal, 21 April 1865, John Ritchie Journal, 21 April 1865, Edward N. Hooper "draft report," Fifty-fourth Regiment Papers, vol. 3, MHS; Emilio, *A Brave Black Regiment,* 307.

72. Fifty-fourth Massachusetts Regiment Letterbooks, RG 94, National Archives; John Ritchie Journal, 25 April 1865, Fifty-fourth Regiment Papers, vol. 3, MHS; Edward N. Hallowell to Mother, 27 April 1865, Hallowell Papers, Haverford College.

73. *WAA,* 5, 19 August, 3 September 1865; John T. O'Brien, "Reconstruction in Richmond: White Restoration and Black Protest, April-June 1865," *Virginia Magazine of History and Biography* 89 (July 1981): 272–73.

74. Albert G. Browne, Sr., to Wendell Phillips, 8 August 1865, Blagden Family Papers, HLHU; see Boston *Evening Transcript,* 12 October 1885, for an obituary of Browne.

75. Albert G. Browne, Sr., to Wendell Phillips, 17 September 1865, Blagden Family Papers, HLHU, emphasis in the original; *Tribune* quoted in *Liberator,* 16 June 1865; *Liberator,* 23 June 1865.

76. Typescript notes of Charles B. Fox Letterbooks, 13, 22 May 1865, Burt G. Wilder Papers, Cornell University; George Thompson Garrison diary notes, 27–30 June 1865, Association of Officers of the Fifty-fifth Massachusetts Volunteer Infantry, box 1, MHS; Albert G. Browne, Sr., to Wendell Phillips, 17 September 1865, Blagden Family Papers, HLHU; Alfred S. Hartwell to L. B. Perry, 7 August 1865, Alfred S. Hartwell Papers, MSL.

77. Boston *Transcript* cited in the *Liberator,* 16 June 1865; *Commonwealth,* 15 July 1865; Laura Matilda Towne, *Letters and Diary of Laura M. Towne* (New York: Negro Universities Press, 1969), 167–68; Richard H. L. Jewett to Eliza Nutting Jewett, 19 March 1865, Richard H. L. Jewett Papers, Boston Athenæum; Bernard E. Powers, Jr., "Community Evolution and Race Relations in Reconstruction Charleston, South Carolina," *South Carolina Historical Magazine* 95 (January 1994): 27–28; Harriet Kershaw Leiding, *Charleston: Historic and Romantic* (Philadelphia: J. B. Lippincott, 1931), 247, 255.

78. Charleston *Courier,* 3, 5 April 1865; Susie King Taylor, *Reminiscences of My Life with the 33d United States Colored Troops Late 1st S.C. Volunteers* (Boston: Author, 1902), 42; Wilbert Lee Jenkins, "Chaos, Conflict and Control: The Response of the Newly-Freed Slaves in Charleston, South Caro-

lina to Emancipation and Reconstruction, 1865–1877," Ph.D. diss., Michigan State University, 1991, 102–3.

79. Charleston *Courier*, 22 March 1865; Jenkins, "Chaos, Conflict and Control," 73, 84.

80. *The Commonwealth*, 17 June 1865.

81. Richard H. L. Jewett to Eliza Nutting Jewett, 13 June 1865, Richard H. L. Jewett Papers, Boston Athenæum; James Redpath to John A. Andrew, 11 July 1865, Executive Department Letters, MSA; Gray and Ropes, *War Letters*, 217; New York *Herald*, 28 June 1865; Charleston *Courier*, 27 February, 8, 25 July 1865.

82. Albert G. Browne, Sr., to Wendell Phillips, 16 July 1865, Blagden Family Papers, HLHU; Charleston *Courier*, 11 July 1865.

83. Albert G. Browne, Sr., to Wendell Phillips, 16 July 1865, Blagden Family Papers, HLHU; *The Commonwealth*, 22 July 1865.

84. Sgt. Charles Lenox to William C. Nell, 20 July 1865, *Liberator*, 25 August 1865; Charleston *Courier*, 11, 13, 18 July 1865; *Army and Navy Journal*, 29 July 1865, Fifty-fourth Regiment Papers, vol. 3, MHS; Jenkins, "Chaos, Conflict and Control," 329–33.

85. Albert G. Browne, Sr., to Wendell Phillips, 16 July 1865, Blagden Family Papers, HLHU; *The Commonwealth*, 22 July 1865; *WAA*, 8 July 1865; *Christian Recorder*, 10 June 1865.

86. Albert G. Browne, Sr., to Wendell Phillips, 16 July 1865, Blagden Family Papers, HLHU; *The Commonwealth*, 22 July 1865.

87. Charleston *Courier*, 24, 27 July, 5, 7 August 1865; George Thompson Garrison diary notes, 20 September 1865, Association of Officers of the Fifty-fifth Massachusetts Volunteer Infantry, box 1, MHS; Jenkins, "Chaos, Conflict and Control," 108–12.

88. Edward B. Emerson to Luis F. Emilio, 15 June 1865, Fifty-fourth Regiment Papers, vol. 4, MHS.

89. Edward N. Hallowell to John A. Andrew, 24 February, 19 June 1864, Stephen A. Swails to John A. Andrew, 17 July 1864, Edward N. Hallowell to Capt. W. L. M. Burger, 1 June 1864, Maj. Gen. J. G. Foster to John A. Andrew, 18 November 1864, Executive Department Letters, MSA; Edward N. Hallowell to John A. Andrew, 19 September 1864, Fifty-fourth Massachusetts Regiment Letterbooks, RG 94, National Archives; C. W. Foster to Edwin M. Stanton, 21 December 1864, Letters Sent, Colored Troops Division, Adjutant General's Office, 3:258–59, National Archives.

90. Stephen A. Swails to Brig. Gen. William Schouler, 2 December 1864, Stephen A. Swails to Richard P. Hallowell, 14 August 1864, Albert G. Browne, Jr., to John A. Andrew, 9, 17 December 1864, C. W. Foster to John A. Andrew, 28 June 1864, Executive Department Letters, MSA; James Monroe Trotter to Edward W. Kinsley, 29 May 1865, Edward W. Kinsley Papers, Duke University; "Sergeant" to William Lloyd Garrison, 26 August 1864, *Liberator*, 7 October 1864.

91. E. D. Townsend for Secretary of War Stanton, Special Order, 15 January 1865, Stephen A. Swails to John A. Andrew, 2 February 1865, Executive Department Letters, MSA; John Whittier Messer Appleton Letterbook, 26

March 1864, John Whittier Messer Appleton Papers, WVUL; John Ritchie Journal, 17 January 1865, Fifty-fourth Regiment Papers, vol. 3, MHS; *WAA*, 4 February, 4 June 1865.

92. Edward N. Hallowell to Brig. Gen. Schouler, Adjutant General, 10 July 1865, Edward N. Hallowell to Maj. W. L. M. Burger, 27 July 1865, Fifty-fourth Massachusetts Letterbooks, Morning Reports, RG 94, National Archives; Jacob Ballard Court-Martial, RG 153, National Archives. Although Massachusetts recognized Stephens's promotion, it had no official standing.

93. Watson Wilberforce to Luis F. Emilio, 8 July 1865, Edward B. Emerson to Luis F. Emilio, 8 June 1865, Fifty-fourth Regiment Papers, vol. 4, MHS.

94. *Liberator*, 8 September 1865; misc. notes, 1–2 September 1865, Fifty-fourth Regiment Papers, vol. 3, MHS; *WAA*, 16 September 1865, quoting Hamilton.

Chapter 4

"I Have Done My Duty"

When Stephens returned home, he went to work as a canvasser for Philadelphia's Union League. Benjamin C. Tilghman, his former patron, helped found the league, like those organized throughout the North during the war to support the national government, and likely assisted him again. The position gave Stephens time to consider his future. Slavery surely had ended, but the work of building freedom had barely begun. He wanted to help fulfill the dreams emancipation had inspired and provide freed people with the education that slavery had denied them. Sometime in late 1866 or early the next year, Stephens resigned his position with the league and started a freedmen's school at Liberty Hill near Port Royal, Virginia.[1]

Whether because of illness, lack of funds, or the opposition of whites to black education, Stephens soon returned to Philadelphia. There, he met Orlando Brown, Virginia's assistant superintendent of education for the Bureau of Refugees, Freedmen, and Abandoned Lands—better known as the Freedmen's Bureau. In October 1867, Stephens contacted Brown seeking bureau aid for another school. He professed his eagerness to teach and advised the assistant superintendent that he had already collected enough books, maps, and supplies for a school of fifty pupils. "I have determined to remove there as soon as I can get ready," Stephens wrote, "and cast my lot and fortunes or misfortunes, as the case may be in the old Dominion."[2]

Education, Stephens contended, more than anything else would best advance the long-term interests of Southern blacks. Northern blacks like Stephens felt a special obligation to teach those who had been in chains. They were, Stephens held, the slaves' "true friend and brother." They, and they alone, should bear the primary responsibility for the former slaves' education. "We can enter into their feelings and attract their sympathies better than any others can," Robert

Hamilton explained. "We can more patiently help and teach, and more jealously defend them. . . . We are manifestly destined for this work of mercy."[3]

With the coming of freedom, hundreds of Northern black men and women streamed south as teachers, missionaries, and political organizers. Like Stephens, many had been soldiers and saw firsthand the work that had to be done. Others had been slaves and keenly felt the need to return home. All went with the mission of remaking millions of slaves into American citizens. As one black teacher resolved, "As a colored man I feel it my duty" to "take up my cross there among my people."[4]

Stephens founded the Tilghman School, named to honor his Philadelphia benefactor, in November 1867 and located it in Tappahannock, Essex County, Virginia, near the Rappahannock River. Eager for education, Virginia blacks attended 366 such schools, 106 managed by African Americans.[5] Stephens's enthusiasm and energy made the effort successful. He fashioned desks and benches from lumber he purchased with his own money and even whitewashed the building himself. More important, he provided all the school's books, writing slates, and an "immense amount of clothing," which he gave to "the needy and destitute." When he requested financial assistance from the Freedmen's Bureau, he made it clear that "not one man black or white in the dist[rict] has contributed one dollar to aid in this thankless and important work—single handed and alone I have struggled on with nothing to cheer me, but the sweet consciousness that I have done my duty."[6]

Despite its ramshackle building, the Tilghman School attracted earnest students. Stephens began his work with only sixteen or seventeen children. Within a month, fifty-eight pupils filled his benches for six-hour lessons, and forty-one more attended night classes. By June, enrollment had shot up to sixty-five. Within nine months, more than 30 percent of his students—primarily the children of former slaves—tackled advanced reading, writing, and elementary geography.[7]

Next to freedom itself, Southern blacks craved learning. "There is one sin that slavery committed against me which I will never forgive," a slave remarked. "It robbed me of my education." Wherever the Union army had liberated slaves, blacks started up a school. They constructed their own buildings, sometimes doubling as church and schoolhouse, and bore aching deprivations so their children could attend.[8] Where no schools existed, blacks flooded the offices of the Freedmen's Bureau just to find something to read. To former slaves, education was "a long denied *right*," a badge of freedom, of citizenship, and the way to gain power. "Many see clearly," Virginia's assistant superintendent of education declared, "that without education their political and social position as well as their material interests will never be advanced."[9]

Stephens received bureau funds for the Tilghman School's rent, but most of his support came from the Pennsylvania branch of the American Freedmen's Union Commission. It financed twenty-two other teachers in Virginia and spent about $4,000 a year for its operations throughout the South. Founded in 1862 as the Pennsylvania Freedmen's Relief Association to assist former slaves at Port Royal, South Carolina, the commission counted some of Philadelphia's leading reformers and philanthropists among its members. The Garrisonian abolitionist James Miller McKim was the corresponding secretary, and Morris L. Hallowell, Edward N. and Norwood P. Hallowell's father, served on its board of directors.[10]

Stephens also received $10 a month from the Peabody Education Fund. Established by the Anglo-American merchant George Peabody in 1867, the fund was the first of several Northern foundations to promote education in the South. It held $2 million in trust, producing well over $100,000 a year in revenue to support its drive to establish public education and teacher training throughout the South for whites and blacks. The Massachusetts aristocrat Robert C. Winthrop served as Peabody's confidential advisor and chair of the fund's board of trustees. Winthrop also appointed Barnas Sears, an able administrator and former head of the Massachusetts Board of Education and president of Brown University, to direct the fund's activities.[11]

Sears, who located his office in Staunton, Virginia, may have visited the Tilghman School and decided to forego the fund's strict rules mandating that local communities provide the bulk of a school's finances and offer Stephens some support. Most small operations like the Tilghman School received nothing from the Peabody Fund and relied on whatever resources the impoverished former slaves could muster. Although Peabody subsidies may have resulted from Stephens's influential contacts, they also testified to his abilities and the extraordinary progress he made with his students. In practical terms, it meant survival. "None but those in my position can fully appreciate the benefit of aid in this form," Stephens advised the bureau. Peabody money pays "my rent and thus enables me to continue. I do not think a better plan could have been devised for the distribution of this noble Bequest."[12]

Stephens notified the bureau that Tappahannock whites "are quite friendly and well disposed" toward his school. Near the beginning of 1868, they had "organized a Sunday School for colored children," he reported. Although that school had closed by the end of the year, Stephens maintained that "the people of both classes are generally orderly." In short, according to Stephens, whites seemed "quite favorable" to black education.[13]

Perhaps some Tappahannock whites did tolerate Stephens's efforts and approved of those educational activities that came under their control, such as the Sunday school. Stephens's surviving letters to Freedmen's Bureau administrators reveal no serious conflict with local whites, much less threats to his life. But Stephens, hoping to retain bureau support, presented a rosy, if not distorted, picture of race relations in Essex County.[14]

In nearby districts, whites defiantly refused to accept the Confederate defeat. Many voiced their intention to wait out the federal occupation and regain their power and their slaves. At the very least, whites believed that "they will be compensated for what they lost by and expended in the 'Confederate Cause.'" Where agent C. G. McClelland labored in Warsaw, Virginia, "The principle business done is, to drink *mean whiskey,* abuse the *'miserable High Hatted Yankees'* the 'nigger' and Congress." Blacks who refused to obey whites, who registered and voted for Radical Republican politicians, lost their jobs or their homes. "Everything that a malicious, rebellious people can invent," McClelland reported, "will be made use of to intimidate the colored people in this county."[15]

Contradicting Stephens's optimistic assessments of race relations in Tappahannock, Freedmen's Bureau records show that blacks endured terrible recriminations from their former masters. Watson R. Wentworth, the bureau agent in Stephens's district, sent his superiors unusually candid assessments of racial conflict in his region. Fraud, political corruption, beatings, rape, and murder kept blacks repressed.[16] Whites revived the old slave patrols and roamed the countryside, intimidating blacks and breaking into their homes in the middle of the night to search for "stolen goods." The white terrorists rarely, if ever, found such items and were not brought "to justice by the civil authorities and," Wentworth concluded, "never will be."[17]

White planters compelled blacks to sign labor contracts that virtually reinstituted slavery. Although Freedmen's Bureau agents were supposed to oversee all labor agreements, Wentworth, helpless in the face of determined opposition, negotiated only one contract in an entire year. "The colored people must starve or steal under the present state of things," he advised the bureau. Some did steal food, mostly corn, and when apprehended fell victim to the white-controlled courts. One hapless man who stole corn and then returned it was rewarded with a life-long labor contract that effectively ended his freedom. Two other blacks caught stealing sheep received a "fair trial" and thirty-nine lashes. Given the real conditions in Tappahannock, when the bureau characterized white attitudes toward black education as "rueful acquiescence" it barely hit the mark.[18]

Stephens not only failed to apprise the bureau accurately of conditions in Tappahannock, but his classroom success also never translated into eased social tensions or financial stability for the school. In February 1868, the Virginia assistant superintendent of education for the Freedmen's Bureau informed Stephens that the government had cut back its support and that he would have to rely on private contributors. "I shall be obliged to leave you henceforth to their tender mercies," R. M. Manly advised him. The bureau nevertheless continued its funding, and when federal money fell short Manly provided Stephens with money from private sources at the bureau's disposal. Other schools in Essex County also suffered and either closed or operated only intermittently as money came available. When Stephens found bureau coffers empty, he operated the school "at my own expense."[19]

By the summer of 1868 Stephens admitted that his effort to educate the former slaves had provoked determined white opposition. In July the school building's owners evicted him. Then he ran afoul of Wentworth, the Freedmen's Bureau agent. Maintaining that the bureau had paid for and owned the school's benches, Wentworth gave them to another black teacher, Richmond Robinson. Robinson, who had arrived in Tappahannock in January, competed for the same students, community support, and bureau money. The resulting clash nearly convinced Stephens to give up his efforts and return home. "My own straightened circumstances have at times almost overwhelmed me," he informed Manly.[20]

Stephens detailed the deteriorating conditions to Manly and insisted that local blacks had pleaded with him to remain. He then requested additional bureau funds to reestablish his school. But Wentworth, who distrusted Stephens, processed all bureau documents in his jurisdiction, sabotaged Stephens's official forms, making him appear negligent or indifferent to bureau regulations. Manly accepted Stephens's explanations of Wentworth's behavior and, along with the Pennsylvania Commission, continued to support him. He was puzzled, though, if not deeply disturbed, by the confusing claims and reports coming out of Tappahannock. From month to month the number of schools reporting to the bureau changed, and Manly never could determine whether Stephens and Robinson, who used the same building, operated different schools or merely different classes, with Stephens serving as principal.[21]

In December 1869 an exasperated R. M. Manly confessed that the bureau would like to support a school in Tappahannock if he could determine how many schools existed there and who taught in them. "I should be glad to extend the trifle of aid which the Bureau can give to some reliable good school in Tappahannock," he wrote to Stephens. "But such is the conflict of testimony at present that I find it is impossible to determine anything." The sour relations between Stephens and Robinson, Wentworth's subterfuge, and the arrival of two more teachers at Tappahannock, proved confounding. Kate Elliot, a black from Fortress Monroe, had been at Tappahannock since December 1868 and had received no pay. Robinson lectured Manly for his "remiss" in providing support for Elliot: "Shame, Shame, Shame," he cried. But Manly labored under the mistaken notion that Elliot worked for Stephens and that he should provide her wages.[22]

When Stephens's wife, Susan, suddenly appeared in April 1869, the school situation in Tappahannock moved beyond comprehension. Stephens then stunned Manly with the announcement that he had stopped teaching altogether and that his wife had taken over his duties. She began receiving funds from the Pennsylvania Commission and the bureau, despite threats that it would curtail its subsidies.[23] In the fall, Stephens won election as Tappahannock's sheriff and received an appointment as postmaster. His nemesis, Richmond Robinson, flooded Manly's office with complaints about Stephens and his wife, attempting to corral all the bureau's financial support. With his school in jeopardy, Stephens resigned his newly won positions and pledged to Manly that he would "devote more fully my time and services to the cause of education." The "improvement of my race, at this juncture, is far more important than political preferment."[24]

Stephens and Robinson continued to battle for bureau patronage, each accusing the other of fraud and malfeasance. Robinson could not tolerate Stephens's political aspirations and the assumption of teaching duties by his wife. Stephens, in turn, denounced Robinson as "ignorant and vicious" and a person who stood "in the way of true progress and reconstruction." Manly temporarily halted payments to Robinson and threatened to cut him off entirely. Whatever Stephens's culpability, Robinson caused Manly the most concern. He suddenly revoked the bureau's support and informed Robinson that he would consider securing him a teaching position elsewhere, but only *"if you will have nothing to do with whiskey."* Before the end of December, Robinson vanished from Tappahannock.[25]

Congress's refusal to fully recharter the Freedmen's Bureau—already weakened by federal cutbacks—in 1869 amounted to a death warrant for the Tilghman School and other bureau-sponsored schools throughout the South. Beginning in May, many closed their doors so that teachers could take advantage of the bureau's policy of reimbursing travel costs and return home. The bureau laid off staff, and the Education Department closed entirely in August 1870, although some funds remained available until 1872 for school construction. The Pennsylvania Commission severely diminished its support and in 1870 assisted only seven schools in all of Virginia. "God help the Freedmen in their rights," one dejected bureau agent wrote.[26]

As bureau support receded and Northern philanthropies abandoned the South, Southern blacks seized control of their own education. Much to Manly's amazement, the more the bureau retrenched the more black schools appeared. By July 1869, black-managed schools had reached a record number of pupils. In Tappahannock, blacks established at least three day schools and four sabbath schools, with African-American teachers instructing 116 students. As Stephens, the bureau, and Northern philanthropists discovered, Southern blacks not only desired education but also wanted to control it. Although grateful for the efforts by others, the former slaves knew what served their interests better than Northerners—black or white—and wanted to "mark out on the map of life with their own hands."[27]

Southern blacks welcomed Northern assistance but rejected Yankee culture and arrogance. Tappahannock blacks refused to support temperance societies, which the bureau sponsored in the area despite the complete lack of evidence of alcohol-related problems. As bureau agents learned, blacks would attend political rallies every night of the week, but they wanted no part of a temperance gathering. They assembled, more often than not, in taverns, which served as convenient meeting places and centers of power.[28] Blacks in Tappahannock, as throughout the South, proved energetic and adept organizers. Despite white oppression and limited resources, they organized a "Beneficent Society," formed their own board of education, erected a new school building, and maintained a flourishing church that sponsored services three times a week. In 1868, they established a Union League and also Union Republican Clubs, which gave local whites apoplexy.[29]

Stephens, a staunch temperance advocate, clashed with the cultural patterns he found among Southern blacks. Although he had viewed them as brothers in chains, he never overcame his belief that slaves were "uncivilized" and "unchristian." As a rule, Northern blacks believed that the "most formidable obstacle to the education of these people" was "their spurious religion." With confidence, Stephens repudiated Southern black religion as "grotesque." Southern black culture alienated him, and his letters to the bureau revealed impatience and intolerance. Although he found the younger children amenable, their parents struck him as dull and stupid. However much he identified with Southern blacks, Stephens could not suppress his conviction that "the bulk of the slaves . . . are infidels."[30]

Black leaders who went South proudly carried their cultural presumptions in their carpet bags. They came as saviors and missionaries who thought they knew best what Southern blacks required. "What they need to learn is the practical principals of domestic economy, the saving of time and money, the laws of health, and the training of children," the *Anglo-African* explained. Northern blacks such as Stephens, the paper advised, should bring the former slaves "the plain but full standard of Christian civilization," which "must be set before their minds, and every effort made to inspire them up to it." They saw Southern blacks as childlike, impressionable, and ready to be molded by proper leadership. Stephens and fellow black teachers hoped to instill Southern blacks with Northern bourgeois sexual and social codes, remaking the former slaves into their own image. It should come as no surprise, then, that Southern blacks resisted the "help" from Northerners almost as much as they fought white domination.[31]

By 1870, the Southern white reaction to the bureau's activities and Reconstruction in general had been set. Torching school buildings, lynchings, and political assassinations became commonplace, especially when blacks assumed more control over local schools and government. "Masked marauders" of the Klan terrorized teachers and black leaders, killing those they could not convince to leave. Northern philanthropies, with the exception of the Peabody and Slater Funds, that underwrote white and black educational efforts, disappeared.[32] In Virginia, blacks had already achieved their greatest political gains, and their political fortunes declined precipitously as white Conservatives drove Republicans and blacks from office. The state's Radical Republicans, black and white, had failed to gain the support of Northern Republican leaders. Even Gov. John A. Andrew preferred white rule and economic development to black suffrage and black political power. Before his death in 1866, Andrew disillusioned many hopeful African Americans when he refused to support black suffrage and declared that "the rebel vote is better than a loyal one, if on the right side."[33]

Alienated from those he came to help, abandoned by liberal reformers, cut off from his sources of financial support, and in debt, Stephens faced a bleak future in Virginia. Although official records say nothing about his financial obligations, quite likely Stephens owed rent for his school building. After pouring out his heart and savings in what he had called "thankless" work, he gave up. One week before Congress readmitted Virginia into the Union and withdrew the remaining federal troops, Stephens left Virginia and his debts behind.[34]

Stephens returned to Philadelphia but remained there for less than three years. Although no details survive, he probably experienced considerable difficulty finding employment. At a time of dramatically increasing racial tensions and declining economic fortunes for Philadelphia blacks, Stephens could not return to cabinetmaking and found other trades closed to blacks. Perhaps worst of all, Manly cut off Stephens from his patrons by advising former members of the Pennsylvania Commission that he had fled Virginia as a "defaulter." Sometime in 1873, Stephens left Philadelphia for a new start in Brooklyn, New York. His wife had died after their return to Philadelphia, and if her children survived, they probably went to live with relatives in York.[35]

Stephens established an upholstery business in a basement on Brooklyn's Hicks Street and in the spring of 1875 married Catherine Tracy, an illiterate Irish laundress whom he met in his shop. On 28 May 1876, the thirteenth anniversary of the Fifty-fourth's departure for South Carolina, George E. Stephens, Jr., was born and on 9 June baptized in Brooklyn's Assumption Catholic Church. The Stephens family lived a marginal existence, moving repeatedly and never accumulating any property.[36]

Stephens remained politically active and as the years passed became increasingly involved with veterans' organizations. In 1867, he had helped organize Philadelphia's National Convention of Colored Soldiers and Sailors and served with William Still, Alfred M. Green, and his minister James Underdue on its business committee. The convention drew black veterans from across the country to promote black rights and advance the "claims of the men who fought for their country." The soldiers believed that their military service had earned them full citizenship. As one former sergeant proclaimed, he considered himself "fully competent to vote a traitor down as to shoot him down."[37]

During the 1880s, when lynchings plagued the South and racial discrimination continued unabated in the North, Stephens sought to preserve the memory of black service during the Civil War. On the twentieth anniversary of the Fifty-fourth's attack on Battery Wagner, veterans of Massachusetts's black regiments paraded down New York City's Fifth Avenue. Stephens, who headed the William Lloyd Garrison Post of the Grand Army of the Republic, marched with Boston's Robert Gould Shaw Veterans Association. Four years later he served on the executive committee of the Grand Reunion of Colored Veterans, which met in Boston on 1–2 August 1887.[38]

With his health declining, Stephens probably did not attend the Grand Reunion. In 1881, he had filed for a disability payment from the federal government. The injury he had sustained at Battery Wagner resurfaced, leaving his arms atrophied and "almost powerless." He applied for his commission as a first lieutenant in 1885, hoping to guarantee his wife and child a larger pension after his death. But the adjutant general's office turned down Stephens's request, despite

1884 congressional legislation awarding Civil War commissions denied on the basis of race. Through persistence and the help of a Washington, D.C., law firm, Catherine Stephens convinced the government in 1891 to reverse its decision and grant the commission. As a final indignity, when the government awarded Stephens her rightful pension it deducted $6—the cost of the rifle her husband had lost at Wagner. Even this victory came too late; after a prolonged illness Stephens died of hepatitis on 24 April 1888.[39]

* ★ *

For modern readers, discovering Stephens's letters can never come "too late." His arduous and sometimes anguished life remains a heroic story, and his writings chart the black struggle for freedom and equality during the era of the Civil War. Through him, we can recapture the aspirations of black soldiers who fought for the Union and against slavery and racial oppression. In 1890, a Boston paper reminded the country that the "inalienable rights" of the Declaration of Independence that God gave to all Americans had been secured in the Civil War by "the blood of black soldiers."[40] It is that message that still thunders from the voice of George E. Stephens.

Notes

1. *Public Ledger*, 5 July 1901; GES to Orlando Brown, 24 October 1867, Unregistered Letters, Records of the Superintendent of Education, Virginia, BRFAL, RG 105, National Archives.

2. GES to Orlando Brown, 24 October 1867; "Reports on Schools, Teachers, & Buildings," 18 July 1866, Records of the Superintendent of Education, Virginia, BRFAL, RG 105, National Archives.

3. "Banneker" to Thomas Hamilton, 23 November 1859, *WAA*, 3 December 1859; GES to Thomas Hamilton, 14 November 1859; *WAA*, 24 June, 3 September 1865; Hamilton is quoted in *WAA*, 17 January 1863; *National Anti-Slavery Standard*, 10 June 1865.

4. Eric Foner, *Reconstruction: America's Unfinished Revolution, 1863–1877* (New York: Harper and Row, 1988), 9–10, 286–91; black teacher's quotation from Joe M. Richardson, *Christian Reconstruction: The American Missionary Association and Southern Blacks, 1861–1890* (Athens: University of Georgia Press, 1986), 192.

5. GES to R. M. Manly, 9 December 1868, Unregistered Letters Received, Records of the Superintendent of Education for the State of Virginia, R. M. Manly to Orlando Brown, 20 February 1868, Monthly Reports of Assistant Sub-Assistant Commissioner and Agents, January 1868, BRFAL, RG 105, National Archives.

6. Watson R. Wentworth to James Johnson, 12 February 1868, Register of Letters Received, Assistant Commissioner for Education for the State of Virginia, GES to R. M. Manly, 9 December 1868, Unregistered Letters Received, Records of the Superintendent of Education for the State of Virginia, BRFAL, RG 105, National Archives.

7. GES to R. M. Manly, 9 December 1868, GES to R. M. Manly, 1 April 1869, Unregistered Letters Received, Records of the Superintendent of Education for the State of Virginia, BRFAL, RG 105, National Archives.

8. James D. Anderson, *The Education of Blacks in the South, 1860–1935* (Chapel Hill: University of North Carolina Press, 1988), 16–18, slave's quotation on 5; Foner, *Reconstruction*, 97–98; R. M. Manly to Orlando Brown, 10 July 1869, Records of the Commissioner of Education, BRFAL, RG 105, National Archives.

9. R. M. Manly to Orlando Brown, [?] March 1868, Records of the Commissioner of Education, BRFAL, RG 105, National Archives.

10. Robert R. Corson to J. W. Alvord, 24 February 1868, Robert R. Corson, "List of Teachers in the Field in December 1868," Miscellaneous Unregistered Letters Received, Education Division, BRFAL, RG 105, National Archives; *Pennsylvania Freedmen's Bulletin*, February, July 1865.

11. Robert C. Winthrop, *Addresses and Speeches*, 4 vols. (Boston: Little, Brown, 1852–86), 4:163–64; William Preston Vaughn, *Schools for All: The Blacks and Public Education in the South, 1865–1877* (Lexington: University Press of Kentucky, 1974), 141–59; Franklin Parker, *George Peabody: A Biography* (Nashville: Vanderbilt University Press, 1971), 160–67; Betty Mansfield, "That Fateful Class: Black Teachers of Virginia's Freedmen, 1861–1882," Ph.D. diss., Catholic University of America, 1980, 215–21.

12. GES to R. M. Manly, 5 February 1869, Unregistered Letters Received, Records of the Superintendent of Education for the State of Virginia, BRFAL, RG 105, National Archives.

13. GES to R. M. Manly, 9 December 1868, Unregistered Letters Received, "Teacher's Monthly School Report," November 1868, Records of the Superintendent of Education for the State of Virginia, BRFAL, RG 105, National Archives.

14. Mansfield, "That Fateful Class," 180–83; Allan Johnston, "Surviving Freedom: The Black Community of Washington, D.C., 1860–1880," Ph.D. diss., Duke University, 1980, 289.

15. C. G. McClelland to Orlando Brown, 31 March 1868, Reports of Operations and Conditions in Virginia, C. G. McClelland to James Johnson, 8 June 1868, Letters Received, Records of Assistant Commissioner of Education for the State of Virginia, BRFAL, RG 105, National Archives; William A. Blair, "Justice versus Law and Order: The Battles over the Reconstruction of Virginia's Minor Judiciary, 1865–1870," *Virginia Magazine of History and Biography* 103 (April 1995): 157–80.

16. "Oath," 20 January 1868, Records of the Assistant Commissioner of Education for the State of Virginia, Watson R. Wentworth to Orlando Brown,

29 September 1866, 1 November 1867, Records Relating to Murders and Outrages, Records of the Assistant Commissioner of Education for the State of Virginia, James Johnson to Orlando Brown, 31 March 1868, W. A. Coulter to Watson R. Wentworth, 5 September 1868, Letters Received, Records of the Assistant Commissioner of Education for the State of Virginia, BRFAL, RG 105, National Archives. Many bureau agents misrepresented the level of racial conflict in their districts to retain their jobs or bureau funding; see William F. Mugleston, ed., "The Freedmen's Bureau and Reconstruction in Virginia: The Diary of Marcus Sterling Hopkins, a Union Officer," *Virginia Magazine of History and Biography* 86 (January 1978): 48–49.

17. Watson R. Wentworth to Orlando Brown, 31 July, 31 October 1868, Reports of Operations and Conditions in Virginia, Watson R. Wentworth to Maj. Gen. Alfred H. Terry, 25 July 1866, Records Relating to Murders and Outrages, Records of the Assistant Commissioner of Education for the State of Virginia, BRFAL, RG 105, National Archives.

18. Mansfield, "That Fateful Class," 222–23; Watson R. Wentworth to Orlando Brown, 1 February, 31 August, 30 November 1868, Reports of Operations and Conditions in Virginia, Records of the Assistant Commissioner of Education for the State of Virginia, Watson R. Wentworth to Orlando Brown, 29 August 1866, Records Relating to Murders and Outrages, Records of the Assistant Commissioner of Education for the State of Virginia, "State Superintendent's Monthly School Report," Records of the Superintendent of Education of the State of Virginia, BRFAL, RG 105, National Archives.

19. R. M. Manly to GES, 6 February 1868, Letters Sent, GES quotation from "Teacher's Monthly School Report," October 1868, Records of the Superintendent of Education for the State of Virginia, Watson R. Wentworth to Orlando Brown, 30 April 1868, Reports of Operations and Conditions in Virginia, Records of the Assistant Commissioner of Education for the State of Virginia, BRFAL, RG 105, National Archives.

20. GES to R. M. Manly, December 1868, Unregistered Letters Received, Records of the Superintendent of Education for the State of Virginia, R. M. Manly to GES, 7 December 1868, Letters Sent, Records of the Superintendent of Education for the State of Virginia, BRFAL, RG 105, National Archives.

21. Ibid.; "Monthly Reports of Schools, Teachers, Societies, Pupils, and Buildings," January–August 1869, Records of the Assistant Commissioner of Education for the State of Virginia, BRFAL, RG 105, National Archives.

22. R. M. Manly to GES, 17 December 1869, R. M. Manly to Kate Elliot, 3 January 1870, Letters Sent, Richmond Robinson to R. M. Manly, 26 April 1869, Unregistered Letters Received, Records of the Superintendent of Education for the State of Virginia, BRFAL, RG 105, National Archives.

23. Susan Stephens's absence from the Philadelphia city directories for this period confirms her move to Virginia. *American Freedman*, April 1869, 16; "Teacher's Monthly School Report," April–November 1869, R. M. Manly to Robert R. Corson, 20 July 1869, Letters Sent, Records of the Commissioner of Education for the State of Virginia, BRFAL, RG 105, National Archives.

24. GES's tenure proved so brief that he never turned up in the federal "blue books" (*Official Register of the United States*) or in other federal lists of state office-holders. GES is quoted in Mansfield, "That Fateful Class," 365.

25. Mansfield, "That Fateful Class," 365; R. M. Manly to GES, 17, 23 December 1869, R. M. Manly to Kate Elliot, 9 December 1869, quotation from R. M. Manly to Richmond Robinson, 9 December, emphasis in the original, 14 December 1869, Letters Sent, "Monthly School Reports," December 1869–February 1870, Records of the Superintendent of Education for the State of Virginia, BRFAL, RG 105, National Archives.

26. Mansfield, "That Fateful Class," 232–35; James Johnson to Orlando Brown, 31 December 1868, Letters Received, Records of the Assistant Commissioner of Education for the State of Virginia, R. M. Manly to Oliver O. Howard, 10 July 1869, Records of the Assistant Commissioner of Education for the State of Virginia, M. E. Sherman to J. W. Alvord, 24 August 1870, Letters Received, Education Division, BRFAL, RG 105, National Archives.

27. R. M. Manly to Oliver O. Howard, 10 July 1869, Records of the Assistant Commissioner of Education for the State of Virginia, "State Superintendent's Monthly School Reports, September 1869–March 1870," Office of the Commissioner of Education for the State of Virginia, BRFAL, RG 105, National Archives; quotation from Anderson, *Education of Blacks in the South,* 9–12.

28. James Johnson to Orlando Brown, 31 December 1867, Letters Received, Watson R. Wentworth to Orlando Brown, 1 October 1867, 3 March 1868, Reports of Operations and Conditions, Records of the Assistant Commissioner of Education for the State of Virginia, BRFAL, RG 105, National Archives; Harold Forsythe, "But My Friends Are Poor: Ross Hamilton and Freedpeople's Politics in Mecklenburg County, Virginia, 1869–1892," paper delivered at the annual meeting of the Organization of American Historians, Atlanta, 1994.

29. GES to R. M. Manly, 9 December 1868, Unregistered Letters Received, Records of the Superintendent of Education for the State of Virginia, Watson R. Wentworth to Orlando Brown, 2 December 1867, 3 March 1868, Reports of Operations and Conditions in Virginia, Records of the Assistant Commissioner of Education for the State of Virginia, BRFAL, RG 105, National Archives.

30. GES to R. M. Manly, 9 December 1868, Unregistered Letters Received, Records of the Superintendent of Education for the State of Virginia, BRFAL, RG 105, National Archives; GES to Robert Hamilton, 13 February 1862; Mansfield, "That Fateful Class," 250–52.

31. *WAA,* 23 December 1865; Richardson, *Christian Reconstruction,* 199, 240–42; Robert C. Morris, *Reading, 'Riting, and Reconstruction: The Education of Freedmen in the South, 1861–1870* (Chicago: University of Chicago Press, 1976), 110–14; Jacqueline Jones, *Soldiers of Light and Love: Northern Teachers and Georgia Blacks, 1865–1873* (Chapel Hill: University of North Carolina Press, 1980), 65–70, 196.

32. Vaughan, *Schools for All*, 16–17, 35–38, 47–49; John W. Alvord, *Letters from the South, Relating to the Freedman, Addressed to Major General O. O. Howard* (Washington: n.p., 1870), 30–41.

33. Jack P. Maddex, Jr., *The Virginia Conservatives, 1867–1879: A Study in Reconstruction Politics* (Chapel Hill: University of North Carolina Press, 1970), 47–54, 198–99; Richard Abbott, *The Republican Party and the South, 1855–1877* (Chapel Hill: University of North Carolina Press, 1986), 117, 123–45, 155–57; Richard Lowe, *Republicans and Reconstruction in Virginia, 1856–1870* (Charlottesville: University Press of Virginia, 1991), passim; Andrew quoted in Dale Baum, *The Civil War Party System: The Case of Massachusetts, 1848–1876* (Chapel Hill: University of North Carolina Press, 1984), 104–6.

34. Richmond Robinson to R. M. Manly, 28 January 1870, Kate Elliot to R. M. Manly, 2 February 1870, Robert R. Corson to R. M. Manly, 4 January 1870, Unregistered Letters Received, Records of the Superintendent of Education for the State of Virginia, BRFAL, RG 105, National Archives; Maddex, Jr., *Virginia Conservatives*, 86–88; Mansfield, "That Fateful Class," 235.

35. Harry C. Silcox, "The Black 'Better Class' Political Dilemma: Philadelphia Prototype Isaiah C. Wears," *Pennsylvania Magazine of History and Biography* 113 (January 1989): 45–66; Mansfield, "That Fateful Class," 366; Death Register, 1873, 1:8, Philadelphia City Archives.

36. The details concerning GES and Catherine Tracy Stephens are contained in GES's pension file, RG 15, National Archives. The file's documents give a variety of dates for Catherine Tracy Stephens's birth but list her death date as 3 March 1921.

37. "National Convention of Colored Soldiers and Sailors," in *Proceedings of the Black National and State Conventions, 1865–1900*, ed. Philip S. Foner and George E. Walker (Philadelphia: Temple University Press, 1986), 1:289–95.

38. New York *Times*, 19 July 1883; New York *Age*, 28 April 1888; New York *Tribune*, 26 April 1888; [Donald Yacovone], *We Fight for Freedom: Massachusetts, African Americans, and the Civil War* (Boston: Massachusetts Historical Society, 1993), 30.

39. Information on GES's marriage, quest for his commission, and death are in his Compiled Service Record, RG 94, and his Pension File, RG 15, National Archives.

40. Boston *Traveler*, 1 April 1890.

Home of William and Mary Stephens, Philadelphia.

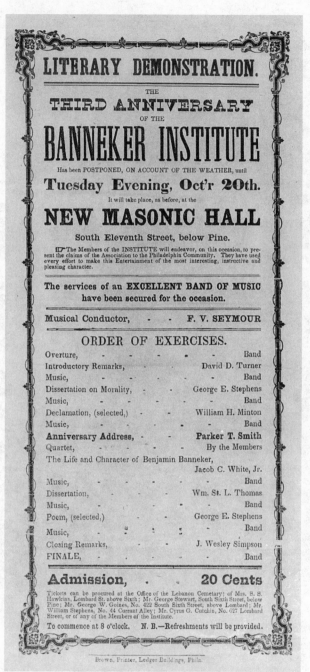

LITERARY DEMONSTRATION.

THE

THIRD ANNIVERSARY

OF THE

BANNEKER INSTITUTE

Has been POSTPONED, ON ACCOUNT OF THE WEATHER, until

Tuesday Evening, Oct'r 20th.

It will take place, as before, at the

NEW MASONIC HALL

South Eleventh Street, below Pine.

☞ The Members of the INSTITUTE will endeavor, on this occasion, to present the claims of the Association to the Philadelphia Community. They have used every effort to make this Entertainment of the most interesting, instructive and pleasing character.

The services of an EXCELLENT BAND OF MUSIC have been secured for the occasion.

| Musical Conductor, | - | - | F. V. SEYMOUR |

ORDER OF EXERCISES.

Overture,	-	-	-	-	-	Band
Introductory Remarks,					David D. Turner
Music,	-		-		-	Band
Dissertation on Morality,		-	-		George E. Stephens
Music,	-		-		-	Band
Declamation, (selected,)	-		-		William H. Minton
Music,	-		-		-	Band
Anniversary Address,	-		-		**Parker T. Smith**
Quartet,	-	-	-	-	-	By the Members
The Life and Character of Benjamin Banneker,					
					Jacob C. White, Jr.
Music,	-		-		-	Band
Dissertation,		-		-		Wm. St. L. Thomas
Music,	-		-		-	Band
Poem, (selected,)			-		George E. Stephens
Music,					-	Band
Closing Remarks,			-		J. Wesley Simpson
FINALE,	-		-		-	Band

Admission, . . 20 Cents

Tickets can be procured at the Office of the Lebanon Cemetary: of Mrs. S. S. Hawkins, Lombard St. above Sixth; Mr. George Stewart, South Sixth Street, below Pine; Mr. George W. Goines, No. 422 South Sixth Street, above Lombard; Mr. William Stephens, No. 44 Currant Alley; Mr. Cyrus G. Cutchin, No. 627 Lombard Street, or of any of the Members of the Institute.

To commence at 8 o'clock. N. B.—Refreshments will be provided.

Brown, Printer, Ledger Buildings, Phila.

Broadside, Banneker Institute. (Banneker Institute Papers, Leon Gardiner Collection, Historical Society of Pennsylvania)

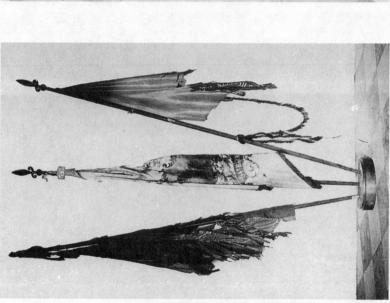

Recruitment Poster, 1863. (Courtesy of the Massachusetts Historical Society)

Regimental Colors of the Fifty-fourth Massachusetts Regiment. (Courtesy of the Massachusetts Historical Society)

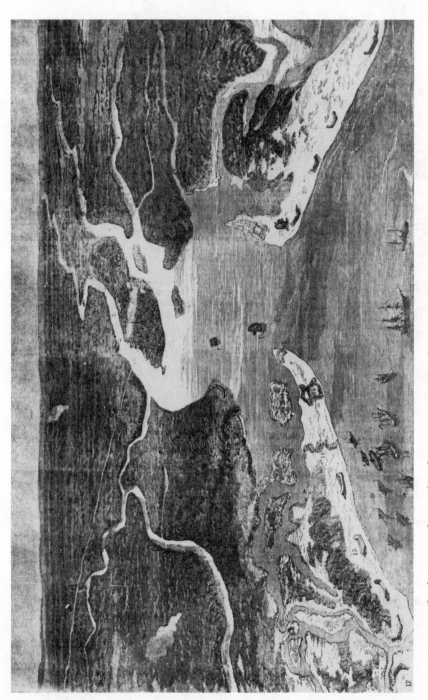

Charleston Harbor and Defenses. Morris Island is on the left; number 13 is Battery Wagner. From *Harper's Weekly*, 15 August 1863. (Courtesy of the Massachusetts Historical Society)

The Approach to Battery Wagner. (Courtesy of the Massachusetts Historical Society)

"Attack on Wagner" by Thomas Nast, 1867. (Courtesy of the Massachusetts Historical Society)

"Bombproof—Battery Wagner" by Haas and Peale. Inside Battery Wagner shortly after the capture. Massachusetts Fifty-fourth soldiers stand at the lower left. (Courtesy of the Massachusetts Historical Society)

"Dress Parade." Unidentified Union troops inside Battery Wagner. (Courtesy of the Massachusetts Historical Society)

Battle of Olustee, Florida, 20 February 1864. From *Harper's New Monthly Magazine*, November 1866. (Courtesy of the Massachusetts Historical Society)

Union Camp near Jacksonville, Florida. (Courtesy of the Massachusetts Historical Society)

GRAND
REUNION OF COLORED VETERANS,

—UNDER THE AUSPICES OF THE—

54th and 55th Infantry, and 5th Cavalry Regiments, and Sailors,

MASSACHUSETTS VOLUNTEERS,

In Boston, August 1st and 2nd, 1887.

* * * " You will never part with that FLAG so long as a splinter of the staff or a thread of the web remains within your grasp." * * * GOV. JOHN A. ANDREW, *on presentation of flag at Readville, Mass., May 18, 1863.*

" The old FLAG never touched the ground, boys ! "—SERGT. WILLIAM H. CARNEY (*severely wounded*), *on the parapet of Fort Wagner, S. C., July 18, 1863.*

BOSTON, Mass., June 1, 1887.

Comrade,—

DEAR SIR, — There will be a reunion of the surviving Veterans of the 54th and 55th Mass. Vol. Infantry Regiments, the 5th Mass. Vol. Cavalry, and Massachusetts Sailors, in Tremont Temple, Boston, August 1st and 2nd, 1887.

The Executive Committee extend a hearty invitation to the reunion to all colored Soldiers and Sailors of Massachusetts and the United States, and sincerely desire to make the occasion a most enjoyable and successful one : renewing old acquaintance, and reviving fraternal feeling among all the old comrades of the country.

You are, therefore, earnestly requested to join with us, and to do all in your power to create an interest among comrades, and also to make every effort for a grand and memorable reunion.

The Committee of Arrangements respectfully and earnestly request that all commissioned officers appear in uniform (coat and hat or cap); non-commissioned officers, (coat or blouse, and hat or cap); privates, (blouse and cap or hat, or G. A. R. uniform.)

All comrades are requested to send their names and addresses at once to Lieut. WILLIAM H. DUPREE, *Chairman of Executive Committee, Station A, P. O. Boston, Mass.,* in order that they may receive a circular-programme, later on, containing full information.

Various Sub-Committees will be appointed as soon as a sufficient number of names, from the different localities, are received.

The Executive Committee would further suggest for the Convention a programme as follows : —

Handbill for the Grand Reunion of Colored Veterans, 1–2 August 1887. Stephens's name is misspelled on the Executive Committee list. (Courtesy of the Massachusetts Historical Society)

Aug. 1.—First Session.—Tremont Temple, at 10 A. M.

1.—MUSIC, BOSTON BRASS BAND, ALSO FIFE AND DRUM CORPS.
2.—CALLING THE CONVENTION TO ORDER BY THE CHAIRMAN OF THE EXECUTIVE COMMITTEE.
3.—PRAYER.
4.—MUSIC.
5.—ADDRESS OF WELCOME BY THE PRESIDENT.
6.—MUSIC.
7.—ADJOURNMENT AND COLLATION.

At 2 p.m., formation on the Common for a parade through the principal streets, which will probably be reviewed by the Mayor of Boston, and the Governor of the Commonwealth. The route will be published in the newspapers and printed on the programmes, which will be distributed in the Temple.

Aug. 1.—Second Session.—Tremont Temple, at 4 P. M.

Addresses to be delivered by commissioned officers and others of the different regimental organizations, also remarks will be made by other invited guests.

Aug. 2.—Third Session.—Tremont Temple, at 10 A. M.

Addresses by commissioned officers and non-commissioned officers of the several regiments, also representatives of the sailors.

A business meeting will be held at Tremont Temple before adjournment, to effect a permanent organization of all colored veterans in the United States.

Company L., 6th Regiment, Mass. Vol. Militia, will be invited to do escort duty for the parade.

The Executive Committee has under consideration an excursion to "Camp Readville," and a sail down Boston Harbor, *visiting and decorating with flowers the grave of Massachusetts' Great War Governor,* JOHN A. ANDREW, at Hingham.

" I will never give up the rights of these men while I live, whether in this world or the next."—*Gov. Andrew's appeal to Government for equal pay.*

" I know not what record of sin may await me in another world; but this I know :— I was never mean enough to despise any man because he was ignorant, nor because he was poor, nor because he was black."—*Gov. Andrew.*

Let the comrades of nearly twenty-five years ago respond to the call of the *Executive Committee,* and meet once more in one grand camp-fire, and revive the memories of our old campaigns

EXECUTIVE COMMITTEE.

Lieut. WM. H. DUPREE, 55th, Chairman, Boston, Mass.
Sergt. BURRILL SMITH, 54th, Secretary, Boston, Mass.
ISAAC S. MULLEN, U. S. Navy, Corresponding Secretary, Boston, Mass.
Lieut. CHARLES L. MITCHELL, 55th, Treasurer, Boston, Mass.

Lieut. JAMES M. TROTTER, 55th, Washington, D. C.
Sergt. WM. H. CARNEY, 54th, New Bedford, Mass.
Sergt. AMOS WEBBER, 5th Cavalry, Worcester, Mass.
Sergt. GUSTAVUS BOOTH, 5th Cavalry, Hartford, Conn.
Chaplain SAMUEL HARRISON, 54th, Pittsfield, Mass.
Sergt. CHARLES W. LENOX, 54th, Watertown, Mass.
Sergt. GEORGE T. FISHER, 5th Cavalry, New Bedford, Mass.
Sergt. WESLEY J. FURLONG, 54th, Boston, Mass.
Lieut. STEPHEN A. SWAILS, 54th, South Carolina.
JAMES H. WOLFF, U. S. Navy, Boston, Mass.
Lieut. FRANK M. WELCH, 54th, Bridgeport, Conn.
Sergt. J. H. BATES, 5th Cavalry, Wilkes Barre, Pa.
WM. HAZARD, 54th (of John A. Andrew Post, G. A. R.), New York City.
WM. B. DERRICK, U. S. Navy, New York City.
Sergt. JOHN DAVIS, 5th Cavalry, Carlisle, Pa.
Sergt. ROBERT M. DORSEY, 55th, Washington, D. C.
Sergt. SAMUEL J. PATTERSON, 5th Cavalry, Wilkes Barre, Pa.
Sergt. E. GEORGE BIDDLE, 54th, Worcester, Mass.
GEO. E. HICKS, U. S. Navy, Boston, Mass.
Sergt. BENJ. W. PHENIX, 5th Cavalry, Boston, Mass.
Sergt. GEORGE E. LEE, 54th, Wellesley, Mass.
JOHN LITTLE, 55th (of Wm. Lloyd Garrison Post, G. A. R.), Brooklyn, N. Y.
Lieut. GEO. E. STEVENSON, 54th (of Wm. Lloyd Garrison Post, G.A.R.), Brooklyn, N. Y.
WM. H. JARVIS, U. S. Navy, Lynn, Mass.

Comrades in organizations of 25 to 500, and over, can get discount from regular rates of 10 to 50 per cent. by applying to " General Passenger Agents " in their localities.

" BOSTON ADVOCATE " Job Print (Grandison & Powell), 65 Hanover Street.

The Citadel's parade ground, where the Fifty-fourth drilled during the occupation of Charleston. (Courtesy of the Massachusetts Historical Society)

Part 2

The Letters of
George E. Stephens

Chapter 5

"We Will See the Anglo-African a Power in This Country"

14 November 1859–15 January 1861

"Speak out in *thunder tones*," advised one early African-American newspaper.[1] The New York *Weekly Anglo-African* heeded that call and led the attack on slavery and racism during the Civil War. Thomas and Robert Hamilton, who published and edited the *Anglo-African* from 1859 to 1865, made it the paper of record for African Americans in the North. It became a crucial forum for debate and sharply analyzed the issues that mattered most to mid-nineteenth-century blacks: colonization and emigration, racism and slavery, and the meaning of the Civil War.

Few issues received more critical scrutiny among blacks than emigration and colonization; no organization drew more rage or organized resistance than the white-led American Colonization Society (ACS). Founded in 1816, the ACS insisted that blacks and whites could never coexist in freedom. Its efforts to resettle free blacks in Liberia on the West African Coast, exponents argued, would remove an unwanted element from American society, uplift blacks, and bring "civilization" and Christianity to Africa. Stephens and most Northern blacks spurned the ACS as a monstrous fraud that perpetuated ideas of racial inferiority and subverted their claims to American citizenship.[2]

During the late 1850s, however, a small but growing number of blacks doubted that they would ever gain equality in this country until they proved themselves in their own. The African Civilization Society (AfCS), founded in 1858 and dedicated to the "civilization and evangelization" of Africa, gained black support through its pledge to end slavery by bringing Christianity and free labor principles to Africa. Led by Henry Highland Garnet, the eloquent black abolitionist and anticolonizationist, the AfCS appeared to offer blacks their best chance to establish a black nationality. To most, Garnet's efforts only replicated the ACS's long-hated attempts to deport them to Liberia. During the Civil War, the AfCS admitted that its association with colonization had inspired widespread distrust and abandoned emigration to help educate the former slaves.[3]

To Stephens, any return to Africa represented a defeat, an admission that blacks could never achieve equality in the United States. He briefly supported Haitian emigration or resettlement elsewhere in the Western Hemisphere as legitimate alternatives for blacks seeking a refuge from crushing American racism. Haiti drew Stephens's attention because it offered the hope of freedom and was, in Frederick Douglass's words, "still within hearing distance of the wails of our brothers and sisters in bonds."[4] Nevertheless, Stephens remained ambivalent over the idea of emigration. He wished to fight slavery and racial prejudice but increasingly found the likelihood of success remote. The Civil War ended his uncertainty and brought Stephens new hope.

1. *Colored American*, 4 March 1837.
2. P. J. Staudenraus, *The African Colonization Movement, 1816–1865* (New York: Columbia University Press, 1961); *BAP*, 3:5–9.
3. *BAP*, 5:3–11; Floyd J. Miller, *The Search for a Black Nationality: Black Emigration and Colonization, 1787–1863* (Urbana: University of Illinois Press, 1975), 170–263; *WAA*, 3 September 1864.
4. David W. Blight, *Frederick Douglass' Civil War: Keeping Faith in Jubilee* (Baton Rouge: Louisiana State University Press, 1989), quotation on 132.

*   *   *

Philadelphia,
Nov. 14, 1859.

Mr. Editor:[1] The great interest I take in all questions pertaining to either the rights, prospects, or condition of our people, urges me, in view of the general attention directed to the recent so-called "African civilization movement," to present these few remarks for insertion in your widely circulated journal.

Every colored man should carefully consider every enterprise the object of which is the mental or moral amelioration of his people; but he should not allow his love of liberty, or his natural determination to excel, to allure him beyond the limits of judgment or reason. It should be remembered that all schemes should be supported only when they are feasible. No man is morally bound to embark in any undertaking the success of which appears to be beyond probability. Our sympathies may be enlisted in its favor, but facts, stern facts, may render it the wildest folly to aid or promote it.

The purity of the motives of those gentlemen who figure as the principles in this affair, cannot be doubted.[2] They are, to the extent of knowledge at command, beyond even suspicion of meanness or dissimulation. But they are men—fallible men—just as liable to err as other men. Gifted and prolific as was the genius of Bacon,[3] he stooped to become the meanest of men. Rich as Gibbon's[4] erudition and genius were he had the mean ambition to be a fine gentleman. So it is with all men: the greatest have the greatest faults, and commit the greatest errors. The most feeble utter sage remarks, and advance at times great truths. Our common frailties serve to remove the hesitancy that other-wise would exist, and gives freedom, so to speak, to the pen, so that we can express the feelings of our hearts without fear or trembling.

In launching out into the boundless ocean of error we must steer by the great compass of facts and reason in voyaging after truth. How necessary is it to have these directing agencies! How much disappointment—how much regret, would they spare us! The colored people require now, more than at any other time, wise counsel. They want men in whom they can place confidence. Where can we look and find a man in whom the people repose the utmost confidence. Here, in this city, those men who have been leading the people for the last fifteen or twenty years have lost all influence. I will guarantee to say that the host who have handled the contributions of the people cannot successfully advance any scheme that involves the payment, on the part of the people, of a single dollar. These so-called leaders have been advocating impracticable schemes, making great promises, collecting large sums of money that, in many instances have not been accounted for. Thus their efforts have brought no results. Had they been guided by reason the colored people would not now be the victims of misplaced confidence.[5]

We are of the number who believe that the destiny of the colored people must be worked out *in the Western Hemisphere.* We believe that any scheme that serves to alienate us from our native land, and more closely rivets the fetters of the slave by removing his true friend and brother, the free black, should be scorned down by us. Our fathers fought in defence of the country, and it is ours by conquest and birth. Our tears and blood have for nearly three centuries enriched the soil, and shall we now desert it? Shall this fair land be the inheritance only of the oppressor? We have struggled successfully against oppression and prejudice, and are now marching onward and upward in the tide of life. While the cares and forebodings of our task-masters are gathering thick and fast, our hopes grow brighter, and the goal of our ambition draws nearer. Why should we feed the prejudices of the self-pampered Caucasian by indulging the hope that the despised negro will migrate to the sunlit shores of Africa? I [several words illegible] years longer, and we will see the Anglo-African a power in this country. Then we can look to the interests of our *African* brethren. We are advancing rapidly—are startling the world with our progress, even crushed and burdened as we are by American tyranny. Fifty or sixty years ago the disfranchised Americans seemed so firmly locked in the embraces of benightedness that centuries would be required to regenerate him. But from the dark depths to which American slavery had plunged him he has, as with a bound, risen to almost full intellectual manhood. We have poets, orators, professors, able and eloquent writers, and divines not inferior to those of the self-styled superior class. Shall we, in view of our unparalleled advancement, countenance African colonization[6]—a scheme that wars with the dearest interests of our people?

Rapid as has been our progress we have still much to achieve. Thousands are yet slumbering, unawakened to the full importance of mental culture. The kind of reading or speaking they prefer is of an exceptionable character—they only glow under the fire-and-brimstone-and-gnashing-of-teeth style of oratory.

All the civilizing influences we can command our children are waiting to receive. They are shut out from colleges and schools to a large extent, and are thus dependent upon their own people for their education.[7] Our people want a taste for study cultivated among them. They should be informed of the blessings and benefits that result from education. The four millions of our brethren in the "Southern prison-house" are depending upon us for their education. Every fugitive who comes among us must be educated by us. Bawdy-houses, tippling houses,[8] and every other place of dissipation, must be robbed of their wretched but precious inhabitants. When we look around us what do we perceive of that mental and moral excellence so necessary to impart learning and Christianity? What a vast field is here presented for the labors of the teacher and reformer! What a rich harvest to be gained would they but sow diligently those civilizing agents. They should remember that charity begins at home. Let them first pluck the beam from their own eye, and then they can see clearly to extract the mote that lay in their brother's eye.[9]

G. E. S.

WAA, 26 November 1859.

1. Thomas Hamilton (1823–65) and his brother Robert, New York City's most important Civil War–era black publishers, owned and edited the *Weekly Anglo-African* and the *Anglo-African Magazine.* Northern blacks honored Thomas Hamilton for his bold assertions of black rights and unfailing denunciations of slavery. The Hamiltons sold the *Weekly Anglo-African* to the Haytian Emigration Bureau, which renamed it the *Pine and Palm,* but quickly reestablished it. Thomas Hamilton also maintained a separate business, publishing books by such black authors as William Wells Brown. *BAP,* 5:27–29, 39–41, 71.

2. GES refers to the support black leaders such as Garnet, William Wells Brown, and James T. Holly gave to the African Civilization Society.

3. Francis Bacon (1561–1626), English philosopher, essayist, polemicist, and member of Parliament, clashed with nearly every important political leader in a relentless drive for power and royal favor. Leslie Stephen and Sidney Lee et al., eds., *Dictionary of National Biography,* 30 vols. (Oxford: Oxford University Press, 1917–), 1:800–832.

4. Edward Gibbon (1737–94), English historian, is best known for his *History of the Decline and Fall of the Roman Empire* (1776–88).

5. GES probably aimed his criticism at William Whipper (ca. 1804–76) and Whipper's business partner Stephen Smith (1797–1873), two of Philadelphia's richest and most influential blacks. Whipper strongly supported the African Civilization Society. Stephens also may have had Ennals J. Adams in mind. Adams, a Philadelphia clergyman, had lectured at the Banneker Institute and was an AfCS agent. *BAP,* 3:129–30n.1, 4:316–17n.1., 320–21n.23.

6. GES denounces the American Colonization Society.

7. Most American colleges barred admission to blacks. Some institutions, such as Dartmouth College, admitted a few, but those who attended faced withering racial prejudice. No institution matched Oberlin College's record— about three hundred African Americans attended Oberlin before the Civil War. Denied education by law or because of prejudice, blacks established their own primary and secondary schools. Their educational efforts also encompassed the activities of churches and Sunday schools; the publication of newspapers, books, and pamphlets; and the scores of literary and debating societies that existed in most black communities. *BAP,* 3:109–13, 259–60, 398–401,

433–34, 446–49; Jane H. Pease and William H. Pease, *They Who Would Be Free: Blacks' Search for Freedom, 1830–1861* (1974, reprint, Urbana: University of Illinois Press, 1990), 132–56.
    8. Bawdy-houses are places of prostitution, and tippling houses are barrooms.
    9. Matthew 7:3–5.

[January 1860.]

Mr. Editor:—In almost every stage of Christian history we find men perverting and subsidizing the principles of religion to effect their base designs. Looking through the gloomy and painful record of the past, we see the terrible agents of the doctrines of heresy, faggot and torch, tortures, excommunications, and inquisition, reddening the earth with blood, and permeating it with a livid terrorism. These engines of intolerance and fanaticism have been consigned, through the influence of Bible evangelization, to history; but they stand forth in all their revolting hideousness as monuments of folly and violence draped with the vestments of religion.

But while the world witnesses the spread of gospel truth and the destruction of many devilish systems and crimes, the religionist has to mourn that the hydra-headed monsters, error and sin, still live and stalk abroad in the land. He has to mourn that after eighteen hundred and sixty years of warfare with the Stygian foe, complete victory has not perched upon the banners of the faithful. He has to mourn that, instead of love and peace reigning amongst men, oppression, hate, and strife prevail. "Whatsoever you would that men should do unto you, do ye even so unto them,"[1] has become a scoff and jest. No wrong seems to be too deeply-dyed to receive the countenance of the so-called Christian. Throughout the entire church thousands of Baalites and Iscariots[2] may be found unblushingly defaming Bible truth with their impious tongues.

Mormonism,[3] that relic of barbarism, boasts of 800,000 votaries to its lecherous system—a shame and a disgrace to the age. "Free-love" and "Spiritualism,"[4] the miserable creations of morbid moral sentiments, are openly and daringly advocated. That arch-infamy, American slavery, a parallel to which cannot be found in the history of the world, are all propagated, sanctioned, and justified by the Bible. The "slaughter of the Jews," the "murder of the innocents," and the "reign of terror"[5] will stand in the annals of crime chiefest in atrocity; but, like a mountain above the hills, American slavery will tower above them all, and will brand the American nation with infamy through coming time.

"Colonization," the offspring and mouth-piece of American prejudice and hatred, under the false plea of christianizing Africa, is using every effort, aided by deluded or avaricious and designing colored men, to propagate emigration to that enervating region, thus blighting the prospects of the sterling and aspiring free negro on American soil. Not content with the stratagems that sophistry and meanness suggest to effect their accursed designs, they have commenced the work of compulsory emigration. State after State has either re-enslaved or banished our brethren from its territories.[6] They seemed determined that the negro shall remain in the country only in the condition of a slave. Take notice, disfranchised Americans! the favorers of this scheme are preparing two dreadful alternatives for you—hopeless bondage in this land, or suffering and death on the arid shores of Africa. And, mark it well! colored men in high places are lending their influence and are urging the motion of their infamous measure.

G. E. S.

WAA, 21 January 1860.

1. Matthew 7:12, also Luke 6:31.

2. The Baalites were one of many rival sects that competed with the ancient Israelites and as early as the ninth century B.C. symbolized worshipers of false gods. "Iscariots" refers to Judas Iscariot, the betrayer of Jesus. Paul J. Achtemeier, ed., *Harper's Bible Dictionary* (San Francisco: Harper and Row, 1985), 84–85, 514.

3. Most Northern blacks shared the nation's obsessions with Mormonism and Catholicism and feared them as agents of secretive, anti-Christian, and anti-republican organizations. David Brion Davis, *From Homicide to Slavery: Studies in American Culture* (New York: Oxford University Press, 1986), 137–54.

4. GES mentions two controversial movements that orthodox Protestants condemned as corrupt or depraved. The Free Love movement took root in antebellum reform communities, especially at Oneida, New York, and challenged traditional family and gender roles. Spiritualism, which began with the antics of two adolescent girls in Rochester, New York, became a wildly popular social and religious movement until the end of the nineteenth century. Its proponents' claim that the living could communicate with the dead found a large following among middle-class women and reformers. Ronald G. Walters, *American Reformers, 1815–1860* (New York: Hill and Wang, 1978), 56–58, 163–78.

5. GES refers to the anti-Jewish pogroms that had punctuated European and Russian history since the Middle Ages; King Herod's order, upon hearing of Jesus' birth, to kill all male infants in Bethlehem to eliminate any possible challenge to his rule; and the executions associated with the French Revolution.

6. Before the Civil War, most Northern states considered or adopted legislation to restrict the settlement of blacks. Northern white anxiety heighten in the 1860s over fears that freed slaves would move north. "Our people," Ohio Republican Senator Lyman Trumbull proclaimed, "want nothing to do with the negro." The Illinois legislature's lower house approved bills to strengthen the state's exclusion laws and even repudiated the Emancipation Proclamation. V. Jacque Voegeli, *Free but Not Equal: The Mid-West and the Negro during the Civil War* (Chicago: University of Chicago Press, 1967), 17–18, 77; Leon F. Litwack, *North of Slavery: The Negro in the Free States, 1790–1860* (Chicago: University of Chicago Press, 1961), 66–74.

Philadelphia,
March 19, 1860.

Mr. Editor:—The "Anglo-African" has become the mouth-piece of the proscribed Americans throughout the Northern States, and if its contemporaries would know the sentiments and feelings of the free Northern blacks, upon almost every subject, they must turn to its columns to find them boldly and manfully enunciated. I rejoice that we can boast of more than one able and influential journal,[1] and will hail the advent of others with joy—those that will vindicate the cause of our wronged and oppressed people.

But, sir, while a journal of the character of the "Anglo" evidently affords the largest latitude to all for the expression of their opinions and sentiments, it has higher and more responsible purposes and duties—to correct error, denounce wrong, and control and direct opinions. No guilt, no dissimulation, no falsehood, should escape its scathing brand. Our contemporaries, though offensive from the very stench of iniquity, are not guilty of all the crime perpetrated in society. We have all sorts of evils existing among us; we have prostitution, intemperance, irreligion, disunion, ignorance, sectionalism, (religious,) and colonization—i.e., civilization—proclivities, and had we been so assiduous in our efforts to attain noble and virtuous qualities as in succumbing to the behests and promptings of the passions and appetites, we would now be wielding an influence powerful to the pulling down of the strongholds of Satan—the above enumerated sins.

The position of the negro in this country springs upon us many anomalies. Those things that would elicit the admiration of the world under other circumstances, now merit scorn and condemnation, and are violative of the best interests of our people; and it is to these evils that lie hid beneath the finely-spun veil of sophistry, that your penetrating glance should be turned to tear asunder the vile covering, and to expose them in all their meanness and contemptibleness to the withering gaze of all men. Then we may look up to your noble sheet as the guide and director that teaches us where lie, and how to shun, the rocks and shoals upon which may be wrecked our dearest hopes.

G. E. S.

WAA, 31 March 1860.

1. Other important black papers publishing during this period were *The Christian Recorder,* 1854–1902; *The Colored Man's Journal,* 1851–60; *Douglass' Monthly,* 1859–63; *Frederick Douglass' Paper,* 1851–60; and the Hamilton's *Anglo-African Magazine,* which was founded in January 1859 and folded in March 1860. Penelope Bullock, *The Afro-American Periodical Press, 1838–1909* (Baton Rouge: Louisiana State University Press, 1981), 57–63; I. Garland Penn, *The Afro-American Press and Its Editors* (Springfield, Mass.: Willey, 1891); Frankie Hutton, *The Early Black Press in America, 1827–1860* (Westport: Greenwood Press, 1993).

Philadelphia,
Jan. 15, 1861.

Mr. Editor:—We are in the midst of sore political tribulation,[1] and the bulls of our people seem to be resting in the most profound indifference; not a ripple disturbs the quiet calm of the wide sea of their contentment. Ominous quiet is this. It is but the breathless stillness preceding a storm big with violence, ruin, and outrage, which will perhaps very soon break with terrible fury on their heads. If I could make my voice heard throughout the length and breadth of this broad land, I would cry from the depths of my soul, "Arouse, free black men! arouse! Act—act in the living present!"

The present crisis in the political world here may partake of the character of the crisis that culminated in 1840 by the election of Harrison to the Presidency,[2] and pass away and be forgotten; but before it does pass away, it may inflict injuries upon our people irreparable. With almost every question that has obtruded itself upon the people of this country except that of slavery, the wildest excitement has subsided into comparative indifference; but the question of slavery seems to gather earnestness and interest. Were it not the foundation and building-walls of the nation, there might be some hope for the ultimate success of our side; but the fluctuation of popular sentiment is what is to be dreaded above all things. The best of men may be sacrificed by a senseless mob; the works of art, the embellishments, the wealth, and the nationality of an empire may be torn down and swept away in the mad moment of popular tumult, which centuries of peace and prosperity have been spent in fashioning and acquiring.

At this time the moral instincts and principles are obscured, and the religious sentiments are stultified, so blinded by fanaticism are men under the frenzy of mob violence that these influences are impotent in damming up the fearful flood of disaster and death. Under the present demoralizing state of affairs, when leading men in the country, by precept and example, are enforcing the idea upon the vicious multitude that black men have no rights that white men are bound to respect,[3] and this with the bloody precepts of old hoary-haired Stockton, and the New York lawyer Brady,[4] are the sown wind which must produce a whirlwind.[5] I fear that we are on the eve of a general mob law, and if the evening should come, we may expect the hideous darkness of its midnight before the light of the new day shall appear, and thousands of us may perish before its butcheries cease. Let us not sleep while the enemies' war shouts are ringing about our ears, or cry "peace, peace when there is no peace."[6] Another great fact must have a tendency to encourage this fear—it is the consciousness of the white man, that every true man of the servile race is bound in his heart of hearts to the sentiment and principle, that "man must be free! if not through law, why then above the law."[7] This axiom wars with everything American; gain is the main spring of American law, learning, religion, politics. Slavery is one of the main sources of her gain—war against slavery, is therefore hostility to everything American. The almighty dollar is the heart and soul, the life blood of the nation. Are we prepared to maintain a conflict with a giant of such colossal dimensions, when it is a question of life or death with him? Are we in the position to hope for anything but disaster? To avert if possible these calamities, the work of preparation must be begun. The forces of slavery are sounding their notes of preparation, and are concentrating their forces; are the forces of freedom—not republicanism, nor abolitionism, nor colonization, but they who say "man must be free"—are they preparing and concentrating their forces?

In the first epistle I ever obtruded upon the public gaze, I arrayed my humble self amongst those who believe that "the destiny of the negro must be worked out upon the Western Hemisphere"[8]—I am more firmly of this opinion. A glorious destiny will be worked out for our people though millions of lives should have to pay the forfeiture. Although conservative col[ore]d, men may raise their feeble voices against concentration of the race to those portions of the continent, those regions where it nominally has the rule, and where we could in a brief period wipe from the shores of America the mightiest despotism that ever wielded its sceptre over mortal man; so sure as God lives, a noble destiny is dawning upon the negro. The mighty American nation conceived as it has been in infamy, maintained and supported by outrage, perfidy, and criminality—the covenant of death[9]—though she shall strike down every right, blast our every hope upon her sin accursed soil, rather than disturb the harmony or jeopardize the perpetuity of her glorious Union; a noble destiny must be worked for him. For the sake of the best interest of wives, children, and our suffering brethren, concentrate, inundate the tropics with strong arms and stout hearts, add your quota to working out a glorious destiny for our struggling race. Remember that ten thousand men under the unfurled banner of insurrection can sweep away the slaves' shackles like a tornado does chaff.[10]

G. E. Stephens.

WAA, 26 January 1861.

1. GES refers to the secession crisis, begun on 20 December 1860, when South Carolina withdrew from the Union after Abraham Lincoln's election. At the time of Stephens's letter, Mississippi, Florida, and Alabama also had adopted secession ordinances. David M. Potter, *The Impending Crisis, 1848–1861* (New York: Harper and Row, 1976), 498.

2. The 1840 presidential campaign, usually dismissed as all "hard cider" and no content, initially sparked the same Southern fears that destroyed the Union in 1861. Radicals warned that William Henry Harrison's election would endanger Southern liberties, subvert the South to Northern economic interests, and threaten the institution of slavery. Eric H. Walther, *The Fire-Eaters* (Baton Rouge: Louisiana State University Press, 1992), 53–54.

3. GES quotes from Chief Justice Roger B. Taney's opinion in *Dred Scott v. Sanford*, 19 Howard 393 (1857). Although Taney's decision did not surprise blacks, its apparent finality represented a crushing blow to their hopes. In

Philadelphia, blacks felt "hopelessly doomed" or saw only a "faint prospect" for change. *BAP,* 4:362–65; Don E. Fehrenbacher, *The Dred Scott Case: Its Significance in American Law and Politics* (New York: Oxford University Press, 1978).

4. GES refers to Democratic politicians John Potter Stockton (1826–1900) and James Topham Brady (1815–69). Stockton, an outspoken New Jersey U.S. senator who supported Lincoln, bitterly opposed emancipation and wartime restrictions on the Democratic press. Brady, a successful New York City lawyer, ran for governor in 1860 as a Breckinridge Democrat. He later supported Lincoln and the war effort.

5. Hosea 8:7

6. Jeremiah 6:14, 8:11.

7. GES quotes the masthead of the *Anglo-African.*

8. *WAA,* 26 November 1859.

9. GES quotes William Lloyd Garrison's January 1843 repudiation of the Constitution and the Union as a "'covenant with death, and an agreement with hell'—involving both parties in atrocious criminality; and should be immediately annulled." Walter M. Merrill and Louis Ruchames, eds., *The Letters of William Lloyd Garrison,* 6 vols. (Cambridge: Harvard University Press, 1971–81), 3:118.

10. GES probably alludes to the bloody Haitian revolution that led to independence in 1804. The revolution symbolized the black nationalist struggle for power and independence.

Chapter 6

Pleasing the "Jealous God of Slavery"

17 October 1861–4 January 1862

Only a few months into the war, Stephens wrote like a veteran correspondent. His observations and opinions displayed the confidence that comes with experience. While Stephens marched with the Army of the Potomac and helped free slaves, black leaders at home still reeled from the government's rejection of their offer to help defend the Union. They contentiously debated the war, many justifiably asking what loyalty they owed a government that denied them citizenship and still supported slavery. Should they even remain in the United States when the government of Haiti offered them equality and free passage to the Caribbean?

Stephens appreciated their quandary but preferred action to debate, believing that events would eventually compel the Union to fight slavery. He did not misconstrue the North's war aims and understood that the Lincoln administration intended to preserve the Union, not emancipate slaves. He did not support Lincoln's election and damned his government as the "fag end" of a series of proslavery administrations. Although Stephens witnessed the war's cruelty firsthand and graphically detailed the Union army's savage treatment of blacks, he saw clearly what the long-term effect of escaping slaves would be on the course of the war in ways that black leaders at home could not. The Union army, Stephens wrote, had "opened up avenues of free intercourse between Northern and Southern black men, [that] compels us to admit their invasion of Southern soil to be grand and beneficent." Despite the atrocities Yankees committed on Southern blacks, he believed that the army ultimately was "on the side of freedom."

The Army of the Potomac occupied southern Maryland to protect the nation's capital from attack, to further its uncertain strategy against Richmond, and to put down secessionist fervor in a crucial border state. Gen. Joseph Hooker commanded a Union division, which included Stephens's Twenty-sixth Pennsylvania Regiment, that sought to immobilize Confederate forces across the Potomac in Virginia, suppress the illegal and damaging cross-river trade, and root out Southern sympathizers. Hooker's division was also one of the first Union commands to confront the problem of fugitive slaves. Although the Lincoln administration enforced the 1850 Fugitive Slave Law to ensure that border slave states like Maryland remained in the Union, implementation proved difficult and troubling to many soldiers compelled to execute it.

Congress's First Confiscation Act of 6 August 1861 authorized Union commanders to seize only slaves of disloyal owners. Loyal slaveowners and those whose treason remained unproven could recover their property under the Fugitive Slave Law until Congress repealed it in June 1864, although enforcement declined after January 1863. Congress's enactment of an additional article of war in March 1862 that outlawed using soldiers to execute the law provided the legal foundation for Union troops to resist the orders of their proslavery officers.[1] Nevertheless, Lincoln remained sensitive to the demands of the border states rather than the moral imperative of the slaves. Although the Fugitive Slave Law provided no role for the military, the Lincoln administration instructed Union officers to cooperate with slave catchers. Gen. Benjamin F. Butler went further and assured Maryland's governor that his federal troops could be counted on to suppress any slave rebellion.[2]

In Hooker's division, the Massachusetts and Pennsylvania troops generally proved sympathetic to the fugitives and hounded the slave catchers who prowled their camps looking for runaways. But regiments from other Northern states, especially New York, acted with sadistic fury. They held blacks responsible for the war and found their repellent racial prejudices confirmed by the deplorable conditions slaves endured. Soldiers' letters harped on the slaves' supposedly "queer" and "disgusting" appearance. Few disagreed with the remarks of one Yankee who said, "I dont think enough of the Niggar to go and fight for them. I would rather fight them."[3] Many did. In Alexandria, Virginia, occupying Union troops shot blacks for amusement, and members of the Ninety-ninth New York Regiment kidnapped others to sell to rebel troops.[4] Blacks who sought freedom and protection behind Union lines, especially early in the war, rarely found it. Instead, they became trapped between the blue-coated demons of the North and outraged masters in the South.

1. Berlin, *The Destruction of Slavery*, 1:22.
2. Ibid., 1:11–36; Stanley W. Campbell, *The Slave Catchers: Enforcement of the Fugitive Slave Law, 1850–1860* (Chapel Hill: University of North Carolina Press, 1968), 188–94.
3. Leon F. Litwack, *Been in the Storm So Long: The Aftermath of Slavery* (New York: Random House, 1979), 122–35, quotation on 127.
4. Reid Mitchell, *Civil War Soldiers: Their Expectations and Their Experiences* (New York: Simon and Schuster, 1988), 120–23.

* * *

Head-quarters Hooker's Division,
near Bladensburg, Maryland,
Oct. 17th, 1861.
Mr. Editor,[1]
This division[2] is composed of Sickles'[3] and Cowden's Brigade,[4] formerly Hooker's Brigade. General Hooker has been raised to the dignity of General of Division.[5]
On last Sunday morning General Sickles reported himself here in our camp to the Commander-in-Chief. He was accompanied by a portion of his staff and a mounted escort of 12 men, and looked like a Spanish brigand that we see represented on the stage of a theatre, with his huge moustache, plumes and boots. His Brigade lies about 5 miles to the eastward of us, and is expected to encamp with us very shortly. Six companies of the 1st Indiana cavalry[6] joined our Brigade to-day, they are a fine looking body of men and splendidly mounted and caparisoned. Our camping ground is a most magnificent one; our camp lies in the form of a crescent, about one mile south of Bladensburg, the extreme right resting on the famous dueling ground,[7] the left on the line of the Baltimore and Washington Railroad. The health of the Brigade has been excellent, there have been but five deaths in two months in this army of between five and six thousand men, three by accident and two by disease.[8]
On last Tuesday General Hooker reviewed the Brigade of General Sickles—on Wednesday General Cowden's. I did not get an opportu-

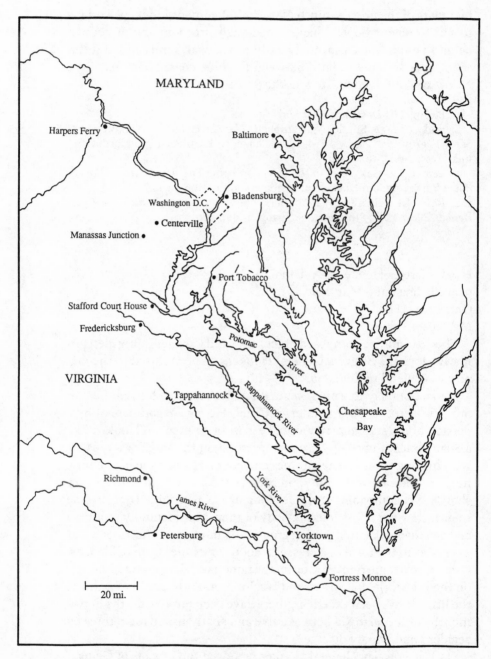

Map 3. Eastern Virginia and Southern Maryland

nity to see the former—the latter was a military pageant. All the regiments were drawn up in line, the army wagons and ambulances to the rear; the regiments comprised the 1st Michigan,[9] 2d New Hampshire,[10] 26th Pennsylvania,[11] and 1st and 11th Massachusetts,[12] and while my eyes were dazzled with the imposing display, the regimental bands were charming my ears with their melodies. Although standing upon a soil polluted by slavery, my heart was lifted up, and this painful reflection which ever burdens it, was momentarily soothed, that man must be a demon that resists successfully the charms of the divine art.

As the most opposite emotions were experienced by me on the following occasion, I will give you an account of it. It was a painful case; a private of the 1st Michigan regiment secured a furlough to visit his family. Full of expectation he prepared himself for the passage, but accidentally fell under the wheels of the car that was to bear him home, was fatally injured and was buried yesterday with military honors. The circumstances of the case, the solemn dirge-like music, the slow measured dead-march, made the obsequies painfully touching; but imposing ceremonials have a strange fascinating influence over us all. I have often wondered why the soldier delights to increase the solemnities of a death: they say it is "Honor to the departed Brave." The soldier's business is to deal in carnage and blood, and these honors are a happy way to preserve a due regard for the value of human life.

While about closing the last paragraph, a man who is dignified with the title of sheriff, rode into camp with a posse of five persons, and seized a little boy about 15 years of age, a fugitive from *slavery*. He dared not attempt to take the boy with his posse, but secured a sergeant and a guard to escort them over the lines and to prevent his rescue. So you see it required 13 men to take one boy of 15 years. Great Heavens, how many men would it require to re-enslave ten thousand full-grown men? But we did all in our power to aid him, but the vigilance of the guards outwitted us. Poor Frank was surrendered up, and now swells the list of the thousands sacrificed upon the altar of the "jealous God of Slavery." We resort to another method now, we hurry the panting fugitive to the Virginia side, and urge him to enter the Federal lines from that direction. But, my dear sir, it is hard to elude the vigilance of Federal man catchers.

The soil upon which our camp is situated belongs to a Mr. McGill,[13] and when the Brigade first commenced its encampment here, he commanded all persons living upon his large farm not to sell one cent's worth of produce to the troops; thus inviting depredations by the soldiers. But a few weeks sufficed to strip his farm of everything eatable, corn, tomatoes, cantelopes, beans, &c. He left his home and joined another farm belonging to him, near Marlborough, leaving the only personal and portable property behind in the shape of two chattels, personal, Washington and Diana.

These poor creatures had nothing to eat, and had to live upon the bounty of the camp. I took Washington with me in my own tent, and engaged him to act as body servant to an officer. About a week after I had thought he had found the society of his comrades in treason, Mr. McGill returned, Dianah had vanished; not a vestige of her was left, not even an old hood or tattered shoe. Washington was found comfortably seated in his tent. Mr. Secesh said, "Come along, Washington, you have been here long enough;" but Washington was not so easily sucked in; he would "neber let no strange man own him." A sergeant's guard was called to convey him to his detested chains, when lo! Washington had vanished like so much thin air. They hunted and called, called and hunted, but the subtle Washington would not take upon himself the much coveted entity of blood, bones and sinew, and he is to-day awaiting that inevitable hour when the decree shall go forth from Capitol Hill proclaiming "Liberty throughout all the land to all the inhabitants thereof."[14] I learn from undoubtful source that passes are issued to Maryland slave-holders to cross over to the Virginia side to search for runaway slaves, while non-slaveholders are denied the privilege of visiting their friends in the camps. This makes the friends of humanity tremble for their cause. How can the American people expect the support of the civilized world, while they thus prove themselves the cringing votaries of the hell-born system? We hear it whispered that the Southern Confederacy will, as the last resort to secure a permanent dissolution, and to save the necks of their leaders, *declare their slaves free.*[15] From a philosophical point of view this is clearly a probability. To whom would the four and a half millions, scorned and rejected by the Northern Confederacy, owe allegiance? I shall give my life to him who enfolds the scroll of emancipation, no matter who he may be, Northerner or Southerner. Did you read the speech of Bulwar?[16] Reproduce it. He breathes the words of inspiration. But we are in the midst of doubts and fears, and must labor hard and wait for the rapid march of events. In my next I shall try to say something in regard to the *Anglo.*

G. E. S.

WAA, 2 November 1861.

1. Robert Hamilton (1819–?), the *Weekly Anglo-African's* editor, became one of the most eloquent advocates of black rights in the North. He organized petition campaigns in support of black suffrage and promoted black temperance. Hamilton urged blacks to withhold their support for the Union until it adopted emancipation as a war aim and then championed the Fifty-fourth Massachusetts Regiment. *BAP*, 5:27–29, 40; *WAA*, 17 January 1863, 13 May, 9 September, 7 October 1865.

2. Hooker's division in October 1861 contained three brigades (twenty-three regiments) led by Brigadier Generals Henry M. Naglee and Daniel E. Sickles and Col. S. H. Starr. Dyer, *Compendium*, 2:277; *OR*, ser. 1, 5:716.

3. Daniel E. Sickles (1819–1914), a New York lawyer and member of Congress (1857–61), became a brigadier general of volunteers in 1862. His large moustache made Sickles readily identifiable to his men. At the time of his visit to Stephens's camp, Sickles commanded the Second—"Excelsior"—Brigade, composed of the Seventieth through Seventy-fourth New York Regiments. *HTIECW*, 250, 594–95; *WWWCW*, 594–95; Dyer, *Compendium*, 2:273.

4. Col. Robert Cowden (1805–74) commanded Hooker's brigade—the Second Division, Third Corps, Army of the Potomac—in August 1862. Colonel of the First Massachusetts, he became a brigadier general in the U.S. Volunteers in 1862. The brigade included the Second New Hampshire, First and Eleventh Massachusetts, and the Twenty-sixth Pennsylvania Regiments. *WWWCW*, 147; Dyer, *Compendium*, 2:273; Compiled Service Records, RG 94, National Archives.

5. Gen. Joseph Hooker (1814–79), West Point graduate and Massachusetts native, lived in California at the war's outset. He served as divisional commander from 3 October 1861 to 13 March 1862. Although popular with his men, Hooker failed to win any major victories and too often lost his nerve in a crisis. *WWWCW*, 317–18; Walter H. Hebert, *Fighting Joe Hooker* (Indianapolis: Bobbs-Merrill, 1944).

6. The First Indiana never served in Virginia. GES probably meant the Third Indiana Cavalry, which was attached to Hooker's division from October 1861 to March 1862. It camped at Budd's Ferry until December 1861, patrolled the lower Potomac region, suppressing rebel sympathizers, and guarded polling stations during the fall elections. Dyer, *Compendium*, 3:1103–5; *OR*, ser. 1, 5:635, 640.

7. Washingtonians favored Bladensburg, Maryland, as a dueling site, especially after 1839, when Congress outlawed the practice in the District. Com-

mo. Stephen Decatur was killed there on 22 March 1820. Warren H. Cudworth, *History of the First Regiment, Massachusetts Infantry* (Boston: Walker, Fuller, 1866), 75–78.

8. Hooker's division included 6,775 infantry, 519 cavalry, and 16 artillery pieces. *OR*, ser. 1, 5:650.

9. The First Michigan Regiment, organized on 16 September 1861, was attached to Hooker's division from September 1861 to February 1862. It lost 337 men in the war and mustered out on 9 July 1865. Dyer, *Compendium*, 3:1281.

10. The Second New Hampshire Regiment, organized on 8 June 1861, remained in Hooker's brigade from August to October 1861 and in Hooker's division until March 1862. The regiment suffered 350 casualties in the war and mustered out on 19 December 1865. Ibid., 3:1347.

11. The Twenty-sixth Pennsylvania Regiment, commanded by Col. William F. Small and Benjamin C. Tilghman of Philadelphia, officially mustered into service on 25 May 1861. It joined Hooker's brigade in August, camped at Bladensburg until 20 October 1861, and then marched to Budd's Ferry, where it remained until 1 April 1862. The Twenty-sixth suffered 706 casualties in some of the most lethal fighting of the war before disbanding on 18 June 1864. Frank Hamilton Taylor, *Philadelphia in the Civil War, 1861–1865* (Philadelphia: City of Philadelphia, 1913), 52–53; Bates, *History*, 1:344–54.

12. The First Massachusetts, organized in May 1861, joined Hooker's brigade in August. It remained in Virginia for most of the war and mustered out on 25 May 1864. The Eleventh Massachusetts served in Hooker's division and also passed the winter of 1861–62 at Budd's Ferry. The unit formed on 13 June 1861 and disbanded on 14 July 1864. *Massachusetts Soldiers, Sailors*, 1:1–2; 735–37; Dyer, *Compendium*, 3:1248.

13. James McGill (1834–?), a wealthy Bladensburg farmer, possessed $45,000 worth of real estate and $250,000 of personal estate. 1860 U.S. Census.

14. Leviticus 25:10.

15. Rumors that the South would emancipate slaves to serve in the army circulated throughout the war. The Confederacy did not seriously consider the move until 1865, and even then military leaders failed to support it vigorously. The Confederate legislature never approved any black units. Slaves occasionally accompanied their masters into battle, and early in the war some slaves and free blacks had been pressed into armed service. Virginia armed a few blacks at the end of the war, but no meaningful effort resulted. James M. McPherson, *Battle Cry of Freedom: The Civil War Era* (New York: Oxford University Press, 1988), 831–37; Arthur W. Bergeron, Jr., "Free Men of Color in Grey," *Civil War History* 32 (September 1986): 247–50; *WAA*, 2 November 1861; Ervin L. Jordan, Jr., *Black Confederates and Afro-Yankees in Civil War Virginia* (Charlottesville: University Press of Virginia, 1995).

16. Edward Robert Bulwer Lytton (1831–91), an English poet and writer, served at a variety of European diplomatic posts during the war. In his 25 September speech to an English agricultural society, Bulwer Lytton predicted that the United States would break up into four or more separate coun-

tries. This would, he believed, eliminate a dangerous empire and foster "civilization" in the former United States. The speech found few receptive ears in the North. Leslie Stephen and Sidney Lee, eds., *Dictionary of National Biography*, 30 vols. (Oxford: Oxford University Press, 1917–), 12:387–92; *New York Times*, 12, 15 October 1861.

Headquarters of Hooker's Division,
Near Budd's Ferry, Doncaster, Md.
Nov. 11, 1861.

Mr. Editor: I promised that I would say something in regard to the "Anglo;" since that promise was penned I have endured all the vicissitudes and fatigue of a long march, suffered a painful illness, and labored under so many other difficulties that the fulfillment of it has been all but impossible. But, my dear sir, we surely can rely on the self-respect, intelligence and public spirit of our people, for that encouragement and support your noble paper so justly merits, without me urging its claims. The most eloquent testimonial that could possibly be offered in its behalf, it bears upon its own face, in its columns. I shall never entertain the thought that the colored people could be so recreant to duty and interest as to allow your paper to perish for want of support. It behooves every one of us in this startlingly eventful period of our country's history, one portion of which is sternly warring for our utter enslavement, the other scorning and rejecting our every manly and patriotic impulse, to unite heart and hand in making the Anglo the Tribune[1] of the Negro. Never let the shameful story go forth that :hree hundred and fifty thousand black men could not support one single newspaper.

The main body of this Division took up the line of march for this place on the 24th ult., accompanied by a numerous artillery and baggage train.[2] The distance from Camp Union to Budd's Ferry is reckoned to be between thirty-eight and forty miles, and the road is the most villainous I ever saw. I call it a road because the folks here call it one. No people in the world, save sloven, brutal, ignorant Marylanders, would dignify this meandering quagmire, this tortuous slough of despondency, with the title of road. It is intersected throughout its entire length with unbridged runs, creeks, and ponds of sandy mud. Our struggling teams would be stalled for hours, and when I call to mind the state of that—I am ready to believe that our arrival here with artillery and baggage safe and sound, is the result of some supernatural interposition.

The scenes along the road were numberless and indescribable. These cold, autumnal nights and wet murky days, the folks at home, seated by blazing, cheerful hearths, may read with perfect *nonchalance* of the soldier's march from one point to another. Little do they dream of the hardships of the march; the travel of miles with nothing to eat but hard biscuit, his trunk packed on his back, on his shoulders forty rounds of ball cartridge and a thirteen pound gun; at night he stops for the bivouac, chops his wood, builds his fire, makes a bed of the earth, accepts the sky for his roof, and sleeps regardless of storms, wind or rain.

The second day after our departure an affair transpired which came near proving fatal to a private of the 26th Pennsylvania Regiment. Colonel Small[3] (who, by the way, is the same individual who furnished the oracular parts of Parson Brownlow's argument with Rev. Abram Pryne, at National Guards' Hall,)[4] ordered that no man should advance alone beyond the regiment. Privates Winters and Brody[5] disobeyed this order, and the Colonel ordered them back. Thinking they did not move quick enough, he fired three shots, one taking effect in the leg of Brody, and another in the spine of Winters, who was left at Piscataway, too badly wounded to be moved farther than that place.

The towns were not to be seen—the villages, few and very far between. I saw two churches on the route, but no school houses. The latter may have been secession ones. Plenty of negroes, dirty, ragged, dreamy-eyed—very few seedy looking, stupid whites. On every hand I saw the evidences of sloth and thriftlessness, the twin sisters or offsprings of unrequited toil.—When a chance offered, some poor fellow would venture to ask a question about the object of the Union troops, so many fugitives having been returned by them that the slaves are almost their enemies. One odd fellow told me that he did not want the Union troops to help him out, but wanted them not to be so anxious to send him back into hard, helpless bondage.

The slaves, to a man, are on the alert. They look upon Union men as little better than secessionists. I thought to myself that many a lesson might have been learned by these Northern soldiers, of the effects of slavery upon a community, but the men of which this army is composed are drawn from the cesspools of society, and are intemperate, brutal and ignorant; pregnant with negro hate, and strangers to every sentiment of honor or justice. They would carry fire and sword to the home of the friend, as well as foe, and never yet have imbibed the first notion of law or humanity. No country in the world furnishes a populace so hatefully mean and violent as that of the United States. On every hand are the traces of wanton destruction of property; hen-roosts, turkey pens, turnip patches, barns, were ransacked and pillaged. I saw a fine fat hog pierced with bayonets, and a hind quarter cut from him while yet alive, the rest left behind. Cattle and sheep were shot down for mere pastime.

A party of men from the Excelsior Brigade went into the house of a free colored man by the name of Isaac Newton, and behaved most shamefully. After eating all they could find, they insulted his wife and daughters. Captain Price, learning that his men were at Newton's, went down to protect him, if possible, when the villains fired on the Captain, wounding a young man who happened to be in his company at the time. The Captain returned the fire with his revolver, mortally wounding one and slightly wounding two others. Mr. Newton was left to himself by his master, who died some three years ago. He informs me that the slaveholders have done everything in their power to ruin him. He owns about one hundred acres of land here in Doncaster. His entire family, a wife, son and three daughters, were left free upon this place, and he has thus become an object of hatred and envy among the slave-driving whites. They have been killing his stock, trampling under foot his grain, annoying him with midnight patrols. Last fall a party of them attacked him with clubs, and for four long weeks he was confined to his bed from the effects of the assault.

Since our arrival here, the 28th ult., we have had no letters, papers or news. The mails are irregular, but in very short time, the General tells us, we will have regular mail facilities.

G. E. S.

WAA, 23 November 1861.

1. Horace Greeley's New York *Tribune*, founded in 1841, became the nation's most influential newspaper. Through its pages, Greeley promoted social reform, abolitionism, and pressured President Lincoln to adopt emancipation. Frank Luther Mott, *American Journalism: A History, 1690–1960*, 3d ed. (New York: Macmillan, 1962), 267–78.

2. Hooker's division left Bladensburg on 20 October. Advance elements began arriving at Budd's Ferry the next day. Bates, *History*, 1:345; *OR*, ser. 1, 5:372–73.

3. William F. Small, a Philadelphia lawyer, organized and commanded the Twenty-sixth Pennsylvania Regiment. He returned to Philadelphia in 1862 after being wounded at the battle of Yorktown. Bates, *History*, 1:344; Frank Hamilton Taylor, *Philadelphia in the Civil War, 1861–1865* (Philadelphia: City of Philadelphia, 1913), 27, 28, 52, 251.

4. GES mentions the 1858 Philadelphia public debate between the Rev. Abraham Pryne (1822–62) and William G. Brownlow (1805–77) of Tennessee, a Methodist minister and the state's most influential editor. Pryne, an abolitionist editor and New York state representative, advocated the immediate end of slavery, while Brownlow maintained that slavery ought to be preserved. GES may have witnessed the debate. Several members of the Banneker Institute attended and later presented Pryne with a series of resolutions praising him as one of the "ablest defenders of human rights." Francis S. Drake, *Dictionary of American Biography* (Boston: James R. Osgood, 1872), 134–35; Walter M. Merrill and Louis Ruchames, eds., *The Letters of William Lloyd Garrison*, 6 vols. (Cambridge: Harvard University Press, 1971–81), 4:594–95n.5; Parker T. Smith, Jacob C. White, and William H. Johnson to the Banneker Institute, 13 October 1858, Banneker Institute Papers, LGC, HSP.

5. The reference is to Pvts. John Winters, Company I, and James Brodie, Company G, Twenty-sixth Pennsylvania. Brodie recovered from his wounds only to die at Chancellorsville on 3 May 1863. Winters also recovered and mustered out on 18 June 1864. Bates, *History*, 1:371, 378.

Headquarters of Hooker's Division,
Near Budd's Ferry, Charles County, Md.,
Nov. 19, 1861.

Mr. Editor:—It has been my fortune to witness much of life in the Southern States. I was arrested in the city of Charleston, S.C., in the year 1858, for merely standing upon that slavery cursed soil, in spite of my regular enlistment in the navy of the United States, as a seaman.[1] Virginia, Florida, Alabama, Louisiana, and lastly Maryland, have all furnished painful scenes and incidents for the imagination to dwell upon. I have seen old grey-haired men of toil-worn frame and tottering step, old women and young women, driven like very beasts to shambles and a market. I have seen wives and daughters torn from husbands and parents, and their charms sold to the highest bidder, to lecherous masters. My own dear father was exiled from Northampton county, Virginia, before I was born—in 1830—by the persecutions which followed the Nat Turner insurrection.[2] From infancy up to my manhood he has been relating the wrongs of my people. Many a tale of woe has he impressed upon my mind and heart. The thousand-fold crimes of this guilty nation against our race, pass in solemn sorrow before me. The fangs of the serpent of oppression has pierced my own bosom until it swells with the hot blood of a revenge which nothing but the blood of a slaveholder can satiate. This is a stern school for a man who has passed the terrible ordeal of life under American slavery and oppression. This land must be consecrated to freedom, and we are to-day the only class of people in the country who are earnestly arrayed on the side of freedom. True it is that thousands of our enfranchised brethren are ready and willing to offer up their lives upon the altar of liberty. Tens and hundreds of thousands would rejoice to see the great national sin eradicated; but could they restore what was supposed to be by the credulous a "Glorious Union," and the Constitution and laws, with all of the crimes and iniquities which hover around it, they would passively submit and forget under the sophistries and blandishments of polished rhetoric, the claims of millions of enslaved men, to all of the blessings and benefits of liberty and civilization. Three quarters of a century of complicity[3] in the guilt of manstealing has demoralized a people who in 1776, for their love of liberty, gained the admiration of the civilized world, secured the valor of Lafayette, DeKalb[4] and others, and called forth the eloquence of England's most popular statesmen. In that memorable struggle for nationality the purest and most imperishable sentiments gushed forth, as if from the fountain-head of liberty. It seemed but the prelude to that great social symphony—Liberty, Fraternity, Equality— which Republican France sounded throughout monarchical Europe when the old State House bell in Independence Hall[5] rung out the declaration of freedom to all. Compare that brilliant epoch with the present. Recount in your minds the noble deeds of "'76," and mark the events of "'61."—Whom of the noble spirits of that age dreamed that in the year of our Lord 1861, the only powerful Republic on the face of the earth was sanctioning, directly and indirectly, those monstrous wrongs against an entire race of men which I have thus meagerly epitomized. Nearly a million of men in arms, one half unblushingly declaring its purpose to be the unlimited extension of slavery; the other half daring not to raise its hands against the iniquitous purpose. Oh, sir, in the present instance the righteous sword is unsheathed, and I honestly believe there are enough freedom loving allies to our cause to keep that sword unsheathed until every wythe[6] that binds the slave shall be cast asunder.

I am perfectly astonished at the many reports which appear in the daily papers about the "Blockade."[7] The reports generally sent from this region are generally unreliable, and will always be so, if all newspaper correspondents do as I see one of the New York Herald[8] correspondents do. Well, he had any quantity of note paper, seated in a captain's tent; the captain spreading himself, and relating all the most extravagant stories he could rattle off, and which are gathered from the thousand and one statements straggling soldiers bring in. The truth is, we know nothing sure of the number, location or purpose of the enemy. With powerful glasses we can discover squads of cavalry and infantry over toward Aquia Creek; can see one rebel battery with S.C. flag flying;[9] two large guns visible, and on an island directly opposite Budd's Ferry fresh earth thrown up, which may be a rifle pit, or boat or raft; building operations to the rear of this; on a bluff is an earthwork with no guns visible. Large rewards are said to be offered to the individual who will make a reconnaissance of the enemy's position, and bring back information of his number and location. There is scarcely any danger of your humble servant's undertaking— the hazardous task. The rebels take great delight in practicing with their big guns. They are constantly throwing shot and shell over on this side, and as we lay some two miles inside, we feel a perfect indifference to their death-dealing missiles. Of our own batteries and entrenchments I dare not say anything. Suffice it to say, they are almost completed. We have river communication regularly with Washington, and our telegraph is completed which connects us with headquarters. General Hooker is all activity, and from what I can learn from him he does not apprehend any attempt to cross. In my opinion, nothing is more desirable than that they should do so. There is not provision enough in all Maryland to support an army of 5,000 men. There are but a very few points from which their guns could command the river; that is where the channel runs close to the Virginia shore. The river varies in width 1½ to 4½ miles; hence should they cross over here in force, and we should all have to take to our heels for dear life, the river could be inundated with gunboats of light draught, and cut off all supplies and re-enforcements. The traitor population of Maryland is already drained of arm-bearing men, and there are no arms in the State to put into the hands of the few which are left.[10] The sycophant croakers say that Maryland is loyal too.—

Well, nothing but disaster or defeat to the rebel army could result from an invasion of the sacred soil of Maryland. The most hypocritical thing in the world is this much talked of loyalty. Everybody you meet says he is "for the Union," and they laugh, talk and drink with you— are even glad to converse and drink with a Northern "nigger!" But hear one withering proof of the utter disloyalty. Just here in the vicinity of Budd's Ferry the rebels used to congregate; they kept up a regular ferry between the two shores, and their engineers had surveyed the positions now occupied by the Union troops, and yet in the face of all this, it is impossible to gather any information from these people here that would be of advantage to us. Can it be possible that they are ignorant of the plans, and purposes, and force and position of their accomplices? The lawyers tell us that the "manner and appearance" of the criminal have great bearing on his case. If this be true, the Marylanders, so far as I have seen of them, stand adjudged guilty of the crime of treason.—Well, I am told a sheep thief is about the meanest looking wretch on earth. Well, take a score of sheep thieves, extract the essence, then the quintessence of all their meanness, and you have pictured in your mind's eye of a hang-dog Marylander—heart and soul an enemy he is—conscious of his entire subjection, in spite of his negro-driving propensities; and although I hate a slaveholder from the inner most recesses of my heart, and also when I consider the doughfaced[11] negro-hating propensities of the horde by which I am surrounded, I must admire his consistency.

The rebel batteries are continually throwing shot and shell over here, but as yet done no harm. They are ugly looking missiles, and I should not wonder if a tap from one of them should do one's physical frame considerable damage.

You will remember that a year or two (I think) ago, it was published in the various papers, and stated publicly, that a man by the name of Harry Green sold three of his children to the far South. I disremember all the details of the story, but I have learned from the woman who gave the children their supper on the night of their departure for Richmond, Va., that is was through the infernal machinations of a wretch by the name of "Skinner,"[12] that this poor man was compelled to sell into bondage his own flesh and blood. I have seated myself at the same table where that last supper to them was partaken; have looked upon the inhuman wretch who was party to the infernal deed. I shall try, at some future time, to give the details of the painful story, if I should be able to seize sufficient time from amidst the whirl and excitement of camp life.

Hopkins, the Sheriff of Prince George county, was up here on a slave hunt. We pointed him out to the Indiana cavalry boys. It would have done your heart good to have heard the jeers and imprecations they heaped upon him. Mr. Lambert Dutrenielle (the General's steward) while he (Hopkins) was seated at the General's table eating cold beef-steak, sat down directly opposite to him, and called for hot steak. By a preconcerted arrangement, one of the white servants asked; "How dare you sit down to the table with a white man?" "I thought this was a colored gentleman, he sticks so close to the colored people." Hopkins dared not whisper, and, if I am not very much mistaken, will not visit these parts again soon.

It gives me great pleasure to announce that the tide of emigration Northward continues to flow, all barriers to the contrary notwithstanding.

G. E. S.

WAA, 7 December 1861.

1. GES misstates his status on the USS *Walker.* He sailed under the authority of the U.S. Coast Survey, not the navy.

2. The date supplied in this letter is most likely a printer's error because the Turner Rebellion took place on 13–23 August 1831 in Southampton County, Virginia. GES was born the next year.

3. GES loosely refers to the history of United States under the Constitution (1789).

4. GES mentions two of the many Europeans who assisted the American cause during the Revolution. The Marquis de Lafayette—Marie Joseph P. Y. R. G. du Motier (1757–1834)—was a French nobleman and advisor to Washington. Johann de Kalb (1721–80), a German-born officer, fell mortally wounded at the battle of Camden on 16 August 1780. Richard B. Morris, ed., *Encyclopedia of American History* (New York: Harper and Brothers, 1953), 95, 103.

5. The reference is to Independence Hall in Philadelphia. The historic hip-roofed brick structure, built between 1732 and 1741, houses the Liberty Bell and served as the setting for the signing of the Declaration of Independence, the Articles of Confederation, and the U.S. Constitution. James Truslow Adams, ed., *Dictionary of American History,* 5 vols. (New York: Charles Scribner's Sons, 1940), 3:85–86.

6. The word is usually rendered *withe*—a band, tie, or shackle made from flexible twigs bound together.

7. GES mentions Confederate "control" of the Potomac River below Washington, D.C., which brought the national government much ridicule, especially from the foreign press. Confederate forces, however, never blockaded the Potomac River, and even slow-moving Union vessels safely negotiated it. Rowena Reed, *Combined Operations in the Civil War* (Annapolis: United States Naval Institute Press, 1978), 98, 116.

8. Founded by James Gordon Bennett, the New York *Herald* (1835–1924) became one of the most vitriolic critics of the Lincoln administration and the Civil War. It took up the antiwar Democratic or "Copperhead" stand and bitterly opposed emancipation. Frank Luther Mott, *American Journalism: A History of Newspapers in the United States through 250 Years, 1690–1940* (New York: Macmillan, 1941), 229–38, 348–50.

9. At least eight regiments from South Carolina served in the Confederate First Corps, Army of the Potomac, commanded by Gen. P. G. T. Beauregard. *OR*, ser. 1, vol. 5, 825.

10. Hooker confirmed GES's observation, stating that "a majority of the young men of the country are with the rebel troops and those remaining are filled with terror." Southern Maryland remained notoriously pro-South, and Union troops spent their time seizing weapons, interdicting smuggling operations, and rooting out spies. Many civilians near Budd's Ferry (in Charles County) had relatives in the Confederate army across the Potomac in Virginia and provided them with supplies and information about Union troop movements. The county seats in Calvert and Prince Frederick Counties openly displayed the Confederate flag, while local rebel sympathizers threaten Union soldiers, brandished weapons, or made treasonous declarations. *OR*, ser. 1, 5:375–76, 386, 640; Charles L. Wagandt, *The Mighty Revolution: Negro Emancipation in Maryland, 1862–1864* (Baltimore: Johns Hopkins University Press, 1964), 20; Warren H. Cudworth, *History of the First Regiment, Massachusetts* (Boston: Walker, Fuller, 1866), 90–92.

11. The word is a contemptuous characterization of a Northern supporter of slavery and the South. John Russell Bartlett, *The Dictionary of Americanisms* (1849, reprint, New York: Crescent Books, 1989), 120.

12. Thomas Skinner was a storeowner and licensed liquor dealer who lived in Nanjemoy on the Potomac. Before the war, his store had been a center for Democratic partisans. As early as 1855, Skinner had been selling slaves to local buyers. Berlin, *The Destruction of Slavery*, 1:376; Wearmouth, *Abstracts from the Port Tobacco* Times, 2:24, 49, 109, 118, 137.

Headquarters of Hooker's Division,
Near Budd's Ferry, Doncaster, Md.,
Nov. 30, 1861.

Mr. Editor:—Although the charges are grave and numerous which we have to prefer against Union troops, the fact that they have opened up avenues of free intercourse between Northern and Southern black men, compels us to admit their invasion of Southern soil to be grand and beneficent. The minds of our brethren of the Southern States have been crowded and confused with the most strange and extravagant stories of life and customs in the North. I find a great many of the people about here who really believe that Northern people intend to sell the negroes of rebels, and all they can get. The wily master points his slave to this returned fugitive and the other, and says—"Now Jim, Sambo, Dick, don't you see these people are opposed to letting you go free? If I was a rebel they would take you and sell you to some outlandish place. Which would you rather do—stay with me or go with them?" The poor slave, who always dreads the auction block, gives the desired answer. If you ask him of what party his master is, Union or Rebel, he will say Union. How can they know the truth, when they see the Northern troops doing the dirty work of their masters, which a gentlemanly Confederate would scorn to do, and they see the Northern troops arresting supposed rebels, and guarding their slaves until executive clemency releases them. For instance, about the time our Division marched down here, the Indiana cavalry arrested a man by the name of Big Dick Posey.[1] This is his universal cognomen. He is the king rebel of Charles county. As soon as the arrest was made, his slaves were placed under guard. He was detected making signals with lights to the rebels on the Virginia shore. A man by the name of John Waite, colored, who was employed to work one of Posey's boats, also testified that he had frequently communicated with the other shore for him, carrying men and provisions. There is not a slave or free man within twenty miles that does not know that this man is in collusion with the enemy, and they see the Union troops holding his slaves while he undergoes the form and ceremony of government arrest. It is hard to convince these people that we are on the side of freedom. Untutored minds are always, more or less, material like the Pagan of India, who believes in no God unless he can feel him and see him with the natural eye.[2] They want the fact and the evidence practically, that we are on the side of freedom. No theory will satisfy them. That innate principal of man—love of liberty—tells them that the rights of man can bear no compromises. Another false notion impressed upon their minds is that the colored people of the North are in a suffering and starving condition. The falsehoods have been so earnestly and unblushingly stated by their masters, and corroborated by others, that there is no wonder their minds are influenced in some degree thereby.

I have taken pains to investigate the customs, living and condition of the folks here about. The houses are generally built of logs, mansions as well as quarters; that of the master sometimes floored, that of the slave the bare earth. One, two, or ten slaves, married and single, male and female, bundle in together. The interior of these hovels present perfect pictures of discomfort, yet the people here are those that talk so glibly of the poverty and misery of the Northern people. No den of misery, or sink of iniquity, in the lowest purlieu of any of our Northern cities, ever presented a scene of squalid misery equal to some of those I have witnessed during my sojourn here. I say again, that the war so far has produced at least one good result for us (if the devil does us a good turn, we must give the devil his due, and say he is a devilish good fellow); all those old false notions are being rapidly dissipated, and we are enabled now in a small degree, to indulge in the pleasure of an interchange of sentiments.

I see by recent advices that the advocates of emigration are hard at work in the preparation of their various schemes, as if affairs at home demanded no attention whatever. I believe emigration to be a good thing if kept within natural bounds, that is, not superinduced by undue and extravagant representations—it will then stimulate society in an industrial point of view, enlarge and extend social and commercial intercourse, unite and harmonize the various great families of men, and thus pave the way to a larger liberty, a more radical fraternity, and perfect equality, morally and politically, as well as socially amongst mankind; but I cannot, to save my heart, perceive the wisdom of raising the hue and cry of emigration about the ears of a nation at a time when we should be working might and main, tearing down a government, if unfriendly to our cause, or, if friendly, building it up.[3]

I find the Anglo to be a welcome visitor even here, in this region of darkness and slavery. One individual could hardly believe when he saw the Anglo, "dat niggers could do dat," and I am importuned continually by men in the army for chances to read your paper. They find in it matter of interest and importance which they can gather from no other source.

I see in Skinner's store a handbill posted which offers a reward of $50 for the return of a slave belonging to a Mr. Cox,[4] who lives near

Port Tobacco,[5] but if I mistake not Mr. Cox need not be so lavish with his money.

Folks across the river continue to pay their addresses to us in the form of shot and shell, but they have been so very frequent we disdain to notice them. I am full of expectancy, for during the coming week we may take up the line of march to join some one of the Southern Expeditions now preparing.[6] This to me is good news, for I long to be transported to the very heart of Cottondom if needs be. Query. Did Secretary Cameron sound the key-note of the war, when he endorsed the speech of Col. Cochran?[7] Times change and men change with them. The question of emancipation is vehemently discussed among the officers; the sentiments uttered by Col. Cochran reflecting those of the majority here. A violent discussion took place between a Colonel and Lieut. Colonel of the regiments a few days ago, during which one of them declared that before he would allow a slaveholder to take a fugitive from his camp he would throw up his commission. Since the Division has been here there has been a marked improvement in the appearance and condition of the men. Access to the whiskey jug is almost cut off;[8] but although the General has done all in his power to prevent the entrance of liquor into camp, still it finds its way there by some unknown means. A sailor and a soldier will do almost anything for a glass of grog. One fellow discovered that his musket barrel would hold just one pint, he straightway gets a pass, has himself and his musket filled, and comes into camp, and fills a famished comrade. Another nearly fills a stone jar, covers the top of it with butter, and passes in. Another buys a sack of potatoes, half of which prove to be whiskey-skins, and so they go, resorting to every device whereby the baneful beverage can be obtained.

G. E. S.

WAA, 14 December 1861.

1. GES probably refers to Richard B. Posey, a wealthy planter and slaveowner but may have confused him with Timothy Posey, who owned as many as ninety-four slaves. The treasonous activities of the Charles County Posey family were well known to Union authorities. A slave, possibly John Waite, hired by Timothy Posey and caught by Union troops crossing the Potomac, reported that Posey sent weapons, horses, and men every day to rebels in Virginia. Posey, whose house was situated on a bluff near Budd's Ferry, allegedly used mirrors or lights to communicate with rebels. Before the end of October 1861, Hooker arrested the family but gained no convictions. *WAA,* 7 December 1861; *OR,* ser. 1, 5:372, 384–85, 630, 632; *ORN,* ser. 1, 4:629, 675;

Walter H. Hebert, *Fighting Joe Hooker* (Indianapolis: Bobbs-Merrill, 1944), 63;
Wearmouth, *Abstracts from the Port Tobacco* Times, 2:13, 20, 57, 62, 115,
118, 141, 162.

2. GES, like most nineteenth-century Protestants, considered the non-
Christian religions of India as primitive, uncivilized, and idolatrous.

3. The Haytian Emigration Bureau, along with the African Civilization Society, attempted to keep black interest in emigration alive from 1860 to 1862.
Although nearly two thousand blacks from Canada and the United States re-
settled in Haiti, enthusiasm for the scheme ended by the close of 1862. Philadelphia, because of its large and relatively prosperous black population, was a
frequent target of emigrationists' appeals. In November 1860, James T. Holly
lectured there for the Haytian Emigration Bureau. Stephens's Banneker Institute debated the merits of Haitian emigration, where, in March 1861, William
P. Powell, the New York black abolitionist leader, denounced the scheme as
the abandonment of the "4,000,000 of your brethren in bonds." *BAP*, 5:108n.13;
WAA, 16 March 1861; Michael P. Johnson and James L. Roark, *Black Masters:
A Free Family of Color in the South* (New York: W. W. Norton, 1984), 284–85.

4. For Samuel Cox, see 10 January 1862 letter.

5. Port Tobacco, Maryland, situated on an inlet off the Potomac River thirty-two miles from Washington, D.C., had been a thriving port during the
colonial era. Union forces employed its fifty-foot wharf to unload supplies.
The town is usually remembered as a stopping point for John Wilkes Booth
after assassinating President Lincoln and as the home of George A. Atzerodt,
another Lincoln conspirator. *OR*, ser. 1, 5:409, 697; Kim R. Kihl, *Port Tobacco: A Transformed Community* (Baltimore: Maclay and Associates, 1982), 7–
8, 16–17, 22.

6. GES alludes to the Union victory at Port Royal, South Carolina, in ear-
ly November and other small-scale operations along the eastern coastline.
James M. McPherson, *Battle Cry of Freedom: The Civil War Era* (New York:
Oxford University Press, 1988), 370–72.

7. Simon Cameron (1799–1889), Lincoln's first secretary of war, eagerly
supported the enlistment of black soldiers. John Cochrane (1813–98), a two-
term member of Congress from New York, commanded the Sixty-fifth New
York Regiment. Cochrane, a staunch Democrat before the war, issued a surprise call on 13 November for the arming of blacks. He exclaimed that the
government should take "the slave by the hand, place a musket in it, and in
God's name bid him strike for the human race." *HTIECW*, 107; *WWWCW*,
131; Nicolay and Hay, *Abraham Lincoln*, 2:422; Benjamin P. Thomas and
Harold M. Hyman, *Stanton: The Life and Times of Lincoln's Secretary of War*
(New York: Alfred A. Knopf, 1962), 133.

8. U.S. Army regulations stated that "one gill of whiskey is allowed daily,
in case of excessive fatigue and exposure." Distribution of alcohol depended
entirely on individual commanders, and few could halt "unofficial" consumption of it. U.S. War Department, *Revised Regulations for the Army of the
United States, 1861* (Philadelphia: J. B. Lippincott, 1861), 244; Charles W.
Reed, *Hardtack and Coffee* (Boston: George M. Smith, 1887), 140–41.

Headquarters of Hooker's Division,
Near Budd's Ferry, Md.,
Dec. 6, 1861.

Mr. Editor:—Thanksgiving day was observed strictly amongst the New England men, which may be attributed to their descent, more directly than the rest, from a Puritan ancestry. One of the noblest peculiarities of their forefathers is love for the worship of Almighty God. I thought to myself as I strolled amongst them, of the days of which history speaks, when the praying Roundhead and the jeering cavalier met in deadly array; when Cromwell and the commonwealth fought against King Charles the First and the kingdom, one for equal rights and the habeas corpus—that great charter of civil and religious liberty; the other for the prerogative, for titles, and for dignities. Here are Massachusetts' liberty-loving sons ready to meet death amid the din and clash of arms, to preserve intact the institutions of their fathers. (I must admit that they battle for Liberty.) Beyond the Potomac stands the proud, haughty Southerner, fighting for and dreaming of real titles, dignities, and the annihilation of the vestiges of Liberty around him. Christianity and progressive civilization are the emblems that adorn the former; barbarism, ignorance, and moral imbecility disgrace the latter; in both instances, and the coincidences with one exception, is complete, we have no Cromwell![1]

The boys searched the country for miles around for turkeys, roasting pigs, geese, ducks, and everything else necessary to make up a holiday dinner, and as you pass their marquees, the olfactories are greeted by savory orders. What with the good dinners, the sermons, exemption from all duty, and the canteens of whiskey smuggled into camps, they enjoyed themselves hugely. The review or inspection of the Division was concluded to-day. The important business was intrusted to the Count de Paris[2] and Major——, of Gen. McClellan's staff. These notables arrived on the 2d instant, and of course were the guests of Gen. Hooker. The inspection was very rigid, and may be the precursor of an early movement of the Division. We may be said to be in Winter quarters, for log huts, wooden chimneys, and camp stoves, have made our canvas walls comfortable, and although you may say living out of doors, we are able to forget the fact, and talk of Christmas, for it comes apace, and before we can gather our senses,

will be here.—Nowhere in the United States did the Christmas holidays pass so gaily as in the Old Dominion; master as well as man
revelled in feasting and the whiskey jug.—Among the slaves it was a
season of happy re-unions, and of rest from a year's incessant toil.[3]
Wives and husbands, parents and children, hired long distances apart,
could then unite in the cordial greeting of Merry Christmas. But how
like a dream; a few days and hours, and the same old heart-burnings
and separations, the same old stripes and scars; perhaps by the next
Christmas many familiar faces are missing. Where is he or she who
was with us last Christmas? Sighing in some rice-field, or sorrowing
upon some cotton or sugar plantation in the far South—and so the
years rolled on—there seemed no help for the captive; but this Christmas finds Virginia a broad bloody battle field, and has become the
arena in which the fate of the nation is to be decided. Will her slaves
and slavemasters assemble in the feast, the song, and dance, this coming Christmas? or will the latter, amid the fresh graves scattered
around them, forget the convivialities of the season? I know the
former are watching the events of the hour, and while the walls of
their prison-house are crumbling to pieces around them, hope lights
up their hearts; bright and all-absorbing visions of liberty and freedom
crowd upon their mind. But how are matters at home? Thousands and
hundreds of thousands of homes are cheerless, the sparkling bumper[4]
will not be passed around so cheerily; the vacant seat will carry the
mind away to the battle-field and to the exposed camp—the whisper-
ing winds tell of the bitter cold and the probable suffering of father,
husband, brother, friend. But, disfranchised American, you, who of
right, feel but little more solicitude for the Northern soldier than for
the illy-clothed Southerner, how is it with you? Will you drink and
make merry while your brethren are hunted like beasts, and are the
hapless victims of cruelty, outrage, and assassination? Rather make
the coming Christmas a season of mourning and prayer, consultation
and organization, and of determined action. The path that leads to
liberty is bloody; prepare to tread its gory depths! Study the practice
and manual of arms—drill, drill, drill, night and day. Black men are
valorous, just give them the art of war, and they will make better
troops than will be furnished of any other people in the Western
Hemisphere, from the pale-faced Caucasian up to the nut-brown
Monteguman.[5]

"Roll on thou cheerful day,
When tyranny's proud sway,
Stern as the grave,
Shall top the ground be hurled,
And freedom's flag unfurled,
Shall wave throughout the world,
O'er every slave."

The news communicated in my last that we should probably be joined to some one of the Southern expeditions now fitting out, turns out to be as I feared, an idle rumor. We are most certainly joined to a Southern expedition, but landward, not seaward. All sorts of rumors are being whispered around. Some think the rebels about to cave in, others that they are meditating some terrible onslaught upon the Unionists. It is generally supposed that they are equal, if not superior to us in numbers. The rumors, coupled with the conscious weakness and timidity of the Northerners, and which the present inaction indisputably displays, make the troops here impatient and dissatisfied. Complaint is universal—doubts, fears, and a general demoralization, are stealing with a fatal certainty o'er them.—An advance of the army of the Potomac must be made, even at the risk of adding to the list another disastrous defeat. Perhaps before this reaches the eyes of your readers, the Federal army will have marched upon the strongholds of Manassas victorious, and the first step made towards the establishment of the Union with slavery; or perhaps instead, the Federal army will be driven back terror-stricken and dismayed; the Confederates panting with hell-born rage in the hot pursuit. Then will come the cry for Liberty and Union; then will emancipation be proclaimed, if not from the National Capitol, from Fortress McHenry;[6] if not from Fortress McHenry, from Independence Hall! It may be said that this is treason, but Christianity, humanity and civilization teaches that this is true patriotism. Perhaps another signal chastisement at the hands of the rebels, may prove by its effects a salvation of the country, and the regeneration of its slaves. Let the American people but say we are their brethren, and the millions of our race will flock to the national defence, and seal with blood their love for liberty, and devotion to the national cause—but call us men and brethren, and all the tears shed and wrongs suffered, all the scoffs, jeers and persecutions meted out to us ever since Crispus Attucks[7] fell the first martyr to the revolution, shall be buried in the very deep of forgetfulness. But I fear, rather than call us brethren, ! the invidious wretches who control the nation would let the rebel chief cover the North even to the St. Lawrence with his unopposed legions; such is the rancor and persistency of their hatred for our race. Millions of treasure, rivers of blood would be saved if the North would fortify themselves on all sides with justice and reconstruct their government upon the foundations of equity and truth. Perhaps Providence is now reserving us for great and important works.—"Thy wisdom, O Lord, is wonderful, it is high, I cannot attain unto it."

It becomes my painful duty to record the death of Mr. I Newton, to whom I have before referred in one of my communications [11 November 1861]. The greater part of his life was spent in bondage. Not until he was 58 did he receive his freedom. And before his manumission by the will of his deceased master four of his children were sold into Virginia. Poor man! he stood before me one week before his death and told me with tears in his eyes of his dear children. Obdurate facts willed that he should never gather those dear children around him. You remember there were some sixty or seventy slaves who escaped from the Virginia shore on board the U.S. steamer Live Yankee;[8] among this number were his three sons, Harry, Joseph and Thomas; the other child, a girl, Divinia, is at Richmond, Va. The tidings of their escape did not reach the family until several hours after his death. O that that news had reached them sooner, so that this fond father might have been soothed in the hour of his death with the consciousness that his children had escaped from their earthly hell!

A few days ago we had a visitor from the rebel camp on the opposite side of the river. It is said that his family is know to Gen. Hooker. He hails from New York. He tells the incredible story that he personally knows of two hundred persons who are ready to desert the rebel flag. He was well dressed, and has received no pay since spring.

The Indiana Regiment arrested two more at the mouth of the Patuxet. One of them is the son of Dr. Stewart.[9] In fact scores of these rebels are stealing home since an armed occupation of their state has become a fixed fact. Guards are posted at Mattawoman Creek and other inlets, to intercept these traitor rebels. It was discovered that the rebels had erected a battery opposite Deep Point, by which they could command the mouth of Mattawoman Creek, the point where the government land provisions. Five steamers and gun boats, among which were the

Harriet Lane[10] and Live Yankee, ran down on the 8th instant and shelled them out beautifully. It was most exhilarating to see the chivalry,

> "Winged with fear,
> Fleet as the wind,"[11]

flying over their sacred hills. The federal gunners proved themselves far superior to theirs. Nearly every shell fell with fatal precision among their teams, while hot shot fired their storehouses and barns. So far as I can learn there were no casualties among the fleet. A little boy was arrested as a fugitive when the division first arrived here, and carried back to Bladensburg, our former camping ground; forty-eight miles is the reckoned distance. He could not get north and has retraced his steps, and is again with us. Does he not deserve his liberty?

G. E. S.

WAA, 28 December 1861.

1. GES recites popular antebellum mythology that compared the American conflict with the English civil war. The chivalrous cavalier evoked images of the English gentry, aristocracy, and feudalism—inspired by the notion that slaves were an American version of the English peasantry. A gentleman of refined taste, the Southern cavalier resisted the encroaching, materialistic, and hypocritical Puritan Yankee. Northerners, especially New Englanders, viewed Puritan Roundheads as an antimonarchical force that defended liberty against the tyranny of the aristocracy and the influence of Catholicism. The English monarch Charles I (1600–1649) was beheaded near the end of the conflict, and Oliver Cromwell (1599–1658) established the English Protectorate. William R. Taylor, *Cavalier and Yankee: The Old South and American Character* (New York: Harper and Row, 1969); Goldwin Smith, *A History of England* (New York: Charles Scribner's Sons, 1957), 321–42.

2. Louis Philippe Albert d'Orleans [Comte de Paris] (1838–94), from the exiled family of the French monarchy, was a captain and aide-de-camp to George McClellan from September 1861 to July 1862. He later wrote the *History of the Civil War in America* (1876–88), a critical study of the Union army. WWWCW, 487; Stephen W. Sears, *George B. McClellan: The Young Napoleon* (New York: Ticknor and Fields, 1988), 115–16.

3. Some masters did not compel slaves to work on Sundays and most considered Christmas a holiday when slaves could visit spouses and family members at neighboring plantations. In many locations, three days were put aside for feasting and relaxation. Slaves might enjoy fruit, plum pudding, gingerbread, coffee, and alcohol that were unavailable the rest of the year. Frederick Douglass argued that slaveowners distributed enough alcohol to keep their slaves compliant. Masters visited slave cabins to distribute sugar to children and other items to adults. Singing and dancing might continue

late into the evening, while at other locations Christmas meant only time off to cultivate a private plot, inspect tools, or to receive a token reward of extra rations. Eugene D. Genovese, *Roll, Jordan, Roll: The World the Slaves Made* (New York: Random House, 1974); Charles Joyner, *Down by the Riverside: A South Carolina Slave Community* (Urbana: University of Illinois Press, 1984), 101–2, 127, 134–36; Donald Yacovone, "The Transformation of the Black Temperance Movement," *Journal of the Early Republic* 8 (Fall 1988): 290.

4. A bumper is a cup or glass, usually containing alcohol and filled to the brim.

5. The word is probably a printer's error for Montezuman, referring to the native people of Mexico.

6. Fort McHenry, famous for its successful resistance to British attacks during the War of 1812, sits on Chesapeake Bay. During the Civil War it housed civilians arrested for disloyalty or treason. Charles L. Wagandt, *The Mighty Revolution: Negro Emancipation in Maryland, 1862–1864* (Baltimore: Johns Hopkins University Press, 1964), 173–75; *OR*, ser. 1, 5:642.

7. Crispus Attucks (1723?-70), escaped slave from Framingham, Massachusetts, died on 5 March 1770 in the "Boston Massacre." For nineteenth-century blacks, Attucks became a symbol of defiance and revolution. Between 1858 and 1870 Boston blacks held annual celebrations to commemorate his death and the black contribution to American liberty. *DANB*, 18–19.

8. GES probably refers to the USS *Yankee*, a side-wheeled tug built in 1860. For a time it served as flagship of the Potomac Flotilla and frequently picked up escaping slaves. The *Official Record*, however, does not note the *Yankee* transporting so large a group. Paul H. Silverstone, *Warships of the Civil War Navies* (Annapolis: United States Naval Institute Press, 1989), 124; *ORN*, ser. 1, 4:662–63.

9. Richard H. Stewart, a staunch Confederate and the richest man in King George County, Virginia, was later arrested under suspicion of harboring Lincoln assassination conspirators John Wilkes Booth and David Herold. *WWWCW*, 625.

10. The *Harriet Lane*, originally built as a federal revenue cutter, was acquired by the navy in 1861. It served briefly in Virginia and on 6 December engaged rebel batteries along the Potomac. Silverstone, *Warships of the Civil War Navies*, 82; *ORN*, ser. 1, 5:3.

11. The quotation is possibly an adaptation of "fear lent wings to his feet" from Virgil's *Aeneid*, viii, 224.

Headquarters of Hooker's Division,
Near Budd's Ferry, Md.,
Jan. 4th, 1862.

Mr. Editor:—The Christmas Holidays in camp have been the fruitful themes of both pen and pencil. Editors, letter-writers, and artists, have burdened the popular fancy with truthful portraitures of the many ways the soldier passed his time. The sentinel on his post, the grotesque group, the blazing camp fire, the merry song, the boisterous dance, and the inevitable game of bluff, are as well conceived by the popular mind as though every man in the country was a soldier, and every town a camp; nothing then should be given, unless it be extraordinary, would we have it interesting.

Typhoid seems to be on the increase; I cannot learn the extent of the mortality, this is kept secret. One thing is certain, there is some disease or other now ravaging our ranks.[1] But by far the most important thing to be commented on, and the greatest evil to be abated is intemperance.[2] Next to slavery in enormity of evil stands intemperance. They are two great sins of the nation which threaten its very existence, the upper and nether millstones which threaten to grind into atoms all its elements of goodness and greatness. One of the first acts of Gen. McClellan when he assumed the chief command of the army was, to suppress the sale of liquors in camp, but no sooner was the order issued than unprincipled men in and out of the army began their successful smuggling and sale of the intoxicating beverages.[3] Hundreds of boxes of liquor find their way down here labelled, "Hair Tonic," "Pickles," "Schniedam Snapps," ect. I know one instance where two casks of "Red Eye" were buried in the ground, and the man who sold it had it so arranged that when he pumped the rum out, one would suppose that it came from the bowels of the earth, and thus he dispensed in copious draughts, disease and death to hundreds and thousands. But do not think, my dear sir, that intemperance is confined to the poor private; this is not the case. Men high in authority are the victims of the rum bottle. Some of the camps here are at times more like that of bacchanals, than enlisted soldiery. Brawls, riots, and midnight orgies, proclaim the supremacy of the drunken god.

On New Years day an officer upon the division staff, was ordered back to his regiment for drunkenness and riot. He is talented and educated, but has suffered rum to steal away his senses and bring disgrace. He must resign or be dishonored. On Christmas night a man by the name of Samuel Rodgers,[4] of Co. D., 26th Reg., Pa. Vol., died from intemperance. Just think of it, a man to die from excessive drinking in the U.S. Army, under the eye of military authority! I really believe that with ten thousand sober men, I could subdue the whole army of the Potomac, just let me have as much whiskey as I shall choose. It is a very common thing for men to get drunk on post and the officers to do the same on duty. A man, Cap.——, in one of the regiments here, is always drunk: it is his natural state. Water would astonish his stomach, just as whiskey would that of a *bona fide* tee-totaler.[5] The officers have what are called "Dial Clubs." The duty of the members is to keep all liquor out of sight by Dan May's process: i.e., throwing the skin of their bellies outside of it. They visit each other often, tatoo, and imbibe until one by one they are overcome by drunkenness; and this practice is not a local one, it reflects the universal practice here.

A word about the "contrabands" which Col. Graham[6] brought off with him from his expedition over in Virginia. A large number of the men are at work unloading the government boats at Liverpool Point;[7] they are well fed and clothed, and paid by the government. Their huts are comfortable and warm, being dug down into the ground about three feet, logged up, thatched with brush, and then daubed with mud. The interiors are neat and clean, and are far more tastefully fitted up than those of the poor whites and slaves any where about here. They are generally quite pleased with their new situations, but have very little confidence in those around them. They all prefer to be farther removed from the vicinity of their recent sorrows and trials.

Night before last a great light was to be seen over towards Aquia Creek. I have a suspicion that the rebels are burning their store-houses, and perhaps are retreating along the whole line of the Occoquan. Mark! when a movement is made it will be a sudden and startling one.

We have had weather cold enough indeed, but not until last night did hoary winter clothe himself in an icy garb, sparkling with chilling transparent gems. About 7 o'clock we had quite a snow storm, with a slight mixture of hail. This morning is beautifully clear; there is "not a cloud to dim the azure of the sky;" the cold is extremely painful. The sensation reminds me of that painful chilliness one feels when sailing to the leeward of an iceberg. It shocks every nerve, penetrates every pore of the skin.

I have learned this moment that the sutler of the 26th Pennsylvania Volunteers has been ordered to close his business instantly. He was detected with a large amount of whiskey labelled "Wigwam Tonic." A man belonging to the Excelsior Brigade—I could not find out his name or the company to which he belonged—of Col. Dwight's Regiment[8] drank of this "tonic," and, in a fit of insanity which it occasioned, blew out his brains. The miscreant! the murderer! he should not only be stopped from selling his goods, but should be incarcerated in Sing Sing[9] for life as a felon and a dangerous man to society.

G. E. S.

WAA, 18 January 1862.

1. Disease killed more soldiers in the Civil War than bullets or bayonets. Most generals assumed they would lose at least two men to disease for every one killed in combat. Dysentery killed the most, followed by typhoid and pneumonia. During the summer months, malaria became a feared killer. James M. McPherson, *Battle Cry of Freedom: The Civil War Era* (New York: Oxford University Press, 1988), 484–89.

2. The temperance movement proved enormously popular in Northern black communities. From the pulpit, the press, and at virtually every public forum, black leaders espoused the benefits of temperance. Stephens's Banneker Institute colleague Jacob C. White, Jr., advised blacks to avoid liquor so that "they should have men to fight their battles, and contend with our enemies for our rights." Donald Yacovone, "The Transformation of the Black Temperance Movement," *Journal of the Early Republic* 8 (Fall 1988): 281–97.

3. Alcohol consumption became chronic in Hooker's division. In December 1861, drunken soldiers from the Twenty-sixth Pennsylvania rampaged through Port Tobacco, resulting in twenty-one arrests. Shortly after McClellan assumed command of the Army of the Potomac, he rationed but did not prohibit whiskey to active troops. In a February 1862 circular, he condemned "the degrading vice of drunkedness" and encouraged "total abstinence." Bell Irvin Wiley, *The Life of Billy Yank: The Common Soldier of the Union* (Indianapolis: Bobbs-Merrill Company, 1952), quotation on 252; Warren H. Cudworth, *History of the First Regiment, Massachusetts Infantry* (Boston: Walker, Fuller, 1866), 104–6; Walter H. Hebert, *Fighting Joe Hooker* (Indianapolis: Bobbs-Merrill, 1944), 64–65; Stephen W. Sears, ed., *For Country, Cause, and Leader: The Civil War Journal of Charles B. Haydon* (New York: Ticknor & Fields, 1993), 89.

4. Pvt. Samuel Rodgers joined the Twenty-sixth Pennsylvania on 1 June 1861 and died of "apoplexy" at Budd's Ferry on 25 December. Bates, *History,* 1:365; Compiled Service Records, RG 94, National Archives.

5. The teetotal pledge signified complete abstinence from all alcoholic beverages. Although the origins of the term are uncertain, by the 1840s teetotalism—or total abstinence—became a mark of purity and respectability to temperance reformers. Ian R. Tyrrell, *Sobering Up: From Temperance to Prohibition in Antebellum America, 1800–1860* (Westport: Greenwood Press, 1979), 135–58, 215–16, 267–68, 298.

6. Historians credit Gen. Benjamin F. Butler with first describing Confederate slaves as "contraband," open to seizure by Union forces. The term soon

applied to all slaves who entered Union lines. Under the First Confiscation Act, Union commanders could seize all "property" used in support of the rebellion but had to return the slaves of loyal masters. Many Union officers remained unsure of what to do with the contraband, some of whom came from owners in Maryland. The federal commander of the navy's Potomac Flotilla sent his contraband to the Washington Navy Yard, where they might work for 40 cents a day plus food and housing. Col. Charles Kinnaird Graham (1824–89) led the Seventy-fourth New York Regiment. A fearless commander, Graham and four hundred of his men invaded Mathias Point, Virginia, on 9 November 1861 in an unauthorized mission. Because he returned without loss and with thirty to forty slaves, Hooker did not punish Graham for acting without orders. Contance M. Green, *The Secret City: A History of Race Relations in the Nation's Capital* (Princeton: Princeton University Press, 1967), 64; Berlin, *The Destruction of Slavery*, 16, 78; *HTIECW*, 161–62; *WWWCW*, 258; *OR*, ser. 1, 5:407–11; Hebert, *Fighting Joe Hooker*, 60–61.

7. Federal troops used Liverpool Point as a supply depot. Its sixty-foot wharf increased the flow of supplies, and Union forces made balloon observations on Confederate positions across the Potomac from the site. *OR*, ser. 1, 5:409–10, 697.

8. Col. William Dwight (1831–88) commanded the Seventieth New York Regiment. At the Battle of Williamsburg, 50 percent of his regiment became casualties, and he was wounded three times. *WWWCW*, 196–97; Warner, *Generals in Blue*, 134–35.

9. Sing Sing, the New York state prison at Ossining, was founded in 1825. David J. Rothman, *The Discovery of the Asylum: Social Order and Disorder in the New Republic* (Boston: Little, Brown, 1971), 79, 89, 101–3, 253–54.

Chapter 7

"Atrocious Deeds" and Heroic Acts

10 January 1862–21 March 1862

George Stephens showed how a war to save the Union became a war to end slavery. His correspondence helped prepare the ground for emancipation by exposing the horrors of slavery and smashing racial stereotypes. Popular depictions of African Americans as savages, barnyard animals, or hopelessly recreant children had filled the Northern press since the beginning of the nineteenth century. Whites, most of whom had never met an African American, held conflicting but universally derogatory views of Southern blacks. Whatever the image, the message remained the same: blacks were unfit for freedom.

Stephens challenged those views and put appealing human faces on the men and women who desperately wanted—and deserved—freedom. The conditions of slavery, not the slaves, he asserted, determined behavior, and when blacks enjoyed freedom they accomplished what whites often would not. "The black man under the incentives of Free labor, pay, and freedom," Stephens wrote on 2 March 1862, "goes blithely and gaily to his task; while the white man under the repulsiveness of forced labor and no pay, lounges about and skulks skulkily away."

Stephens's vivid portrayal of fugitive slaves who risked death to reach Union lines shattered popular notions of the contented slave. Although slave masters blamed Union troops for stealing their "property," the torrent of escaping humanity discredited those accusations with finality. Countless Virginia slaves who had fled bondage heroically recrossed the Potomac to rescue those left behind. A sympathetic Union officer warned one slave against returning to retrieve his family: capture meant certain death. But no warnings, no dangers could dissuade the man from his mission. He was "bound to get them," the officer discovered, "or die in the attempt."[1]

The Union army attempted to avoided the issue. If unwanted slaves appeared in Union camps, generals such as Joseph K. Mansfield, commander of the Department of Washington, ordered that they should not "be in any way harbored in the quarters and camps of the troops." George B. McClellan commanded his subordinates to exclude blacks from Union lines and repeatedly assured Maryland slaveowners that the army would do what it could to return their missing "property."[2]

But runaway slaves complicated the army's plans. Union troops could not readily determine which slaves belonged to loyal owners and which served the Confederate war effort and, thus, should be confiscated. Union officers found themselves besieged by irate slaveowners clamoring for their slaves and denouncing Yankee soldiers who either refused to help them or who assisted the runaways. The further the Union army pushed into rebel territory the more slaves entered its lines and the more annoying slave catchers, and the more haughty slaveowners, became. Union soldiers increasingly sympathized with the slaves' plight. "Two years of war," one soldier wrote in 1863, "have made more abolitionists than the lectures of Wendle Phillips and Gerit Smith and Wm Lyod Garison would have made in one hundred years."[3]

Many Yankees enjoyed watching masters brutalize the slaves they recovered from army camps. Some even participated in the beatings. Others became sickened by the inhumanity and, as Stephens documents, chased the slave catchers from their camps. In one astonishing case, New York troops who saw masters flogging recaptured slaves released the blacks and thrashed the owners. Those soldiers who resented the role of slave catchers, forced upon them by men of questionable loyalty or by military decree, found powerful allies back home. Newspapermen such as Horace Greeley provoked debate over fugitive slaves by denouncing orders that compelled soldiers to assist slave catchers. Gov. John A. Andrew spoke with equal fervor and informed the secretary of war that "Massachusetts does not send her citizens forth to become the hunters of men."[4]

1. Reid Mitchell, *Civil War Soldiers: Their Expectations and Their Experiences* (New York: Simon and Schuster, 1988), 124.
2. *OR*, ser. 2, 1:760; Berlin, *The Destruction of Slavery*, 1:161–65.
3. Mitchell, *Civil War Soldiers*, 104.
4. Barbara Jeanne Fields, *Slavery and Freedom on the Middle Ground:*

Maryland during the Nineteenth Century (New Haven: Yale University Press, 1985), 104; Berlin, *The Destruction of Slavery,* 1:353–54.

* * *

Headquarters of Hooker's Division,
Near Budd's Ferry, Md.,
Jan. 10th, 1862.

Mr. Editor:—Our bitter cold has been succeeded by a season of mildness and sunshine, and any quantity of mud and water is spread out around us, that we may perform laborious feats of pedestrianism. Oh, omnipresent mud! soft, fathomless mud! grey, red, saffron colored. The swine are in ecstacies, and the negro drivers are joyous; but the soldiers are cheerless. One takes a step, down goes the inevitable left deeper, deeper. One then begins to think, to what muddy depths will the foot descend before it finds bottom; then we move step by step, sounding for bottom with one foot as we walk, like the leadsman on shipboard, we to avoid deep bottom, he the shallow.

The talk of war with England absorbs all other topics of conversation;[1] the enemy in our face is forgotten, the belching cannon are unheeded. The voluminous details of miniature battles remain unrehearsed, all the usual amount of braggadocio, American white men indulge in, burden the ear. To hear them talk, they can whip the whole civilized world, and the barbarous too, including the Southern Confederacy. Of course this is all nonsense, and comes with a bad grace from men who have borne insult upon insult to their national flag; who have been kicked and cuffed by Southern gentlemen (!), whose ephemeral military fame has waned, whose love for liberty has grown cold, and who stand gazing with terror and dread on the entrenchments of an insurgent foe whom they dare not face. But a war with England is, I think the most improbable thing imaginable. It is the old hue and cry to kindle into a flame the scattered embers of Unionism.[2] I have no doubt but that the Administration will magnify all differences between the two governments, perhaps step to the very verge of hostilities to all appearances; but to engage in actual war, never! But a war with England, to the eye of emancipationists is no very calamitous contingency; for the four millions of newly made freemen of the country alone, could defend the United States against any and all forces the other could array against them. I know that the temporizers are tremulous—they know that a war with Great Britain is an edict for emancipation, or, if not, it is defeat, bankruptcy and a dismembered Union. All of these suggestions show one thing: that is, the negro is a power, and I confess to one thing; namely, I cannot imagine which would be the best for us, Union with emancipation, or disunion without. Where are our black leaders? Why don't they give some light on this subject? Query. Will the Southern Confederacy very soon be recognized as an independent power by the United States authorities?[3]

I learned to-day that the firing heard towards Aquia Creek, mentioned in my last, proceeded from the guns of some of the Federal gunboats. It is said they attacked the rebel depot at the mouth of the Creek and laid it in ruins, destroying a large quantity of stores and provisions, and peppering the batteries most profusely. These fellows cannot stand the gunnery of negroes, for very many of the boats are manned by them.[4]

The contraband goods trade is still kept up by the rebels down the river. The General received notice of the fact and sent scouts out to arrest any person found engaged in unlawful practice. They came upon a party of men who attempted to make their escape, when they came upon the goods already piled up on the beach; blankets, shoes, medical stores and flannel. Everything necessary to the comfort of the slaveholder's army were found nicely packed away in boxes. Three army wagon loads were brought over to the Commissary department here on last Monday.[5]

One of the most cruel and atrocious deeds of the barbarous slavemaster was perpetrated by one Samuel Cox,[6] living five miles below Port Tobacco, who is said to be an ex-state representative, a returned rebel, the Captain of a Calvary company organized for the rebel army, but disbanded by the Federal troops, and a contraband trader. When Col. Dwight, of the Excelsior Brigade, scoured that portion of the country with his regiment, Jack Scroggins, a slave, reported to the Colonel that Cox and his confederates had secreted quite a large amount of ammunition and arms, and true enough, these arms and ammunition were found in Cox's house and in an adjoining marsh. The regiment moved down to its present encampment above Hilltop. Jack joined them, and this was about eleven miles from his home. Cox dared to lay claim to his slave, and under the promise that he would not harm the slave he was surrendered up to him, but not without difficulty, for the men protested and forcibly rescued him when an officer rode up and declared he would shoot the first man that again interfered with the master, and thus was this man returned to bondage by an officer of the United States army. Such was the reward of disinterested loyalty. Cox, the cursed fiend, tied the man to his horse and rode at a rapid rate, the poor slave running to keep up behind him. When he left the regiment he had on a pair of good shoes, but when he reached his master's house his shoes were gone, and his bleeding feet were found to be bursting open from coming in contact with pebbles and stones. He had been dragged eleven miles behind his master's horse! They arrived home in the evening about 11 o'clock on a Friday. He tied him to a tree and called his overseer, Franklin Roby and a man by the name of John Robinson.[7] They commenced whipping him about twelve o'clock and whipped him until three o'clock, three hours taking turns with the whip, when one was tired and breathless another would apply the lash. The only words he uttered up to two o'clock were, "I shall not live after this." "Oh, no you rascal I intend to kill you!" said Cox. "Mr. Cox," said Robinson, "he is dying." "No he is not. He is stout-hearted and able-bodied. He can stand as much more. However, give me the whip, let his blood be upon my head," replied Cox. The lash was then applied until about two hours before day. Say the narrators about 3 o'clock he was cut down and sank to the earth insensible. He had on a new cotton shirt when they began to whip him, and when they were done there was nothing left of it but the collar-band and the wristbands. Then commenced the rubbing down to bring back sensibility, but all of no avail. Their unfortunate victim breathed his last before sun-down on Saturday evening. Thus perished a loyal negro at the hands of a traitor. Oh, what a terrible reward for patriotism; death in its worst, and hideous form, by torture! Yet the villain who did this is at liberty! This is the way United States officers treat traitors. They would plunge all of the country's wealth, learning and prosperity in a vortex of ruin; yes even hurl it from amongst the family of nations. But my dear sir, when I dwell on the diabolism of the deed my hand trembles, my nerves lose their steadiness, my mind its self-possession.

Another of these Southern hounds a Dr. Smoot,[8] crossed the Potomac last May and returned in the latter part of November. He lives in the same neighborhood with Cox. He has a "safeguard" he says and crosses the river in a professional capacity; plausible is it not? Well he had been home a short time when he felt it necessary to whip one of the children of his slave named Nace Dorsey. The boy managed to get away when Smoot ordered the father to catch him and bring him back. This the father refused to do, when Smoot called for his gun and said he would shoot him. The poor man tried to get away, when Smoot levelled his piece and killed him in his tracks! The murderer was arrested but released on his patrol of honor!

A short time before Smoot killed Nace Dorsey he attempted to kill a man by the name of Henry Young. He ordered Young to his barn to get flogged, when the latter told him he would not allow him to flog him. Smoot had a double barrelled gun in his hand, and Young kept close to him, that he might not level it at him, and followed him to the barn. When they reached it Smoot stepped back and levelled his piece, when Young with the agility of a cat sprang upon him, wrenched it from him and shivered the breach to pieces over his head.[9] Carrying the stockless barrels with him he fled across the river and was arrested by the Virginians as a runaway slave and locked up in the Rappahannock gaol.[10] He remained there four days with four others besides himself, broke gaol, released his comrades, and found his way to the banks of the Potomac, signaled a passing steamer, was taken on board and carried to Washington, and I heard that he had returned to his home within a week or so. He is a brave man, and one of more than ordinary intelligence. There are many of the same sort about here.

I learned to-day that a captain in one of the regiments here is *particeps criminis*[11] of kidnapping a free colored boy who joined the regiment when at Bladensburg and whose mother lives in Washington city.[12] Should this meet the eye of any friend of the cause in that city perhaps he may be able to forward to the office of the Anglo her address. I know the boy well. He can be found no where. He was spirited away during my temporary absence from camp. We are determined to have him and to bring to justice the guilty parties if there is any justice for them to be brought to.

G. E. S.

WAA, 18 January 1862.

1. On 8 November 1861, the U.S. Navy's *San Jacinto* stopped the British mail steamer *Trent* on the high seas and seized two Confederate commissioners, James M. Mason and John Slidell, in violation of Britain's neutral rights. Public meetings throughout England urged retaliation. Although they settled the incident amicably, for months the two nations verged on war. Gordon H.

Warren, *Fountain of Discontent: The Trent Affair and the Freedom of the Seas* (Boston: Northeastern University Press, 1981).

2. GES was not alone in speculating on this possibility. In April 1861, Seward secretly advised Lincoln that a foreign war, perhaps over French and British intervention in Mexico, might help unify the country and avert civil war. Lincoln ignored the outrageous proposal. Benjamin Thomas, *Abraham Lincoln: A Biography* (New York: Alfred A. Knopf, 1952), 253–54.

3. GES refers to the central diplomatic problem facing the Lincoln administration. The North never accepted the legitimacy of secession and maintained that the war was an internal domestic conflict. But the government's imposition of a blockade—a weapon of war used against sovereign states—implied to foreign powers that the North accepted Southern independence. Furthermore, the conduct of the war, such as prisoner exchanges and adherence to internationally accepted rules of war, also suggested that the conflict was not a civil war but one between nations. James M. McPherson, *Ordeal by Fire: The Civil War and Reconstruction* (New York: Alfred A. Knopf, 1982), 218–19.

4. Almost ten thousand blacks served in the Union navy during the war and probably many more worked as government laborers. Although the navy relegated blacks to the lowest ranks, it did not discriminate in pay or maintain segregated vessels. Berlin, *The Black Military Experience*, 14n.22, 18n.30, 53.

5. Illegal trading continued throughout the war and was especially strong along the Potomac River.

6. Samuel Cox (1819–?), a wealthy Charles County tobacco planter, railroad promoter, Democratic politician, and a notorious slaveowner, brutally murdered Jack Scroggins. Cox admitted to killing his slave, whipping him to death for escaping, but Union authorities never prosecuted him. The Scroggins case came to the nation's attention through articles in the New York *Tribune*, the Baltimore *American*, and the *WAA*. Berlin, *The Destruction of Slavery*, 1:348; *WAA*, 5 April 1862; *The Biographical Cyclopedia of Representative Men of Maryland and District of Columbia* (Baltimore: National Biographical Publishing, 1879), 412; Wearmouth, *Abstracts from the Port Tobacco Times*, 2:49–50, 128–29, 3:67.

7. Frank Roly was Cox's overseer and with the help of two other men—perhaps also Cox's employees—participated in Scroggins's murder. Berlin, *The Destruction of Slavery*, 1:348.

8. Dr. Andrew J. Smoot owned Green Spot Plantation in Charles County. His troubles with runaway slaves began as early as 1857, and during the Civil War Smoot frequently attempted to retrieve runaways from Union camps. On one occasion, he complained to the War Department that soldiers from the Twenty-sixth Pennsylvania had hounded him out of camp, showering him with stones and yelling, "Shoot him, bayonet him, kill him, pitch him out, the nigger Stealer the nigger driver." Smoot and other white Charles County leaders survived the war with their power and continued to dominate local politics into the 1870s. *WAA*, 24 August 1861; Kim R. Kihl, *Port Tobacco: A Transformed Community* (Baltimore: Maclay and Associates, 1982), 90; Bar-

bara Jeanne Fields, *Slavery and Freedom on the Middle Ground: Maryland during the Nineteenth Century* (New Haven: Yale University Press, 1985), 102, 233n.36; Berlin, *The Destruction of Slavery*, 1:360–362; *ORN*, ser. 1, 5:302; Wearmouth, *Abstracts from the Port Tobacco* Times, 2:49, 140; 3:67.

9. The Port Tobacco *Times* provided a more sinister version of the Smoot-Young incident. It claimed that Smoot had chastised "Harry" Young, his plantation foreman, for a minor act of insubordination. Young then ignored Smoot's orders and stalked off into the woods with an axe. The next day, the shotgun-toting Smoot confronted Young, who apologized for his behavior. Satisfied with his slave's contrite remarks, Smoot laid down his gun and walked away. Young then seized the weapon and shattered its stock over Smoot's head. *WAA*, 24 August 1861, citing the Port Tobacco *Times*, 8 August 1861.

10. Gaol is a variant spelling of jail.

11. The term means "partner in crime."

12. The boy and his mother were James Henry Barnes and Sarah Barnes; see 29 January 1862 letter.

Hooker's Division,
Near Budd's Ferry, Charles Co. Md.,
Jan. 20, '62.

Mr. Editor: The weather here is very disagreeable—warm, sultry and damp; and the mud is the same fathomless and boundless sea referred to in my last. Within the month past there has not been much firing by the rebels. They seemed to have at least realized the utter folly of wasting ammunition, when their national finances, like our own, are bankrupt; but the monotony was suddenly disturbed on last Saturday night when the Pensacola[1] passed their batteries; but, although they hurled messengers of death and destruction at her quick and fast, she passed unharmed.

There is an order here from headquarters to return all slaves to their masters, and to exclude them from the lines.[2] There are upwards of two hundred fugitive slaves hovering around this camp, to which may be added some seventy employed at Liverpool Point by the government unloading vessels, etc. When the division moves, if ever it does, a black army will move with it, and all the Sewards[3] and McClellans in the country cannot halt that army. A case was brought to the notice of the General, which I think compelled him to ask for information. Let me remark here that Gen. Hooker is sound on the question of the vigorous prosecution of the war. He is a regular officer; but mark

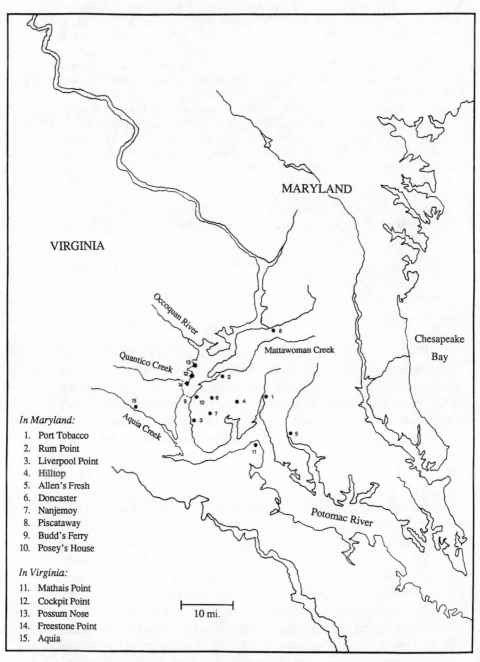

MARYLAND

VIRGINIA

Occoquan River

Quantico Creek

Mattawoman Creek

Chesapeake
Bay

13
12
14
2
8
15
9
10 6 4 1
3 7
5
11

Aquia Creek

Potomac River

In Maryland:
1. Port Tobacco
2. Rum Point
3. Liverpool Point
4. Hilltop
5. Allen's Fresh
6. Doncaster
7. Nanjemoy
8. Piscataway
9. Budd's Ferry
10. Posey's House

In Virginia:
11. Mathais Point
12. Cockpit Point
13. Possum Nose
14. Freestone Point
15. Aquia

10 mi.

Map 4. Maryland and Virginia along the Lower Potomac River

me, he will make his mark should he ever get his command on the enemy's soil. The case I refer to was that of the slaves of a man by the name of Stonestreet,[4] who owned some nine hundred or a thousand acres of land between Mattawoman Creek and Piscataway, and claimed ownership to about thirty persons. He joined the rebel army last May, and by power of attorney transferred his claim to one Jenkins; and when this place was occupied by the Federal troops, all of that portion of the estate which may be called "moveable," disappeared, with the exception of an old man, a woman and four children. These few that were left behind only because they could not get away, were robbed of all their provisions by some of the members of the Excelsior Brigade, and they were left in a starving condition. No one dared to lay claim boldly to them, and they were forced to come into camp to see whether they could not be sent to Washington, there to be employed by the government. The general could not pass them to Washington because they were the slaves of a citizen of a loyal State, but would give them employment at Liverpool Point. He could take no action on United States soil. As a military commander he could not adjudicate a civil case. The instructions he has received from the Commander-in-Chief to investigate the cases of slaves in his lines, and to employ those whose masters have employed them or are engaged themselves in the rebel service, gives him power, if he chooses to exercise it, to confiscate them. This old man, the woman and children, are now near Port Tobacco, living with some of Stonestreet's family. Parties here have done their utmost to give them a safe passage, but there is so much to do in this direction that they are unequal to the task. We long for a movement anywhere, we don't care where, Northward or Southward.

We have at least one man who is a martyr, so far as position in the army goes. A little boy belonging to a man somewhere in Nansenov[5] ran away from his master, and was kept by the teamsters of the 11th Massachusetts Regiment. He was captured by the slave-hunters; came back, and ran away the second time. The slavehunters reported to headquarters that the boy was again amongst them. Col. Van Dyke,[6] of the 26th Regiment of Pennsylvania Volunteers ordered Isaac Coburn of the 11th Massachusetts Regiment,[7] who was boss teamster of the 26th, to search for the boy and bring him to his tent; Coburn refused, declaring that he did not enlist in the army to hunt slaves, nor would he hunt them for any one, and the slavehounds have tried to disgrace him: they have reduced him to the [words missing], but instead of this being a disgrace to him, it is an honor; and he may live to see the day when he can look down with contempt on the cringing, cowardly enslavers of men. They took the boy, and will perhaps whip him to death, as was poor Jack Scroggins. If they do not whip him to death he will be back here very soon. There is quite an audible murmur here about the return of fugitives. I expect to see the time very shortly when more than one slavehunter will bite the dust. An officer of high rank told one of them some time ago that in a very short time he would not guarantee his (the hunter's) life five minutes in the lines on a slave hunt.

Last evening the death like stillness which has brooded over the rebel batteries since the passage of the Pensacola, was broken by the most deafening volley of artillery I have heard since I have been here. The sight was truly beautiful. Flash after flash would burst out away across this broad river away in mid air like rockets—the shells would fly exploding with as great a concussion as the piece that discharged them. As the shells pass through the air the sound is startling. As they sonorously ring and whistle one feels as if they were fell demons flying through the air seeking whom they can devour. You may form some idea of their destructive power, when I tell you that if they will burst at the point of contact, say 64 pounder shells, they will plow up the earth to the depth of four feet and form a well three feet in diameter. There must have been an unusual number of vessels passing last night to have called forth such a pyrotechnical display.

I have noticed in the "Anglo-African" on the 4th inst., a letter from Dr. M. R. Delany[8] to Dr. J. M'Cune Smith,[9] and headed "Important movement." I had made up my mind to call upon our leading men to guide our steps in the present dark and gloomy political wilderness. A convention of leading negroes at this time would wield a moral and political influence in this nation second to none other before convened.[10] The higher the order of talent displayed by its members, the weightier will be its influence. It should not be too Democratic: that is, it should not be composed of a numerous membership; three persons from each state; you would thus keep out babblers and asses who wish to hear themselves talk. We want those of our representative men who have shown their ability to grapple with the mighty and momentous issues upon which is suspended the destiny of the teeming millions of our race. The age we live in is truly said to be one of ideas, and it is the aggregation of ideas that constitutes the aegis of power. Three members from each state would be select and sufficiently numerous. Every organized society, whether religious, social, or benevolent, should be taxed with a sufficient sum to publish thousands of copies of the deliberations to be scattered over the world, as the collected wisdom of a people who have resisted and triumphed over the most unyielding despotism the world ever saw—the despotism of American Slavery, and that the time has come when they can dictate terms to the trembling autocrat. I know what I am saying; the eternal logic of facts tells me that the negro henceforth and forever, holds the balance of power in this country. And I exultingly declare it, and what is more, he is destined to achieve more for the cause of christianity and progressive civilization than the mean money loving Saxon. The loftiest type of human progression cannot be reached by the Saxon. Civilization but makes his barbarism exquisite. Who but polished savages could have spent whole lives in rearing up that monument of shame which the pro-slavery literature of this country forms. I can speak of one body in Philadelphia, a responsible body, the "Social, Civil, and Statistical Association,"[11] having the learning and wealth of that city amongst its membership, that should choose three delegates for Pennsylvania. What do you think of it gentlemen?

G. E. S.

WAA, 1 February 1862.

1. The USS *Pensacola*, built in 1858, carried about twenty guns of varying sizes. On 12 January 1862, at 5 A.M., rebel batteries at Cockpit Point fired on the ship as passed in the dark but inflicted no damage. Paul H. Silverstone, *Warships of the Civil War Navies* (Annapolis: United States Naval Institute Press, 1989), 37; *OR*, ser. 1, 5:698, 1032; *ORN*, ser. 1, 5:16–17.

2. In December 1861, Hooker asked McClellan what he should do with the increasing number of fugitive slaves entering his camps. McClellan informed him that all slaves who had not been employed as workers for the Confederate army "are to be dismissed from your camp." *OR*, ser. 1, 5:642, ser. 2, 1:813–14; Berlin, *The Destruction of Slavery*, 80, 174–75.

3. William H. Seward (1801–72) served as secretary of state in the Lincoln and Andrew Johnson administrations. His declarations during the 1860 campaign that African Americans might not be capable of self-government proved bitterly disappointing to black leaders. *BAP*, 5:88–89.

4. GES may refer to either Nicholas or Benjamin G. Stonestreet, members of a prominent Charles County family and local Democratic politicians. Wearmouth, *Abstracts from the Port Tobacco* Times, 2:50, 3:67.

5. This probably refers to Nanjemoy, a small town southwest of Port To-bacco on the Potomac River.

6. Lt. Col. Rush Van Dyke joined the Twenty-sixth Pennsylvania on 5 May 1861 and was discharged on 11 April 1862. He was held under arrest for unspecified causes before his release on 27 July 1862. Compiled Service Records, RG 94, National Archives; Walter H. Hebert, *Fighting Joe Hooker* (Indianapolis: Bobbs-Merrill, 1944), 65.

7. Neither an Isaac Coburn nor a George Coburn—GES corrected the name in the 29 January 1862 letter—served in the Eleventh Massachusetts. Stephens may have meant Gridley B. Coburn of the First Massachusetts Regiment, which also camped at Budd's Ferry. Coburn enlisted on 22 May 1861 and was discharged for disability on 20 April 1863. *Massachusetts Soldiers, Sailors*, 1:24.

8. Martin R. Delany (1812–85), black nationalist and African emigration-ist, published the Pittsburgh *Mystery*, an antislavery newspaper, from 1843 to 1848 and coedited Frederick Douglass's *North Star*. Disillusioned by American racism, Delany moved to Canada West, made plans to found a black settlement in West Africa, and lectured throughout the North, Canada, and Great Britain to promote his venture. In 1863 he abandoned his scheme to join the Union war effort. He became a recruiter and a major in the U.S. Army, the highest rank achieved by a black during the war. GES mentions Delany's *Anglo-African* letter that called upon black leaders to sanction both sides of emigration question, supporting the right of blacks to decide their own des-tiny. "Is it true," he wondered, "that we are not to be permitted anywhere to govern ourselves, but must have white rulers? Have we no other destiny?" *BAP*, 4:129–30n.6; *WAA*, 4 January 1862.

9. James McCune Smith (1813–65), the son of former slaves, became one of New York's most influential black leaders. He attended Scotland's Glas-gow University and eventually earned three academic degrees, including doctor of medicine. He helped lead the effort to win black suffrage in New York and ably represented black interests at many state and national black conventions. Smith became a fierce opponent of colonization and all emigra-tionist schemes, especially Delany's African emigration venture and the Haytian Emigration Bureau. *BAP*, 3:350–51n.8, 5:100–105.

10. The convention GES called for did not take place until 1864. The National Convention of Colored Men met on 4–7 October 1864 in Syracuse, New York. Delegates from eighteen states founded the National Equal Rights League, an organization that promoted black suffrage, civil rights, and a thor-ough reconstruction of the South. It formed auxiliaries in most states and in Pennsylvania helped end the Jim Crow transportation system and restore black suffrage. *BAP*, 5:304–7.

11. Philadelphia's Social, Civil, and Statistical Association, founded in 1860, counted such wealthy blacks as William Still and Stephen Smith and some Banneker Institute members among its ranks. It fought to integrate the city's public transportation system and became an important civil rights or-

ganization. The group continued the battle for black rights after the war but disintegrated when influential black leaders such as Robert Purvis, who opposed anything that smacked of separatism, withdrew their support. Jane H. Pease and William H. Pease, *They Who Would Be Free: Blacks' Search for Freedom, 1830–1861* (1974, reprint, Urbana: University of Illinois Press, 1990), 168; James M. McPherson, *The Struggle for Equality: Abolitionists and the Negro in the Civil War and Reconstruction* (Princeton: Princeton University Press, 1964), 233; Philip S. Foner, *Essays in Afro-American History* (Philadelphia: Temple University Press, 1978), 59, 61, 66; Robert Purvis to Parker T. Smith, 22 February 1867, box 2G, LGC, HSP.

Hooker's Division,
Near Budd's Ferry, Charles Co. Md.,
Jan. 29, '62.

Mr. Editor,—It seems to me that the elements do really conspire against the Union arms. It was said, and with apparent good reason, that so soon as the frost hardened the roads sufficiently to admit the transportation of artillery and baggage trains, the Grand army of the Potomac would make an advance. But since this declaration was made Jack Frost has become refractory, in the dark hours of twilight he breathes a fragile firmness, a sort of crust over the soft yielding mud, which is dispelled by the sun's first rays. This alternate thawing and freezing does more to render the road impassable than if the atmosphere continued above the freezing point. Thus Jack Frost has become, instead of an ally, an alien to the Federal cause.

If Manassas Gap, or even Richmond, the metropolis of rebeldom presented an easy conquest, this army, this "slumbering giant," could not budge an inch: here it would have to lie at its huge length, barricaded in the mud.

I committed an error in my last, please correct. Francis Coburn, should read George Coburn. I will make a few remarks upon this case, so that there shall be no misunderstanding of it. An order was sent up to the 26th Regiment Pa. Vols., by Gen. Hooker, to send outside the lines a boy who was claimed as a fugitive from slavery; this was the extent of that order. Lieut. Col. Van Dyke, who is ever ready to do the bidding of slave master and kidnapper, transcended the intent and spirit of that order by ordering this teamster to bring the boy to his tent, for the purpose of handing him over to the pretended master; thus constituting himself without any authority a judge and a civil magistrate. His duty, according to General Hooker's own statement was to have dismissed the slave catchers, to have had no communication whatever with them, and to have sent the boy with a corporal's guard outside the regimental lines; but the poor, old, imbecile fellow was so ignorant that he did not know his duty in a case so plain as this. George Coburn knew that General Hooker nor Colonel Van Dyke had any shadow of authority to command him to become the enslaver of men, and he peremptorily refused to obey the order of Colonel Van Dyke; and it was for disobedience of this infamous order that he was disrated. Mr. Coburn belongs to 11th Regiment Mass. Vols. (Col. Blaisdell).[1]

We have the boy who was kidnapped through the connivance of a certain officer belonging to the division, again with us. He was discovered about fifteen miles from here, in the custody of one James Maddock, a regular kidnapper, an associate with Skinner. This Skinner has already served a term at the Richmond jail for kidnapping. I may remark here that this Maddock was in company with the parties whom Van Dyke surrendered the above mentioned slave. As soon as the boy was discovered they removed him from Maddock's house to Skinner's. Col. Small, on hearing of the boy's disappearance became highly indignant, and sent over to Skinner's and had the boy brought over to camp in a most deplorable condition. He met with a terrible accident playing with a miniature cannon. He received a whole charge of powder in his face, and will lose the sight of both his eyes. This is most terrible. He is an intelligent boy and about twelve years of age. I will give his own statement verbatim.

"My name is James Henry Barnes. My mother and father are dead. Her name was Sarah Barnes. Before she died we lived at 110 Massachusetts Avenue, Washington city; after her death I was sent to the poor house. I left there and came into Camp Union last October, and have been with the division ever since. Maddock asked me whether I would like to live with him, and said he would give me a horse to ride, plenty of good things to eat, plenty of fine clothes to wear, and he bought me about a half dollar's worth of cakes and candies. He asked me to get in his wagon; I got in; he took me to his house, which is about fifteen miles from here; I staid there about three weeks; he sent me from there to Skinner's, and about an hour before I was brought away from Skinner's I got my face hurt. Captain Webb and Lieutenant Snow[2] were at Maddock's house when I was there; they told me to take care of their horses. Captain Webb and Maddock are old cronies; I overheard Maddock say that I was worth one hundred and eighty-five dollars."

This is the lad's statement, which was not even shaken by cross-examination. While the case is a plain one, and the facts prove beyond a shadow of doubt that this boy was kidnapped, yet it is impossible to bring the parties to justice. But while justice sleeps the moral turpitude of this act fastens upon the participators in the deed the ineffable scorn of all true and honest men. I pity the boy—for he is doomed never to see the light of day—he is stone blind for life. He is well cared for however, and is attended by a skillful army physician who takes great interest in his case.

G. E. S.

P.S. Jan. 30th. A couple of "Secesh" ladies were brought into camp this morning. Upon information of a slave by the name of "Jim," they were arrested for furnishing aid and comfort to the rebels.[3]

Among other things, about thirty pairs of stockings were found on their premises already labeled C.S.A. One of them admitted that she had a brother in the rebel army, and when they rode past the Union flag one of them turned up her nose in contempt for the stars and stripes. The slave catchers are expected here next Saturday in pursuit of "Jim," but a thousand hearts are pledged to secure him his freedom. Returning fugitive slaves is growing daily to be up hill work.

G. E. S.

WAA, 8 February 1862.

1. Col. William Blaisdell (1817–64) served in the Eleventh Massachusetts from 13 June 1861 until 23 June 1864, when he was killed near Petersburg while in command of the Corcoran Legion. Compiled Service Records, RG 94, National Archives; *Massachusetts Soldiers, Sailors,* 1:737.

2. GES mentions Newton L. Webb and William B. Snow of the Twenty-sixth Pennsylvania, Company I, both of whom joined the unit on 31 May 1861 and resigned in January 1862. Bates, *History,* 1:375.

3. The arrest of women was not uncommon nor without cause. In one case, the wife of a Maryland secessionist singlehandedly procured enough arms, cartridges, and supplies to equip five hundred men. John Thomas Scharf, *History of Maryland from the Earliest Period to the Present Day,* 3 vols. (Baltimore: John B. Piet, 1879), 3:445–47.

Hooker's Division,
Near Budd's Ferry, Charles Co. Md.,
Feb. 6th, '62.

Mr. Editor.—Since my last we have had quite a little snow storm, which hid the mud for once at least. The snow commenced to fall on the evening of the 2d instant, and on the afternoon of the following day when it ceased, it lay to the depth of four inches. You may judge what a charming relief this must have been to us. I expect you have been blessed with a like visitation. It never snows but I think of a beautiful snow song, published this winter a year ago in the Anglo. You know sleighing days are the gala days of hard, stern winter. How the boys dance and sing, the girls gambol, the women laugh, and the sleigh bells jingle when the snow falls thick and fast! For the first time in my life have I seen the ground covered with snow without hearing the sleigh bells ring. I cannot say, positively, that sleighriding is an institution unknown to Dixie's land, but there is at least no sign of it in this portion of Dixie's vineyard.

The whole division is now engaged repairing the roads. In a few days the teams will be able to pass to and fro with comparative ease. They can do nothing until the roads are corduroyed. If they are allowed to remain as they are, in a few days whole regiments might be in a state of starvation. This may seem incredible, when it is known that provisions lay in abundance at Liverpool Point, three miles distant, and Rum Point,[1] five miles; but it is nevertheless the most probable thing imaginable. You will remember that the allied army lost twenty thousand horses, when in the harbor of Sebastopol[2] there lay, loaded with forage, ships whose crews threw it overboard to get rid of it; it could not be carried over the roads; not until they constructed a railroad which ran into their very trenches were they able to supply their army, and maintain that memorable siege. A lesson might be learned from this example. It would be cheaper to construct a railroad at once, for when the government comes to foot the wood bill, and the wear and tear of teams and wagons is accounted for, it would be found more economical than the corduroy road.

There was quite an exciting time in one of the camps this morning. The slave hunters did not come for "Jim, the negro spy," on last Saturday as they said they would do, but they put it off until this morning. I suppose they thought they would by this little delay, put him off his guard; but no, no, it seems that these fellows who have serious objections to serving a master, have learned intuitively that "Eternal vigilance is the price of liberty."[3] When a man's limbs have been bruised by the galling chains, he knows how sweet it is to be able to step forth free and unencumbered, and he will run fast and kick hard should any one attempt to reinvest him with those chains. Well, about twelve o'clock three Maryland magnates—slave hunters—rode into camp, provided with abundant dingy looking papers. A crowd was of course assembled in double quick time, without any regard to either right or left dress. There stood James, looking on in calm dignity. One asked, "Why don't you take him?" "I want the officer to let me take him," stammered the frightened hunter.

"Why you fool, there is not an officer in this whole division that dare give this man to you as a slave."

"Put 'em out! put 'em out! Ride 'em on a rail!" went up from every quarter. In a twinkling of an eye they were in their saddles. Groans, hisses, and snowballs were showered on their devoted heads, and the last that was seen of them was when they were making Maryland mud fly in ignoble style.

I noticed in the National Republican[4] of Washington city, a short time ago, a statement to the effect that Mr. Redpath, the editor of the Haytian Emigration newspaper—the "Pine and Palm"—had proposed to the United States authorities to transport all the contrabands of war to Fortress Monroe, for the modest sum of $20 per head. I was amazed and startled; I hoped that this was a mis-statement, and have been waiting for a denial. The source from which it comes, and the denial not having been made, we must accept it as true.[5]

This last crowning usurpation compels us to pause and look around us, and see how we stand. About a year ago the announcement was made that an agency had been established at Boston with a white man at the head of it. A running contest was kept up by the agent and his aids with all who dared to dissent from the scheme. The foulest epithets were applied to those who had been foremost in the fight against oppression. The Anglo-African became the Pine and Palm, and the free discussion of the emigration question crushed. The only paper the masses could call their own was prostituted to the advocacy of a scheme which had already proved more disastrous to the colored people than anything in their history except slavery itself. I will venture to say that the amount of property sacrificed by the colored people of Philadelphia alone, in 1824, when citizen Granville and Frederick Hinton led them to emigrate to Trinidad and Hayti would amount to millions of dollars. Large tracts of land were owned by colored people in the heart of our city, and are now worth millions, but it was all sacrificed upon the altar of emigration.[6] I was confident that although Redpath might pay out Haytian gold lavishly, and shut his columns to every dissenting word that might be uttered against his scheme, would fail, not taking into consideration the course pursued by him and his parasites, which was overbearing and arrogant. To day sees Haytian Emigration stillborn on the hands of its fathers and progenitors, and, as if by some strange fatality to make its failure doubly sure, he dares to propose to trample in the dust all that is left of our liberties. No colonizationist ever dared to proceed to the length Redpath has, in his proposition to remove the freedmen at Fortress Monroe, regardless of their will of choice, to bind their hands and feet, if needs be, to make good his shipping contract.

Now that the slavery question is about to pass from the arena of political disputation, the question of expatriation will be thrust upon it. It can be seen looming up in mighty proportions in the distance. It is the next great barrier the enemies to human freedom, negro equality, and progressive civilization propose to build up. They have abundant and suitable materials to work with—these are the millions who have been schooled in that code of political ethics, the cardinal maxims of which are that the negro is inferior to the Caucasian, that he never can attain to equality with the dominant class in this country, and that his natural normal condition is slavery! They are determined to enslave or transport us if they possibly can, for they hate us cordially. Redpath has allied himself to these. It would be most disastrous to us at this stage of the contraband question to have the government do as he proposes. When I say us, I mean, of course to include the four millions of American slaves whose destiny is, to all appearances, suspended upon the decision of this question. Against those accursed ideas, these natural, moral, religious and political heresies, the anti-slavery men have waged an incessant war. Their only mission has been to give the lie to these infamous assumptions. My dear sir, if we look back to the past, and recall the struggles, the trials, and the triumphs of anti-slavery men, then turn to the noble words of Phillips and Sumner, hear Whittier sing, muse over the philosophy of Emerson, wonder at the genius of the lamented Parker,[7] turn again to our distracted country, where war, bloody and merciless is precipitated by the slavery power, in a paroxysm of rage hoping thus to stay the overwhelming tide of public opinion, which this record of suffering and these noble words have created, can we look with any degree of allowance on any man or clique who indirectly calls this a farce? No, sir, we stand on the broad platform of the universal brotherhood of man. I expect to see the day when negro representatives unite in the halls of legislation. I believe, as a writer has beautifully said, that "the animosities are mortal but the humanities live forever."[8] Redpath must be reckless, indeed, when knowing that he is repudiated by the colored population of the northern States attempts to take advantage of the dependence of those people who have been freed by the exigencies of this war. Just as they have been raised to the dignity of manhood, and a new life of hope and promise lies spread out before them, and are revelling in the exuberant joyfulness of a new life of freedom, Redpath proposes to expatriate them! If Haytian emigration was not already defunct, this act of Redpath would so completely annihilate it that it could never have a resurrection.

G. E. S.

WAA, 15 February 1862.

1. Hooker's men constructed a large supply depot at Rum Point on Mattawoman Creek. Wagons could be turned around on the three-hundred-foot wharf they built. Walter H. Hebert, *Fighting Joe Hooker* (Indianapolis: Bobbs-Merrill, 1944), 57; *OR,* ser. 1, 5:697.

2. The allied campaign against Russia on the Crimean Peninsula (1854–56) proved a deadly lesson in futility and ineptitude. The army's "transportation system," its horses, mules, oxen, and even camels, died by the score, forcing soldiers to carry their supplies through oceans of mud. Balaclava's harbor became a appalling cesspool of human bodies, the carcasses of pack animals, dogs, and cats, and the detritus of an army in chaos. Alan Palmer, *The Banner of Battle: The Story of the Crimean War* (New York: St. Martin's Press, 1987), 173–76, 233–34; Christopher Hibbert, *The Destruction of Lord Raglan: A Tragedy of the Crimean War, 1854–1855* (Boston: Little, Brown, 1961), 205–18.

3. Although usually attributed to Thomas Jefferson, the quote originated with John Philpot Curran (1750–1817): "The condition upon which God hath given liberty to man is eternal vigilance." "Speech . . . on the Right of Election of Lord Mayor of Dublin . . . [1790]," in *Speeches of John Philpot Curran,* 2 vols. (New York: I. Riley, 1811), 2:236.

4. The *National Republican,* founded in 1860 and edited by W. J. Murtagh, was a staunch Republican organ that remained loyal to the Johnson admin-

istration. It halted publication in 1888. Frank Luther Mott, *American Journalism: A History, 1690–1960* (New York: Macmillan, 1962), 451.

5. James Redpath (1833–91), Scottish-born abolitionist and reporter for Greeley's *Tribune*, became commissioner for the Haytian Emigration Bureau in 1859. His relentless advocacy of Haitian emigration stirred intense resentment among many black leaders. Mary Ann Shadd Cary, the fiery Canadian journalist, denounced him as "James Blackpath" the slave trader and his agents as "maggots in the Haytian carcass." In June 1861, Redpath tried to convince Secretary of War Cameron to cooperate in his Haitian scheme and turn Fortress Monroe—near the mouth of the James River in Virginia—where thousands of "contraband" had gathered since the beginning of the war, into his personal supply depot. *BAP*, 2:37–38, 449, 456–57n.7; Robert F. Engs, *Freedom's First Generation: Black Hampton, Virginia, 1861–1890* (Philadelphia: University of Pennsylvania Press, 1979), 3–7, 18–22; James M. McPherson, ed., *The Negro's Civil War: How American Negroes Felt and Acted during the War for the Union* (New York: Random House, 1965), 77–89; Louis S. Gerteis, *From Contraband to Freedman: Federal Policy Toward Southern Blacks, 1861–1865* (Westport: Greenwood Press, 1973), 17.

6. Haitian President Jean-Pierre Boyer sent Jonathan Granville (1785–1839) to the United States in 1824 to promote resettlement in Haiti. He first stopped in Philadelphia, obtaining the endorsements of such prominent white leaders as Nicholas Biddle and the influential *Niles Register*. Between six and seven thousand blacks from Philadelphia, Baltimore, New York, and Cincinnati sold their property and moved to Haiti. Several hundred Philadelphia blacks accompanied the African Methodist leader Richard Allen to Haiti to escape racial prejudice. The project immediately faltered as conditions in the island nation proved deadly. Before the end of 1825, many blacks had returned. Frederick A. Hinton (1804–49), a North Carolina-born free black, was a respected and successful Philadelphia barber and a leader of the city's growing black abolitionist community. In 1839 he became an agent for British colonial officials, one of several black leaders urging resettlement in Trinidad. Embittered by racism, Hinton even considered moving to Liberia. Julie Winch, "American Free Blacks and Emigration to Haiti, 1804–26," *Working Paper* no. 33, Centro de Investigaciones Del Caribe y America Latina (Río Piedras, Puerto Rico: Universidad Interamericana de Puerto Rico, 1988), 1–31; Julie Winch, *Philadelphia's Black Elite: Activism, Accommodation, and the Struggle for Autonomy, 1787–1848* (Philadelphia: Temple University Press, 1988), 47–48, 64–66; Gary B. Nash, *Forging Freedom: The Formation of Philadelphia's Black Community, 1720–1840* (Cambridge: Harvard University Press, 1988), 243–45; *BAP*, 3:197–98n.17.

7. GES names Massachusetts's and the North's best-known reformers and abolitionists: Wendell Phillips (1811–84), an orator and Garrisonian abolitionist; Charles Sumner (1811–74), a lawyer, scholar, and Radical Republican senator; John Greenleaf Whittier (1807–92), a Quaker poet and pacifist; Ralph Waldo Emerson (1803–82), a Transcendentalist philosopher, poet, and essay-

ist; and Theodore Parker (1810–60), a Transcendentalist-Unitarian minister and supporter of John Brown.

8. The writer is Christopher North [John Wilson] (1785–1854), in *Noctes Ambrosianae*, no. 35 (August 1834).

Head Quarters, Hooker's Division,
Near Budd's Ferry, Md.,
Feb. 13th, 1862.

Mr. Editor:—Doctor Bell[1] the Division surgeon died in camp, the 11th inst., of pleurisy. His remains were conveyed with military honors to Rum Point for transportation eastward. Of the biography of Dr. Bell I know nothing. Last October when Gen. Hooker was assigned to the command of this Division, the Doctor received the appointment of Division Surgeon. At the time of his promotion he was Surgeon of the 1st Massachusetts Regiment,[2] and was with this Regiment at the battle of Bull's Run,[3] and gained the highest encomiums for his courage and attention to the wounded in that remarkable contest. It is related that a wounded rebel was brought into the hospital to have his wound dressed, when supposing that the doctor's animosities were as great as his own, plaintively cried, "Dr. I am your enemy, I am your enemy!" The Dr. straightened himself to the fullest extent of his lengthy proportions, looked on to the bleeding rebel benignly, and answered: "You were my enemy, you are now my patient." He was a man of large and varied information and stood among the highest in his profession. No man in the Division had a larger influence or commanded more respect in it than Dr. Bell.

While I write, the news of the capture of Roanoke Island by Gen. Burnside[4] and the defeat and capture of the rebels is going around the camps. Ten o'clock tatoo has already sounded—the soldiers are in delirium of joyful excitement—the bands are playing the National Songs. It does one's heart good to hear the Massachusetts boys cheer.

I would give the world if I could cheer, if my heart unclouded by the thoughts of my bondage would be free and buoyant and swell with patriotic fervor. I cannot, I will not cheer at the success of any man or nation that sanctions human bondage. Suppose Beelzebub and Belial should engage in mortal combat, which victor would Gabriel cheer?[5] Would he not turn from the combatants and pray to that God against whose people they have jointly warred, and whose laws they have mutually violated; that they, these personifications of disorder and ruin, perfidy, and deceit, might like wounded and envenomed serpents sting each other to death!

Since my last the officers referred to by young Barnes in his statement, have both resigned. The first named is one of the most despicable scoundrels that ever disgraced human kind; the other cannot read or write, yet he was commissioned as 1st Lieutenant in company I, 26th Regt., P. V. The first named was a companion of Walker's in Nicaragua,[6] as was also Lieut. Col. Van Dyke, which recommendation, however potent in its claims upon the Federal administration, will not ensure to the possessor of it an entrance into the third Heaven.[7]

Here is a little circumstance to which I would call special attention. It is well known that there are among the officers of the Excelsior Brigade as grand villains as ever went unhung, but little did I think that even the clergy were tainted with corruption and meanness. Of the five Regiments composing this Brigade, there is one that has a Roman Catholic Priest as chaplain. I do not know the reverend father's cognomen. A fugitive slave entered the camp where this notable exercised spiritual jurisdiction—the slave, like a great many in this region, was also a Roman Catholic. Well, true to the practice of the religion, he went to confessional, and while there the Reverend villain wrung from the slave the fact that he had left his master, and also the name of the master and where he lived, made the slave promise that he would return, and sent a letter to the master instructing him to come and get his slave. The poor fellow, when telling this, by his manner and tone, revealed the conflict that was going on in his mind between his religious superstition and his sense of right and justice. I asked him "why did you confess to a thing that should have been kept secret in your own bosom?" "My dear sir," said he "I thought it was a sin to tell a lie." "Yes it is a sin," said I, "to tell a lie; but when you found that the truth would harm you, why did you not refuse to answer?" "We are not allowed to keep any thing secret." I asked: "do you think you would have violated the laws of God had you refused to answer the priest?" "No sir, no sir!" But when this poor fellow found that the priest was about to sacrifice him he made good his retreat and I have no doubt that he is now convinced that a clerical garb does not always cover a pure, honest or christian heart. It is one of the most difficult things in the world to find a christian negro in the South. They go to church, participate in the excitement of their grotesque religious gatherings. But they have no ideas of the sublime principles of christianity and its bearings on human actions. Of course the master does not permit the christian religion to be preached to his slaves.[8] I will guarantee that the bulk of the slaves in the Southern States are infidels—they believe that their freedom is to come. This is universal. The christianity they are taught teaches that slavery is their natural lot and condition, and that obedience to the master is obedience to God. Their liberty is first and their religion second, and sooner or later they will show to the world another lesson. Religion, if its advocates would have it cover the earth as the waters of the great deep, must be so comprehensive, so pure and unsullied, that liberty and justice can become its hand-maids. It is hard to be a christian if we stop to look around us and note to what infamous depths the expositors and representatives of religion sink themselves. If we could find the majority of them on the side of truth and right, we might pass their great derelictions of duty by and hope for better things in the future; but the majority to-day of clergymen, if they are not on the side of slavery, they are not on the side of freedom, and this sin of omission is at this moment of peril as deep and damning as though they were on the side of slavery. It is not a difficult matter to convince men that religion is a farce, but it is impossible to convince men that liberty is a chimera and not worth loving above all else known to rational beings.

General Hooker is again at his post.[9] The rumor is floating around that a movement will take place some time next week. The rebels are evidently frightened, they are firing continually. Five sloops ran the blockade the other night, and although twenty-five or thirty shot were sent after them they passed unharmed.

I see that Mr. Edward M. Thomas[10] is still at work encouraging art and artists amongst the Anglo-Africans. I have the honor of an acquaintance with several gentlemen in Philadelphia, possessed of artistic skill of no mean order. Mr. Wm. Dorsey, Mr. A. Burr, one of the descendants of Aaron Burr of U.S. history, and Mr. David B. Bowser.[11] There are others not now in my mind's eye who are struggling manfully to become proficient with the pencil. Mr. Dorsey is now revolving in his mind the project of joining a company of young men in a business trip to Africa. He thinks that original sketches of life and landscape in that interesting country would be rare and valuable. Indeed I had myself some notion, if I could raise the "wind," to join the party, but my dear sir I find the "wind" to be the hardest thing in the world to raise.

G. E. S.

WAA, 22 February 1862.

1. Dr. Luther V. Bell (1806–62), director of the McLean Asylum for the Insane, joined the Eleventh Massachusetts on 13 June 1861 and reported to Hooker's brigade on 21 September. He fell ill on 5 February and died six days later. George E. Ellis, "Memoir of Luther V. Bell," *Proceedings of the Massachusetts Historical Society* 7 (April 1863): 27–99; Personal Papers of Medical Officers, Adjutant General's Office, box 44, RG 94, National Archives.

2. This should read *11*th Massachusetts Regiment.

3. The First Battle of Bull Run or First Manassas took place on 21 July 1861 and ended with a humiliating rout of the Union army. The South suffered 1,982 casualties while inflicting 2,896 on the North. *HTIECW*, 91–92.

4. Gen. Ambrose E. Burnside (1824–81), corps commander and then leader of the Army of the Potomac, proved a tragic disappointment. At Fredericksburg, his inflexibility cost thousands of Union lives. On 7–8 February 1862 Burnside and 15,000 troops landed on Roanoke Island, North Carolina, capturing 2,500 Confederates in a one-sided engagement that gave the Union an important southern base and a much-needed victory. Warner, *Generals in Blue*, 57–58; *HTIECW*, 636.

5. Beelzebub—or Baal-zebub—the "prince of demons" and Belial is Hebrew for worthlessness or wickedness, implying a choice between two devils. Paul J. Achtemeier, ed., *Harper's Bible Dictionary* (San Francisco: Harper and Row, 1985), 86, 102.

6. GES refers to Captain Webb and Lieutenant Snow. In 1855 William Walker (1824–60) and sixty followers—"filibusters"—helped inflame a civil war in Nicaragua. He became a hero to Southerners who envisioned a Caribbean slave empire. A Honduran firing squad ended his adventures in 1860. James M. McPherson, *Battle Cry of Freedom: The Civil War Era* (New York: Oxford University Press, 1988), 110–15.

7. Islam and Buddism refer to various levels of heaven and the New Testament contains a reference to "third heaven," but this reference probably comes from Dante's *Divine Comedy* Canto VIII: "With one circle, with one circling and with one thirst we revolve with the celestial Princes to whom you in the world did once say, 'You who move the third heaven by intellection'; and we are so full of love that, in order to please you, a little quiet will not be less sweet to us." 2 Corinthians 12:2; Dante Alighieri, *The Divine Comedy: Paradiso*, trans. and ed. Charles S. Singleton (Princeton: Princeton University Press, 1975), 85.

8. Many Southerners denied their slaves any religious instruction and tried to extinguish the practice of African religious ceremonies. Most masters probably permitted their slaves to attend Christian services—always supervised

by whites—where the sermons dwelled on the duties of servants to their masters. In the slave community, however, especially along the South Carolina coast, African rituals freely merged with elements of Christianity. Black abolitionists such as GES repudiated the Christianity of slaveowners and dismissed African-influenced slave religion as paganism. Kenneth M. Stampp, *The Peculiar Institution: Slavery in the Ante-Bellum South* (New York: Random House, 1956), 156–62; Sterling Stucky, *Slave Culture: Nationalist Theory and the Foundations of Black America* (New York: Oxford University Press, 1987), 3–97.

9. Hooker went to Washington, D.C., several times during the first two months of 1862. He met McClellan in January and spoke with Lincoln at the White House on 5 and 22 February. Walter H. Hebert, *Fighting Joe Hooker* (Indianapolis: Bobbs-Merrill, 1944), 68–71.

10. Edward M. Thomas (1820?–63) lived in Washington, D.C., during the Civil War and was president of the Anglo-African Institute for the Encouragement of Industry and Art. GES refers to Thomas's 16 December 1861 letter in the *Anglo-African* concerning a black art show he sponsored. Such displays, Thomas believed, demonstrated black ability and inspired other blacks to express themselves through art. James de T. Abajian, comp., *Blacks in Selected Newspapers . . .*, 5 vols. (Boston: G. K. Hall, 1977–85), 3:472; David W. Blight, *Frederick Douglass' Civil War: Keeping Faith in Jubilee* (Baton Rouge: Louisiana State University Press, 1989), 138; *WAA*, 8 February 1862.

11. William Henry Dorsey (1837–1923), part of Philadelphia's black elite and a well-known artist, painted many portraits, landscapes, and historical subjects but never traveled to Africa. David Bustil Bowser (1820–1900), a Philadelphia black abolitionist and postwar civil rights advocate, also enjoyed success as a portrait painter and commercial artist. Many of Bowser's clients were white, some from the ranks of anti-Catholic and anti-foreign Nativists and fire companies in Philadelphia and Baltimore. In addition to portraits and landscapes, he did decorative banners, caps, and flags for black Civil War regiments. A. Burr was probably the son of John P. and Hetty Burr, active Philadelphia abolitionists. John P. Burr claimed to be the son of Aaron Burr of American Revolutionary fame and his Haitian-born governess. Roger Lane, *William Dorsey's Philadelphia and Ours* (New York: Oxford University Press, 1991), 1–2, 110–16, 120–25; *BAP*, 3:195–96n.13; Bustil-Bowser-Ashby Collection, 127, Moorland-Spingard Research Center, Howard University.

Head Quarters, Hooker's Division,
Near Budd's Ferry, Md.,
March 2d, 1862.

Mr. Editor.—We have had high winds for the last two or three days, interspersed of course with rain, but if the rain would cease these driving March winds would soon dry up the roads, and the grand army of the Potomac would be able to walk dry shod over into the unhappy land of Canaan, (Dixie's land.)

The rumor has reached us that Gen. Banks has been defeated, and his forces completely routed on the upper Potomac.[1]

Professor Lowe[2] has been unable to make his usual daily balloon reconnaissance on account of the high wind. The wind blew so violently on Tuesday last that he was compelled to disinflate his balloon, but will reinflate it as soon as the winds subside.

We are reliably informed that the rebels immediately in front of us have received large reinforcements; they evidently anticipate an attack.

Brigadier General Naglee,[3] of Pennsylvania, arrived in camp on the 17th ult., and took command of 1st Brigade, in place of Col. Cowdin, of the 1st Massachusetts regiment, who returns to his command.

Captain Page who has commanded at Liverpool Point, where the contrabands are employed unloading vessels, etc., and where the army supplies are stored, relates that two of these contrabands undertook and accomplished the boldest feat of the war, thus furnishing us with another irrefutable evidence of the courage, daring and skill of the negro, when brought face to face with danger; the strength and permanence of his affections, which is the noblest evidence, too, of a pure, perfect and elevated nature. These men belong to the party Col. Graham brought off when he made his inroad into Virginia. The captain says that one of them came to him and asked permission to recross the river to rescue his wife, declaring that he was almost certain that he could bring her off safely. The captain thought the fellow mad, but he plead so earnestly that he gave him permission, and gave notice of the fact to the commander of the flotilla, to prevent his being fired upon by the gun boats. He left Liverpool Point on a dark night, in a small skiff with muffled oars. His wife lived some six or seven miles up the Occoquan Bay. He reached her, brought her off safe, gathered much valuable information of the strength and position of the enemy, and returned the following night to Liverpool Point with his companion, safe and unharmed. This man is a true type of the negro; jet black, erect and athletic. The other man, a type of the mixed blood, seeing the triumph of his comrade, asked and received permission to secure his wife, and not having as far to go, brought her off triumphantly and returned the same evening that he went upon his errand. When it is remembered that the rebels are very vigilant on account of the expected attack of our forces, and that the beach is lined with sentinels from Martha's Point to Occoquan Bay, whose bivouac fires can be seen every night with common glasses, and also that if they had been detected nothing but instant death would have been meted out to them, we must accord these two of the most daring ventures and successful exploits of the war. If these men and their brethren were allowed to become active instead of passive co-operators with the Union forces, how long would treason be able to so impudently defy the federal powers?[4]

Here is an item I give you for the special benefit of your fair readers. The more susceptible of the sterner sex may also gather whatever satisfaction this little story of love, struggle and triumph, may give. One of the most painful of the revolting sights one sees when sojourning in this land of slavery, is the universal prostitution by their masters of beautiful slave women. There are scarcely any farms or plantations in the south that can boast of no pretty women. They are prized, petted, bartered and sold according to the nature and extent of their charms. Beauties rivaling those of the Caucasian are sold in the slave marts of the U.S. No matter how loathsome to her the purchaser of her charms may be, the hard remorseless necessities of her position compel her to yield.[5] Mary Thomas, a beautiful negress, the slave of a man by the name of Henry Eglon, living near Newport, belonged to this class. Her master had already engaged her to an old lecherous scoundrel. She fell violently in love with an Anglo-African in one of the companies. Longing to be free, and to escape that living martyrdom, the life which her master had marked out for her, and also unite her destiny with that of her lover, she made a bold stroke for life, love and liberty. She did not clothe herself in male apparel, like many of the paler heroines and amazons have done, but maintained a distinction of sex.[6] She had not gone far before Ferrel, a slave master near Port Tobacco, arrested her and locked her up in the jail at that place. Her lover broke the jail open and released her. She had not been released five minutes before Johnny Shackelford,[7] a noted slave hunter, re-arrested her; but the girl fought him bravely. Her lover and the soldiers could not quietly look on such a contest as this; they came to the rescue, and just barely left life in the hunter. And why should she not triumph? Did not she turn her back on slavery and ruin, while the path which she proposed to tread was illuminated with the bright hope of salvation, liberty and love? I rejoice to say that Mary Thomas to-day is free!

There is nothing more galling to a black man than the iteration and reiteration of the foul misrepresentations which the advocate of man-stealing, man-torturing, and man-slaughtering slavery urge against him. There never has been a time in the history of this country, when there was such a scarcity of material to build these heartless lies on. They may oppose us and deny us rights, but our friends and ourselves will soon settle the contest of ideas; but when our enemies add "insult to injury" it incites in us the desire to cut their throats or give them a taste of the horrors of the system they so much love. Although the Government has spurned the loyalty of the negro more pointedly and peremptorily than it has the treason of these slaveholding dogs and their Northern tools and accomplices, they have, as by some unseen power, become active and prominent in this great civil contest, and have impressed the indelible truth upon the minds of the thinking portion of this nation that he is a dreadful power for evil or a grand and noble one for good.

Rum Point and Liverpool Point, as I have often before remarked, are the points where the supplies are landed. Before the contrabands were brought here, details from the various regiments were made to unload the vessels and to store the provisions; these details generally numbered about a hundred men—a whole company. The soldiers were not allowed for this special duty any extra compensation; so the result was, that they skulked out of as much work as they could, upon the principle that it is far more agreeable and much more reasonable to play for nothing than to work for nothing. They were certain to get their $13 per month, and this poor pay and poorer fare formed no incentive to hard manual labor. Since the 30 or 40 muscular blacks have arrived at Liverpool Point it is made the principle depot for stores and Rum Point is made the passenger depot; and these 30 or 40 men do more in the same space of time than a hundred white men—thus reversing the order of things. The black man under the incentives of Free labor, pay, and freedom, goes blithely and gaily to his task; while the white man under the repulsiveness of forced labor and no pay, lounges about and skulks sulkily away. They are also temperate and cleanly; are comfortably housed, clothed and fed by the Government, wives, children, and all; and are to receive ten cents a day pay, which is small—but when the housing, clothing and feeding of a man and his family are considered, his pay is nearly as good as the enlisted soldier; it can all be saved up by them, and will make a small start for them when they shall be released by the authorities.

G. E. S.

WAA, 15 March 1862.

1. No battle involving Banks's troops took place in the upper Potomac. His thrust to seize Winchester and begin the long-awaited Union flanking movement against Richmond—which would have sent Hooker's division across the lower Potomac—failed to commence because of poor planning. Stephen W. Sears, *George B. McClellan: The Young Napolean* (New York: Ticknor and Fields, 1988), 156–57; Rowena Reed, *Combined Operations in the Civil War* (Annapolis: United States Naval Institute Press, 1978), 114–17.

2. Thaddeus Sobieski Constantine Lowe (1832–1913) pioneered the use of balloons in combat and was chief of army aeronautics. Lowe's balloons lost favor with Hooker after his defeat at Chancellorsville. Lowe resigned on 8 May 1863, and the army unwisely terminated the Balloon Corps. *HTIECW*, 451–52; *WWWCW*, 397.

3. Gen. Henry Morris Naglee (1815–86) commanded Hooker's Brigade from 3 October 1861 to 13 March 1862. While serving in the District of Virginia he ran afoul of Union Gov. Francis H. Pierpont and was forced out of the service in 1864. Dyer, *Compendium*, 2:277; Warner, *Generals in Blue*, 340–41.

4. GES probably knew of many other similar acts of bravery. The Union army, and Hooker's division in particular, depended upon local blacks for estimates of rebel troop strength and positioning. On 11 January 1862, for example, one black on the USS *Freeborn* had penetrated Confederate lines, rescued his wife and family, and reported on rebel positions. *OR*, ser. 1, 5:697.

5. Black and white abolitionists recoiled at the plight of Southern black women and the impact of this especially sordid side of slavery on African-American families. Conditions endured by individual women varied by region and owner, but all female slaves were subject to the unchecked control of their masters. The cruelties inflicted by a James Henry Hammond or the sufferings of a Harriet Jacobs were hardly exceptions under the slave regime, and any slave woman could easily find herself raped or sold as a prostitute. New Orleans traders, for example, specialized in light-skinned female slaves who tragically ended up in the lucrative "fancy-girl" market. Eugene Genovese, *Roll, Jordan, Roll: The World the Slaves Made* (New York: Random House, 1974), 416–17, 422–31; Drew Gilpin Faust, *James Henry Hammond and the Old South: A Design for Mastery* (Baton Rouge: Louisiana State University Press, 1982), 69–104; Harriet Jacobs, *Incidents in the Life of a Slave Girl, Written by Herself*, ed. Jean Fagan Yellin (Cambridge: Harvard University Press, 1987).

6. GES probably refers to the famous case of Ellen Craft (1826–90). On 26 December 1848, the light-skinned Georgia slave disguised herself as a Southern gentleman, with her face partially obscured by tinted glasses and a poul-

tice and one arm in a sling to preclude requests for a signature. With her slave husband, William Craft (1824–1900) acting as a servant, the two traveled a thousand miles to Philadelphia by feigning a search for medical treatment. The Crafts' ingenious and heroic escape, recorded in their *Running a Thousand Miles for Freedom* (London, 1860), catapulted them into international fame. *BAP,* 4:36–37.

7. GES may refer to John L. Shackelford, a Charles County constable, tax collector, businessman, and political leader. Wearmouth, *Abstracts from the Port Tobacco* Times, 2:1, 105, 141, 149, 128–29.

Head Quarters, Hooker's Division,
Near Budd's Ferry, Maryland,
March 4th, 1862.

Mr. Editor: If General Sickles, or perhaps Col. Graham, chose to do so they would verify the general truth of the statements of my letter of January 10th. Gen. Sickles has now in his possession a white stallion which he seized from Cox, the murderer of poor Jack Scroggins. The treason of Cox is unmistakable, and this horse with other things were seized by virtue of his treason. Cox was maltreated by the soldiers when he came after Scroggins, and he would never have been able to take him, had not an officer in either Col. Graham's or Col. Dwight's Regiment returned him. My letter makes no charge against Col. Dwight, but only against that officer through whose order a loyal negro was surrendered to one of the most notorious traitors of this Pandemonium of treason and slavery. "An officer of the 1st Excelsior Brigade"[1] is rather hasty in his defence, and championship, of Col. Dwight. He reminds me of that verdant thief who being caught at one of his light fingered tricks, denies his guilt before a charge was made against him. It has been my fortune to meet Col. Dwight on more than one occasion; and I have found him an officer and a gentleman, and I am pleased to bear my humble testimony to his efficiency in subduing, in connection with General Sickles and Col. Graham, the bold, active and insolent treason so rampant in the lower counties of this State.[2] I am familiar with one instance at least, where a trio of Secessionists from Newport prevailed on General Hooker to prefer charges against Col. Dwight; but the committee appointed to investigate the affair bear the highest testimonial to the justness and correctness of Col. Dwight's actions and conduct. So notorious was the treason of Cox, that whenever the steamers touched at Chappel Pt., on Port Tobacco River, they always searched his house; and when Colonel Dwight's Regiment moved down in that vicinity and encamped on Dr. Rob Ferguson's farm, Mulberry Grove,[3] they searched and found nothing worth mentioning; they, however seized some of his things and returned them. But Col. Graham moved down there and encamped at Allen's Fresh; another and last search was made, and sufficient things were found in a swamp, between Cox's and William Nesbit's farm, buried in the earth to justify the seizure of the greater part of Cox's stock, which fact must be totally unknown to "an officer of the 1st Regt. Excelsior Brigade." "An officer" would have subserved the cause of his country, and therefore of truth, had he confined himself to the vindication of the officers of his Regt. Not content with that he pronounces my letter "wholly incorrect" in all its statements, treating as a farce one of the most astounding and guilty crimes, which has covered the authors and abettor's of this Rebellion with the blackest infamy!

Over two months have elapsed since I penned the letter "an officer" refers to. At the time I wrote it, it was almost impossible to ascertain positively in which of the Regt.'s referred to, the 1st or 5th, the rendition took place. Knowing Colonel Dwight, and having facts in my possession which could enable me to make the amend honorable should this Regt. be the wrong one, I gave his name, almost confident that there must have been some one officer there who would set me right, but he has not yet shown himself. I have certain proof that Col. Graham's Regt. was the 2nd one that encamped near Port Tobacco, Col. Dwight's being the 1st that went there, and that Scroggins joined the 2d one which had encamped at Allen's Fresh. After they commenced the march down to Hill Top, Cox and eight or ten friends went in pursuit, and overtook them about six miles on the march at a white house, where a man by the name of Joe Walters lived. Among Cox's friends was a man by the name of James Neale,[4] who was elected to the State Legislature last fall. Cox rushed in the ranks and seized Scroggins, when the men with Scroggins beat him badly. An officer rode up and rescued Cox, and made the men surrender the slave up upon the promise that he would not harm him. I have tried to find out the name of the officer, but I find it almost impossible. Is there no honorable man in the 1st or 5th Regiment or anywhere else who will give the name of the officer? I heard that it was the Major of the 5th Regt.

G. E. S.

WAA, 22 March 1862.

1. The unidentified officer wrote on 4 March 1862 to the New York *Tribune*, denying Stephens's allegations concerning Scroggins's murder and claiming that Colonel Dwight never knew anything about Cox or the Scroggins case. Moreover, he claimed that Scroggins never gave Dwight information concerning Cox's treasonous activities and that Cox never appeared in camp to claim his slave. *WAA*, 15 March 1862.

2. Under Sickles's orders, Colonels Dwight and Graham arrested prominent Southern sympathizers and broke up hostile local militias. The Maryland coastline, with its innumerable coves and inlets, provided convenient cover for spying and smuggling operations. Eager to halt such treasonous activities, Dwight and Graham destroyed the property of rebel sympathizers and seized their slaves. These actions alienated local whites, and, "Complaints of this command were universal." Many civilians fled across the Potomac to escape arrest and loss of all their "property." *OR*, ser. 1, 5:388, 609–10, 614.

3. Dr. Robert Ferguson owned the Mulberry Grove Plantation and was president of the Charles County Agricultural Society, an organization supported by many county leaders. Wearmouth, *Abstracts from the Port Tobacco Times*, 2:24, 34, 140.

4. James Henry Neale (1802–72), a wealthy Charles County planter, possessed $16,000 in real estate and $41,000 in personal estate. Although not a state legislator, he often served as county commissioner and attended the 1861 county convention that supported secession. Harry Wright Newman, *The Maryland Semmes and Kindered Families* (Baltimore: Maryland Historical Society, 1956), 314–15; 1860 U.S. Census; Wearmouth, *Abstracts from the Port Tobacco Times*, 1:29, 111; 2:49–50; 3:67, 110.

Head Quarters, Hooker's Division,
Near Budd's Ferry, Md.,
March 12th, 1862.

Mr. Editor: The rebels have raised the siege of the National Capital. The U.S. flag now waves majestically, if not triumphantly, over the ramparts of the famous Cock-Pit Point Battery.[1] On the evening of the 8th inst., about 10 o'clock, two fugitives from Slavery escaped from the Virginia shore in a small dug-out, and fell into the custody of picket guard No. 3 of the 8th Reg. N. J. Vols.[2] They reported that orders had been received by the rebels to abandon their works. About 3 o'clock on the 9th (Sunday), the gunboat Anacostia[3] crept down to the rebel batteries and commenced shelling them, and receiving no response, sent a boat on shore and found the works deserted. The second boat ran the flag up amid the cheers of the thousands of soldiers; while this was going on the steamer George Page[4] could be seen enveloped in flames, as was also two schooners, her prizes. Far back could be seen numerous minor explosions; and about 4 o'clock the works on Shipping Point blew up with a great concussion. Boats commenced to run frequently between the two shores, and by night-fall five hundred men must have straggled over there. As your correspondent has been cautioned against furnishing information of the movements of the division I must be extremely cautious, or, like Dr. Ives,[5] the champion of Northern treason, I may suddenly find myself in *durance vile.*[6] I shall not refrain primarily but only incidently on this account, for although the Government has spurned and rejected us, and has pampered and petted its bitter foes, yet for the love and gratitude I bear for the millions in the free North who are standing between the slave and the slave-master, I am determined to be loyal, and to lose the insignificant life before one single word of mine will jeopardize the interests of the service. Now that the rebel blockade of the Potomac has been raised the valuable fishing grounds will be accessible to the fishermen.[7] The Potomac fisheries are worth thousands of dollars; and thousands of souls now in the throes of starvation will be furnished with food both savory and nutritious. There was such a continued communication kept up by the *quasi* Unionists of Maryland with the Virginia shore that the authorities were compelled to destroy nearly all the seine boats on the river, and these will have to be replaced before seine-hauling can be resumed. The fishing season commences about the 10th of March, at which time the gillers commence to take in the shad. About the last of March or the first of April seine-hauling commences. The shad season closes about the last of May; the seine-hauling about the 10th of May. Herring is the principle yield of these fisheries.

The brand new General Naglee, like the old dough-faces of old, has summoned all the military power he possesses to advance the interests of slavery; but he belongs to a by-gone race.[8] They stood and looked on with blanched cheek when Sumner was beaten down in the Senate Chamber;[9] they were bullied and kicked by imperious slaveholders; they plead and begged the free North to spread inhumane bondage over the entire North; their mean cringing narrow souls longed for this; their big soft bellies yearned for it; and after Sumter fell[10] and the national flag dishonored and the rebel ensign unfurled over nearly every fort, arsenal and custom-house in the Southern States, they prayed to their God that "Jef. Davis"[11] might extend his dominions to even Bunker Hill and Faneuil Hall, so that free-speech might become a crime. There are but few of them left, Vallandigham,[12] Diven,[13] and several little Generals. They are traitors. There is no such thing as an uncompromising loyalist and a slave-holder whether in fact or in heart. Any man who ever apologizes for slavery apologizes for treason, and so long as slavery exists so long will secession remain unsubdued. This is as true as that God lives and reigns. I see in the "Anglo" an extract from the columns of the "New York Tribune," which gives the special order No. 24 with comments,[14] and which calls forth these remarks: these are very common things, and I can furnish you with any quantity of such orders. But the peculiarity of this order is its bold and unqualified assertion of the loyalty of Samuel W. Adams,[15] which is false, gloriously false. This man, who commanded Brigadier General Naglee and whom Brigadier General Naglee instantly obeyed, lives at a place called Smith Point, on the Potomac, and which is directly opposite to Aquia Creek. He was the owner of several boats, and last summer used them to convey goods and men to the Virginia shore, and his house was a sort of rendezvous for the pilgrims to secessia. For this his boats were seized and he was arrested, carried to Washington, and of course released. For this man General Naglee proposes to employ the whole force of his Brigade, nearly 4,000 United States soldiers, to crush if possible by any manifestation of sympathy for the oppressed or love for freedom; but the power he thus dares to insult will overwhelm him if he dare oppose it. The negro he would have re-enslaved by New England men, was rescued and set free under his very nose and would have been under his eyes. So much for the brand new Brigadier General Naglee, of Pennsylvania.

In your report of the Congressional debate on the bill establishing an additional article of law for the Government of the U.S. Army, Mr. Diven is reported to have said, I want to ask the gentleman (Mr. Bingham)[16] to specify where any military officer has hunted down any fugitive slave for the purpose of returning him to his master? Now, sir, I would have given the world if I could have had a chance to make the specifications referred to. I can give the data for scores of cases; one case, particularly, where an officer, Col. Van Dyke, of the 26th Pennsylvania Volunteers, had sent a guard outside the regimental lines beating the bushes for a negro boy, while the hunter in search of him was imbibing bad whiskey with the colonel; and a captain still in the same regiment approached a lieutenant and inquired of him whether he would not like to make twenty dollars. The lieutenant, of course, said yes; when he was told that he must help him to catch and re-enslave a panting fugitive from inhuman slavery, he indignantly rejected the offer and reported the captain to his superiors. So you are already aware I might go on to enumerate. The one case alone of the return of Jack Scroggins by the Major of Col. Graham's Regiment is enough to choke Mr. Diven of itself.

G. E. S.

WAA, 22 March 1862.

1. Union troops grossly overestimated the strength of Confederates along the Potomac and then allowed them to withdraw unnoticed on 8 March 1862. On 9 March they shelled abandoned positions. McClellan claimed the rebel retreat as a victory, but the Northern press disagreed and condemned the Union army's lackluster performance. Rowena Reed, *Combined Operations in the Civil War* (Annapolis: United States Naval Institute Press, 1978), 114–21.

2. The Eighth New Jersey Regiment, organized on 14 September 1861, served in Hooker's division until March 1862 and chased Lee with the Army of the Potomac until Appomattox. It lost 286 men in the war and mustered out on 17 July 1865. Dyer, *Compendium*, 3:1360.

3. The USS *Anacostia*, a 217-ton gunboat built in 1856, served in the Potomac Flotilla throughout the war and engaged rebel river batteries beginning 1 January 1862. Paul H. Silverstone, *Warships of the Civil War Navies* (Annapolis: United States Naval Institute Press, 1989), 103.

4. The CSS *George Page*, a 410-ton troop transport built in 1853, was seized by Confederates in May 1861. Retreating rebels burned it on 9 March to prevent its recapture. Silverstone, *Warships of the Civil War Navies*, 243.

5. Malcom Ives, an arrogant and quick-tempered New York *Herald* reporter, headed the paper's Washington, D.C., office. His relationship with McClellan gave him access to detailed information concerning the Union war effort, but the general could not protect him from the secretary of war, who imprisoned Ives for violating censorship rules. Stephen W. Sears, ed., *The Civil War Papers of George B. McClellan* (New York: Ticknor and Fields, 1989), 160–61; J. Cutler Andrews, *The North Reports the Civil War* (Pittsburgh: University of Pittsburgh Press, 1955), 56–58.

6. The term means a long imprisonment.

7. The U.S. Navy authorized fishing and commercial crafts to use the Potomac River. *ORN*, ser. 1, 5:21.

8. GES's criticism appeared justified. In November, Naglee abolished all black schools in Yorktown, Virginia, advising John Oliver, a black American

Missionary Association teacher, that "all persons who are in gaged in this enterprise are ruining the Colored people, and retarding the progress of the Government." *BAP*, 5:159, 163n.1.

9. Beginning on 19 May 1856, Sumner delivered his famous "Crime against Kansas" oration, reviling South Carolina Sen. Andrew P. Butler as the Don Quixote of American slavery who had chosen the "harlot" slavery as his "mistress." Three days later, Rep. Preston S. Brooks, also from South Carolina and a relation of Butler, beat Sumner into unconsciousness with his cane. The event fueled sectional tensions and marked an important stage in the movement toward civil war. David Herbert Donald, *Charles Sumner and the Coming of the Civil War* (Chicago: University of Chicago Press, 1960), 282–300.

10. The Civil War began at 4:30 A.M. on 12 April 1861, when South Carolina secessionists under Gen. P. G. T. Beauregard began their bombardment of Fort Sumter in Charleston Harbor. Two days later, the fort surrendered. *HTIECW*, 279–80.

11. Jefferson Davis (1808–89) became president of the Confederacy on 18 February 1861.

12. Clement L. Vallandigham (1820–71), a member of Congress from Ohio, became the North's most notorious antiwar Democrat (Copperhead).

13. GES reacts to comments by Alexander S. Diven (1809–96), a New York lawyer and member of Congress. Diven, however, supported the abolition of slavery in Washington, D.C., and later introduced the first legislation to authorize the recruitment of black troops.

14. GES cites the *Anglo-African* reprint of a New York *Tribune* article entitled "ORDER FOR NEGRO HUNTING." The paper reprinted General Naglee's Special Order No. 24, 1 March 1862, to Colonel Cowdin of the First Massachusetts, ordering him to find Martin Tolsin, a runaway slave belonging to Samuel W. Adams, "a citizen of Maryland and loyal subject of the United States." Greeley's *Tribune* denounced Naglee's attempt to transform soldiers into "nigger catchers." *WAA*, 8 March 1862.

15. Samuel W. Adams, a Nanjemoy slaveowner, served on a committee in 1857 that sought to restrict the liberty of free blacks and proposed to enslave those found without homes. *ORN*, ser. 1, 4:740; Wearmouth, *Abstracts from the Port Tobacco Times*, 2:52, 76.

16. Under the headline "OUR SOLDIERS NOT TO BE USED AS SLAVE HOUNDS," the *Anglo-African* reported the 24 February House debate on a bill of Francis P. Blair, Jr., that prohibited the army from returning fugitive slaves. John A. Bingham (1815–1900), a Republican member of Congress from Ohio, amended the bill to include all branches of the military service. Diven refused to believe that U.S. officers had returned individuals to slavery. "I want the gentleman from Ohio," he exclaimed, "to specify where any military officer has hunted down any fugitive slave for the purpose of returning him to his master." *WAA*, 8 March 1862; *Biographical Directory of the American Congress, 1774–1971* (Washington: Government Printing Office, 1971), 593.

Head Quarters, Hooker's Division,
Lower Potomac,
March 21st, 1862.

Mr. Editor:—The stupendous retreat of the Confederate army from the whole line of the Potomac, must be conceded by every man in the grand army to be a bold and hazardous military feat. An army of seventy thousand men in the face of nearly one hundred and fifty thousand, encumbered with thousands of civilians, with their moveable property and slaves, carrying all off successfully, leaving behind them a desolate and depopulated country which the grand army, when it takes upon itself sufficient vitality, may take possession of. When this is formally done, I suppose orators will proclaim the wonderful achievement of slumber and inertness, poets will canonize it.[1] The immortal McClellan, the pet young American general, the hater, Young America-like, of abolitionists, good morals, manners, and of liberty, who could not take it into his heart to hurt the poor rebels, or to take from them their dear "niggers," nor, would not a "nigger" see inside the lines of his pickets, unless he has sent a bullet into the heart of some poor mudsill, has become the founder of a new school of warfare.[2] Future generals may emulate his novel tactical genius, those stray imps of the demon of treason and slavery who have escaped the tender mercies[3] of the grand army, and have kept up communication with their satanic emissaries, in spite of glittering bayonets, passports, and frowning cannon, who have robbed the nation of its commerce, its trade, its manufactures, its power, and its fair fame; who have spilled the blood of the best men of the nation; who have robbed four millions of human beings of life, liberty, and the pursuit of happiness, may dance with hellish glee and exultation in the lurid glare of burning cities and towns, and while the hundreds of thousands of national troops have been sleeping in their quarters and silently gazing on rebel entrenchments, the rebels have been preparing a stupendous movement of concentration which they could never have done if the army of the Potomac had two months ago attacked and routed the main army in front of it. But the fortuitous moment has passed, and the grand army is demoralized and to-day is more inefficient than they were three months ago. I will guarantee they are not a whit more efficient or better drilled at least.[4] But I see in it the finger of God. In ninety days the rebels will be concentrated and hidden in the interior and the mountain fastnesses, and the war will be protracted to such a length that the black Unionists will have to step in at last and settle the question. This they will cheerfully do, although how? Montgomery Blair, in the capacity of prophet, declares that in the event of such an action, the result would be a war of extermination.[5] I think so too, a war of extermination of slaveholders as a class: there would not be a soul left who stood in the way of liberty, and union! Mr. Blair, the negro has something to say about this matter as well as yourself, though you hold in your possession the portfolio of a cabinet officer.

Although the rebels have abandoned their entrenchments, we still lie here, and we dare not put our feet on the Virginia shore unless we have a pass signed and countersigned by the commanding officer. Day before yesterday I took two hours to myself in the vicinity of Cockpit Point battery. For some reason or other the guards would let me make but a short stay. I saw many deserted log huts, and quite a large number of tents, on one which was marked in large illy-shaped letters, "No quarters for the Yankees," and quite a large well furnished mansion which a poor white women told me had generally been used as the quarters of the commanding officer. I saw the table at which he sat eating his dinner when the Gunboats commenced to shell the batteries. One of the shells fell in the centre of the room. He left his plate, knife and fork and scampered off; his dinner half eaten on his plate, so sayeth a poor white women. The name of the officer I could not learn. Another women stated that the rebels had treated her very badly. On the day before they left, they took her last hog. While she related this, a big fat porker stuck his nose in the door and grunted a contradiction. The woman colored up, and if we had not been so black we might have colored up also, but we thought to ourself and looked black. We found numerous secesh specimens, such as ragged coats, wornout shoes, hideous looking knifes, buttons, miserably written letters, of which I would fain send you specimens did space allow. Scores of freedmen are coming in. There are now some seventy or seventy-five at Rum Point, and some twenty or twenty-five more at Liverpool Point, added to those who were already there. They are principally from Stafford County, and were forced to secrete themselves in the woods and hedges, to escape being run off to Richmond. Some come in wifeless and childless; some husbandless and fatherless. Wives, husbands, children, and parents, have been run off to aid

the cause of slavery, and treason. They are generally intelligent. Quite
a number can read. One of the most communicative, whose name is
Peter King, was held to service and labor by George Moncure, of Kelsea
farm, Stafford County. He has a wife and two children, whom he desires to take with him to the North. His sister and grandmother were
seized by the retreating rebels and carried off. He states that he has a
mother living at Altoona, Pa., whose marriage name is Maria Alexander; Lieut. Baum,[6] of the 26th Regt., the ordinance officer of the
division, in company with a telegraph operator ventured too far outside the lines, and were made prisoners by the rebel pickets, and he
states that he saw them en route for Fredricksburg, Va., under a guard
of twelve men. This is some relief to the uncertainty of their fate, as
it was feared that they might have been murdered by the bush-whack-
ers. One man was found three or four days ago with his throat cut from
ear to ear.

It is a sight to see these men and women who, though born and bred
in slavery, boldly grapple with death itself for the sake of freedom.
They tell me they were not badly fed or poorly clad, that there is an
abundance of provisions in secession. All they seem to desire is liberty. I heard some of them telling some officers that they fared very
badly, and, on investigation I found it to be a rule amongst them to
so represent their cases, shrewdly knowing that in the majority of
cases the white man's idea of the wrongness of slavery, lies in the bad
treatment of the slaves. Their idea is, if he could be convinced that
the slaves were well fed, clothed, and housed, he would forget that
man has an unalienable right to liberty, and believe slavery to be a
sublime and beneficent institution because its victims could revel in
hog and hominy. This is one of the lessons slavery teaches. Here is
another specimen of the deceptions which the necessities of the
slave's condition compels him to resort to. Henry Morsul, the slave
of R. H. Eglin, was overseer on his master's plantation. The master
one day, revolving in his mind the probability of his whole human
stock deserting him, asked Henry whether he intended to leave him
like the hundreds who had already left good masters. Henry became
terribly enraged, and even shed tears because his master had allowed
such a thought to enter his mind. The master pleased and delighted
pronounced him a faithful, and a noble fellow. "Indeed I is massa,"
declared the faithful Henry. That night about 12 o'clock a large ro-
bust, deeply colored specimen of manhood, might be seen making

steady and rapid strides towards Rum Point. The next evening about the same hour the same specimen, who we may call Henry Morsul, might be seen walking up Broad street, Philadelphia, snuffling free air. Mr. Eglin says he "don't care a d—m for all the niggers in the country;" declares that "they will run away in spite of h-ll, they will 'fore God!" A little boy about 12 years of age who had made his escape, sent word to his mother and two little sisters that he would soon be in a free country where he could earn money for himself, and that he intended to save his money and buy them out of bondage. When boys of twelve years are animated by such thoughts as those, what must be the thoughts that dwell in the minds of hardy and sturdy manhood?

G. E. S.

WAA, 5 April 1862.

1. GES reflects common Northern criticism of McClellan and the Army of the Potomac for failing to engage Confederate forces. Stephen W. Sears, *George B. McClellan: The Young Napoleon* (New York: Ticknor and Fields, 1988), 118–20.

2. The term *Young America,* coined by the expansionist Edwin de Leon, symbolized the hypernationalism of the 1850s that imitated similar European movements. McClellan's views on race, slavery, and abolitionists were well known. Although he personally may have disliked slavery, McClellan believed that the Constitution guaranteed it, and he would never fight to end it. He despised abolitionists and once wrote of blacks, "I confess to a prejudice in favor of my own race, & can't learn to like the odor of either Billy goats or niggers." David M. Potter, *The Impending Crisis, 1848–1861* (New York: Harper and Row, 1976), 182–84; Sears, *George B. McClellan,* 116–18, quotation on 116.

3. Proverbs 12:10.

4. GES's criticism strikes at the heart of McClellan's image as an efficient organizer and strategist who whipped the Army of the Potomac into shape, demanding the best-trained and best-equipped men in overwhelming numbers before he would engage an enemy. Sears, *George B. McClellan,* 68–76; James M. McPherson, *Battle Cry of Freedom: The Civil War Era* (New York: Oxford University Press, 1988), 348–50.

5. GES refers to Postmaster General Montgomery Blair (1813–83), an avid colonizationist, who often warned that the Civil War would become a race war. Blair wished to deport blacks to Central America. See Stephens's 7 August 1863 letter.

6. Lt. William J. Baum, Company G, Twenty-sixth Pennsylvania, joined the unit on 28 May 1861. Official records state that rebels captured him on 24 March 1862 at Dumfries, Virginia, and he was exchanged on 15 October 1862. Compiled Service Records, RG 94, National Archives.

Chapter 8

"A Power That Cannot Be Ignored"

5 April 1862–31 December 1862

Northern blacks heard the same cry countless times: "This is a white man's war." But Stephens's letters show that the Civil War never had been entirely a "white man's war." Blacks had served valiantly in the Union navy since 1861, and the army depended upon military information provided by fugitive slaves. Even Gen. George B. McClellan, a fierce racist, admitted that his most reliable intelligence about the enemy came from blacks. Jefferson Davis's own coachman fled to Union lines and provided the North with as intimate a look at the rebel government as it would ever get. Union generals repeatedly ordered fugitive slaves expelled from army encampments and then ignored those directives when they discovered the information runaways possessed. "They are acquainted with all the roads, paths, fords and other natural features of the country," one Union general confessed, "and they make excellent guides. They also know, and frequently have exposed, the haunts of Secession spies and traitors, and the existence of rebel organizations."[1] They were, as Stephens wrote, a "spy in every household of the enemy." As spies, scouts, seamen, and stevedores, blacks had made an indispensable contribution to the Union war effort.

But the assistance of Southern blacks could not compensate for inferior generalship. From Bull Run to Fredericksburg, Union forces met with disappointment or disaster. So-called Union "victories," such as the Confederate evacuation along the Potomac River, only brought ridicule from the foreign and domestic press. Frightful Union defeats punctuated by prolonged inertia incited a clamor for new generals. At one point, Stephens exclaimed that he preferred another defeat to indecision and inactivity. Even when the massive Army of the Potomac did move, as in the daring amphibious assault of the

Peninsula Campaign, McClellan quickly lost his advantage. Rebel leaders appeared prescient in their ability to read Union intentions and rush fresh troops to the front. At Fredericksburg in December 1862, a new Union commander, if anything, only increased the monumental waste of human life. One officer who survived the battle wrote a terse and accurate assessment of the action: "13,000 men killed & wounded without a shadow of good resulting therefrom, is the result. Nothing but murder."[2]

Yet the end of 1862 proved the truth of Stephens's earlier predictions about the course of the war. Bled white by savage fighting, the North needed more men. The black man was a power the North could no longer ignore. As Frederick Douglass argued, the North "fought the rebellion, but not its cause. The key to the situation was the four millions of slaves; yet the slave, who loved us, was hated, and the slaveholder, who hated us, was loved. We kissed the hand that smote us, and spurned the hand that helped us."[3] The Emancipation Proclamation capped a two-year process brought about by stout rebel resistance and the presence of four million slaves.

Stephens was not alone in pondering the meaning of the watch-night of December 1862 when he wrote to the *Anglo-African* after Fredericksburg. He and his abolitionist allies wondered if President Lincoln would keep his promise of September to issue the Emancipation Proclamation on the first of the year. When the First of January broke, jubilation erupted across the North. In Boston, William C. Nell, the city's black abolitionist leader, reminded the throng at Tremont Temple that New Year's Day had been known as "Heart-Break Day" in memory of the thousands of slave families ruined on the auction block. But with the proclamation, that day had been reborn, "invested with new significance and imperishable glory in the calendar of time." Frederick Douglass sang "Blow yet trumpet, blow," and the entire assembly declared that "Jehovah hath triumphed, his people are free."[4] Stephens, who witnessed the war at ground level, remained circumspect but seized the opportunity Lincoln now provided.

1. Benjamin Quarles, *The Negro in the Civil War* (1953, reprint, New York: Da Capo Press, 1989), 80–83, quotation on 83.

2. Robert Garth Scott, ed., *Fallen Leaves: The Civil War Letters of Major Henry Livermore Abbott* (Kent: Kent State University Press, 1991), 154.

3. Frederick Douglass, *Life and Times of Frederick Douglass* (New York: Collier Books, 1962), quotation on 351–52.

4. Quarles, *The Negro in the Civil War*, quotations on 171–73.

* * *

Budd's Ferry, Md.
April 5th, 1862.

Mr. Editor.—After weeks and months of tedious rest and painful suspense we find ourselves at last on the march to meet the enemy.[1] We do not wish to make your readers think that we are anxious to meet death on the battle field that we are pawing here in the muddy valleys of Maryland smelling the battle afar off, or to use the language of a contemporary, "go out as gaily to meet death as to our bride,"[2] but we came here to brave danger, and even before we united our destinies with the Union cause we counted the cost. Fancy pictured to us all the dangers, all the horrors of bloody war. We felt that we were but unknown and insignificant; that thousands like us might be swept away in the ensanguined flood, unwept, unhonored, and unsung. Although we loved our country, "Our own our native land,"[3] and revered her flag, we left behind us dear relations and cherished friends and all the comforts and pleasures of home. But what are these when liberty is imperilled; when this corner-stone of progressive civilization is threatened with an upheaval? Although we rushed with ready hands and willing hearts to the defence of that liberty, we were told to stand back!

Denied the privilege of taking up arms against traitors and assassins, or to defend our country, which stood on the very brink of the yawning gulf of anarchical ruin. But there is a logic in this denial; the enfranchised man seems to tell us, "Negro, you have endured and suffered enough. Burnings, tortures and death have been meted out to you with a fiendish lavishness;—the cup of your misery is filled to overflowing. Stand aside while we take our draught of the poisoned chalice." Every tear shed by the bereaved widow and orphan, every sigh for the departed brave, form the sad and mournful atonement and portion, and are sanctifying the motto "Liberty and Union"—soon to adorn our flag. Thus the blood and the tortures of the slave blending with the blood and tears of the free, promise eventually to insure universal freedom and a peaceful and united country.

But the strangest thing of all is that although all the power of the nation (those in authority) have signally failed, and in spite of that power the negro has and is playing his part in the bloody arena. He is the spy in every household of the enemy. He conveys from every point the information without which the military operations of the United

States would be ineffective. When the Union soldier meets the negro in the enemy's country he knows him as a friend and asks him to strive for freedom in spite of fugitive-slave laws, proclamations and orders. He must play his part in spite of men and devils. He is a power that cannot be ignored. Yesterday afternoon Gen. Naglee issued an order that no colored man from a southern state should accompany the officers in the capacity of servant, that there were several hundred of Maryland slaves in the camps, and every officer who did take one such would be guilty of pillage! What folly to waste paper writing such orders. How many northern colored men could be found to risk their lives for nothing? They are bound to take these men, and who will Gen. Naglee get to prevent them? The thing works very nicely; they stay long enough to get a start and then they make tracks to more congenial regions, and others take their place. So the regenerating process goes on.

There is one thing to which the attention of the authorities at Washington should be called. There are about 350 freedmen here. They have received no pay from the government, although they have done all the shipping and unshipping of goods at Liverpool Point— some of them for the past five months. They have no one to instruct them, and seldom do any of the Lord's shepherds hereabouts trouble themselves about them. I rode over again to Liverpool Point the other day to see Mr. James Lawson, the negro scout, but he had gone over into Virginia, in company with some twelve or fifteen freedmen, and Gen. Sickles and some part of his command. Cornelius, his comrade, whom James reported dead, returned some time ago, safe and sound. He successfully accomplished the mission on which he was sent bringing back papers and valuable information. He has pluck, and had he not greeted the rebel pickets with a shot the whole party would have been taken. Jim's story about the picket's firing at Cornelius seems to have been forced on the imagination by excitement. Cornelius kept on, and made a successful reconnaissance to Fredericksburg, and has been highly complimented by Gen. Hooker. The fugitives still continue to flock in, and I think they should be looked after. There is one remarkable fact that has come under my observation: it is the dissimilarity between the slaves of Virginia and those of Maryland. The people of the latter are stupid, careless, and shiftless, while those of the former are intelligent, cleanly, and are able to talk on political matters with as much judgment as ordinary people in the free states. I account for this in this way; those who brave death are those who have obtained light, and consequently value liberty, and willingly dare to brave death for the sake of it, while the best of the latter have already left for the North and the debris is left behind.

Some of the most stirring tales of adventure are told by these people, of suffering of hair-breadth escapes. The man who crossed the river for his wife and family is the First Lieutenant of the freedmen at Liverpool Point. His name is Dennis Bland. His elder brother is the captain. When he brought his wife and two little children he also brought two young girls and a man. His noble and heroic wife gave a little idea of her trials after her husband came away. She said the moment her husband made his escape she commenced to plan her own. She, with a female companion hired two slave men to build a boat, promising to give him a passage. She and her comrade carried over four miles the boards to build the boat down to the river side. They labored in the night, so that they could not be found out. When the boat was put together they took their scissors, after buying tar and hemp, and caulked it. They fixed a night for the hegira, they gathered all the children and a little provisions and started. They passed the pickets and safely reached the appointed spot—when, Heavens, the boat was gone! The men they had paid to build it had stolen it and made their escape. Back that unfortunate night to their houses they had to travel. When she got home she was overcome by excitement and fatigue, and relieved her almost broken heart with soothing tears. Some one ran in and told her that Dennis was there!—She lived again, for she knew he came to rescue her. That night Dennis brought off his charges safely, wading waist deep out in the river on a December night, carrying that wife and those children he loved so well. She said, "I did not get angry when I found the boat was gone, but I prayed to the good Lord. I knew he saw my struggles and knew my desires, and I felt that he could not desert me in the trying hour." Such faith as this will remove a mountain of difficulty.

A court-martial has been assembled in the 11th Massachusetts' Regt. for the trial of Col. Wm. F. Small,[4] 26th Regt. Pennsylvania Volunteers.

G. E. S.

WAA, 26 April 1862.

1. With Confederates abandoning their positions along the Potomac, on 10 March 1862, McClellan's entire army—112,000 strong—moved toward Win-

chester in the north and Manassas and Centreville in the south. *OR*, ser. 1, 5:740–41; Stephen W. Sears, *George B. McClellan: The Young Napoleon* (New York: Ticknor and Fields, 1988), 163.

2. The contemporary writer to whom GES refers probably paraphrased Shakespeare: "But I will be a Bridegroom in my death, and run into it as to a lover's bed." *Antony and Cleopatra*, 4.12.99.

3. Sir Walter Scott, *The Lay of the Last Minstrel* (London: Longmans and Constable, 1805), 5:13.

4. In April 1862, Small was court-martialed for insubordination, making a false muster roll, and whipping an enlisted man. Hooker ordered an investigation by company officers, which Small quashed, but at the price of helping to bring about his trial and conviction. Lt. Col. Benjamin C. Tilghman, GES's patron and the judge-advocate in this case, provoked Small's charges that Tilghman was an atheist and part of a conspiracy against him. McClellan overturned the conviction, and Small resumed command of the regiment but resigned after the battle of Yorktown. General Court Martial Case Files, RG 153, Office of the Judge Advocate General (Army), National Archives.

Hooker's Division,
Before Yorktown,
April 19th, 1862.

Mr. Editor: On the 17th inst. our division was thrown out to the extreme front and within pistol shot of Gen. McClellan's headquarters. We keep the rebels in continual alarm. They dare scarcely show themselves above the ramparts of their entrenchments.[1] The preparations of Gen. McClellan are progressing with marvelous rapidity. On the 17th about 5 o'clock in the afternoon the enemy threw a shell into our lines while Lieut. Wagner[2] of the Engineer corps was just finishing a sketch of their works, which exploded with terrible effect, killing private Barrier[3] of the 57th Penn. Volunteers; fatally wounding Jerry Luther[4] of the 2nd. Rhode Island; shattering the left arm of Lieut. Wagner, and slightly wounding three others. The chart was spread out upon a table, the group standing around. When Dr. Mintzer[5] rode over to the Lieut. he politely waived his right hand and facetiously remarked "Doctor, I have met with a little accident," and conversed with the officers until his arm was amputated which was skillfully done by Dr. Judson[6] of Gen. Naglee's staff and Mintzer of the 26th Penn. Vols. Lieut. Wagner says he is willing to use the other arm in the service of his country. Luther still lives. When the Doctor asked him whether he had any message to send to his mother, he gave a comrade a piece of shell which he himself had taken from his own bowels to be sent to her, and requesting that his dead body be forwarded to her. The Doctor asked him whether he was married—he answered, "Nary time." His left arm was amputated this morning by Dr. Mintzer.

We took a walk out to the extreme outposts yesterday afternoon to see our artillerymen stir the rebels up. They threw sundry shell after them scattering them like frightened sheep. They returned the compliment. Their skirmishers drove us away, which turned out to be quite fortunate for our physical comfort for the rebels had just got our range and sent an iron missile which struck the very spot where we stood but a minute before. At the time it struck Genl. Naglee and his aid were riding within fifteen paces of that spot.

We heard heavy firing on our left last evening; I could not learn the particulars of it. It is supposed that the rebels attempted a sortie upon our approaches. In less time than I have occupied in penning these three lines this vast army was under arms and ready for mortal combat.

G. E. S.

WAA, 26 April 1862.

1. Confederates positioned about 31,500 men at Yorktown, Virginia, with their main force under Joseph E. Johnston west of Fredericksburg. Johnston anticipated McClellan's move to the Peninsula and on the night of 3 May 1862 evacuated Yorktown, destroying what could not be carried away and leaving McClellan with another hollow "victory." Herman Hattaway and Archer Jones, *How the North Won: A Military History of the Civil War* (Urbana: University of Illinois Press, 1983), 159–62, 172–75; Rowena Reed, *Combined Operations in the Civil War* (Annapolis: United States Naval Institute Press, 1978), 122, 157–60.

2. Orlando G. Wagner (1829–62) served as assistant top engineer during the Peninsula Campaign. He was wounded while surveying rebel positions at Yorktown and died on 21 April 1862. George W. Cullum, *Biographical Register of the Officers and Graduates of the U.S. Military Academy,* 2 vols. (New York: Van Nostrand, 1868), 2:483.

3. No one by this name served in the Fifty-seventh Pennsylvania.

4. Pvt. Jerry Luther, Jr., Company G, Second Rhode Island Regiment, entered the service on 5 June 1861 and according to official records died on 18 April 1862. Compiled Service Records, RG 94, National Archives.

5. Dr. St. John Mintzer, Twenty-sixth Pennsylvania Regiment, joined the unit on 27 May 1861 and left the service on 18 June 1864. Compiled Service Records, RG 94, National Archives.

6. National Archives records and nineteenth-century medical cyclopedias do not reveal a Dr. Judson. Stephens may refer to a hospital steward.

26th Reg. Pa. Vols., Sickles' Division,
Union Mills, Va.,
Nov. 20, 1862.

Mr. Editor.—A sudden, unexpected, and brilliant change of directions has been given to the grand Union Army, now in full advance on the Rebel Capital. Three days ago, the transhipment of the vast amount of army stores concentrated at Manassas Junction, and along the line of the Orange and Alexandria railroad,[1] even so far as Warrenton, commenced from front to rear and the last burthen train passed this point about 3 o'clock. Our troops commenced falling back to the line of Bull Run Creek last night, destroying [bri]dges and culverts, rendering the road utterly useless for rebel purposes. The rebels occupy various points as we evacuate them.[2]

The Excelsior Brigade, and the New Jersey Brigade[3] fell to the rear this morning. The rain is now falling in torrents and we are guarding the front against surprise. The base of operations is the City of Fredericksburg. The Union Generals are too wily to allow the rebels to draw them into a fox and goose chase up and down the hills and ravines of the Shenandoah Valley.[4]

As is ever the case when our troops fall back from the enemy's country, large numbers of contrabands or fugitive slaves follow in our wake. At the last battle of Bull Run, this whole region was depopulated of its slaves. None remain but the aged, infirm, young, and a few of that class of treacherous, pampered and petted slaves, known as house servants. Large numbers are flocking around us here, they come from Fauquier Co. Women and children are walking, as if for dear life, to reach Washington, which is considered by every negro within the boundaries of the Old Dominion, as his city of refuge.[5] There is one case which may be worthy of notice. George and Kitty Washington, and four remaining children belonged, with seventy others, to a man named Joe Weaver, living near Warrenton Junction. Our forces evacuated that place yesterday morning. Weaver had carried off to Richmond two other children of Washington but our troops came on him before he could get the rest away. Kitty knew that as soon as the Union soldiers left that she and her children would be carried down South, so she took as many of her things as she and her husband could conveniently carry, and turned her steps northward. Her little children walked so slowly that the rebel cavalry watching the movements of our troops came near capturing them; but they struck [for] the woods, and reached here in the drenching rain about 12 o'clock. They say they saw a great many others on the way. They also stated that all negroes caught attempting to escape are ordered to be shot.

A rebel deserter has just come in. He says he belongs to Stewart's Flying Artillery. Stewart left Culpeper last Monday morning with his whole command, cavalry and artillery, for some point in the vicinity of Fredericksburg. He says [he] don't know the force of the cavalry— Stewart always takes his whole command to make his raids.[6] The deserter who is a Prussian by birth, states that he has been in the army since last May one year, and is now tired of fighting, has no objections to fighting if he can get enough to eat. Stewart's battery consists of a new breech loading Whitworth gun, two Parrotts, and two Napoleons.[7] I have no doubt that Stewart is hovering around our flank between here and Fredericksburg to harass us with bold and unexpected raids on any undefended points. The deserter states that the rebels curse old Joe Hooker just as they do Butler[8] at New Orleans, and pronounce Sigel[9] a devil.

G. E. S.

WAA, 6 December 1862.

1. Virginia's Orange and Alexandria Railroad, owned by the former member of Congress and senator John S. Barbour, Jr., ran from beyond Charlottesville to Culpepper Court House, northeast to Manassas Junction, and terminated at Alexandria. Robert C. Black III, *The Railroads of the Confederacy* (Chapel Hill: University of North Carolina Press, 1952), 26–27.

2. McClellan's bloody trek up the Peninsula brought the Army of the Potomac to the outskirts of Richmond but no closer to victory. Pope's convincing defeat at the Second Battle of Bull Run (29 August) and the rebel victory at Chantilly (1 September) sent Hooker's division back over ground recently gained during the Confederate retreat from the Potomac. The Twenty-sixth Pennsylvania camped near Alexandria and did not fight at Antietam (17 September). The first week of November it was ordered to Union Mills to secure the northern part of the Orange and Alexandria Railroad. William Swinton, *Campaigns of the Army of the Potomac* (New York: Charles Scribner's Sons, 1882), 112–93; Bates, *History*, 1:344–48.

3. Commanded by Col. S. H. Starr, the New Jersey brigade in Hooker's division contained the Fifth through Eighth New Jersey Regiments. *OR*, ser. 1, 5:524–25, 716.

4. During the late spring and early summer of 1862, Stonewall Jackson's seventeen-thousand-man force ran riot through Virginia's Shenandoah Valley, hammering Union troops and capturing much-needed supplies. The North's inability to halt Jackson reinforced popular belief in the Union ar-

my's ineptitude. James M. McPherson, *Battle Cry of Freedom: The Civil War Era* (New York: Oxford University Press, 1988), 454–60.

5. Since the beginning of the war, blacks escaping slavery flocked to Washington, D.C., and to military camps along the city's perimeter. Many suffered, especially during winter, but philanthropic efforts begun in the summer of 1862 by Elizabeth Keckley, Mary Todd Lincoln's black personal attendant, helped many. Before the war's end, more than forty thousand freed slaves passed through government shelters—mostly on property confiscated from Robert E. Lee. Constance M. Green, *The Secret City: A History of Race Relations in the Nation's Capital* (Princeton: Princeton University Press, 1967), 58–64; *BAP*, 5:248–52.

6. Gen. James Ewell Brown Stuart (1833–64) became the South's most flamboyant and successful cavalryman. At the time of this letter, he commanded 603 officers and 8,551 troops. GES mentions Stuart's famous 12–16 June 1862 circuit completely around McClellan's army with only 1,200 cavalrymen. Maj. John Pelham commanded Stuart's mounted artillery, consisting of four Virginia batteries and one from South Carolina. On 18 November, Stuart established his headquarters near Fredericksburg and spread his growing force along fifty miles of the Rappahannock River. *WWWCW*, 631–32; *HTIECW*, 727–29; Emory M. Thomas, *Bold Dragoon: The Life of J. E. B. Stuart* (New York: Harper and Row, 1986), 187, 189, 191–94.

7. Deadly accurate, the English-made, hexagonal-bore Whitworth was one of the few breech-loading cannons employed during the war. Although favored by the Confederates, Hooker's division received two Whitworths on 20 February 1862. Parrott guns, reliable muzzle-loading artillery employed by both armies, carried a thick reinforcing band around the breech. The Napoleon, or model 1857 cannon, became the war's most prized fieldpiece. Warren Ripley, *Artillery and Ammunition of the Civil War* (New York: Van Nostrand, 1970), 142–48; *HTIECW*, 520, 558; Warren H. Cudworth, *History of the First Regiment, Massachusetts Infantry* (Boston: Walker, Fuller, 1866), 126; *OR*, ser. 1, 5:525, 725.

8. Benjamin F. Butler (1818–93), member of Congress from Massachusetts and a controversial general, commanded the Department of the Gulf, where he earned the undeserved title of "Beast." *WWWCW*, 96–97; Warner, *Generals in Blue*, 60–61.

9. Franz Sigel (1824–1902) rallied German Americans for the Union. Confederates did not fear his mediocre military talents but abhorred his abolitionism. Warner, *Generals in Blue*, 447–48; Berlin, *The Black Military Experience*, 341.

Camp near Fredericksburg, Va.,
Dec. 19 [1862].

Mr. Editor: I would fain be silent but my duty compels me to record what fell under my notice in the great battle of Fredericksburg, which has resulted in the total defeat of the Federal Army.[1] On Thursday morning the 11th inst., about four o'clock, the heavy booming of cannon and continual volleys of musketry told in no mistakable terms that we were on the eve of a great battle. These premonitions were not unexpected for orders had been received two or three days previous to the above date, for every man to be supplied with four days cooked rations and to be prepared for marching at a moment's notice. The whole army, which for many dreary days had been laying literally gazing on the growing rebel entrenchments, was awakened from its slumber and inactivity, to bustle, activity and enthusiasm, and by daylight vast columns of infantry, immense trains of artillery, might be seen deploying to the right, to the left, to the front and the rear. The pale but stern countenances of the men, and their quick firm step, kindled within me a certainty of victory. Delays are said to be dangerous, and as days succeeded days, I have asked myself the question, "Why does not the army move?" Every day must render more remote the chances of victory. The day of advance came—the air was cold and bracing—the sun shone brightly, a week's wintry weather had frozen the roads hard, and the heaviest artillery could be readily transported. The day of battle came and no one doubted that in a little while the rebel horde would be flying dismayed before our victorious arms.

The right was assigned to General Sumner, the left to General Franklin, the centre to General Hooker whose main force was held as a reserve.[2] The action was opened by the rebel sharpshooters firing on the pontoon builders, who suffered severely in the attempt to throw a bridge across the river opposite the city. These sharpshooters took refuge in some old shanties in suburbs of the town, and could not be dislodged until our artillery opened on the town and sent their hiding places whizzing about their heads. General Hooker called for volunteers to cross in boats and effectually dislodge them, when the 7th Regiment of Michigan[3] crossed the river and took some hundred prisoners, and won the honor of being the first troops to stand on the Richmond side of the Rappahannock. While this was going on our pontoons were thrown across about three miles below the city opposite Bell Plain, and about 12 o'clock General Franklin's grand division commenced to cross under the cover of the guns of our artillery, and by Friday afternoon the whole of Sumner's and Franklin's corps had crossed, and a general skirmish between the heavy guns along the whole line ensued to cease entirely on Friday evening, when both armies rested as if [to] gather strength for sterner and more vigorous s [word missing].

Saturday came smiling and beautiful, [word or words missing] most delightful day of the season. The wind favored us, for the frosty mists obscured our movements. Away on the opposite hills long dark lines of rebel infantry were drawn up like great black serpents; and the forces of General Sumner might be seen slowly advancing, the musketry seemed to grow more and more distant, but the action now began to extend along the whole line. I imagined I heard the shrieks of the wounded above the dreadful noise. Soon the biers, the ambulances, crowded by; the pale, limping, and emaciated wounded commenced coming in. Up to 2 o'clock there seemed to be no lull in the action. Sickles' Division[4] was ordered to cross the river, which they did and entered the field about 3 o'clock. Birney's Division[5] were to make the movement which was to decide the fate of the day. Sumner had hurled his Brigade against the rebel strongholds on the right dashing them to pieces like waves against a rocky shore. Franklin's forces charged the enemy and drove him headlong before him. This was on the left centre. The importance of this movement will be understood when it is known that the railroad runs parallel with the river.[6]

Franklin's attack was made about 12½ o'clock. Shortly afterwards our division (Sickles') crossed the river, entered the field, threw out skirmishers, and the action began. Meade's and Gibbon's divisions formed the attacking column.[7] They drove the rebels across the railroad, out of the first skirt of woods, into an open field beyond, kept them at bay for half an hour but not being reinforced were compelled to fall back leaving their dead and wounded on the field. Their loss was much heavier from falling back than from the advance. All along this ravine were rifle pits but they formed no impediment to the impetuous advance of our soldiers. Where was Franklin that he did not support this heroic and successful attack? Why did he not hurl his fifty thousand, if need be, against this vulnerable point?

When Mead and Gibbons fell back, the rebels advanced and poured into their ranks a most galling fire, and in a short time attempted a flank movement and opened with terrible precision with artillery on the left. In the first skirt of woods they succeeded in getting a battery in position, but in less than fifteen minutes our cannoneers had silenced it. Our division lost considerably in skirmishing, but aided materially in staying the rebel attack. We could stand on the plains and see great heaps of dead, and while our artillery was playing among the enemy, no matter where you turned your eye along the lines, you might see them fall. On Saturday night the pickets kept up an continual exchange of shots. A squad of rebel cavalry tried to penetrate our lines in front of Sickles' Division. Our pickets fired on them and killed one and wounded two leaving them on the field. They thought, no doubt, that our forces had already commenced to recross the river; but they were mistaken. We rested Saturday night on the field and we heard the rebels felling trees and heard their artillery moving. They had been taught by Saturday's attack that this was a weak point. They were busy strengthening it. On Sunday morning, immediately after daylight, the rebels rained a perfect shower of shot and shell on us. It is marvelous that so many escaped unharmed. No matter where you would turn your eye these terrible missiles were seen plowing up the ground. Our artillery replied vigorously and the battle gradually subsided until 9 o'clock when it totally ceased. No one, at first, could tell what caused this until a long train of ambulances began to move to and fro with the wounded, and fatigue parties began the work of burying the dead. Some say the truce was exchanged, but common sense tells us that Burnside asked for time to bury his dead as a *ruse* to cover his retreat across the river. It was a masterly move to cross the river under the guns of the enemy. It tells us that a master will commands the army.

The battle of Fredericksburg was splendidly planned but bunglingly executed. Had certain subordinates exhibited the average degree of executive ability, the battle would have been, instead of a defeat, a signal victory. There seems to be no lack of enthusiasm or any dissatisfaction among the men. They would fight just as determingly and willingly now as they did at the four days battle of Fredericksburg. It is estimated here that our loss will amount to less than 10,000 killed and wounded and missing; the wounded largely predominating. Straggling to any extent was for once prevented. There was no use in it, for there was not a foot of ground on the other side of the river which the rebel guns did not command, and the pontoons were guarded; so a fellow who wanted to straggle away out of danger, had to swim the Rappahannock. This, of course he would decline doing at this season of the year. There were no boats or even a bit of plank on which a fellow with shaky nerves could float.

We now occupy the old camp, wishing in our heart of hearts that John Rebel would come over and meet us on an open field.

A few short weeks ago when our division left Fairfax Seminary[8] there was a young man just married. His young wife bade farewell to him expecting to see him Christmas. I saw that young man on Saturday sick, not able to carry his knapsack. He threw it to one side of the road, saying: "I shall soon have no use for it." Sure enough, the first man struck in the line was this young man. Although sick he would not be excused from duty; would rather go out and meet death like a man.

Passing by the hospital (Bernard's House)[9] I saw a crowd of men standing around one of the surgeons. "Are you all wounded, men?" A dozen voices answered, "Yes, sir!" "Ah, yes! your feelings are wounded by your being so badly frightened." This may account for the long lists of wounded and the short lists of killed. The 10th Mass. Vol.[10] reported 40 wounded; none killed. Poor fellows! wounded feelings. Seeing a number of litters pass with forms upon them I stopped to give them a passing glance, when one of the hospital attendants asked, "What have you got there, men?" "Only a few more dead," was the answer. "Take them down to the end of the field yonder, and lay them with the rest." The work of removing and burying the dead has become so common and tame that the lifeless body of a man was looked upon as nothing more than that of a brute. I have learned of but one colored man being killed. His name I could not find out. He was struck on the head with a shell.

There are comparatively few people who have taken refuge among us, and they are principally free colored people. The slaves were all run off. There were twenty-five or thirty slaves of Bernard left behind. They did not succeed in making their escape when we retreated, the movement was so suddenly and quickly performed.

The Hawkins Zouaves[11] are distinguished for their rowdyism and brutality to colored men. They form one of the regiments of Sickles' old Division. More than one poor slave has met his death at the hands of this mob. It is a common boast, "I licked a nigger!" The day of our departure one of these men had some difficulty with one of the colored teamsters, and seized a bar of iron and commenced a furious attack on the teamsters indiscriminately, and his comrades were on the point of joining in the assault, when the boss teamster, a white man, drew a revolver and threatened to shoot the rascals if they did not desist. They all ran yelling with the news to the regiment, which had halted a few paces from my own, seized their arms and with upwards of fifty more returned to the attack to murder in cold blood a few unarmed negroes. The men got wind of their intentions and concealed themselves. The boss teamster stood his ground, would not surrender but walked before them into camp, when Gen. Taylor[12] ordered his release and gave him credit for his action.

I am informed that during the heavy firing on Saturday afternoon the 20th Reg. N. Y. Vols.[13] took refuge behind some embankments, and some of the colored servants also took shelter from the enemy's shells, when the officers and men drove them out at the point of the bayonet saying, "Let the damned nigger be killed—how dare they come here among white men." There, sir, in the very jaws of death, they did not forget to hate our brethren. Sir, in the bottomless pit, when the flames are parching their tongues they will lisp and stammer curses on the race.

G. E. S.

WAA, 3 January 1863.

1. Gen. Ambrose E. Burnside surprised Lee with a quick move toward Fredericksburg on 15 November but squandered his advantage waiting for pontoons to bridge the Rappahannock River. Lee then concentrated about seventy-five thousand men and three hundred artillery pieces in a virtually impregnable position to await the Union advance. The horrible slaughter begun on 13 December, especially at Marye's Heights, cost 12,653 Union casualties, whereas the Confederates suffered only 5,309. Herman Hattaway and Archer Jones, *How the North Won: A Military History of the Civil War* (Urbana: University of Illinois Press, 1983), 303–8; Edward J. Stackpole, *Drama on the Rappahannock: The Fredericksburg Campaign* (New York: Bonanza Books, 1957).

2. Gen. Edwin Vose Sumner (1797–1863) commanded the "Right Grand Division"—Second and Ninth Army Corps and a cavalry division—and led the assault. Gen. William B. Franklin (1823–1903) commanded the "Left Grand Division," comprising the First and Sixth Corps and a cavalry brigade. Burnside unfairly blamed him for the defeat at Fredericksburg. Hooker led the "Center Grand Division"—Third and Fifth Corps and a cavalry brigade. Warner, *Generals in Blue*, 159–60, 489–90; Stackpole, *Drama on the Rappahannock*, 78, 235–37; Hattaway and Jones, *How the North Won*, 307.

3. Organized on 22 August 1861, the Seventh Michigan also saw action at Antietam and Chancellorsville and helped put down the New York City draft riots. It lost 397 men in the war and mustered out on 5 July 1865. Dyer, *Compendium*, 3:1284–85.

4. Sickles commanded the Second Division, which included Stephens's Twenty-sixth Pennsylvania and twenty-two other regiments and artillery batteries from New York, New Jersey, and Massachusetts. *OR*, ser. 1, 21:54.

5. Gen. David Bell Birney (1825–64), son of the abolitionist leader James G. Birney, headed the First Division under Hooker. Accused of disobeying orders, Birney actually performed well. Warner, *Generals in Blue*, 34; *OR*, ser. 1, 21:53.

6. The *Anglo* noted here that "a portion of our correspondent's letter failed to reach us. Ed."

7. Gen. George Gordon Meade (1815–72), later commander of the Army of the Potomac, led the Third Division under Franklin. Gen. John Gibbon (1827–96) led the Army of the Potomac's Iron Brigade, commanded the Second Division under Franklin, and was wounded in the battle. *HTIECW*, 309, 482–83; *OR*, ser. 1, 21:58.

8. GES probably refers to the Virginia Theological Seminary near Alexandria, founded in 1823 by the evangelical wing of the Episcopalian church. Federal troops used its grounds for a cemetery. William Wilson Manross, *The Episcopal Church in the United States, 1800–1840: A Study in Church Life* (New York: Columbia University Press, 1938), 92–93; Robert W. Prichard, *A History of the Episcopal Church* (Harrisburg: Morehouse Publishing, 1991), 169.

9. Bernard's plantation house, about two miles south of Fredericksburg on the west bank of the Rappahannock River, served as General Franklin's headquarters. Confederate shelling destroyed it. Stackpole, *Drama on the Rappahannock*, 108, 162–63, 184, 237, 254.

10. Organized in May and June 1861, the Tenth Massachusetts Regiment remained in reserve at Fredericksburg but fought at the second battle there on 3 May 1863 and sustained heavy losses. The unit mustered out in July 1864. *Massachusetts Soldiers, Sailors*, 1:682–83.

11. The Ninth New York Regiment, formed on 23 April 1861, abandoned the Zouave uniform early in the war. It lost ninety-six men during the conflict and disbanded on 20 May 1863. Dyer, *Compendium*, 3:1408–9.

12. Gen. Nelson Taylor (1821–94) originally led the Seventy-second New York Regiment in Sickles's Excelsior Brigade but at Fredericksburg commanded the Third Brigade, Second Division, First Corps. *WWWCW*, 642–43.

13. Popularly know as the United Turner Regiment, the Twentieth New York was organized on 6 May 1861, fought mostly in Virginia, and mustered out on 1 June 1863. Dyer, *Compendium*, 3:1412.

26th Penn. Regiment, Sickles' Division,
Camp near Fredericksburg, Va.,
December 31, 1862.

Mr. Editor:—I know of no moment so opportune and suggestive as the present one with which I might occupy myself. Thus, you know it is said that men generally regard moral and religious duties more attentively as they grow in years, and as year by year pass away, I am the more deeply impressed with the fleetness of time and the rapid approach of the eternity beyond the tomb; and as the annual watch-night[1] approaches, thinks I to myself, have any of the christian graces adorned the conduct of the receding year? Has faith strengthened? Is the devotion to the cause of God and my fellow-man more firm? And am I prepared to brave the storms and conflicts of the hour, or willing to sacrifice interests, home, comfort, or life if need be for God and liberty? These are some of the suggestions of the watch-night of December 31, 1862.

If we who have been prating for so many long years of our inalienable right to liberty, have not prayerfully and tearfully pondered over these questions, oh, let us this night, if possible, transform ourselves, forget little narrow, mean, contemptible self, and resolve to accept the dangers and the consequences of the new year willingly. New Year's Eve has ever been a season of prayer among the colored people from my earliest age. I have participated in those annual greetings. It has always seemed like a period for moral and religious reckonings, when the errors and misdeeds of the past year are tearfully and prayerfully remembered, and a new leaf is turned over and we resolve to live better in the future.

The "Anglo-African," which is read and reread until its folds are worn in parts, informs us that noble efforts are being made to celebrate the proclamation of freedom in the rebellious States. The "Anglo" has clothed herself in a new year dress to commemorate this glorious and most momentous event.[2] Your beauty and tastefulness, "Anglo," fascinates me. May you win the patronage of ten thousand new subscribers for a new year's gift. I long to be present to participate in this great jubilee; to listen to the stirring words that fancy shall kindle on the glowing tongue of eloquence, and to cry with my brethren of the North—"Jehovah hath triumphed; the people are free!"[3]

There cannot be a more appropriate season for our assembling together to recount the doings and to mark the changes of the past year. What changes have been wrought since last new year['s] watch-night! Thousands who joined in the festivities and solemnities then, are forever absent. One short year of time is pregnant with great and wonderful results; and the coming year may form the epoch which shall regenerate our race and shall reduce to poverty, beggary and ruin that insolent faction which has brought humiliation, disgrace and a bloody civil war upon the country, and in the frenzy of a confirmed diabolism, proclaimed to the christian world that the slavery of my people is morally, politically and religiously right.

This December 31st, the watch-night of 1862, may be the watch night which shall usher in the new era of freedom. It may, after all, be the season for a national reckoning, and the crimes and misdeeds which have accumulated during the period of eighty odd years may be tearfully and prayerfully remembered and a new resolve made to adhere strictly to national duty. Oh! may the nation pause and reflect, and remember her pride, avarice and injustice. Do not nations have to suffer for misdeeds as well as individuals? And should they not have a season of moral reckoning? I know of but one act in the whole history of this country which furnishes any evidence of national duty performed, viz; the abolition of slavery in the District of Columbia.[4] No other act of her's illumines the national record. Her wealth is built on the labor of slaves. Her religion, clothed with the garb of divinity, the hideous deformities of involuntary servitude; and her law, after establishing the outlawry of my race, culminated in the remarkable and gratuitous declaration of R. B. Taney—"black men have no rights that white men are bound to respect." Would to God that the nation could say like England, "We have baptized free every atom of our soil," or like Russia, "We have manumitted our serfs," or like little Denmark, "We have emancipated our slaves."[5]

The history of the United States since the adoption of the Constitution, must be most humiliating to those enlightened statesmen who have struggled to make America the freest as well as the most enlightened nation on earth. But their tears and entreaties were unheeded, and a broken, distracted country, the desolations of civil war and distracted councils are the bitter fruits of this disregard for national duty.

Of the President's proclamation of freedom in the rebellious States we can scarcely say anything, for the pro-slavery pressure on him must be very great. Since the recent elections have unmistakably indicated that the pro-slaveryites are immensely in the majority, I should not be disappointed if the proclamation be withheld. If military necessity, three months ago, required emancipation, the military necessity of the present time must require it still the more. The battle of Fredericksburg placed it beyond a doubt, and if it be withheld, it will be because slavery is preferred to honor, country, or right. When the proclamation comes it will be the signal for a commencement of the

war, and those men who are now spurned by the constituted authorities, must then be armed, and in the name of High Heaven the sorrows, tears, and anguish of millions shall be revenged. A proclamation will necessitate a general arming of the freedmen.[6]

Christmas day passed off quite gaily, if getting drunk and keeping
up a terrible uproar furnish the popular notion of gaiety. Immense
quantities of government whiskey were consumed on that day in the
camps. I saw more drunken men on that day then I have seen since
last winter in Washington. The only disturbance that I know of occurred in the 2nd New Hampshire Volunteers. The sutler of the regiment would not sell his whiskey to the privates and they attempted
to take it by main force. The 26th Penn. and 11th Mass. were kept in
readiness to repel any depredations, and a strong guard was placed
around the sutler's tent until the following morning, when everything
resumed its usual order.

A grand Christmas dinner was given at the headquarters of Major
Gen. Hooker. The arrangements were ample and sumptuous. There
were present among some twenty-five guests, Brig. Gens. Mott, Revere, Hooker and A. A. Gen. Joseph Dickinson.[7] Toasts on toasts were
drank to the old hero, and so pressing were the attentions that he was
compelled to make a few remarks. Gen. Stoneman[8] would have been
present, but was quite unwell, and has been sick for some time. The
toast to which Gen. Hooker responded, and which was drank standing, was:

"General Hooker, the future Commander of the Army of the Potomac."[9]

Gen'l. Hooker said:—"I don't know, my friends, whether you are
my friends or not when you wish me to take command of the army;
for this army is, so to speak, at the bottom of a well, while, the enemy is at the top, and it must be extricated before it can be expected
to perform what its force and strength should perform. I do not know
how to thank you for the expressions in reference to myself. If I should
take command of this army, I should take command of it as I would
of a forlorn hope, and should strive to do with it all that I could to
crush this rebellion. When the rebellion broke out I left California and
came here. I had left the army, as I supposed, forever; but that flag had
been outraged. I resolved to do as much as any one individual can do
to resent that insult, and to give my life, if need be, to crush treason.
But no matter who commands this army, I shall strive hard to defeat

the enemy. I care not who commands, I do not care for rank—if a lieutenant had command I would cheerfully do my duty."

During the dinner, one of the brigade bands played the most splendid music. The dinner was given in two large wall tents. Three large chandeliers were formed of evergreens and bayonets, into which were placed candles. Every arm of the service in the Center Grand Division was represented.[10]

There are great preparations making for celebrating New-Year's day. The 40th N.Y., Mozart,[11] have near their camp an enclosure where a greased pole is to be set up with ten dollars pinned to the top—and there is to be foot-racing, horse, mule, and sack racing for prizes. It is astonishing how few men are sick hereabouts and what splendid spirits (not ardent) and condition the army seems to be in.

G. E. S.

WAA, 17 January 1863.

1. Watch-night services, held in slave communities, black churches, and among evangelical whites, offered singing, preaching, and fervent prayer for God's blessing of the new year. On the night before Lincoln officially decreed the Emancipation Proclamation, interracial meetings across the North anxiously awaited the telegraphic message that declared slavery's death warrant. William H. Wiggins, Jr., "January 1: The Afro-American's Day of Days," *Prospects: An Annual of American Cultural Studies* 4 (1979): 331–53; Frederick Douglass, *Life and Times of Frederick Douglass* (New York: Collier Books, 1962), 353–55.

2. The *Anglo-African* changed typeface and size, giving the paper a sharper, clearer appearance.

3. Stephens quotes from the popular English author, poet, and song writer, Thomas Moore (1759–1852). Moore's "Miriam's Song," also called "Sound the Loud Timbrel," was frequently invoked by antislavery advocates. In part it reads, "Sound the loud timbrel o'er Egypt's dark sea! Jehovah has triumphed,—his people are free." Thomas Moore, *Melodies, Songs, Sacred Songs, and National Airs* (New York: George Long, 1821), 214–15.

4. Henry Wilson's measure to abolish slavery in the District, proposed on 4 December 1861, was adopted on 16 April 1862. It provided compensation to loyal masters, and only 36 of the 966 petitions—covering 2,989 slaves—that sought reimbursement for slaves freed under the act failed to receive money. Henry Wilson, *History of the Antislavery Measures of the Thirty-Seventh and Thirty-Eighth United-States Congresses, 1861–64* (Boston: Walker, Wise, 1864), 37–78, 198–202; Berlin, *The Destruction of Slavery,* 164–65.

5. GES refers to the Dred Scot case, the Somerset case and the 1833 Emancipation Act in England, Russia's ending of serfdom in 1861, and Denmark's abolition of the slave trade in 1804.

6. GES's prediction proved correct. Although Lincoln had authority to enlist black troops under the Second Confiscation Act, he did not seek such action until issuing the Emancipation Proclamation. Berlin, *The Black Military Experience*, 68–69.

7. GES mentions Gen. Gershom Mott (1822–84), just recovered from wounds suffered at Second Bull Run, who resumed command of the Third Brigade, Second Division, Third Corps; Gen. Joseph Warren Revere (1812–80), who led Mott's brigade at Fredericksburg, was later court-martialed and removed from command for an unauthorized retreat at Chancellorsville; and Joseph Dickinson, Hooker's adjutant. *WWWCW*, 460–61, 538.

8. Gen. George Stoneman (1822–94), appointed chief of the cavalry under McClellan, commanded the First Division of the Third Corps at Fredericksburg. His "daring" cavalry dashes usually produced no significant results. Warner, *Generals in Blue*, 481–82; *WWWCW*, 627–28.

9. Hooker, openly critical of Burnside's generalship, used his contacts in the Lincoln cabinet to become head of the Army of the Potomac. Appointed on 26 January 1863, he was relieved on 28 June. Warner, *Generals in Blue*, 234; *WWWCW*, 317–18.

10. Hooker commanded the Center Grand Division, Army of the Potomac, from 16 November 1862 to 26 January 1863. *WWWCW*, 317.

11. The Fortieth New York Regiment ("Mozart Regiment" and "Constitution Guard"), organized on 27 June 1861, lost 410 men in the war and mustered out on 27 June 1865. Dyer, *Compendium*, 3:1418–19.

Chapter 9

"Better to Die Free, Than Live Slaves"

18 March 1863–1 May 1863

Few whites acknowledged the slavery of racial prejudice. Denied the vote, derided in the popular press, barred from public assemblies, banished to segregated schools, relegated to the lowest paying jobs regardless of education or ability, and often driven from their homes by seething mobs, northern blacks lived without freedom. While their subjugation paled compared to Southern slavery, neither did they have the fundamental liberties whites took for granted. New York editor and black abolitionist Samuel E. Cornish gave voice to the importance Northern blacks placed on fighting racism. "The time has come when the question has got to be met. Prejudice against color, after all, is the test question—at least among us. The mere and direct question of slavery is not. For every man here says—'I am as much opposed to slavery as you are. But as for these *Niggers*, we don't want them here—let them go home to their own land.'" This constant refrain convinced blacks that slavery, however heinous, was not their true enemy. "The real battleground between liberty and slavery is prejudice against color."[1]

Black leaders wrote thousands of essays, pamphlets, and books and gave countless speeches to refute charges of racial inferiority and prove black ability. To the degree that racial prejudice grew out of ignorance of black accomplishments, African-American leaders had done all they could to inform a skeptical public. The Civil War offered another way to confound prejudice and prove black worth.

When the Lincoln administration consented to Gov. John A. Andrew's request to form a regiment of African-American troops, blacks such as Stephens took the lead. Scores of black recruiters volunteered their time and energy in the spring of 1863 to organize the Fifty-fourth Regiment of Massachusetts Volunteer Infantry. As Stephens proudly claimed, "Every one of us felt it to be a high and holy duty to organize the first regiment" of black troops in the North. Men from every free state, Canada, Great Britain, the Hawaiian Islands, and even Africa enlisted in the unit to destroy the idea of racial inferiority, win full citizenship, and crush slavery. Although the dangers were obvious and the rewards might prove limitless, the responsibility was enormous. Speaking for Northern blacks, the *Anglo-African* put the matter bluntly: "The eyes of the whole world are upon you, civilized man everywhere waits to see if you will prove yourselves. . . . *Will you vindicate your manhood?*"[2] The Fifty-fourth's most fervent white supporters, including its commander Robert Gould Shaw, harbored at least momentary apprehension. Not one black soldier, however, ever doubted the outcome.

1. *Colored American,* 9 June 1838, in *BAP,* 3:265–66.
2. *WAA,* quoted in *BAP,* 3:59.

*   *   *

Philadelphia,
March 18, 1863.

Mr. Editor:—I was not a little surprised at your Boston correspondent's, G. L. R.'s,[1] severe criticism on Wm. Wells Brown's new book.[2] I think he overlooks entirely the purpose for which the work seems to have been written:—a text book, a book for the times, an argument for the race which cannot be refuted. It should be circulated all over the country, to aid in the great and good work of dispelling the sin-begotten, infatuated notion—negro inferiority. The animus of G. L. R.'s criticism lies in this, that there are so many men of genius and distinction "left out," such as Stephen Smith,[3] Joseph Turpin,[4] and a few others, or perhaps G. L. R. has his own crow to pick with this book. This principal objection to the "Black Man," that everybody was not recorded within its pages, has cumulated in a most intense feeling. I have just seen a letter from a well-known colored gentleman who says, "there is a prejudice against the work here, created by those who are *'left out,'* and what have those left out ever done to give them a place in this or any other book?" This shows the little appreciation that colored men are capable of placing upon the writings of their own race.

Ralph Waldo Emerson says, "Mr. Brown's book is the best argument ever put forth in defence of the negro."[5] It is a marvel that Mr. Brown has achieved so much with such scanty means.

Slavery and caste has so stultified our progressive tendencies, and the "demands of society" upon us for scientific or literary attainments have been so limited that we have been compelled for the sake of daily bread to devote ourselves to plebeian avocations, and if perchance distinction were achieved, it must be traced to fortuitous circumstances with scarce a hope of honor or emolument, and without the stimulus of manly competition in the arena of letters. Is it a dishonor to the race that there are few great men amongst us? No! But it is an honor to the race that Mr. Brown has with his limited material given to the American people a work, which tells them that we possess the foundation material, on which we are about to build a superstructure of pure Christian civilization.

Your Boston correspondent predicts that some person in the future will hand down to posterity his fame by doing or undoing what Mr. Brown has done in his work. This coming biographer could be famed for nothing, but his folly. The deeds and achievements for which the negro is destined, will wrap the terrible and humiliating history of the past two hundred years, in a brilliant wreath of martial and intellectual glory.

But Mr. Brown's book does not claim to be a biography, but a sketch book of our most distinguished characters, and he transcended no prerogative, when he presented a strong array of characters. But our critic will not be comforted. He in almost the one and same breath complains that Mr. Brown gives too many names—too much pork for a shilling, and denounces the book, because he left out such remarkable geniuses as Stephen Smith, Joseph Turpin & Co.

As a text book it is invaluable, and it has been pronounced by intelligent men, white and colored, to be the best argument in favor of the black man's ability yet published. Did G. L. R. read the sketch of Miss C. L. Forten with those gems of prose and poetic offshoots of her pen?[6] a sketch which of itself is worth the price of the book. Did he forget to peruse the sketch of Benjamin Banneker,[7] a literary effort which, I think, has done our great mathematician better justice than any other sketch? The intrinsic value of the work lies in the fact that he has brought out so many new characters. Frederick Douglass,[8] Toussaint L'Ouverture,[9] Nat Turner,[10] and such men have been so frequently written about, that their names have become household words. But the young artists, Wm. H. Simpson,[11] Edwin M. Bannister,[12] with all their genius were never known to the public, till the "Black Man" made its appearance. Prof. Wilson[13] and Alex. Crummell[14] are fortunate in having Mr. Brown as their exponent. This work contains the first sketch ever published of Crispus Attucks,[15] though his name and deeds have often been in print. Mr. Brown exhibits the genius of nearly every one of his characters, either by quoting some of their writing or speeches, and this forms an interesting feature in the many beauties of his most important work.

G. E. Stephens

WAA, 28 March 1863.

1. G. L. R., a regular Boston *Anglo-African* correspondent, was the Virginia-born black George Lewis Ruffin (1834–86). In 1863, Ruffin attempted to join the Fifty-fifth Massachusetts but failed the physical examination. He later graduated from Harvard Law School, entered the Suffolk County Bar in 1869, served in the State House and on Boston's common council, and won appointment to the municipal court in Charleston. In his *Anglo-African* letter, Ruffin asserted that the time had long since passed "when a colored man was not thought capable of writing" a book. Thus, Ruffin believed that all books should be judged on their own merits, and he found William Wells Brown's *The Black Man: His Antecedents, His Genius, and His Achievements* (New York: Thomas Hamilton, 1863) superficial, "too much pork for a shilling." He also criticized it for leaving out such black leaders as Stephen Smith, Joseph H. Turpin, Amos G. Beman, and H. Ford Douglas. *DANB*, 535; *WAA*, 7 March 1863.

2. William Wells Brown (1814?-84), born a slave in Lexington, Kentucky, rose to become, next to Frederick Douglass, the most eloquent and influential black abolitionist. A prolific author, Brown wrote *Clotel* (1853), the first novel by an African American. Responding to his critics, Brown explained that his book offered information relevant to *"the present crisis."* The book's success—ten printings in three years—confirmed Lewis Tappan's declaration that this "is just the book for the hour. It will do more for the colored man's elevation than any work yet published." William Edward Farrison, *William Wells Brown: Author and Reformer* (Chicago: University of Chicago Press, 1969); *WAA*, 8 August 1863; James M. McPherson, *The Struggle for Equality: Abolitionists and the Negro in the Civil War and Reconstruction* (Princeton: Princeton University Press, 1964), 139.

3. Stephen Smith (ca. 1797–1873), who gained a fortune through his lumber, coal, and real estate businesses, was also an AME minister. He put his financial resources at the disposal of a number of black causes, attended black national and state conventions, helped found the American Moral Reform Society, and supported the Institute for Colored Youth. GES probably resented Smith for his failure to aid the men put on trial for the abortive rescue of the fugitive slave Moses Horner in 1860. *BAP*, 4:316–17n.13; *DANB*, 566; *WAA*, 21 April 1860.

4. Joseph H. Turpin was an African-American daguerrian who worked in Boston. *North Star*, 28 January 1848.

5. The source of Emerson's statement remains elusive. Because he rarely reviewed books or published promotional statements, he may have praised *The Black Man* at an antislavery meeting or a fund-raiser for the Fifty-fourth Massachusetts. GES probably was not in Boston at the time of Emerson's remarks but may have heard of them through antislavery colleagues. I wish to thank Joel Myerson and Len Gougeon for their help.

6. Charlotte L. Forten [Grimké] (1837–1914), diarist and member of Philadelphia's important black antislavery family, during the Civil War taught former slaves at Port Royal, South Carolina. She knew Robert Gould Shaw and helped care for the Fifty-fourth's wounded after the attack on Battery Wagner. In 1878 she married Francis J. Grimké, step-brother of the South Carolina-born abolitionists Sarah and Angelina Grimké. Brown reprinted two Forten poems, "A Parting Hymn" and "The Angel's Visit." Her anonymity, Brown believed, resulted from racial prejudice. If she was white, he announced, the country would have recognized her "as one of its brightest gems." Edward T. James, Janet Wilson James, and Paul S. Boyer, eds., *Notable American Women, 1607–1950*, 3 vols. (Cambridge: Harvard University Press, 1971), 2:95–97; Brown, *The Black Man*, 190–99.

7. Benjamin Banneker (1732–1804), self-taught mathematician, astronomer, surveyor, and author of a popular almanac, gained national attention by publishing his correspondence with Thomas Jefferson. He quickly became a symbol of black achievement. Brown's biographical sketch of Banneker proudly heralded the learned mathematician as a pure African with not a "drop of Anglo-Saxon" blood. *DANB*, 22–25; Brown, *The Black Man*, 51–58.

8. Frederick Douglass (1818–95), an escaped Maryland slave, rose to become the most influential African American of the nineteenth century. His *Narrative of the Life of Frederick Douglass* (1845) propelled him to international celebrity. A brilliant orator and gifted writer, his three antislavery newspapers, the *North Star, Frederick Douglass' Paper*, and *Douglass' Monthly*, established him as the nation's most successful black editor and the unrivaled leader of the black antislavery movement. He pressed the Lincoln administration to emancipate the slaves and in 1863 recruited for the Fifty-fourth and Fifty-fifth Massachusetts Regiments. William S. McFeely, *Frederick Douglass* (New York: W. W. Norton, 1991); Brown, *The Black Man*, 180–87.

9. Toussaint L'Ouverture (1748–1803) was the slave-born leader of the 1791 revolt against French rule in Haiti—then the colony of Saint Dominque. For most blacks, L'Ouverture represented "a tower of strength to his friends and a terror to his foes." Brown contrasted the Haitian revolutionary to his American counterpart, George Washington: "Toussaint liberated his countrymen; Washington enslaved a portion of his." C. L. R. James, *The Black Jacobins: Toussaint L'Ouverture and the San Domingo Revolution* (New York: Random House, 1963); Brown, *The Black Man*, 92–105.

10. Nat Turner (1800–31), a Southampton County, Virginia, slave preacher, in August 1831 organized the bloodiest slave revolt in American history. Brown,

a former Garrisonian abolitionist, saw Turner as a model for black action. "Every eye is now turned towards the South, looking for another Nat Turner." Stephen B. Oates, *The Fires of Jubilee: Nat Turner's Fierce Rebellion* (New York: New American Library, 1975); Brown, *The Black Man*, 59–75.

11. William H. Simpson (1830–72), a Buffalo-born black artist, moved to Boston in 1854 and gained fame for his compelling portraits of such leaders as John T. Hilton and Charles Sumner. Simpson remained in Boston until at least 1866. Brown, *The Black Man*, 199–202; James A. Porter, *Modern Negro Art* (New York: Dryden Press, 1943), 51–52; Wade Baskin and Richard N. Runes, eds., *Dictionary of Black Culture* (New York: Philosophical Library, 1973), 402.

12. Edward M. Bannister (1828–1901)—often misidentified as Edwin—was the New Brunswick-born, Boston artist. His landscapes and portraits made him the first important regional black painter. He moved to Boston around 1850 and quickly established a prosperous business. His marriage to Christiana Cartreaux, a popular Boston wigmaker and hairdresser, brought him contacts in the antislavery community. *DANB*, 25–26; Brown, *The Black Man*, 214–17.

13. William J. Wilson (1818–?), a New York bootmaker and educator, gained renown for his many pseudonymous "Ethiop" contributions in the *Anglo-African Magazine*, the *Weekly Anglo-African*, and *Frederick Douglass' Paper*. During the 1840s and 1850s, he taught in New York City's segregated school system and became a leader in the statewide fight for black suffrage. Beginning in 1863, Wilson taught freedmen's schools and during the 1870s worked at Howard University. To Brown, Wilson represented "a sense of our capabilities." *BAP*, 4:144–45n.11; Brown, *The Black Man*, 230–35.

14. Alexander Crummell (1819–98), the Brooklyn-born black graduate of Queens College and Cambridge University and an Episcopal priest, spent twenty years as a Liberian missionary. Throughout his life, Crummell spoke out in defense of black rights and urged education, self-help, and moral improvement on blacks. A theologian and scholar, Crummell, according to Brown, was "one of the best and most favorable representatives of his race." Wilson J. Moses, *Alexander Crummell: A Study in Civilization and Discontent* (Oxford: Oxford University Press, 1988); Brown, *The Black Man*, 165–69.

15. William C. Nell had treated Attucks and his role in the "Boston Massacre" earlier in *Colored Patriots of the American Revolution* (Boston: Robert F. Wallcutt, 1855), 2–20; Brown, *The Black Man*, 106–10.

Philadelphia,
April 2, 1863.

Mr. Editor:—One of the most impudent assumptions of authority and a long string of the basest misrepresentations have been perpetuated by a number of white men under the leadership of one Frishmuth,[1] an illiterate German, on the people of the State of Pennsylvania; men who possess no record on the question of anti-slavery, and have not the shadow of a claim to the confidence and support of the colored men of this State, and are regarded by every intelligent colored man in the city as irresponsible militarily, pecuniarily, politically, and socially. Many of these men claim to have held quite recently commissions in either the regular or volunteer service of the United States, and rumor, which seems to be well founded, says that at least three of these men were cashiered or dismissed from the service.

It will be remembered that just as soon as Gov. Andrew[2] had obtained authority from the War Department at Washington to raise colored regiments, a simultaneous response of the colored men of every State in the North was made to the call of the noble old Bay State. Every one of us felt it to be a high and holy duty to organise the first regiment of the North at once, so that the irresistible argument of a first-class regiment of Northern colored men *en route* for the seat of war, might overwhelm or, if possible, scatter to the four winds the prejudice against enlisting colored men in the army, and at the same time giving cheer to the hearts of good and loyal men everywhere. But no sooner did that hateful political reptile, the copperhead, discover the generous response and patriotism which this call elicited, than the insidious and guilty work of counteracting or neutralizing these pure and earnest manifestations, commenced. Every influence has been applied to dishearten us; mobbed, as at Detroit[3] and elsewhere, and in every town and village kicked, spit upon and insulted. The wily enemy knows full well that if they can impress on the minds of the masses the notion that the whites of the North are as bitter enemies as those of the South, it would be impossible to get a regiment of Northern colored men; then they would deride Massachusetts and the colored men, as they do Gen. Jim Lane[4] of Kansas, for failing to realize certain promises and expectations regarding the promptness of our people to enlist, and yell like madmen, "niggers won't fight!"

I am right glad that the black brigade is rolling up so bright a record. May they continue to drive before them the buzzard foe! You meet these copperheads at every step, and when violence is not resorted to, they come [with] the friendship and counsellor dodge. They ask, "Are you going to enlist in the army?" Of course, you answer "Yes!" They continue, "Any colored gentleman who will go down South to fight, is a fool. Every one of them that the rebels catch will be hanged, or sent into the Indigo mines, or cut up into mince-meat, or quartered and pickled, or spitted, or—or— What good is it going to do the colored people to go fight and lose their lives? Better stay home and keep out of harm's way."

These are the arguments that the copperheads insinuate into the ears of the credulous, the ignorant, and the timid. They do not tell you that the measure of the slaveholder's iniquity is completed; that the accumulated wrongs of two centuries are a thousand-fold more horrible than two centuries of war and massacre. They do not tell you that it were "better to die free, than live slaves"—that your wronged and outraged sisters and brethren are calling on you to take up arms and place your interests and your lives in the balance against their oppressors—that "your dead fathers speak to you from their graves," or "Heaven, as with a voice of thunder, calls on you to arise from the dust,"[5] and smite with an avenging hand, the obdurate, cruel, and relentless enemy and traitor, who has trampled in the dust the flag of his country and whose life and sacred honor are pledged to wage an interminable war against your race.

Oh no, to tell us these truths would be to nerve our arms and fire our hearts for the noble struggle for country and liberty. Men and brethren! for the sake of honor, manhood and courage—in the name of God, of country, and of race, spit upon the base sycophants who thus dare to insult you. But these are silent influences which are at work. The open, tangible, bolder ones are now at work in Pennsylvania. She presents a wide theater for operations. Her colored population is more numerous than that of any other Northern State;[6] and if the copperheads can neutralize this State, half of the object has been accomplished and the system has been thoroughly organized. Ever since Frederick Douglass' address[7] appeared in the daily journals, these men have been holding meetings and stuffing the Philadelphia papers with false accounts of their glowing successes and influence over the colored people.

A few weeks ago they caused an article to appear in the *Evening Bulletin*[8] which stated that sixty thousand dollars had been promised to them by colored men in this city. At a meeting of colored men held at Philadelphia Institute on last Wednesday two weeks ago, and upon which meeting Frishmuth and his associates introduced themselves, Mr. Rob't Jones,[9] the secretary of the meeting, read this article and demanded who the parties were that had subscribed this money. The whole gang were confounded. Not a name could be offered and not one colored man said that he reposed any confidence in those men. They forced themselves upon us, and spoke of the inadvisability of colored men enlisting in the Massachusetts regiment; that there would be authority given to them the next day to organize a colored brigade in Pennsylvania; that President Lincoln and Gov. Curtin[10] were only arranging the preliminaries.

Frishmuth said he loved the colored man and wanted to be "de Moses ob de cullerd population"—forgetting that Moses belonged to the race which he led out of the house of Egyptian bondage. There were many colored ladies present at the meeting, yet one of those unprincipled men used the most profane and disgusting language. They belong to that ignorant class of white men who, knowing nothing of the sentiments and intelligence of colored men, labor under the hallucination that they can lead where they will we should go, and that if a white man should say to us, "You are a good nigger," we will be immediately overwhelmed with gratitude for the gracious condescension.

They have printed circulars scattered among the colored people in Philadelphia and adjoining counties, calling on them to join the 1st Colored Penn. Brigade.[11] They hold "officers' meetings" and report their proceedings to the daily papers. They told a friend this morning that they had not yet received authority to enlist colored men. Of course not. By what authority do they thus call upon the men of color of Pennsylvania to take up arms and thus mislead them and deceive the public? By these misrepresentations all through the State, the efforts of our people, in a military point of view, have been neutralized. Even so far west as Pittsburgh, the copperhead bait has been successful. Even Geo. B. Vashon[12] has been gulled into participating in a war meeting in Pittsburgh, in response to what they were led to believe by the Philadelphia press, was a genuine call of Pennsylvania. We shall tear the curtain away, and expose to the people these gross frauds, and base attempts to deceive and mislead them.

Many men were disposed to regard these men favorably, but all sympathy was lost when they placed themselves in opposition to Massachusetts, the cradle in which the sickly puling infancy of American liberty was nursed; who has made colored men equal before her laws; who has been the protectress and benefactress of the race; who in the darkest hour of adversity, when every other State seemed bound, hand and foot, at the feet of slavery, proclaimed the right of petition against slavery; whose representatives have been insulted, abused, and their persons violated, in the halls of Congress for thundering against the citadel of Human Wrong the burnished shafts of truth and eloquence, and for her unswerving devotion to liberty, the rebel sympathizing democracy, conscious of the irresistibility of truth and justice, and that this noble old State will never furl her banner of right while a single vestige of human wrong shall disgrace the country, are now striving to reconstruct the Union, leaving her and her sister States of New England out in the cold.

Now, these men can see no potency in these claims of Massachusetts. When these facts are presented to them, they claim that we should have "State pride." I would to God that they could have heard Isaiah C. Wears' and Prof. Green's[13] scathing rebukes to even the presumption of State pride for Pennsylvania in the breasts of colored men—a State which, instead of restoring our stolen rights, stripped us of the elective franchise, and even within the last two weeks, passed in one branch of the legislature a law excluding colored men from the State.[14] There is no meaner State in the Union than this. She has treated the families of her soldiers worse than any other State, and with her confirmed negrophobia could we expect the treatment of dogs at her hands? But in spite of all this, if such men as J. Miller McKim, Judge Kelley,[15] or Col. Wm. F. Small should obtain authority to raise a regiment or brigade in Pennsylvania, I would give my heart and hand to it; but knowing, as I do, that no other colored regiment will be raised in the North until the Massachusetts one is placed in the field, I say, let every man lend his influence to Massachusetts. If, by any means, the 54th should fail, it will be a blow from which we Northern men would never recover. We would be ranked with the most depraved and cowardly of men. Our enemies, infuriated as they are beyond measure, would hunt us down like so many wild beasts, while our friends, shamed and humiliated by our criminal cowardice and imbecility, would be compelled to become passive witnesses of their unbridled violence.

Look at our brethren in the South! Those who have endured all of the horrors of the Southern prison-house, defying the menaces of the besotted tyranny, taking up arms to achieve with their valor those rights which Providence has designed that all men should enjoy. Has freedom stultified our sterner aspirations, and made us forget our duty? Has the Copperhead obtained an influence over us? If we thought that of what little freedom, we of the North enjoy, has had a tendency to nourish a disregard for our own and the rights of our fellow men, it were better that the mob-fiend drive us from off the face of the earth, to give place to those noble freedmen who are now bravely and victoriously fighting the battles of their country and liberty. We have more to gain, if victorious, or more to lose, if defeated, than any other class of men. Not abstract political rights, or religious and civil liberty, but with all these our personal liberties are to be secured. Many of us are insensible to the stern realities of the present hour, but they are here thundering at our very doors, and the sooner we awaken to their inexorable demands upon us, the better for the race, the better for the country, the better for our families, and the better for ourselves.

G. E. Stephens.

WAA, 11 April 1863.

1. William Frishmuth represented one of several groups of white officers who tried to organize a Pennsylvania black brigade in the spring of 1863. Frishmuth previously commanded the 113th Pennsylvania Regiment. In the 24 March 1863 issue of the Philadelphia Evening Bulletin, Frishmuth announced that city blacks supported his efforts and that several of Philadelphia's wealthy black leaders had agreed to donate $60,000 to outfit his brigade. Philadelphia Evening Bulletin, 21, 24 March 1863; Frank Hamilton Taylor, Philadelphia in the Civil War, 1861–1865 (Philadelphia: City of Philadelphia, 1913), 170, 187.

2. John A. Andrew (1816–66), the wartime Republican governor of Massachusetts, was a committed abolitionist and close friend of Boston's black community. The state's black soldiers respected Andrew and trusted him to protect their interests. Henry Greenleaf Pearson, The Life of John A. Andrew: Governor of Massachusetts, 1861–1865, 2 vols. (Boston: Houghton, Mifflin, 1904).

3. Rioting against black communities plagued the years before and during the Civil War. In the 1860s, antiwar Democrats (Copperheads) and a virulently racist press enflamed whites by blaming blacks for the conflict. On 6 March 1863 about two hundred whites attacked Detroit's black community, killing two, injuring twenty, and incinerating more than thirty buildings. Local police failed to quell the riot, which Union soldiers eventually put down. Leon F. Litwack, North of Slavery: The Negro in the Free States, 1790–1860 (Chicago: University of Chicago Press, 1961), 100–102, 159, 219; John C. Schneider, "Detroit and the Problem of Disorder: The Riot of 1863," Michigan History 58 (Spring 1974): 5–23.

4. James H. Lane (1814–66), U.S. senator from Kansas and a "Jayhawker" guerrilla during the bloody Kansas wars of the late 1850s, formed the First Kansas Regiment of Colored Volunteers in September 1862. Lane had recruited blacks since the fall of 1861 and voiced his support in the Senate chambers for the general enlistment of black soldiers. He did not receive official authorization for his regiment; nevertheless, in October 1862 the First Kansas met and repulsed a larger force of Missouri rebels. *HTIECW*, 424–25; *WWWCW*, 373; Dudley Taylor Cornish, *The Sable Arm: Negro Troops in the Union Army, 1861–1865* (New York: W. W. Norton, 1966), 69–78.

5. GES quotes from Henry Highland Garnet's famous 1843 "Address to the Slaves of the United States of America" delivered at the National Convention of Colored Citizens at Buffalo, New York, on 16 August 1843. Abolitionists considered Garnet's address so incendiary that only John Brown dared to publish it—but not until 1848 and not in its original form. Just before Stephens wrote this letter, the *Anglo-African* reprinted the speech on its front page without the qualifying sentences that contradicted Garnet's call for violent slave rebellion. In its original version, Garnet's address was the most radical call for the downfall of American slavery ever delivered. *BAP*, 3:403–12; *WAA*, 28 March 1863; Sterling Stucky, *Slave Culture: Nationalist Theory and the Foundations of Black America* (New York: Oxford University Press, 1987), 138–92.

6. In 1860, Pennsylvania's black population totaled 56,949, the largest in the North. U.S. Bureau of the Census, *Negro Population in the United States, 1790–1915* (Washington: Government Printing Office, 1918), 57.

7. "Men of Color to Arms!" was an editorial and broadside that first appeared in the March 1863 issue of *Douglass' Monthly* and was widely reprinted by the Northern press. Douglass directed blacks to join the Fifty-fourth without delay, throw open the gates of oppression with "one gallant rush," and free "four millions of our brothers and sisters." New York *Tribune*, 5 March 1863.

8. GES refers to Frishmuth's 24 March 1863 announcement. The staunchly Republican *Evening Bulletin*, edited by Gibson Peacock, was the city's first successful evening paper. Frank Luther Mott, *American Journalism: A History, 1690–1960*, 3d ed. (New York: Macmillan, 1962), 350n; *A Checklist of Pennsylvania Newspapers: Philadelphia County* (Harrisburg: State of Pennsylvania, 1944), 57–58.

9. Robert Jones (1817?–90), a Philadelphia barber, migrated to Hamilton, Canada West, but returned to the city at the start of the Civil War. A militant black abolitionist, Jones had organized Queen Victoria's Rifle Guards, a black militia unit, and feverishly promoted black recruitment during the Civil War. His son joined the Sixth USCT. *BAP*, 5:203.

10. Andrew Gregg Curtin (1817–94), Pennsylvania governor and one of Lincoln's strongest supporters, raised 270 regiments for the Union army. Curtin eventually lifted the state's ban on black troops and organized eleven black regiments at Camp William Penn near Philadelphia. *WWWCW*, 159; Frederick M. Binder, "Pennsylvania's Negro Regiments in the Civil War," *Journal of Negro History* 37 (October 1952): 383–417.

11. GES refers to what would become the Third USCT, the first black regiment raised in Pennsylvania, formed in August 1863 and commanded by Benjamin C. Tilghman. It served alongside the Fifty-fourth in South Carolina and Florida, conducting forays into the north Florida back country, destroying rebel property, and freeing slaves. One sergeant in the unit, Henry James, led a squad of thirty men on a daring raid that freed ninety-one slaves and successfully fought fifty rebel cavalry, killing twenty. General Gillmore praised the heroism of James's adventure, one of the few independent black-led assaults of the war. The Third mustered out on 30 October 1865. Maj. Gen. Quincy A. Gillmore, General Order no. 42, Department of the South, Albert G. Browne Papers, MHS; Emilio, *A Brave Black Regiment*, 149, 155; Edwin S. Redkey, ed., *A Grand Army of Black Men; Letters from African-American Soldiers in the Union Army, 1861–1865* (Cambridge: Cambridge University Press, 1992), 56–59; Bates, *History*, 5:925–26.

12. George Boyer Vashon (1824–78), abolitionist, lawyer, and educator, was the first African American to receive a bachelor of arts degree from Oberlin College and became New York's first licensed black attorney. After the war, Vashon worked for the Freedmen's Bureau and gained the right to argue cases before the U.S. Supreme Court. Stephens may refer to Vashon's 15 January Pittsburgh oration on presidential war powers, where, based on the views of John Quincy Adams, he maintained that Lincoln had the power to emancipate slaves as a war measure. *BAP*, 3:321–22; *WAA*, 31 January 1863.

13. Isaiah C. Wears (1822–1900), a leading Philadelphia black abolitionist, Republican politician, and barber, fought colonization and the African Civilization Society. He first opposed participation in the Civil War but in 1862 urged blacks to join whatever units would accept them. After the war, he served as president of the Social, Civil, and Statistical Association. Alfred M. Green (1833–?), AME minister and peripatetic lecturer, helped found the Banneker Institute. In 1860, Green served a harsh prison term for his role in the Moses Horner rescue attempt. An early advocate of black recruitment, Green hotly debated opponents of black participation in the war, helped recruit for the Fifty-fourth Massachusetts, and later joined the 127th USCT. *BAP*, 4:318–19n.17, 5:125–27n.7; *WAA*, 9 June, 14 July 1860.

14. On 6 March 1863, a state senate committee voted down a proposal to ban blacks from settling in Pennsylvania. The Democratic-controlled house approved the same measure on 25 March, but the senate rejected it. Thomas A. Sanelli, "The Struggle for Black Suffrage in Pennsylvania, 1838–1870," Ph.D. diss., Temple University, 1978, 137–38.

15. J. Miller McKim (1810–74), a founding member of the American Anti-Slavery Society and a leader of the Pennsylvania Anti-Slavery Society, the Pennsylvania Freedmen's Relief Association, and the American Freedmen's Union Commission, worked closely with Philadelphia black leaders. William D. Kelley (1814–90), a Radical Republican congressman from Philadelphia, ardently supported black recruitment. Stephens may have known both men personally, and the Banneker Institute once invited Kelley to address its members. Walter M. Merrill and Louis Ruchames, eds., *The Letters of Wil-*

liam Lloyd Garrison, 6 vols. (Cambridge: Harvard University Press, 1971–81), 4:92; Hans L. Trefousse, *The Radical Republicans: Lincoln's Vanguard for Racial Justice* (Baton Rouge: Louisiana State University Press, 1968), 32, 302, 314, 327–28; Russell F. Weigley, ed., *Philadelphia: A Three Hundred Year History* (New York: W. W. Norton, 1982), 411.

Camp Meigs, Readville, Mass.,
May 1, 1863.

There is quite a stir in the camp to-day. Mayday has adorned herself in sunshine and garlands of green. Hundreds are flocking here from Boston and its environs to witness the military evolutions of the 54th Reg. Mass. Vol., and never did they acquit themselves so admirably. They moved with the regularity and precision of Regulars. The gay concourse of visitors of both classes of our citizens seemed stirred with admiration and pleasure at the rapid progress of this splendid regiment in this school of the soldier. I do not exaggerate when I say that there is no regiment superior, if equal to this in physique and aptitude of its men. I suppose, in the upwards of a thousand men now ready to be mustered into the service of the United States, there are twelve men who will yield to the severest vigors of a campaign in the field. Out of upward of fourteen hundred men, these nine hundred or a thousand have been chosen; the rest have been rejected because they did not come up to the highest standard of mental and physical proficiency.

Governor Andrew visited our camp yesterday[1] and reviewed the regiment, and with other distinguished citizens expressed great satisfaction at the condition of the men and the police of the camp. I noticed among the guests on this occasion our distinguished citizens Dr. J. B. Smith[2] and Lewis Hayden Esq.[3] I never saw a body of men who seem to be so perfectly at home in camp and have so many ways to divert and amuse themselves. Singing, dancing, foot-ball, cricket, wrestling and many innocent games with the parades and drills, dispel *ennui* and dull monotony and keep our camp in a perfect whirl of animating scenes.

There are a few essentials needed, however, to the comfort of these men, who have in the face of the most disheartening influences taken up arms in defence of their country and liberty. There are many of the essentials to the soldiers toilet which the government does not furnish to her troops: such as coarse towels, needles, pins and buttons, besides some items of reading matter, such as testaments (pocket), newspapers, tracts, *etcetera*. A great many of the friends furnish them at times with tobacco, pipes and some few dainties, but those things I have above enumerated are very essential, absolutely so. Will the fair friends at home withhold their regards from the noble 54th and refrain from giving them some few of these testimonials of their admiration and respect? The Social, Civil and Statistical Association of Philadelphia have made an appropriation to purchase some of these items. Fair readers of Philadelphia will you not form your Sewing Circles to make for these men whatever may be necessary?

While that Governor Andrew has made this regiment one which will reflect honor to our race, and as it has become the representative of the men of color in the North, it becomes the indispensable duty of every one at home to cheer and encourage them with sympathy and esteem, and to give them a tangible earnest of a cheerful cooperation with and support to, in this good cause. Ladies it would be strong evidence of your patriotism, intelligence and noble heartedness, did you organize your Sewing Circles in every locality from whence your friends have come to unite their destinies with the 54th.

We desire to have a goodly number of copies of the Anglo-African sent to the address of our chaplain, for this shall be the medium through which all of the affairs of the regiment of public interest, shall be made known. When any sickness, accident or anything else shall take place, the friends and relatives of those in it can know all, learn all, through the columns of the Anglo-African.

Another item of interest is that the regiment is now fully armed with new Springfield Rifles. They were only partly supplied with old Harpers Ferry Muskets.[4] The men can be seen everywhere going through the manual of arms, in which they are already quite proficient. There are already two colored men who are commissioned and attached to this regiment: Dr. John V. De Grasse[5] of Boston, and Rev. Wm. Jackson[6] of New-Bedford, recently of Philadelphia and a Baptist by profession of faith. Dr. De Grasse is only to be temporarily connected, it is understood, with the regiment, to be detached for some other field of action; and, it is expected that Dr. Bachus,[7] the previous acting Hospital Steward, will be commissioned as assistant surgeon of the regiment. So the great pathway to honor and emolument is opening wide to colored men.

The health of the men is good, particularly so. There are in the hospital the week ending to-day, Clark, Wellesly, Harrison, Chas. Owens, Miller, Toote, Shorter, and Phillips,[8] and these are all the cases or ordinary diseases and are nearly all convalescent.

G. E. S.

WAA, 9 May 1863.

1. In the afternoon of 30 April, Governor Andrew, Secretary of War Salmon P. Chase, Samuel Gridley Howe, Robert Dale Owen, and William Lloyd Garrison reviewed the troops at Readville. Emilio, *A Brave Black Regiment,* 23.

2. Joshua B. Smith (1813–79), Boston's preeminent caterer, helped organize the fight to desegregate the city's public schools. Smith served as sutler for the Twelfth Massachusetts Regiment, helped lead the effort to raise a monument to Robert Gould Shaw, and in 1873 served in the state senate. *BAP,* 3:304–5n.10.

3. Lewis Hayden (1811–89), born a slave in Lexington, Kentucky, became one of Boston's most influential black leaders. In 1858, Republicans appointed him messenger in the Massachusetts secretary of state's office, a post he retained for decades. Hayden became a close associate of Governor Andrew and convinced him to raise the Fifty-fourth. His influence during the crisis over unequal pay helped avert a mutiny. Hayden continued the fight for civil rights after the war and in 1873 was elected to the state legislature. *BAP,* 4:268–69n.3.

4. The Fifty-fourth received the English-made Enfield rifle, not the American-manufactured Springfield, on 30 April 1863. The .577–caliber Enfield was used extensively by the North and South. The Harpers Ferry Model 1841, or Mississippi rifle—.54 caliber—was the U.S. Army's first standard issue weapon, and both sides used it during the first years of the Civil War. Luis F. Emilio Diary, 30 April 1863, Philip and Betty Emilio Family Collection; *HTIECW,* 243–44, 342.

5. John V. S. De Grasse (1825–68), eminent Boston physician, attended Aubuk College in Paris and Bowdoin College, where he received his medical degree with honors in 1849. He practiced in New York for two years before moving to Boston, where in 1854 he became the first black member of the Massachusetts Medical Society. De Grasse did not serve in the Fifty-fourth but joined the Thirty-fifth USCT (First North Carolina). Although cashiered for being drunk on duty, De Grasse's dismissal more likely resulted from the protests of the regiment's white surgeons who refused to serve with a black physician. *DANB,* 169; Joseph T. Glatthaar, *Forged in Battle: The Civil War Alliance of Black Soldiers and White Officers* (New York: Free Press, 1990), 189; Richard Reid, "Raising the African Brigade: Early Black Recruitment in Civil War North Carolina," *North Carolina Historical Review* 70 (July 1993): 278, 294.

6. William Jackson (1818–?), born in Norfolk, Virginia, served various churches in Delaware, New York, and Philadelphia before ministering to the

Salem Baptist Church in New Bedford, Massachusetts. A recruiter for the Fifty-fourth Massachusetts, Jackson served as acting chaplain for the unit at Readville, beginning on 23 March 1863. He shared duties with William W. Grimes (1824–?), a Virginia-born itinerant AME minister. Andrew appointed both as camp chaplains, with only one to follow the unit south. Grimes, insulted at having to share the position, resigned his post; Jackson failed to accompany the regiment and in July became the chaplain for the Fifty-fifth Massachusetts. *WAA*, 2 May 1863; *Christian Recorder*, 24 August 1861; Fifty-fourth Massachusetts Company Letter Books, 23 March 1863, RG 94, National Archives; [Charles B. Fox], *Record of the Service of the Fifty-fifth Regiment of Massachusetts Volunteer Infantry* (Cambridge: John Wilson and Son, 1868), 101; William W. Grimes, *Thirty-three Years' Experience of an Itinerant Minister of the A.M.E. Church* (Lancaster: E. S. Speaker, 1887); Edwin S. Redkey, "Black Chaplains in the Union Army," *Civil War History* 32 (December 1987): 332.

7. This probably refers to Theodore J. Becker (1831–70?) of Fitchburg, Massachusetts, the regiment's hospital steward. He joined the unit on 23 April 1863 and died in Charleston, S.C. James L. Bowen, *Massachusetts in the War, 1861–1865* (Springfield: Clark W. Bryan, 1889), 672–73.

8. GES probably refers to Isaac Jefferson Clark (1843–?) and William Henry Harrison (1827–?), two married farmers from Philadelphia who joined Company B on 9 March; Charles A. Owens (1839–?), an unmarried cook from New Orleans who enlisted in Company E on 4 April; John Miller (1838–?), a single barber from Philadelphia who joined Company B on 21 February; John Shorter (1847–?), a single farmer from Amboy, Michigan, who mustered into Company G on 9 April; and Jeremiah Phillips (1835–?), an unmarried laborer from Marshall, Michigan, who joined Company H on 21 April 1863. Toote and Wellesly are unidentified. Emilio, *A Brave Black Regiment*, 345, 346, 347, 362, 371, 376.

Chapter 10

"Give Them 'Greek Fire'"

June 1863–September 1863

George E. Stephens and the Fifty-fourth Massachusetts Regiment spearheaded the assault against Battery Wagner on the night of 18 July 1863. "The grape and cannister, shell and minnies swept us down like chaff, still our men went on and on," Frederick Douglass's son, Lewis, recorded two days after the attack. "If I die tonight," he wrote, "I will not die a coward."[1] Indeed not. The swirling chaos of smoke, shot, and death ended in defeat for Stephens and his comrades, but not failure.

The Fifty-fourth had left Boston on 28 May 1863, exhilarated by all the noble honor the city could muster. The regiment had anticipated trouble from Boston's rabble and the condescending enemies of black freedom. But few incidents marred the day, and the scornful mostly confined their racist sneers to morocco-bound diaries. The inspired crowds stood in awe of the magnificent regiment, its handsome colonel, and the cause for which they had pledged their lives. The state's leaders had committed their honor to one thousand black men, and the governor had staked his personal reputation on the regiment. For Stephens and the other black troops whose hearts swelled when Governor Andrew called them "fellow citizens," this outpouring of support seemed almost unimaginable.

The regiment arrived in the South eager to fight. If Stephens is any guide, the men resented their orders to torch the dreamy little port of Darien, Georgia, but did not dwell on the destruction of rebel property. Their concerns centered on what role the army planned for them. Would they be relegated to guerrilla-style fighting, which would bring them no honor; would they be compelled to exchange their rifles for pikes and shovels? An answer seemed to come on 16 July, when rebels attacked Union forces on James Island. The Fifty-fourth gained the respect of many soldiers when it saved a white regiment from capture or extermination. Two days later, the Fifty-fourth's heroics in the doomed assault on Battery Wagner won it the admiration of the North. The New York *Tribune* declared that Battery Wagner would become for blacks what Bunker Hill was for whites, forgetting that blacks served there as well. The Fifty-fourth's valor discredited racist accusations that blacks could not or would not fight. After 18 July whites no longer considered the regiment a doubtful experiment. The battle became a turning point, opening the way for the enlistment of nearly 180,000 black troops—about 10 percent of all Union forces.[2]

Yet, as the men of the Fifty-fourth Massachusetts vindicated black worth and defended the Union on Wagner's parapets, resurgent racism spoiled the hard-won glory. White mobs in New York City who opposed the military draft beat or murdered scores of blacks, destroyed their homes, and forced thousands to flee in the worst race riot in American history. William P. Powell, black abolitionist leader and owner of the city's Colored Seamen's Home, fled from roof to roof with his family to escape the homicidal mob. Powell, a successful businessman and a devoted supporter of the Union, had a son in the army. "What more could I do?" he implored "What further evidence was wanting to prove my allegiance?"[3] Word of the horrifying riots shocked and astonished the regiment. The despair was palpable. "Have we not been loyal to the country, in season and out of season, through good report and evil?" Stephens wrote. "Is there no justice in America?"

The tragic riots in New York, and elsewhere in the North, and the devastating losses suffered in the Wagner assault left the regiment demoralized. Union commanders furthered the black soldiers' despair by forcing them to perform arduous fatigue duty, far more than they assigned to whites. When the army refused to promote enlisted men to replace the white officers who had been killed or severely wounded at Wagner, the sense of gloom deepened. "Col[ore]d. men have nothing to hope for here in the way of promotion," Stephens lamented.[4] More important, the government went back on its promise of equal pay. Although promised the same $13 a month pay given to white soldiers, the War Department authorized only $10 a month, and $3 of that would be for uniforms.

The Fifty-fourth Massachusetts led the protest over unequal pay and for eighteen months refused to accept any money until the national government provided them with full and equal pay. The soldiers' stand caused intolerable hardships for their families and led to desperate acts of mutiny. The crisis preoccupied Stephens because it embodied the government's callous disregard for the rights of black soldiers and symbolized his struggle against slavery and racial discrimination. In September 1863, James Henry Gooding, a corporal in Company C, wrote to President Lincoln to voice his opposition. He reminded the president that black soldiers fought and died just like white ones. Black families suffered as grievously as "Anglo-Saxon" ones when husbands and sons died in battle. "The patient, trusting Descendants of Afric's Clime have dyed the ground with blood, in defense of the Union, and Democracy," he wrote. "Men, too, your Excellency, who know in a measure the cruelties of the Iron heel of oppression."[5]

1. Lewis H. Douglass to Frederick and Anna Murray Douglass, 20 July 1863, in *BAP*, 5:241.
2. Benjamin Quarles, *The Negro in the Civil War* (1953, reprint, New York: Da Capo Press, 1989), 20–21; Duncan, *Blue-Eyed Child of Fortune*, 53.
3. *BAP*, 5:229–32.
4. GES to William Still, 19 September 1863, LGC, HSP.
5. Virginia M. Adams, ed., *On the Altar of Freedom: A Black Soldier's Civil War Letters from the Front* (Amherst: University of Massachusetts Press, 1991), 118–20.

★ ★ ★

[June] 1863.
Mr. Editor:—Our regiment has been on the move ever since our arrival at Beaufort.[1] Our active and brave leader, Col. Montgomery,[2] gives none under his command time to rot, sicken and die in camp. No sooner does he accomplish one object than he has already inaugurated the necessary steps for the accomplishment of another. The 54th, as you, no doubt, have been apprised ere this, has made a successful raid on the coast of this State, capturing and burning the town of Darien and spreading terror to the hearts of the rebels throughout this region. The expedition which accomplished this, consisted of the U.S. steamer John Adams,[3] Harriet A. Weed and two transports, having on board part of the 2nd S. C. Vol.[4] and eight companies of the 54th Mass. Vol.

We left here on the 10th, reached Darien on the 11th, about 4 o'clock in the afternoon. The John Adams led the way, approaching the town cautiously, shelling the suburbs to the right, left and rear of it. A considerable number of rebel cavalry appeared in sight, but the guns of the J. A. and Weed put them to flight. The town was found to be almost entirely deserted by its inhabitants.[5]

The 2nd South Carolina were the first to land and the 54th followed. Cattle, sheep, pigs, poultry, and many things of use and comfort were secured. One rebel was killed by a shell, and the only persons we saw were one old colored woman and two whites, who requested to be left behind. When we left at sundown the whole town was enveloped in flames, and as we steamed gaily down the river, the Weed greeted the outbuildings with sundry iron missiles.

Darien, before the rebellion, was one of the principal outlets for the lumber trade of the State. I glanced at the books of the principal lumber-merchants here, Davis & Shina. They shipped their timber to French ports, principally.[6]

The regiment or expedition did not lose a man. The regiment has enjoyed remarkably good health since our sojourn in this sickly portion of the Sunny South. We lost one man on the 4th inst., being the only death since the 1st of May and the fifth since the regiment was started in recruiting in March last.[7]

Mr. Walton[8] of our regiment has just informed me of the arrival of Miss C. L. Forten at Hilton Head.[9] There is no telling when we shall return to Port Royal, our occupancy of St. Simon's Island looks so much like a permanent one.[10]

The first rebel flag captured was captured by the 54th, on 11th inst., in Darien, by my company (B).[11]

G. E. S.

WAA, 4 July 1863.

1. The Fifty-fourth landed at Beaufort on 4 June 1863 at 5 A.M. and camped in a field belonging to the Thompson plantation but remained only four days. Emilio, *A Brave Black Regiment*, 37–38.

2. Col. James Montgomery (1814–71), Second South Carolina Volunteers, commanded the brigade that included the Fifty-fourth. An early supporter of black recruitment and a Kansas warrior in the 1850s, Montgomery proclaimed himself a "friend of the negro." Yet he harbored deeply racist views of blacks, and his summary executions for infractions of military regulations earned him the enmity of black troops and sharp—but private—criticism from Colonel Shaw. Dudley Taylor Cornish, *The Sable Arm: Negro Troops in the Union Army, 1861–1865* (New York: W. W. Norton, 1966), 149–50; Duncan, *Blue-Eyed Child of Fortune*, 337n.5, 362–64, 370, 378–79.

3. The *John Adams* was an armed troop transport. Emilio, *A Brave Black Regiment*, 40.

4. Organized at Beaufort on 22 May 1863, the Second South Carolina Volunteers participated in various actions in the Department of the South, including the siege of Battery Wagner and Honey Hill, South Carolina. The unit was incorporated into federal service in February 1864 and became the Thirty-fourth USCT. Dyer, *Compendium*, 3:1636, 1729.

5. Originally, about 500 whites and 1,500 blacks lived in Darien, but most had fled the previous year to escape the harassing raids of federal troops. Montgomery's force probably shelled the Twentieth Georgia Cavalry, about five miles away from the town, and shot at about twenty Confederate soldiers in town. Spencer B. King, Jr., *Darien: The Death and Rebirth of a Southern Town* (Macon: Mercer University Press, 1981), 66–67; Peter Burchard, *One Gallant Rush: Robert Gould Shaw and His Brave Black Regiment* (New York: St. Martin's Press, 1965), 105.

6. Darien had been a thriving shipping center for lumber, rice, and cotton. Most of the lumber processed in the town's mills was long-leaf yellow pine. King, Jr., *Darien*, 4–5, 14, 66.

7. George J. Reader, Theodore D. Thenton, and William Roberson of Company E; William Davis of Company F; and Thomas Beverly of Company I died before the regiment reached South Carolina. Fifty-fourth Massachusetts Records, Regimental Books, RG 94, National Archives.

8. James Morris Walton (1838–74), a Philadelphia lawyer and recruiter for the Fifty-fourth Massachusetts, mustered in as a lieutenant of Company B on 28 March 1863. He was promoted to captain after the attack on Wagner and to major on 11 July 1865. Emilio, *A Brave Black Regiment*, 9, 34, 51, 132–33, 329.

9. Forten had been teaching former slaves in the Sea Islands since October 1862.

10. The Fifty-fourth camped on the grounds of the old Gould plantation near Frederica. The island's romantic beauty and the fine tables and stuffed chairs sacked from Darien made a luxurious camp until the regiment left on 24 June. Emilio, *A Brave Black Regiment*, 44–46.

11. Luis F. Emilio sent a Confederate battle flag and the key to Darien's jail to his home in Massachusetts. The key is fraught with symbolism because masters often sent their slaves to city jails for punishment. Philip and Betty Emilio Family Collection.

Morris Island, S.C.,
July 21, 1863.

Mr. Editor: The month of July has been an eventful one for the 54th. We left our camp at St. Helena on the—inst., and landed at James Island on the—, fought the second battle of James Island[1] on Thursday,

16th, escaped the snare which eight thousand rebels had prepared to entrap us with, by silent midnight retreat through bogs, marshes, and dense woods, reaching Morris Island beach on Saturday morning, 18th; marched directly to the front, and made (what has been conceded by every one to be) a heroic charge on Fort Wagner.

In the engagement at James Island we lost 45 killed, wounded and missing. Among the killed are Corporal Holloway,[2] a nephew of Bishop Payne[3]—a brave, intelligent, Christian soldier. Also Sergeant Wilson,[4] Company H, of Chicago. He fought four rebel cavalrymen, slew three, but the fourth gave him a mortal wound. Sergeant Vogelsang[5] of the same company was ordered by a party of rebels to surrender. His answer was, "Never!" and received, it is feared, a mortal wound.

The battle commenced at daylight. Companies B, H and K were thrown out about two miles on picket. During Wednesday night and Thursday morning the rebels made repeated advances on our picket line, but were kept at bay by our unerring rifles. At the peep of day all was activity among them. Their long, dark line of battle could barely be discerned. Capt. Russell[6] of Co. H ordered us to fall back on our reserve, at the same time, deploying as skirmishers, the whole rebel line advanced full eight hundred strong. Our picket line retired slowly and reluctantly, delivering their fire as if on a skirmish drill. The rebels yelled and hooted, but they could not drive us, and advanced only as our picket line retired.

The 10th Connecticut regiment[7] was encamped on our extreme left. Had our pickets retired precipitately, as pickets generally do, this regiment would have been captured; but they were enabled to take shelter under the gunboats. When our picket line reached the reserve it had all skedaddled, and we were forced to withstand this attack of superior numbers until we reached the main body of our regiment drawn up in a line of battle, supported by the 1st Connecticut artillery.[8] On the rebels came. Volley after volley was poured into them, and after a contest of two hours they fled precipitately. They must have suffered terribly. They carried cart loads of dead off the field.[9]

Although there were a great many other troops on the Island, none but the black regiment of Massachusetts fired a gun. The 54th stood between the foes and our white comrades. A great many of the white soldiers were killed and wounded by the enemies shells. Sergeant Merriman[10] of Co. B was shot in the leg. He says the rebels bound it up for him, and gave him water to drink and to bathe his wound. This seems to ill accord with some of the atrocities they are known to have been guilty of.[11] On that day many of the wounded were killed, and Sergeant Vogelsang was pursued and shot like many others on the banks of an adjoining creek, which is very marshy. The only way that we could secure their bodies after the fight was by boat up the creek. Many of our wounded were shot while lying on the ground. Albert Walls,[12] one of the missing or killed, did not hear the order to fall back and remained at his post and fought until killed or taken prisoner!

It is rumored that the enemy lost a general in the fight. They are known to have an officer killed, but his rank cannot be ascertained.[13] We took eight rebel prisoners. One of our spies penetrated their lines, and found their force to be upwards of eight thousand men.[14] They anticipated inflicting on us another James Island disaster, but our retreat saved us and disappointed them. They did not know that our forces had evacuated the Island until ten o'clock Friday morning. The official report of the killed, wounded and missing has already reached you.

Capt. Simpkins[15] of Co. K, a brave officer, had his life saved in the engagement. He was attacked by two rebel cavalrymen, when one of his men shot one dead and bayoneted the second one. Every man that fell, fell fighting with his face to the foe.

We left the lower end of Morris Island Saturday morning, and marched slowly and steadily to the front until in sight of Fort Wagner. We had heard of the previous attempt to take it by storm, and knew that nothing but hard fighting, with great sacrifice of life, could result in a successful storming of it.[16] Gen. Strong,[17] the hero of the attack of Saturday, when our regiment reached within range of the shells of the fort, rode out bravely a hundred yards in advance of us and reconnoitered the fort and its surroundings. Rode back to us and briefly addressed us, and asked, "Massachusetts men, are you ready to take that fort?" The universal answer was, "We will try." "They are nearly played out. They have but two effective guns," said he. About sundown we were ordered to advance at the double quickstep, cheering as if going on some mirthful errand. The rebs withheld their fire until we reached within fifty yards of the work, when jets of flame darted forth from every corner and embrasure, and even Fort Sumter poured solid shot and shell on our heads. The 54th, undaunted by the hellish storm, pushed up to the work, down into the moat, and like demons ascended the parapet, found the interior lined with rebels soldiers who were well sheltered and fought them one hour before we were re-enforced;

and when the regiment reached us, the 3d New Hampshire, which was presumed to be our re-enforcements, they, to a man, emptied their rifles into us. Thus we lost nearly as many men by the bullets of our presumed friends as by those of our known enemies.[18]

Some few entered the fort, and when they got in, it was so dark that friends could not be distinguished from foes, and there is no doubt but that many a Union soldier was killed by his comrades.

On the whole, this is considered to be a brilliant feat of the 54th. It is another evidence that cannot now be denied, that colored soldiers will dare go where any brave men will lead them. Col. Shaw,[19] our noble and lamented commander, was the bravest of the brave. He did not take his thirty paces to the rear, but led the column up to the fort, and was the first man who stood on the parapet of the fort. When he reached it he said, "Come on, men! Follow me!" and he either received a mortal wound and fell over the wall, or stumbled into the Fort and was killed. If he still lives, it is miraculous, for he must have fell on glistening bayonets. One of the rebel prisoners says that he is wounded and still lives, but for my part I do not believe it.

Gen. Strong, seeing that the rebels were in too great a force, ordered the retreat, and now comes another chapter which I would fain pass, but my duty tells me that I must advert to it. There were large quantities of whiskey to be had, and the guard placed to guard the line of retreat and to prevent straggling imbibed rather freely. Some of the men of the skedaddling white regiments were fired on and killed, and when some of our wounded were passing to the rear they were murdered by these drunken wretches. One of our Sergeants was shot dead by a private of this guard in the presence of an officer of our regiment who immediately shot the private dead. Dozens of our wounded were drowned. The only good approach to the fort is by the beach. The tide was low when we made the charge, and before we could secure our dead and wounded the tide came up, and such as could not crawl away were drowned.[20]

Our total loss cannot be positively ascertained. It is placed at about 300 killed, wounded and missing: 75 killed, 125 wounded, 100 missing.[21] It is supposed that Sergeant R. J. Simmons[22] of your city is among the killed. Major Hallowell[23] is badly wounded.

G. E. S.

WAA, 8 August 1863.

1. The regiment left St. Helena on 8 July, leaving one company behind to protect its camp. This landing at James Island was intended as a diversion for the primary assault on Morris Island and the seizure of Wagner. But, anticipating the attack that came on 16 July, Beauregard reinforced his positions on James Island. The First Battle of James Island—the Battle of Secessionville—was fought on 16 June 1862. Union forces were soundly repulsed, with nearly seven hundred casualties. Emilio, *A Brave Black Regiment*, 51–57; E. Milby Burton, *The Siege of Charleston, 1861–1865* (Columbia: University of South Carolina Press, 1970), 98–111.

2. GES accurately reported the Fifty-fourth's losses: fourteen killed, eighteen wounded, and thirteen reported missing. Cpl. Charles M. Holloway (1839–63), Company K, was an unmarried student at Wilberforce, Ohio. He joined the regiment on 12 May 1863 and was killed on 16 July. Emilio, *A Brave Black Regiment*, 63, 385.

3. Daniel A. Payne (1811–93), educator, abolitionist, and president of Wilberforce University, became the African Methodist Episcopal Church's most famous bishop. The son of freeborn South Carolina blacks, he filled various ministerial and educational positions before his election as bishop in 1852. During the war, he pressed President Lincoln to adopt emancipation as a war aim. *DANB*, 484–85.

4. Sgt. Joseph D. Wilson (1838–63), Company H, an unmarried farmer from Chicago, had previously served with Ephraim E. Ellsworth's Zouaves. He joined the Fifty-fourth on 21 April 1863 and was killed at James Island on 16 July. Misidentified in Emilio's book, Wilson fought with spectacular bravery during the James Island battle and kept as many as five rebels at bay before falling. Emilio, *A Brave Black Regiment*, 58, 378.

5. Peter Vogelsang (1815–87), born in New York City, worked as a druggist and dry goods shipping clerk. He enlisted on 17 April 1863 and became a quartermaster sergeant on 1 December. During the James Island attack, Vogelsang and about eight men tried to escape the oncoming rebels by crossing a creek. Some were killed in the attempt, and Vogelsang was shot trying to surrender. Although he suffered a gaping chest wound, Vogelsang survived and compiled a distinguished war record. Governor Andrew approved his commission as an officer, but the War Department refused to promote him because of his race. Intense lobbying gained Vogelsang his commission in June 1865, and he mustered out on 20 August 1865 as a first lieutenant. He returned to New York, where he worked as a customs clerk until his death. Emilio, *A Brave Black Regiment*, 315, 330, 339; Luis F. Emilio biographical notes, Philip and Betty Emilio Family Collection; Peter Vogelsang to Luis F. Emilio, n.d., Fifty-fourth Regiment Papers, 1:145, MHS; *WAA*, 22 August 1863.

6. Cabot Jackson Russell (1844–63), captain of Company H, joined the Fifty-fourth as a first lieutenant on 23 March 1863. He was promoted to captain on 11 May and died at Wagner. Emilio, *A Brave Black Regiment*, 83, 91, 331.

7. The Tenth Connecticut Regiment, organized on 22 October 1861, served in the Department of the South until April 1864, when it transferred to Vir-

ginia. It suffered 282 casualties during the war and disbanded on 15 August 1865. Dyer, *Compendium*, 3:1011; Emilio, *A Brave Black Regiment*, 59–61.

8. The First Battery Connecticut Light Artillery, organized on 26 October 1861, served in the Department of the South from 13 January 1863 to April 1864. It lost 25 men in the war and mustered out on 11 June 1865. Dyer, *Compendium*, 3:1007.

9. In his official report of the engagement, General Beauregard grossly under-reported his losses as only three killed, twelve wounded, and three missing. *OR*, ser. 1, pt. 1, 28:75; Emilio, *A Brave Black Regiment*, 63.

10. Sgt. George F. Merriman (1841–63), an unmarried farmer from West Chester, Pennsylvania, enlisted on 4 March 1863. His wound eventually proved fatal, and he died at Beaufort, South Carolina, on 1 August. Emilio, *A Brave Black Regiment*, 347.

11. At first, Emilio believed that rebels had committed atrocities on wounded or dead members of the unit, but he later concluded that the unspecified offenses had been committed by fiddler crabs. As scavengers that often congregate in thousands, crabs can mutilate corpses but could not have inflicted gross damage in a brief period of time. There was evidence of Confederate atrocities that Emilio either ignored or failed to uncover. Samuel Willard, captain of GES's company, believed that "the enemy had in many cases offered gross indignities to the bodies of the killed and in one or two cases bayonetted the wounded." Vogelsang saw or was told about two members of his party who had surrendered and were found "tied and shot." Ibid., 62; Samuel Willard to Luis F. Emilio, 20 January 1884, Fifty-fourth Regiment Papers, 1:143, MHS; Peter Vogelsang to Robert Hamilton, 6 August 1863, *WAA*, 22 August 1863. My thanks to C. Douglas Alves, Jr., and his staff at the Calvert County, Maryland, Marine Museum for providing information about marine biology.

12. Pvt. Albert Walls (1834–63), Company B, an unmarried farmer from Philadelphia, joined the unit on 14 March 1863. He was neither killed nor captured during the Battle of James Island and later accompanied GES in the attack on Battery Wagner, where he was listed as missing and presumed dead. Emilio, *A Brave Black Regiment*, 348.

13. Pvt. Preston Williams of Company H saved Captain Russell's life when he shot a Confederate officer, of undetermined rank, in the neck. Ibid., 58–59.

14. Confederate forces on James Island actually totaled about three thousand men; six became prisoners. Burton, *The Siege of Charleston*, 160; Emilio, *A Brave Black Regiment*, 63.

15. Capt. William Harris Simpkins (1839–63), an unmarried clerk from West Roxbury, joined the Fifty-fourth on 23 March 1863. He died with Captain Russell in the Wagner attack. Emilio, *A Brave Black Regiment*, 331.

16. The first infantry assault against Battery Wagner took place at daybreak on 11 July. Elements of the Seventh Connecticut, the Seventy-sixth Pennsylvania, and the Ninth Maine charged headlong at the fort, recently reinforced with additional men in anticipation of a Union attack. The sickening slaugh-

ter—339 casualties—should have provided a useful lesson to Union commanders. Only 88 of the original 196 Connecticut troops returned to camp. Burton, *The Siege of Charleston*, 154–58.

17. Brig. Gen. George Crockett Strong (1832–63), a West Point graduate, commanded the Second Brigade, Second Division, Tenth Corps that attacked Wagner. Wounded during the battle, he contracted "lockjaw" [tetanus] and died. *WWWCW*, 630–31; Warner, *Generals in Blue*, 483–84.

18. The Third New Hampshire Regiment, organized in August 1861, arrived in the Sea Islands in April 1862 and remained until April 1864. It suffered 352 casualties during the war and mustered out on 25 July 1865. Stephens was not sure which regiment shot into the Fifty-fourth—an event not uncommon in battle—and years later suggested that the Ninth Maine had been at fault. Because of night-time conditions and the confusion of close-quarters battle, probably more than one Union regiment fired into its own men. The Forty-eighth and 100th New York Regiments probably bore prime responsibility because they disobeyed orders by loading and capping their weapons before the charge. Dyer, *Compendium*, 1347–48; Emilio, *A Brave Black Regiment*, 93; Peter Burchard, *One Gallant Rush: Robert Gould Shaw and His Brave Black Regiment* (New York: St. Martin's Press, 1965), 140; Charles P. Lord to Sister, 20 July 1863, Charles P. Lord Papers, Duke University Library.

19. Col. Robert Gould Shaw (1837–63), scion of the well-to-do Boston reform family, overcame initial doubts about leading the Fifty-fourth to become a competent and enthusiastic commander. The circumstances surrounding his death, especially rumors that rebels had gleefully buried Shaw in a trench "with his niggers," fueled enormous popular interest and helped make him a hero. Although his parents requested that no attempt be made to recover their son's body, officers of the regiment revisited Wagner ten months later and searched for Shaw's remains. Duncan, *Blue-Eyed Child of Fortune*; Burchard, *One Gallant Rush*; Emilio, *A Brave Black Regiment*, 98–103; Boston *Daily Advertiser*, 31 July 1863; notes from John Whittier Messer Appleton Papers, 25 May 1864, Fifty-fourth Regiment Papers, vol. 2, MHS.

20. Capt. John Whittier Messer Appleton verified Stephens's charges that Union soldiers shot retreating troops and claimed that he had stopped the killing. Other Union troops, however, made heroic efforts to recover the wounded that night, and some courageous souls crawled up to the slopes of Wagner in search of survivors. Union commanders, knowing the extra hazard blacks faced, ordered that wounded blacks be brought in first. Undated notes, Appleton Letterbooks, 64–66, John Whittier Messer Appleton Papers, WVUL; Emilio, *A Brave Black Regiment*, 103.

21. The Fifty-fourth's total casualties were 34 killed, 146 wounded, and 92 captured or missing—272 men. A majority of the captured and missing were either bayonetted by rebel troops or died in captivity. *OR*, ser. 1, pt. 1, 28:210; Emilio, *A Brave Black Regiment*, 431.

22. Sgt. Robert John Simmons (1839–63), Bermuda-born veteran of the English army, knew Shaw's father, was recruited by the black abolitionist

William Wells Brown, and mustered into the regiment on 12 March 1863. He was wounded and captured in the Wagner assault and died in Charleston after the amputation of an arm. The Hallowell family later collected money for the relief of his family. Emilio, *A Brave Black Regiment*, 93, 348; misc. notes, Fifty-fourth Regiment Papers, 1:187, MHS; donation receipts, 11 September 1863, Minot Family Papers, box L, MHS.

23. GES mentions Lt. Col. Edward N. Hallowell (1836–71), affectionately referred to as "Major" by the enlisted men. From the ardent antislavery family of Philadelphia and West Medford, Massachusetts, Hallowell joined the Fifty-fourth on 6 March 1863 and was shot during the Wagner assault. After recovering from his wounds, he took command of the regiment. Hallowell's commitment to the regiment and the antislavery cause was, if anything, stronger than Shaw's. Emilio, *A Brave Black Regiment*, 328–29; Luis F. Emilio, biographical notes, Philip and Betty Emilio Family Collection.

In Camp,
Morris Island, S.C.,
Aug. 7, 1863.

Mr. Editor: Since I wrote my last letter the startling news of the mobs, riots, incendiarism, pillage and slaughter, recently so rife in the North, particularly in New York City,[1] has reached here. You may judge what our thoughts and feelings were as we read bulletin after bulletin depicting to the life the scenes of violence and bloodshed which rivaled and even surpassed in their horrors, those which were perpetrated in Paris, during the bloody French Revolution, for we are yet to find an instance there where the orphan was ruthlessly assailed, or women and children murdered and maltreated without cause or provocation, simply for belonging to another race or class of people.

What cause or provocation have the New York rabble for disloyalty to their country, and for their bloody, atrocious assaults on my countrymen? Are we their enemies? Have we tyrannized over them? Have we maltreated them? Have we robbed them? Are we alien enemies? And are we traitors? Has not the unrequited labor of nearly four million of our brethren added to the country's wealth? Have we not been loyal to the country, in season and out of season, through good report and evil? And even while your mob-fiends upheld the assassin knife, and brandished the incendiary torch over the heads of our wives and children and to burn their homes, we were doing our utmost to sustain the honor of our country's flag, to perpetuate, if possible, those civil, social, and political liberties, they, who so malignantly hate us, have so fully enjoyed. Oh! how causeless, senseless, outrageous, brutal, and violative of every sentiment of manhood, courage and humanity these attacks on our defenseless brethren have been!

Fearful as these mobs have been, I trust they may prove to be lessons, though fearful ones, to guide the popular and loyal masses in the country, in all times of national emergency and peril, for when the services of every citizen or denizen of the country are imperatively required to defend it against powerful and determined foes, either foreign or domestic, and there can be found a strong minority ready and willing to subvert the government by popular violence and tumult or a base submission unworthy the meanest varlet of some monarchy; much less the boasted citizens of this great and magnificent country, it will bring still more forcibly to their minds the truism that "eternal vigilance is the price of liberty."

These mobs are the stepping-stones upon which base traitors and demagogues hope to mount into arbitrary power, and to overawe and subvert liberty and law. They seek anarchy; and despotism, they think, must succeed. First anarchy, then despotism. They make the negro the catspaw or victim; but the loyalist and the friend of law and order cannot fail to see that every blow directed against the negro is directed against them. Our relation to the government is and has been that of unflinching, unswerving loyalty. Even when the government, by its every precept and practice, conserved the interests of slavery, and slaves were hunted down by United States soldiers and surrendered to traitorous slave-masters, the conduct of the negro was marked with distinguished loyalty. The instances are too numerous to cite of their braving the most fearful dangers to convey valuable information to the Union armies, and for this, the half yet untold, such has been our reward. Does not Milliken's Bend and Port Hudson furnish a chapter of valor and faithful loyalty?[2] Is there no justice in America—or are we doomed to general massacre, as Mr. Blair[3] said we would be, in the event of the issue of the President's Emancipation proclamation? If this be our doom let us prepare for the worst.

The siege of Charleston has not yet commenced. The preparations of Gen. Gillmore[4] are very ample. There is no doubt that this citadel of treason will fall. Every one is impatient at the delay; but the siege of a stronghold upon which all of the engineering skill of the rebel Confederacy has been lavished, cannot be planned and matured in a day. They harass our fatigue parties considerably with their shells, but they only succeed in killing and wounding one or two men a day. These shells are very disagreeable at first, but after one is under them a while he can learn to become accustomed to them. The men sing, dance, and play cards and sleep as carelessly within range of them as if they were no more harmful than so many soap bubbles.

This Morris Island is the most desolate heap of sand-hills I ever saw. It is so barren that you cannot find so much as a gypsum weed[5] growing. Our situation is almost unbearable. During the day the sun is intensely hot, and this makes the sand hot; so we are sandwiched between the hot sun and the hot sand. Happily, the evenings are cool and bracing—so much so, that woolen blankets are not uncomfortable. The bathing is most delightful. I think Morris Island beach the most magnificent on the whole Atlantic coast. Had we in the North such a bathing shore, it would soon eclipse Newport, Atlantic City or Long Branch,[6] and the other bathing resorts. The beach at some points is at least one-third of a mile in width, descending at an almost imperceptible angle into the more refreshing breakers.

There is quite a stir in the camp of the 54th just at this moment, created by an attempt on the part of the Paymaster and Col. Littlefield[7] of the 4th Connecticut volunteers (who has been temporarily assigned to the command of our regiment since the death of Col. Shaw, our lamented commander) to pay us off with the paltry sum of $10 per month, the amount paid to contrabands. Col. Littlefield had the men drawn up in their company streets, and addressed them in a style something like this: "Gentlemen, I know that you are in want of money. Many of you have families who are dependent on you for support. The Paymaster refuses to pay any of the colored troops more than $10 per month. I have no doubt that Congress, when it meets next December, will pay you the balance of your pay. The government, in paying you this sum, only advances you this amount—it is not considered paying you off."[8] Only one company consented to take this sum. The rest of the regiment are highly incensed at the idea that after they have been enlisted as Massachusetts soldiers, and been put into the active service of the United States government, they should be paid off as the drafted ex-slaves are. The non-commissioned officers are to be paid the same as the privates.

There is to be, according to the Colonel's and Paymaster's arrangement, no distinction. Our First Sergeants, Sergeant-Major, and other Sergeants are to be paid only $10 per month. Now, if this $10 per month is advanced by the Paymaster, and he is so confident or certain that the next Congress will vote us the pay that regularly enlisted soldiers, like the 54th, generally receive, why does he not advance the privates and non-commissioned officers their full pay? Or does he not fear that the next Congress may refuse to have anything to do with it, and conclude that if we could receive $10 and make out until then, we could make out with that amount to the end of our term? To offer our non-commissioned officers the same pay and reducing them to the level of privates, is, to say the least, insulting and degrading to them.

Then, again, if we are not placed on the same footing with other Massachusetts soldiers, we have been enlisted under false pretenses. Our enlistment itself is fraudulent. When Gov. Andrew addressed us at Readville on the presentation of our colors, he claimed us as Massachusetts soldiers.[9] Frederick Douglass, in his address to the colored people to recruit the 54th, and who penned it by the authority of Gov. Andrew, declares that we form part of the quota of troops furnished by the State of Massachusetts.[10] If this be the case, why make this invidious distinction? We perform the same duties of other Massachusetts troops, and even now we have to perform fatigue duty night and day, and stand in line of battle from 3 to 5 A.M. with white soldiers, and for all this, not to say anything of the many perils we necessarily encounter, we are offered $10 per month or nothing until next December or January! Why, in the name of William H. Seward, are we treated thus? Does the refusal to pay us our due pander to the pro-slavery Cerberus?[11] Negroes in the navy receive the same pay that the Irish, English, German, Spanish or Yankee race do, and take it as a matter of course. Why, sir, the State of Massachusetts has been rebuked and insulted through her colored soldiers, and she should protect us, as Gov. Andrew has pledged his word she would. Since our regiment has been in this department, an attempt has been made to substitute the dark for the light-blue pantaloons of the U. S. army. This was at St. Helena. Col. Shaw rejected them, and we continue to wear the uniform of the U.S. Infantry corps.

The ever-memorable anniversary of British West India Emancipation[12] was observed by the non-commissioned officers of the 54th, by calling, on the 1st instant, a meeting, and passing a series of resolutions. This meeting was organized by the appointment of Sergeant-Major Douglass, Chairman, and Sergt. Fletcher, Co. A, Secretary.[13] A long list of Vice-Presidents were appointed, representing nearly every State. Commissary-Sergeant Lee[14] represented South Carolina; Sergt. Grey,[15] Massachusetts; Sergt. Swails, Pennsylvania.[16] A Committee, consisting of Sergts. Francis, Stephens, Barquet, Johnson and Gambier,[17] presented the following resolutions, which were passed:

1. Resolved, That we look with joy upon the example set by Great Britain twenty-nine years ago in liberating the slaves in her West India Islands, thereby making a long stride in the pathway of civilization, and eliciting the gratitude of enthralled millions everywhere—contributing largely to influence the people of this country to seek the overthrow of that system which has brought the nation to the verge of dissolution. We hail with more than gratification the determination of our government to follow her great and good example as evinced by that glorious instrument of January 1st, 1863, proclaiming freedom to slaves of rebels in Southern States—the desire to purchase those in loyal States—the decision of Attorney-General Bates,[18] and the calling to its aid the strong arms and loyal hearts of its black citizens.

2. Resolved, That we have another day added to our small family of holidays; we hail the 1st of January as twin-sister to the 1st of August; and as we have met together within six miles of the birthplace of secession to commemorate this day, we trust that on the 1st day of January next, by the blessing of God on our arms, the city of Charleston will ring with the voices of free men, women and children shouting, "Truly, the day of Jubilee has come."

3. Resolved, That while we look forward with sanguine hope for that day, and have the arms in our hands to help bring it about, we will use them, and put forth all our energies, and never cease until our ears shall hear the jubilant bell that rings the knell of slavery.

4. Resolved, That in our humble opinion the force of circumstances has compelled the loyal portion of this nation to acknowledge that man is physically the same, differing only in the circumstances under which he lives, and that action—true, manly action, only—is necessary to secure to us a full recognition of our rights as men by the controlling masses of this nation; and we see in the army, fighting for liberty and Union, the proper field for colored men, where they may win by their valor the esteem of all loyal men and women—believing that "Who would be free, themselves must strike the blow."[19]

5. Resolved, That we recognize in the brilliant successes of the Union armies the proofs that Providence is on our side; that His attributes cannot take sides with the oppressor.

Private John Peer,[20] Co. B, died at 6 o'clock P.M. this instant.

G. E. S.

WAA, 22 August 1863.

1. From 13 to 17 July 1863, white mobs protesting military conscription plunged New York City into the worst race riot in American history. Whites killed at least eleven blacks, injured countless others, and committed heinous atrocities on several of their victims. Nearly a hundred people died as a result of the rioting, and scores of others lost their homes. Tragically, Sgt. Robert J. Simmons's family suffered grievously; his mother's home was destroyed, and his nephew was killed. Iver Bernstein, *New York City Draft Riots: Their Significance for American Society and Politics in the Age of the Civil War* (New York: Oxford University Press, 1990), 3–42, 288–289n.; Emilio, *A Brave Black Regiment*, 93, 348.

2. The battles at Port Hudson (27 May 1863) and Milliken's Bend (7 June 1863), Louisiana, which sent the Corps d'Afrique and the Louisiana Native Guard against well-entrenched or more numerous rebel forces, marked the first large-scale use of black troops in combat. After Milliken's Bend, one Union officer remarked that it was "impossible for men to show greater gallantry than the negro troops." The stunning heroism convinced many Union commanders that blacks could make superior soldiers and helped change white attitudes concerning black recruitment. Dudley Taylor Cornish, *The Sable Arm: Negro Troops in the Union Army, 1861–1865* (New York: W. W. Norton, 1966), 137–40, 142–45; Joseph T. Glatthaar, *Forged in Battle: The Civil War Alliance of Black Soldiers and White Officers* (New York: Free Press, 1990), 123–35; Boston *Post*, 13 June 1863.

3. GES reacts to George Lewis Ruffin's 2 July 1863 letter in the *Anglo-African* complaining about Postmaster General Blair's obsessive interest in colonization. In his 20 May 1863 address to a Union meeting in Cleveland, Blair had defended Lincoln's earlier offer of compensated emancipation to the South as "a deliverance by colonization from a war of races which could only end in the extermination of the negro race or amalgamation with it." New York *Times*, 24 May 1863; *WAA*, 25 July 1863.

4. Gen. Quincy A. Gillmore (1825–88), originally with the Army Corps of Engineers, took command of the Department of the South in July 1863. He planned and coordinated the siege of Charleston. *HTIECW*, 310–11.

5. The reference is to gypsophila paniculata (babies' breath).

6. GES refers to the East Coast's most famous pleasure and health resorts, Newport, Rhode Island, and two spots on New Jersey's Atlantic Coast: Atlantic City, near Philadelphia, and Long Branch in Monmouth County. Angelo Heilprin and Louis Heilprin, eds., *A Complete Pronouncing Gazetteer* (Philadelphia: J. B. Lippincott Co., 1922).

7. GES misidentifies Milton S. Littlefield (1832–99), the politically appointed commander of the Fourth South Carolina Volunteers (Twenty-first USCT), who briefly led the Fifty-fourth after the Wagner attack and sparked much hostili-

ty. Advisors to Governor Andrew denounced Littlefield as a "rogue" and charged that he would "endanger the regiment to serve his own interests." He later became a superintendent of black recruitment and was court-martialed for skimming bounty payments. Littlefield apparently won his case and was mustered out of service in April 1866. Complied Service Records, RG 94, National Archives; Emilio, *A Brave Black Regiment*, 107, 117, 176; Edward W. Kinsley to John A. Andrew, 9 February 1864, Edward W. Kinsley Papers, Duke University; Albert G. Browne to Wendell Phillips, 28 October 1864, Blagden Collection, HLHU; Alfred S. Hartwell Letterbooks, 29 January 1866, Alfred S. Hartwell Papers, box 1, MSL; "Recollections of Col. Leonard B. Perry," December 1912, Alfred S. Hartwell Papers, Hawaii State Archives.

8. The War Department had no plans to equalize pay and did so only as a result of congressional legislation.

9. The Fifty-fourth received its colors on 18 May 1863. In his address, Governor Andrew recognized the men as "citizens of Massachusetts." *Liberator*, 22 May 1863; Boston *Commonwealth*, 22 May 1863.

10. In his original recruitment call, Douglass asserted that "I am authorized to assure you that you will receive the same wages, the same rations, the same equipments, the same protection, the same treatment, and the same bounty, secured to the white soldiers." Philip S. Foner, ed., *The Life and Writings of Frederick Douglass*, 4 vols. (New York: International Publishers, 1952), 3:317–19.

11. Cerberus was the three-headed dog of Hades, one of several Greek mythological beasts that guarded the realm of the dead and tormented souls as they passed through the gates of the underworld. Pierre Grimal, *The Dictionary of Classical Mythology* (New York: Basil Blackwell, 1986), 96.

12. Although slavery in the British West Indies ended on 1 August 1834, by the Emancipation Act of 1833 blacks actually entered an apprenticeship program that left them in bonds for another six years. American blacks annually honored the First of August with street parades, speeches, and other festivities to emphasize the hypocrisy of July Fourth celebrations. William A. Green, *British Slave Emancipation: The Sugar Colonies and the Great Experiment, 1830–1865* (Oxford: Oxford University Press, 1976), 99–127; Benjamin Quarles, *Black Abolitionists* (New York: Oxford University Press, 1969), 116, 123–28.

13. Lewis H. Douglass (1840–1908), eldest son of Frederick Douglass, joined the regiment on 25 March 1863 and was promoted to sergeant-major a month later. He survived wounds received in the Wagner assault but caught typhoid fever and was discharged in May 1864. Francis H. Fletcher (1841–?), a Salem, Massachusetts, clerk, helped recruit for the regiment and served from February 1863 to August 1865. William S. McFeeley, *Frederick Douglass* (New York: W. W. Norton, 1991), 222–26, 234–36, 247–49, 258; *BAP*, 5:244–45; Emilio, *A Brave Black Regiment*, 13, 339, 340.

14. Arthur B. Lee (1834–?), Company A, a South Carolina harnessmaker, was promoted to commissary sergeant on 23 April 1863. Emilio, *A Brave Black Regiment*, 339.

15. William H. W. Gray (1825–?), a New Bedford seaman, was first sergeant of Company C. He joined the regiment on 14 February 1863 and was wounded at Wagner but served for the rest of the war. Ibid., 350.

16. Stephen A. Swails (1832–1900?), originally from Columbia, Pennsylvania, had labored on canals and railroads since the age of fourteen. At the time of enlistment on 8 April 1863, he worked as a boatman in Elmira, New York. In January 1865, after a bitter fight with the War Department, Swails became the army's first official black commissioned officer. He moved to Kingstree, South Carolina, after the war, where he became a Freedmen's Bureau agent and taught under the auspices of the New England Freedmen's Aid Society. Swails, a member of the 1867 state constitutional convention, was elected to the state senate, became a clerk for the Treasury Department, and served on the board of trustees of the University of South Carolina. *Freedmen's Record*, December 1866; Emilio, *A Brave Black Regiment*, 336; Luis F. Emilio notes, Philip and Betty Emilio Family Collection; Robert C. Morris, *Reading, 'Riting, and Reconstruction: The Education of Freedmen in the South, 1861–1870* (Chicago: University of Chicago Press, 1976), 104–5, 106.

17. Sgt. Joseph H. Barquet (1823–?), a mason from Galesburg, Illinois, was born in Charleston, South Carolina. He joined Company H on 26 April 1863 and mustered out on 20 August 1865. Barquet, who also wrote for the *Anglo-African*, was court-martialed for one missive that criticized army food. Sgt. Frederick Johnson (1838–?), an unmarried Boston hairdresser, joined on 11 March 1863 and served until 20 August 1865. The *Anglo-African* garbled the names of Barquet, Swails, Francis, and Gambier. The last two are unidentified. *WAA*, 16 September 1865; Fifty-fourth Massachusetts Regiment, Record Books, Company H, RG 94, National Archives; Edwin S. Redkey, ed., *A Grand Army of Black Men: Letters from African-American Soldiers in the Union Army, 1861–1865* (New York: Cambridge University Press, 1992), xii; Emilio, *A Brave Black Regiment*, 351, 373.

18. Edward Bates (1793–1869) was a member of Congress from Missouri and Lincoln's attorney general. GES refers to Bates's opinion of 29 November 1862, implying that black men were citizens of the United States. Nicolay and Hay, *Abraham Lincoln*, 6:419–20; Berlin, *The Black Military Experience*, 372, 374.

19. The quotation is from Lord Byron's *Childe Harold's Pilgrimage* (1818), canto 2, stanza 76.

20. John W. Peer (1842–63), a Philadelphia barber, enlisted on 18 February 1863. He succumbed to dysentery either on 6 or 7 August at Morris Island. Emilio, *A Brave Black Regiment*, 347.

Morris Island, S.C.,
Sept. 4, 1863.

Mr. Editor: There is so much of exciting interest to communicate, and there is so much danger of violating the orders of Gen. Gillmore regarding "contraband information,"[1] that one scarcely knows where to commence or where to end. The recent order from headquarters declares that "the severest punishment known to the military law and usage in the field, will be inflicted on any citizen or soldier who gives information that will be of service to the enemy, or without permission from headquarters of U.S. forces in this department." I have no desire to do this thing, and if there were no order touching the matter, my earnest desire for the speedy triumph of the cause would be amply sufficient to deter me from saying anything that would, in the least, give aid or comfort to the enemy.

The first item of interest to be referred to is the grand review of Gen. Stevenson's Brigade,[2] to which the 54th belongs, on the 16th ult. Ours is the only colored regiment in this brigade, and were drawn up in line, colors flying and marched with the other Massachusetts and also New York soldiers, and reviewed by Gen. Gillmore and staff, Gen. Terry,[3] and Gen. Stevenson and staff. Gens. Gillmore and Stevenson expressed the utmost satisfaction at the fine appearance of the regiment, and when on the march from camp, Gen. Terry met Col. Littlefield and said that no other regiment in the brigade made a finer appearance or marched better than the 54th. Even the privates in some of the regiments conceded that we outmarched them. When we passed Gen. Gillmore, he sat uncovered and could not fail to discover that the desire of every soldier in our regiment was to create a favorable impression on his mind. The good and faithful soldiers courts the favor and approval of his superior officer.

The question of our pay continues to be the topic of conversation and correspondence. Numerous letters have reached us from distinguished friends in the State of Massachusetts, all expressing the utmost confidence that we will receive all of our pay and have secured to us every right that other Massachusetts soldiers enjoy. His Excellency Gov. Andrew, in a letter dated "Executive Department, Boston, August 24th,"[4] and addressed to Mr. Frederick Johnson,[5] an officer in the regiment, says:

"I have this day received your letter of the 10th of August,[6] and in reply desire, in the first place, to express to you the lively interest with which I have watched every step of the Fifty-fourth Regiment since it left Massachusetts, and the feelings of pride and admiration with which I have learned and read the accounts of the heroic conduct of the regiment in the attack upon Fort Wagner, when you and your brave soldiers so well proved their manhood, and showed themselves to be true soldiers of Massachusetts. As to the matter inquired about in your letter, you may rest assured that I shall not rest until you have secured all of your rights, and that I have no doubt whatever of the ultimate success. I have no doubt, by law, you are entitled to the same pay as other soldiers, and on the authority of the Secretary of War,[7] I promised that you should be paid and treated in all respects like other soldiers of Massachusetts. Till this is done I feel that my promise is dishonored by the government. The whole difficulty arises from a misapprehension, the correction of which will no doubt be made as soon as I can get the subject fully examined by the Secretary of War.

I have the honor to be your obedient servant,

John A. Andrew,
Governor of Massachusetts."

The trouble seems to be something like this: The Paymaster General,[8] whoever that may be, has directed the paymasters to pay all negro troops, of African descent, $10 per month, the pay allowed to contrabands by statute when employed in the Commissary or Quartermaster's Department. There seems to have been no provision made to pay colored soldiers.[9] There may be some reason for making distinction between armed and unarmed men in the service of the government, but when the nationality of a man takes away his title to pay it becomes another thing. Suppose a regiment of Spaniards should be mustered into the service of the United States, would Congress have to pass a special law to pay Spaniards? Or, suppose, a regiment of Sandwich Islanders should do duty as soldiers of the United States, would it be necessary to pass a law to pay Sandwich Islanders? Does not the deed of muster secure the services and even life of the man mustered into the service to the government? And does not this same deed of muster give a man a title to all pay and bounties awarded to soldiers bearing arms? I believe that "by law, we are entitled to the same pay as other soldiers," and the "misapprehension arises" from this. The Paymaster General will not have the colored soldiers paid under the law which pay white soldiers, and virtually creates in his own mind the necessity for the passage of a special law authorizing them to be paid. Is there a special law on the statute books of the National Legislature touching the payment of colored men employed in the naval service?

In my last letter I made the types say that Col. Littlefield, our present commander, was of the 4th Connecticut Volunteers—it should have been 4th South Carolina; and for fear that my letter may create an impression that Col. Littlefield is not the friend of the colored soldiers, I will say that since Col. L. assumed command of our regiment he has done as much in the power of one man has, to maintain the character and discipline, as well as the comfort, of the men.[10] Col. Littlefield is a martyr for the cause—an exile from his home, and holds a commission as Colonel of a negro regiment, the 4th South Carolina, now in process of formation. After the siege of Charleston he will make an active and efficient organizer of colored men. Few men are more capable of active, vigorous service, or have a higher appreciation of the services and efficiency of colored soldiers.

Since I wrote my last letter, the 54th has been assigned to a most perilous duty. A certain regiment in this department has been assigned to dig in the foremost parallels, but it was a new one and unaccustomed to sweeping grape and canister and bursting shells. The Commanding General sent word to Col. Littlefield that the aforesaid regiment, its officers as well as men, could not stand fire, and assigned the duty to the 54th. We are to do nothing else. It is a duty of the greatest danger. The men have to dig under the fire of rebel sharpshooters and all the rebel batteries on Morris and James Island. Every man "for duty" in our regiment has to suffer the ordeal eight hours out of every thirty two. We operate under the protection of our sharpshooters. You talk about your charges on Fort Wagner! It is a "pull Dick, pull Devil," between them and the foremost parallels. But the labor must be done, and I feel proud that we are thus honored with the post of danger. Since we have been engaged thus we have been peculiarly fortunate. It seems that Divine Providence has willed that we have suffered enough in loss of life, for the 3d Pennsylvania Volunteers, colored,[11] have lost considerably. The casualties in the 3d Pennsylvania up to this date are:

COMPANY A.
Corp. Edward Powell, killed.
Private Andrew Jackson, killed.
Private Joseph Harris, wounded.
Corp. Denny, wounded severely. All of Philadelphia.[12]

COMPANY D.
Sergt. Hardy, wounded severely.
Corp. Denton Lox, killed.
Private Alfred Fenley, killed.

Private Alfred Rothwell, killed.
Private James Gray, killed.[13]

COMPANY F.
Benj. Williams, slightly wounded.
Rich. Turpin, slightly wounded.
John Harris, slightly wounded.[14]

COMPANY G.
Isaac Goddart, slightly wounded.[15]

COMPANY K.
Daniel Jones, killed.
Israel Jones, wounded.
Francis Jackson, wounded slightly.
Benj. Bradley, wounded slightly.[16]

Casualties in the 54th Massachusetts Regiment.

COMPANY D.
John Alfred Green, wounded.[17]

COMPANY F.
Corp. Joseph Stilles, wounded slightly.
Private Horace Bennett, wounded slightly.
Private Jas. Postley, wounded slightly.
Private Aaron Croger, wounded dangerously in back.[18]

COMPANY K.
Geo. King, leg blown off, since died.[19]

COMPANY H.
Geo. Vanderpool, Coxsackie, N.Y., killed.
Alex. Hunter, wounded in head severely.[20]

G. E. S.

WAA, 19 September 1863.

1. Despite military regulations, an enormous amount of important intelligence found its way into newspapers on both sides of the Mason-Dixon Line. General Gillmore attempted to staunch the flow in his district and may have had the Fifty-fourth in mind when he issued his warning on 7 August 1863. Two unnamed men in the regiment were "placed at hard labor in the trenches for violation" of the order. Brig. Gen. Quincy A. Gillmore to Com-

mander, Fifty-fourth Massachusetts, 7 August 1863, Company Letterbooks, Fifty-fourth Massachusetts Regiment, RG 94, National Archives; Luis F. Emilio to Mother, 12 August 1863, Philip and Betty Emilio Family Collection.

2. The Third Brigade, Tenth Corps, Department of the South had six white units and one black—the Fifty-fourth Massachusetts—until November, when the Second South Carolina and Third USCT joined. Gen. Thomas Greely Stevenson (1836–64), a Boston native, led the brigade from 19 July to 19 September 1863. In April 1864, he transferred to Virginia and fell at Spotsylvania. Dyer, *Compendium*, 2:368; *WWWCW*, 624.

3. Gen. Alfred Howe Terry (1827–90), a Connecticut lawyer, commanded the Tenth Corps at Morris Island, South Carolina, from 19 July to 18 October 1863. Terry and Gillmore reviewed the brigade on the beach at Morris Island on 23 August. *WWWCW*, 645–46; Emilio, *A Brave Black Regiment*, 106, 114.

4. John A. Andrew to Sgt. Frederick Johnson, 24 August 1863, Executive Department Letters, vol. 35, MSA.

5. Sergeant Johnson had read Andrew's letter to the noncommissioned officers, which assured them of the state's full support for their cause and ended disquieting rumors concerning what the state intended to do about the pay issue. Emilio, *A Brave Black Regiment*, 351; Sgt. Frederick Johnson to John A. Andrew, 4 September 1863, Executive Department Letters, vol. 59, MSA.

6. In his letter to Andrew, Johnson declared that the men felt "duped" by the government. Rather than accept the state's offer to make up the difference between black and white pay rates, he suggested that the regiment be called back to serve as a home guard. His lobbying efforts were supported in Boston by the wife of Johnson's minister, Mrs. Leonard A. Grimes, who also wrote to Andrew to plead for equal pay. Sgt. Frederick Johnson to John A. Andrew, 10 August 1863, Mrs. Leonard A. Grimes to John A. Andrew, n.d., Executive Department Letters, vol. 59, MSA.

7. Early in 1863, Andrew obtained Secretary of War Stanton's assurance that the Fifty-fourth would receive the same pay as white troops. Although Andrew accepted that contraband units might receive lower pay, no question existed concerning the pay of black regiments raised in the North. Andrew also advised George T. Downing, the Rhode Island black leader—in a letter widely reprinted in the reform press—that Stanton had promised the same "pay, equipments, bounty, or any aid and protection" given to whites. John A. Andrew to John Wilder, 23 May 1863, Executive Department Letters, box W17, MSA; John A. Andrew to George T. Downing, 23 March 1863, *WAA*, 18 April 1863; Henry Greenleaf Pearson, *The Life of John A. Andrew, Governor of Massachusetts, 1861–1865*, 2 vols. (Boston: Houghton, Mifflin, 1904), 2:85–86.

8. Timothy Patrick Andrews (?-1868), a career military officer, became paymaster general in December 1862 and held this position until retiring on 29 November 1864. Andrews implemented but did not set War Department policy. *WWWCW*, 14.

9. Stephens correctly stated the Fifty-fourth's legal limbo. If the government had recruited blacks under the 1862 Militia Act—Stanton's promise notwithstanding—black troops could legally be paid only $10 a month. On the other hand, if blacks had been enrolled under the 1862 Confiscation Act, rightful pay remained uncertain because the act authorized black recruitment without mentioning pay. The War Department's solicitor, William Whiting, had issued a narrow ruling stating that blacks had entered the service under the Militia Act and so could receive only $10. GES, however, asserted that no special enabling legislation was required to recruit them and that the unit should be treated as any other state regiment. The issue was further complicated by an 1816 army regulation that excluded blacks from service. Herman Belz, "Law, Politics, and Race in the Struggle for Equal Pay during the Civil War," *Civil War History* 22 (September 1976): 197–213.

10. GES's positive view of Littlefield remains curious because he did not fully support the men on the pay issue and believed that Governor Andrew "had spoiled" the regiment through overattention. Mary E. Clark to John A. Andrew, 15 November 1863, Executive Department Letters, box 59, MSA.

11. GES refers to Tilghman's Third USCT by its popular name. The regiment was officially in the U.S. service and was not a state unit. "War Letters of Charles P. Bowditch," *Proceedings of the Massachusetts Historical Society* 57 (May 1924): 436.

12. Cpl. Edward Parnell joined the Third on 26 June 1863 and was killed on 3 September; Pvt. Andrew Jackson enlisted on 26 June 1863 and died on 22 August; and Pvt. Joseph Harris served from 26 June 1863 to 31 October 1865. Harris was promoted to corporal on 6 April 1865. No one named Denny enlisted in the Third. Bates, *History*, 5:925–42.

13. Sgt. Crawford Hardy enlisted on 4 July 1863 and served until 27 April 1864, when he received a medical discharge. All of the following enlisted on 4 July 1863 and were killed at Battery Wagner on 26 August: Cpl. Denton Lox, Pvt. James Fenley, Pvt. Alfred Rothwell, and Pvt. James Gray. Ibid., 5:925–42.

14. Pvt. Benjamin Williams enlisted on 10 July 1863 and received a medical discharge on 26 April 1864; Pvt. Richard Turpin mustered in 11 July 1863 and died at Morris Island on 11 December; and Cpl. John Harris joined on 10 July 1863 and was promoted to corporal on 19 August and sergeant on 1 October 1864, just thirty days before mustering out of the army. Ibid., 5:925–42.

15. Pvt. Isaac Goddard enlisted on 13 July 1863 and died of his wounds at Beaufort, South Carolina, on 14 September 1863. Ibid., 5:925–42.

16. Daniel Jones enlisted on 15 July 1863 and was killed at Morris Island on 27 August; Israel Jones joined on 18 July 1863, was wounded on 27 August, and received a medical discharge on 15 May 1864; Francis Jackson mustered on 18 July 1863 and obtained a medical discharge on 6 June 1865; and Benjamin Bradley remained in the unit from 18 July 1863 until 31 October 1865. Ibid., 5:925–42.

17. John Alfred Green (1845–?), an unmarried Brooklyn, New York, farmer, joined the Fifty-fourth on 16 March 1863 and received a discharge on 30 June 1864. Emilio, *A Brave Black Regiment*, 355.

18. Two men from Middletown, Pennsylvania, were Joseph Stilles (1838–
?), a married laborer who served from 8 April 1863 until 20 August 1865, and
Horace B. Bennett (1838–?), a married farmer who enlisted on 8 April 1863,
received a promotion to sergeant, was wounded at Boykin's Mills, S.C., and
was discharged on 8 June 1865. Pvt. James Postley (1844–?), a single laborer
from Elmira, New York, joined the unit on 8 April 1863, also was wounded
at Boykin's Mills, and served in the army until 12 October 1865. George
Aaron Croger (1834–?), another single laborer from Elmira, enlisted on 8 April
1863, was promoted to corporal, and mustered out with the regiment on 20
August 1865. Ibid., 364, 366, 367.

19. George King (1833–63), a single laborer from Toledo, enlisted on 5 May
1863 and died from wounds received on 1 September 1863. Ibid., 385.

20. George Vanderpool (1845–63), a single laborer from Cocksackie, New
York, enlisted on 17 April 1863 and was killed on 4 September. Alexander
Hunter (1835–?), a single laborer from Cleveland, joined the Fifty-fourth on
29 April 1863, was wounded on 17 August, and discharged on 30 June
1864. Ibid., 375, 377.

[Sept.] 1863.

Mr. Editor: Fort Wagner has fallen! The stronghold which bade
defiance to every assault, and received for forty days the peltings of
iron missiles vomited from the heaviest ordinance employed in modern warfare, has submitted to patient toil and labor with the spade.[1]
The enemy have admitted that Wagner was the key to Charleston,
and our lights say that the reduction and occupancy of Sumter was
an impossibility while it (Wagner) remained in possession of the enemy. These notices have been iterated and reiterated until the fall of
Fort Wagner has become to be regarded by those far removed from the
scenes of active operations as great an achievement as the capture of
Fort Sumter, or the formidable Sullivan's Island batteries. Fort Wagner and Battery Gregg, with some one hundred prisoners and a considerable amount of commissary stores, with seven or eight pieces of
artillery, are our only trophies of victory.[2]

For a week previous to the evacuation of Fort Wagner by the rebel
forces, they had been removing their arms and ammunition, and when
our forces took peaceable possession of it, the magazine was found
to be empty, or nearly so. Their prisoners say no power on earth could
keep us out of Fort Wagner or any other fort that could be approached
by parallels. From the first landing of troops on Morris Island[3] it has
been regarded as lost. They admit that the city of Charleston can be

destroyed by our combustible shells, and the rebel authorities seem to dare our commanding General to burn the city. For what are all those rebel batteries erected? To save the city of Charleston from destruction and to prevent its occupation by our forces. If we burn the city, half the necessity for rebel batteries has been taken away. And another thing: if Beauregard,[4] or whoever else may have command, when he or they found that there was a fixed determination to burn it, if not surrendered, we would have [had] but very few of their insolent parleyings. I would spare the aged and infirm, the women and children, and give them ample time to go beyond the reach of danger, but the city I would burn to ashes. Not one stone of its buildings would I leave upon another for active rebels, armed and unarmed, I would dig graves beneath its smoldering ruins. It is not very likely that the rebels would occupy their works after the material interests of the city were destroyed. If the old nest which contains and has hatched out so many secession serpents was destroyed, the country would be spared many troubles, and a new order of beings not branded with treason or infatuated with slavery could find a home and habitation. The course would in the end be found to be one of the grandest steps toward restoring loyalty and peace, and remove the necessity of a standing army in South Carolina. For the sake of humanity, peace and victory give them "Greek fire,"[5] the torch and shell, not in anger or for revenge, but as a just, well merited punishment for treason, violation of the law, and other crimes.

From present appearances Charleston will not be burned, and the reduction of the other forts and batteries in Charleston harbor is as great a military problem as ever. There is a question between the relative activity of the land and naval forces now engaged in the sieges. The army claim to have achieved all the successes thus far, and that the navy have failed to fully co-operate with them. In the first place, with justice to the navy, it may be said to have been the right arm of the Federal service, and has been the safeguard of the army. The land forces have on many occasions owed their salvation to the naval. It seems to be unjust to deny the navy the high honors it deserves. What if victory has been achieved by the co-operation of the navy? One thing I think is demonstrated in the present siege: the superiority of the Ironsides over the Monitors for such operations.[6] Rapidity of firing is just as essential as great weight of metal. Complete invulnerability cannot be attained. That is, an iron vessel could not be floated with

a hull strong enough to resist steel-pointed shot of the weight modern improved guns can propel against it. Nothing but huge sandbanks
can withstand these terrible missiles. During the siege of Fort Wagner, when the Ironsides would run up into the very jaws of their batteries on Sullivan's Island, right in the face of Wagner and Sumter, she
invariably silenced them. One shell would not explode before another would take its place to fill the atmosphere with death. She did not
give them breathing time. They could not take shelter from one shell
and man and fire their guns before another could reach them, as they
can easily do when engaged with the Monitors.

It is contraband to write of present operations, but I am privileged
to have my say about the operations which led to the evacuation of
Wagner and Gregg. We have lost as much of blood and suffered as
much in toil as any other regiment in the Department in the performance of this task, and I presume that when the commanding General shall come to sum up his report of this affair, he will give us the
credit we deserve.[7] The truth cannot always be learned from newspaper correspondence, there is such wide scope for the ventilation of
sentiments of prejudiced and irresponsible men. This may be "like
pot calling kettle black," but I must say that after we have done as
much as any other soldiers here, our flag should have been alongside
the rest. Serrill's Engineers,[8] who deserve the highest honor, planted
their flag on the works, as did the 3d Rhode Island.[9] If we had demanded to have our flag and urged its claims to a place there, as Col. Shaw
would have done, it would have floated there. But not one suggested
the propriety of it.[10]

The main portion of our regiment was in line of battle, on the right
of Montgomery's Brigade.[11] Detachments from the 54th Massachusetts, 2d South Carolina, 100th New York,[12] 10th Connecticut and the
Marine Corps[13] intercepted three of the rebel barges which contained
the last remains of Gregg's and Wagner's garrison, numbering about
one hundred men.[14] One of the rebel barges escaped. Some of the
rebels in their fright and excitement jumped overboard. There were
some drowned, but the greater number were rescued. There were
some few men found scattered around the works who seemed to court
capture. Our pickets were apprized by a rebel soldier of the evacuation of Wagner about midnight, but before he could make it known
that he bore information for us some of the pickets shot him. The
detachment which captured these retreating rebels was part of a pro-

gramme of movements to take Wagner by assault. The part they had to play was to intercept re-enforcements during the assault, and it was not until we had marched them away down to the Beacon House[15] that one of their principle men admitted that the works had been abandoned. They, to a man, deny having been in the fort on the 18th. They say they relieved the men who held the battery at that time. About a week ago they conversed freely with us negroes, and seemed to have vague notions of retaliation. They all said that they belonged to the Charleston Battalion[16]—were boatmen carrying provisions over to Cummings's Point. There was an officer with them who said that he was only assistant surgeon, but his rank is higher and he does not belong to the medical corps. He cut a mighty sorry figure as he marched at the head of his comrades, and on each side of them the silent, moody negro guard. Now and then the Sergeant would give out the stern command, "Close up!" and Mr. Reb did not have to be told a second time.

Quite a considerable number of colored refugees have come into our lines since the capture of the whole of Morris Island. Ten persons made their escape on last Friday night: four children, one women and five men. They came from the city and confirm the report of the destructiveness of shells charged with "Greek Fire." They say that the citizens are running off their slaves by the thousands.[17] They towed their boats down the harbor in safety, and the mother says that just as they got opposite Sumter the little baby broke out in shrill screams and would not be comforted. They gave up all for lost, but the heroic mother instantly made a wad of a shawl and filled its little mouth, and when they landed on the beach and surrendered to our pickets, the poor little things were almost suffocated. She thinks "it better die den all be slave."

I cannot resist the temptation to refer to the conduct of the colored soldiers digging in the approaches. Says Sergt. Barquet: "Men born and reared on Southern plantations who never saw a gun can now talk as glibly as you please of planes, augers, ranges and distances, and the entire military vocabulary is becoming familiar to them. I overheard the following conversation between two contraband soldiers: 'Sam, Cohorn mortar[18] trow shell great range; to fetch him, reb wastes much powder.' 'Ah! Jim, Cohorn mortar wuss den grape and schrapanel; grape shell come straight in trench—de odder bound to go ober.'" What a fund of information these men have gained, and what a grand school for the soldier is here opened to them! Eight hours out of thirty-six toiling and laboring in the face of death, shell from front and flank, Minnie bullets, grape and shrapnel plunging, whizzing and plowing up the earth on all sides. Some one of the officers of the Engineer Corps has to superintend the work of the fatigue parties.

Barquet gives the following scrap which will show how reckless and profane a man can be under the intoxicating influence of rum, and, is, to say the least, an incident worth telling: The fifth and last parallel had been reached; the rebels seemed to be frenzied with alarm, and their sharpshooters and heavy guns kept up an incessant play on the fatigue parties. An Irish Lieutenant of Serrill's Engineer Corps had charge of the operations on that night. The perilous march had been made without any casualties. When our fatigue reached the point of operations, the following colloquy occurred between the Irish Lieutenant and the men who had the dangerous duty to perform:

"Who comes there?"

"54th fatigue party!"

"Arrah, there should be here at this late hour a brigade of fatigue men. Now listen. There was niver a man hurt wid me," the shot then nearly blinding the men with their fizzing, fuming glare. "I want two parties of sappers and miners[19] of four men each. First party come forward!" The men came. "No. 1 you're a sapper. No. 2, you're a miner. No. 3, you're a sapper. No. 4, you're a miner. No. 1, you're kilt! No. 2, you take his place. No. 3, you're kilt. No. 4, you must take his place." No. 1's and 3's feelings may be better imagined than described. As a sort of climax to this arrangement, the inebriated officer said, "All I ask is two gabions[20] to a man, and by to-morrow morning we'll be in the gates of Fort Wagner and the jaws of death and hell."

The boys went to work with a will, and before daylight an indignant rebel in the riflepits, just behind our parallel, was forced to exclaim to our boys, "You black Yankee sons of b—s intend to bury us in sand, don't you?" On this night poor young Vanderpool was killed, three of the 104th Pennsylvania volunteers,[21] and several wounded.

The Rev. Samuel Harrison[22] has been appointed Chaplain of our regiment. This is most fortunate. Our regiment has felt the need of a chaplain. We have had but four sermons preached to us since we left the camp Readville, Mass.—one by Rev. James Lynch[23] at St. Helena, and one on St. Simon's by the Chaplain of the 2d South Carolina Volunteers, and two on Morris Island by an able and eloquent agent of the American Tract Society,[24] now home in the North, and whose name I disremember. Prayer-meetings are regularly held in our camp and I think there are a few evidences of a revival. These meetings are very boisterous, and many who believe in deep, fervent, devotional worship cannot take as active a part in them as they would if there was less excitement and fewer of their unearthly yellings.

Gen. Gillmore has commenced granting furloughs. To-day some ten or twelve of the 54th go North in the steamer that bears this letter. Your humble servant defers his visit North to a more convenient season. Sergt.-Major Douglass, Sergt. Barquet, and Sergt. Gray of New Bedford, are among this first installment of absentees.

I have just seen another letter from Gov. Andrew, to the effect that there is no law which prevents our receiving full pay—that the Paymaster is not a competent judge in the matter, and that free colored men, citizens of Massachusetts, regularly enlisted as Massachusetts volunteers, cannot be less than citizen soldiers whom the Paymaster has no right to know but as soldiers, and advising us to take ten dollars a month under protest only. The law referring to persons of African descent employed in the army cannot refer to us. There is no proof that any of our fathers are Africans. If they adopt this rule there is no such thing as an American in the country, for all whites and blacks are not aborigines.

G. E. S.

WAA, 10 October 1863.

1. Confederates abandoned Wagner at 1:30 A.M., on 7 September 1863. Recognizing that Morris Island could not hold out against the Union siege, General Beauregard ordered a secret withdrawal. Gillmore had planned a third assault on Wagner for 9 A.M. that day, but a Union reconnaissance discovered it abandoned. Emilio, *A Brave Black Regiment*, 120–23.

2. Union forces actually captured about twenty-five artillery pieces and an undetermined number of muskets, pikes, and spears from Batteries Wagner and Gregg. Ibid., 124–25.

3. Union troops under General Gillmore made their first assault on Morris Island on 10 July 1863 and before nightfall had captured all the island south of Wagner. Ibid., 51–53.

4. Gen. Pierre Gustave Toutant Beauregard (1818–93), who directed the attack on Fort Sumter that began the Civil War, commanded the Department of South Carolina, Georgia, and Florida from August 1862 to April 1864 and led the Confederate defense of Charleston. *WWWCW*, 43–44.

5. Union cannoneers fired off about forty-one experimental, incendiary artillery shells—"Greek fire"—against Charleston. Invented by Levi Short of

Buffalo, New York, the volatile rounds were manufactured by Short and Duer of Chester, Pennsylvania, in solid and liquid versions. All variations proved unreliable, and the army abandoned it. The weapon's antecedents were first used in the sixth and seventh centuries, C.E., by the Byzantine Empire against invading Muslims. *OR*, ser. 1, 28:33–34; *The Press* (Philadelphia), 11 March, 7 April 1863; Robert V. Bruce, *Lincoln and the Tools of War* (New York: Bobbs-Merrill, 1956), 228–29, 241–248; Alex Roland, "Greek Fire," *MHQ: Quarterly Journal of Military History* 2 (Spring 1990): 16–19.

6. GES refers to the USS *New Ironsides* and the controversial *Monitor*-class ships. The *Ironsides*, built in 1862, proved slow and ungainly, but its sixteen eleven-inch Dahlgren cannon, two two-hundred-pound Parrott guns, and four twenty-four-pound howitzers made it well suited for infantry support. The *Monitors*, a design often described as a cheesebox on a raft, became the navy's pet because of the USS *Monitor's* famous engagement with the CSS *Virginia*. Poorly designed and largely unseaworthy, the ships' massive fifteen-inch Dahlgren cannon took up to ten minutes to load and shoot. Edward W. Sloan III, *Benjamin Franklin Isherwood Naval Engineer: The Years as Engineer in Chief, 1861–1869* (Annapolis: United States Naval Institute Press, 1965), 248–49n.1; Rowena Reed, *Combined Operations in the Civil War* (Annapolis: United States Naval Institute Press, 1978), 282–83; Emilio, *A Brave Black Regiment*, 70, 112, 120, 121, 138, 195.

7. Although black regiments made up only one-tenth of the total number of Union troops in the Department of the South, they did about half of all fatigue work. They worked harder and longer and took fewer sick days than white units. The chief engineer's report stated that probably in "no military operations of the war have negro troops done so large a proportion, and so important and hazardous fatigue duty, as in the siege operations on the island." On 15 September 1863, Gillmore praised their heroism, thanking them for enduring "untold privations and dangers," "unremitting and exhausting labors," and "severe and disheartening reverses." Emilio, *A Brave Black Regiment*, 125–27.

8. Col. Edward W. Serrell (1826–1906), an British-born civil engineer, commanded the First New York Engineers until February 1862 and served as chief engineer, Tenth Corps, Department of the South through April 1864. He put his talents to work in 126 battles during the war. *WWWCW*, 580–81.

9. The Third Rhode Island Regiment, organized in August 1861, was redesignated the Third Rhode Island Heavy Artillery on 19 December 1861. Most of its twelve batteries served in the Department of the South and mustered out by battery in 1864 and 1865. Dyer, *Compendium*, 3:1628–30, 1634.

10. The engineers' signal flag and the banner of the Thirty-ninth Illinois Regiment were, apparently, the first Union flags to fly over Wagner. According to the New York *Herald*, the Fifty-fourth planted the state flag on Wagner's parapets. New York *Herald*, 15 September 1863, Fifty-fourth Regiment Papers, 1:254, MHS; Emilio, *A Brave Black Regiment*, 123–24.

11. Montgomery's old Third Brigade disbanded on 19 July. The new one, organized on 24 July, included the Fifty-fourth, Second South Carolina, and

the Third USCT. Emilio, *A Brave Black Regiment,* 114; Dyer, *Compendium,* 2:368.

12. The 100th New York Regiment ("Eagle Brigade"), organized in January 1862, joined the Department of the South in February 1863 and remained until April 1864. The unit suffered 397 casualties before mustering out on 28 August 1865. Dyer, *Compendium,* 3:1444–45.

13. Neither the *OR* nor the *ORN* mention action by the Marine Corps, but GES may refer to a 502–man marine battalion commanded by Maj. Jacob Zelin stationed on Morris Island. Stephen R. Wise, *Gate of Hell: Campaign for Charleston Harbor, 1863* (Columbia: University of South Carolina Press, 1994), 151.

14. Although rebels evacuated Wagner without alerting Union troops, two barges holding about fifty-six men and another vessel holding about eight sailors fleeing Wagner and Gregg were captured. Emilio, *A Brave Black Regiment,* 124–25; *ORN,* ser. 1, 14:557–58.

15. Beacon House was a wood-frame structure on the beach at the south end of Morris Island, behind the first Union line. The house had been stripped of its siding and stood as a skeletal landmark until it collapsed on 25 May 1864. Emilio, *A Brave Black Regiment,* 189.

16. The soldiers probably belonged to the city's defense forces and were assigned as relief troops after 18 July. The "Charleston Battalion," commanded by Lt. Col. Palmer C. Gaillard, helped defend against the 18 July attack, and some of its members had formed a human flag pole to replace one shattered by Union shells. E. Milby Burton, *Siege of Charleston, 1861–1865* (Columbia: University of South Carolina Press, 1970), 161–63.

17. Most of the city's wealthier civilians had fled to Summerville and Orangeburg. All others, ironically including most of the city's free blacks, endured the lethal shelling. Burton, *Siege of Charleston,* 253; Alfred S. Hartwell, "Forty Years of Hawaii Reminiscences," typescript in Alfred S. Hartwell Papers, Bishop Museum Archives, Honolulu.

18. Mortars played a pivotal role in siege operations throughout the war. The "coehorn" mortar, among the smallest used by the army, caused considerable damage inside Wagner. *HTIECW,* 512.

19. Soldiers or conscript laborers dug "sap lines" (trenches) toward enemy fortifications to plant explosive devices under fort walls or move assaulting troops more safely toward their objective.

20. An ancient device to protect infantry or reinforce fieldworks, gabions are wicker cylinders filled with dirt or stones. They were also rolled in front of sap lines to protect soldiers from enemy fire. *HTIECW,* 295.

21. The 104th Pennsylvania Regiment, organized on 16 October 1861, remained in the Department of the South until August 1864 and participated in the 18 July attack on Wagner. It suffered 185 casualties during the war and was mustered out on 25 August 1865. Dyer, *Compendium,* 3:1609.

22. Samuel Harrison (1818–1900), the Philadelphia-born son of Georgia slaves, filled pulpits in Rhode Island and Maine before settling at Pittsfield, Massachusetts's Second Congregational Church. Governor Andrew named

him regimental chaplain on 8 September 1863, and he arrived at Morris Island on 12 November but resigned the following March because of ill health. Harrison's demand for full pay as a chaplain and an officer fortified the regiment's demand for equal pay. After considerable protest, Harrison won his case. *WAA*, 9 April 1864; *Liberator*, 13 May 1864; Luis F. Emilio biographical notes, Philip and Betty Emilio Family Collection; Dennis Dickerson, "Reverend Samuel Harrison: A Nineteenth Century Black Clergyman," in *Black Apostles at Home and Abroad*, ed. David W. Wills and Richard Newman (Boston: G. K. Hall, 1982), 147–60.

23. James Lynch, who attended Dartmouth College, was a Baltimore black abolitionist and clergyman. He conducted one of his first sermons for the regiment on 5 July 1863. On 24 October 1864 the Fifty-fourth's officers elected Lynch as chaplain, but he was not mustered. Luis F. Emilio diary notes, 5 July 1863, Fifty-fourth Regiment Papers, 1:135, MHS; Emilio, *A Brave Black Regiment*, 50, 232; Duncan, *Blue-Eyed Child of Fortune*, 375–76n.6.

24. Founded in 1825 by evangelicals, the influential American Tract Society distributed millions of religious pamphlets and books throughout the country. Its refusal to enter the controversy over slavery and publish antislavery materials forced its Boston branch to secede. John R. McKivigan, *The War Against Proslavery Religion: Abolitionism and the Northern Churches, 1830–1865* (Ithaca: Cornell University Press, 1984), 111, 120–23, 175, 188, 286n.50.

Chapter 11

"Let Us Vindicate Our Manhood by Our Conduct"

3 October 1863–20 August 1864

"Our destiny is united with that of the country—with its triumph we rise, with its defeat we fall." Stephens identified his quest to end slavery and racism with devotion to the Union. But the federal government proved an unworthy ally. Although it had promised blacks equal pay, the Lincoln administration belatedly determined that it could not give black and white soldiers the same wages. This decision, far more dispiriting to black soldiers than the rebel threat of summary execution, struck at the heart of their motivation to serve. If blacks could not receive equal treatment as soldiers, how could they hope to gain equality as men?

Stephens raged at the sadistic racism that plagued African Americans. As black soldiers fought to defend the Union, Northern mobs pillaged their homes and beat or murdered their families. Union commanders praised the regiment's heroism but then rewarded it with relentless fatigue duty. Although men such as Stephens had proven their ability to command, the army refused to commission black officers. Most contemptuous of all, the Fifty-fourth's brigade commander repudiated the regiment's demand for equal pay and derided the men as savages. "You are a race of slaves," Col. James Montgomery exclaimed soon after the Wagner assault. Attempting to coerce the men into accepting the government's pay offer, he berated them with scurrilous insults, especially the obnoxious charge that light complexions exposed some men as the offspring of interracial "rascality."

The soldiers' resentment ran deep. Stephens denounced Montgomery's speech and published it so that fellow blacks might see for themselves the attitudes of white military leaders. Sgt. Peter Vogelsang never forgot the anguish he felt, especially because of Montgomery's slurs concerning skin color. Whenever the colonel rode into camp, the men groaned loudly and turned away. Even the Fifty-fourth's white officers denounced Montgomery for that "insolent, egotistic speech." Lt. John Ritchie hardly could believe his ears. "Oh! for even the boots of Col. Shaw," he grieved in his diary.[1]

Stephens kept Northern blacks fully apprised of the discrimination black troops suffered. At the Battle of Olustee, Florida, on 20 February 1864, the Fifty-fourth's tenacity saved a Union defeat from becoming a catastrophic rout. As one eyewitness remarked, *"had it not been for the glorious Fifty-fourth Massachusetts, the whole brigade would have been captured or annihilated. This was the only regiment that rallied, broke the rebel ranks and saved us."*[2] The regiment twice ignored its commander's order to withdraw and stood its ground to allow the wounded time to reach safety.[3] Nevertheless, whites accused black troops of breaking under fire and causing the Union defeat.

Stephens documented the fury that swirled through the black regiments during the eighteen-month campaign against unequal pay. Still, neither Stephens nor anyone else in the Department of the South ever revealed the true depths of the pay crisis or how close the men had come to a general mutiny. Pvt. Wallace Baker of the Fifty-fifth Massachusetts was executed for leading a mutiny sparked by the pay crisis. Several men in the Fifty-fourth who protested their pay were shot—although not killed—by white officers to maintain discipline. Other soldiers received harsh prison sentences for related acts of insubordination. Relations between white officers and the men sank precipitously.

"We've been humbugged long enough," Samson Goliath of the Fifty-fifth Massachusetts exclaimed. Goliath, probably a former slave from Kentucky, found service under heartless white officers an all-too-familiar experience. "You Massachusetts men have been humbugging us long enough," he cried out, "we are going to do as we please." Goliath, who had refused orders to keep silent, was tied up. Fellow enlisted men released him, and in the resulting brawl Goliath struck an officer. Although Goliath could have been shot, the Fifty-fifth's commander, Col. Alfred S. Hartwell, recognized that discontent over unequal pay lay at the heart of the incident. An officer from the Fifty-fourth Massachusetts served at Goliath's court-martial and proved instrumental in winning him leniency.[4] If not for the antislavery sentiments of some white officers, possibly dozens of men in the two regiments would have stood before firing squads.

Not long after Stephens wrote his final letter to the *Anglo-African* in August 1864, the Fifty-fourth received its full pay. Jubilation swept through the black regiments as the men staged a celebration to commemorate their long struggle to vindicate their rights. Stephens remained with the Fifty-fourth for the rest of the war. He helped liberate hundreds of slaves in the South Carolina backcountry and was one of the first black soldiers to enter Charleston after its evacuation by Confederate troops. Yet, he did not publish his reaction to the victory over unequal pay and never wrote another account of his experience in the war. The loss is inestimable; his silence, perhaps, is understandable given the story he told.

1. Luis F. Emilio interview with Peter Vogelsang, 24 May 1886, and John Ritchie diary notes, Fifty-fourth Regiment Papers, 1:263, MHS.

2. Unidentified newspaper clipping, Norwood Penrose Hallowell Papers, MHS, emphasis in the original.

3. Louden S. Langley to the Burlington *Free Press,* 9 March 1864, in Donald Wickman, "Their Share of the Glory: Rutland Blacks in the Civil War," *Rutland Historical Society Quarterly* 22 (1992): 37–39.

4. Samson Goliath, Courts-Martial Records, RG 153, National Archives; Fifty-fifth Massachusetts Regiment, Descriptive Books, RG 94, National Archives.

* * *

Morris Island, S.C.,
Oct. 3, 1863.

Mr. Thomas Hamilton—Dear Friend: It has been a long time since I wrote you in my old-fashioned way.[1] I have not sent you a line since my advent as a soldier. I thank God that I am at last in a position to learn to be a soldier. I believe that since the chieftains of the slavery party have sought and obtained the arbitrament of the bullet in their question of control of power with the Freedom party, every man should become a soldier, ready to do and to die in defence of freedom. Every Christian and enlightened man desires to see great principles and measures triumph through peaceful means, where reason rules her just sway, and amenity, conciliation, and love, take the place of hatred, passion and revenge.

The present century has been immortalized with the grandest reforms. From the abolition of the slave trade in 1808 down to the freeing of the Danish colonies,[2] peaceful reform seems to have marched steadily on. Science, art and invention, a noble sisterhood, sat in counsel and astonished the world with their achievements. The very elements seemed to pay homage to the genius and skill of man. No man dare say what human ingenuity may not accomplish. The enlightened statesmen have in America hoped to secure the annihilation of every wrong and injustice through the agency of that power which Talleyrand considered more irresistible than the proudest and most powerful potentate, namely "public opinion."[3] The slavery party is arraigned at the bar of "public opinion." Its vile vision is tortured and haunted by the wild spirit of reform. This is a subtle spirit. The engines of warfare cannot impede its progress. It is deathless and omnipresent. It underlies all the pageantry and misery of this gigantic war. The slavery party aims to plunge the country into disorder and anarchy and to establish by force of arms their hell-born system. There is but one alternative left to the freedom party if it would avert terrorism, proscription, and humiliation: 'Tis steel for steel; bullet for bullet; life for life; man for man; blood for blood.

These are some of the notions that led me to join the 54th Mass. Volunteer Infantry. And again I thought that the true interests of all classes of men in our country depended on the success of our party. That they were the true representatives of the newest and best form of government ever established for the government of mankind and are the highest, noblest, and most progressive type of civilization. I can not see on what ground any man can discourage enlistments. Some urge that the treatment of colored citizens is exceptionable— that the guarantees of freedom vouchsafed to us by the government are tardy and doubtful—that some of our representative men, those who are considered the exponents of the principles of the freedom party are as bitter in their assaults on our race and as prejudiced as those of the slavery party. This is true, but these questions are only incidental in their character and cannot effect the general and fundamental principles and theories of the party: It must be remembered that the other class have suffered a slavery of the mind, just as brutalizing, just as debasing as that physical or social thraldom our class are suffering. It is prejudice and a disregard of the inalienable rights of their fellow men. Their notions of justice are so blinded they can without the least remorse rob their fellow-men of every sacred right. These men are to be elevated and their mental or moral condition must be ameliorated, just the same as the condition of those of our class who are debased by slavery should be ameliorated. They deserve the same pity and commiseration that the poor black slave does and we should "pass their imperfection by" just as willingly. Let us be charitable and contend only for the principles of liberty, government and civilization.

The siege of Charleston drags its slow length. Morris Island can never be retaken by the enemy. Fifty thousand men could be swept away in fifty minutes by our guns. Our fatigue parties are somewhat annoyed by the rebel shell, but our labor progresses. The casualties are very few, I had prepared for your satisfaction a complete list of them, but lost my notes. The health of our regiment is bad. We average one hundred and fifty sick per day, caused no doubt, by excessive fatigue duty.

You have also heard I suppose of this matter of pay, it has caused a great deal of trouble, and if it is not adjusted one of the best regiments that ever left the Massachusetts will become utterly demoralized. The tribulations of our regiment have been many since we arrived in this department. The first business we were called on to participate in was the burning of Darien, Ga. Our officers, Col. Shaw among the rest, disapproved of the wanton destruction of that town defenseless and unoccupied as it was by the enemy. The men of this regiment have a distaste for this sort of warfare—we want to enter the field honorably—to fight a legitimate warfare. After our return from this expedition, we were sent to St. Helena. While there a proposition was made to take our arms from us and give in their stead long pikes. Col. Shaw expressed his disapprobation of this scheme. Then there was an offer made to pay us ten dollars per month less three for clothing, in other words pay us seven dollars per month.[4] The men were enlisted as a part of the Mass. State quota of troops and never dreamed that any other pay but that of other Massachusetts soldiers would be given them. We have been urged and urged again to accept seven dollars a month, all, sergeant-major down to the humblest private to get no more. There are respectable and well to do men in this regiment, who have accepted positions. It is insulting to them to offer them about half the pay of a poor white private.

To give you an idea of the feelings of some of the officers here with regard to us on this point, I will give you a short speech made Sept. 30th by Col. James Montgomery, 2d South Carolina Vols., of Kansas

fame, and Commander of the Brigade to which we have been recently joined. Col. Montgomery was not in command of the brigade. He
has been sick some time past. The paymaster was in Col. Littlefield's
tent. Some ten or twelve officers of our own and other regiments were
present. The men had not accepted their pay and the well men were
on fatigue duty, at Battery Shaw and Wagner.[5] Col. M. had those who
were left in camp drawn up in line and addressed them as follows:

"I want to speak to you. You want plain talk and I shall give it to
you. I am your friend. I made the first anti-slavery speech ever made
in Kansas. I was the first man that employed negroes in the United
States service.[6] I fought six years in Kansas for nothing and I do not
come here for pay. I can make $5,000 a year. I get only $2,200 here. I
sacrifice my ease and comfort (for I enjoy myself at home). I have
fought United States soldiers. There is a General now in the Rebel
service whom I fought, killed his horse from under him and took him
prisoner when in the United States service. I would have been hung
long ago if I had held still. Old Jimmy Buchanan[7] offered a reward for
my head. It was a very mean one to be sure, and I was very indignant.
He offered only a yearling nigger worth about two hundred and fifty
dollars. If he had offered a full-grown nigger I would not have cared
so much. You ought to be glad to pay for the privilege to fight, instead
of squabbling about money. A great many of you are fugitive slaves,
and can by law be returned to your masters. The government by its
act in setting you free has paid you a thousand dollars bounty. I know
what the trouble is: the noisy Abolitionists have been telling you you
are better than anybody else. They are your worst enemies. You have
two classes of friends: those who tell you what you are and those who
sees in the Ethiopian a symbol of injured innocence. I have seen a
hundred regiments but I never saw one so fully equipped as this. Look
at your tents and cooking stoves. You want to be placed on the same
footing as white soldiers. You must show yourselves as good soldiers
as the white. For all anybody knows you did very well here. You must
show it by bravery in battle. I should be glad to make you as good
soldiers as the white. You are a race of slaves. A few years ago your
fathers worshipped snakes and crocodiles in Africa. Your features
partake of a beastly character. Your religious exercises in this camp
is a mixture of barbarism and Christianity. I am disgusted with the
mean, low habits you have learned from the low whites. I hear them
say to you, 'bully boys, bully boys, don't take this pay.' What do they

mean by this? Do you mean to bully the government out of your money or that you are stubborn as bulls? You would rather go out here and dig in the trenches than stay here in camp and be paid off. Gov. Andrew advises you to take this money and Frederick Douglass also.[8] I have a letter here from Fred. He has been on a tour to Washington and had an interview with Sec. Stanton on the subject of enlistments.[9] He advised that all that was needed was to treat the negro as a man. There are two classes of colored men: the indolent and careless; the industrious and ambitious. He (Douglass) called on Senator Pomeroy,[10] but did not call on Jim Lane. He perhaps had found Lane out. There are two Senators from Kansas. Pomeroy is a pretty fair sort of man, but Jim Lane is at present a noisy Abolitionist. Some time ago he wanted to buy some lands, utensils and niggers, but not having any money had to do without the niggers. He will buy and sell a nigger as quick as anybody else, but since the majority are in favor of liberty, he is very loud-mouthed. Fred Douglass is far above the mass of his race; but he is not equal to the great men of this country, such as Wendell Phillips, Ralph Waldo Emerson, Sumner, and others. You can be improved by education. Irishmen come to this country and in a few years become the same as other white men. Education expands the brain and improves the features. Your features can be improved. Your beauty cannot recommend you. Your yellow faces are evidences of rascality. You should get rid of this bad blood. My advice to you is the lightest of you must marry the blackest woman. You owe your sutler[11] nearly $2,000 and your refusing to take your pay show that you intend to cheat him out of his goods. You went to his agent after he had gone away, and because he would not trust you broke open his place and robbed him. The men that robbed him should be hung. He had no right to trust you and could be handled for it. It is mutiny to refuse to take your pay, and mutiny is punishable with death."

The Colonel spoke nearly an hour and I cannot stoop to give all the bad epithets directed to our regiment.[12] We had not the remotest idea that he entertained such a spirit of hatred for our regiment. Had he scarcely left the bench on which he stood while addressing the men, when Col. Littlefield who was in command of the Brigade at the time stood up and said: "Men, I cannot let this opportunity pass. The regiment has endeared itself to me. You have done your whole duty. You have written your names on the scroll of fame and any man who defames this regiment defames me. Such a man is my enemy and if I have any fighting to do I will defend you. I do not urge you to take this money, but I am willing to give you a pledge of my honor that you will get your full pay. I have made a promise of $1,000 to Gen. Saxton for a monument to Col. Shaw, and I would have you take this money and make up this sum to commemorate the name of your noble leader."[13]

This instantly dispelled the bad effects of Col. Montgomery's remarks. I am astonished that some insubordinate demonstration was not made, but Col. M. is our superior officer and our boys respect their superior officers. The speech of Col. M. has fixed the determination in the minds of the men to await calmly and patiently. If we thought that our enemies would make this course on our part a ground of assault against colored soldiers, I for one should go for taking $7 per month, nay $2 would be enough, but as the Colonel says, all the private soldiers here are vehement in urging us to refuse this paltry pay. They say if we take this money they will want to cut down their wages next. I have never yet heard a man say that we have failed to perform our duty. We have been complimented for our arduous labor in the trenches and whenever paraded have cleaner clothes, cleaner arms, better polished equipments than any other colored regiment on the Island. In truth there is no negro regiment compared to the 54th. In the last review the palm for martial bearing, accurate marching, and *cleanliness* is disputed with the 54th by the 100th New York Volunteers. The crime that has unfortunately incurred the displeasure of our General is that we do not sign the pay rolls, and the pay-master will not give us money unless we sign and thus give him receipt in full for pay up to the 1st of August. The words of Col. Montgomery fell with crushing effect on the regiment. We did not enlist for money but we feel that the men who enlisted us and those who accepted our service never intended that we should be treated different from other Massachusetts men. If the government had been too poor to pay us we would have been willing to give our services for nothing. But the government seems fully able to pay her soldiers, for just on the threshold of this great war she increased their pay.[14]

We are told that by law we are slaves and can be returned to our masters. This I deny. But a few years ago when the slavery party controlled affairs, fugitives were hunted like so much wild game all over the country, and it was quite a paying business. A few years ago the same party, so the speech shows, made him an outlaw and would have hung him. Their power is broken and we are now United States soldiers and he a responsible citizen and high official. It would be just as incorrect—just as cruel, to call him an outlaw amenable to the law, as to call us fugitive slaves returnable to our masters by law. In truth there are necessarily some few fugitives here, but is the 54th made up of fugitive slaves?[15] No, there are hundreds that have been blessed with a New England education, and have learned their duty as freemen, and know their rights and dare stand up for them, and if they cannot get their rights they can have the manly satisfaction that they stood up for them. Col. Montgomery unfortunately has been accustomed to the negro as a slave or freedman. It startles and astonishes him to see him stand erect with intelligence beaming in his countenance. He perhaps never saw a negro approach a white man except with hat in hand and bowed head. He says further, that he wishes to make us as good soldiers as the white. How can this be done if every stimulant to heroic actions are denied? The only hope of the negro soldiers as his status now appears, is half pay and the name not the rank of sergeant. To urge us to be good soldiers without throwing around us the influences which alone make the soldier, without which the noblest races will become varlet, is grossly absurd. But there seems to be an intimation here that we are not as good soldiers as whites. Is there to be a new theory developed? Everybody, citizens, soldiers, and the rest of mankind say, "thus far the negro soldier has done his whole duty." Does Col. M. deny this? Is his services in ratio of value as $7 is to $13. It is said that the Government supports the worn-out and non-combatant slaves, but I understand that all of these classes of slaves or freedmen are self-supporting—that the government is now realizing an income from the Southern plantations.[16] And does the government not expend hundreds of thousands in subsistence to the families of rebels in arms?[17] Should those rebels return to their allegiance and espouse the Union cause would Uncle Sam ask them to work and fight for $7 a month?

Then again "we should be glad to pay for the privilege to fight." After we have endured a slavery of two hundred and fifty years we are to pay for the privilege to fight and die to enable the North to conquer the South—what an idea! to pay for the privilege to fight for that tardy and at best doubtful freedom vouchsafed to us by the government. For what are we to be grateful? Here the white man has grown rich on our unpaid labor—has sold our children—insulted our wives—shut us out from the light of education, and even kept the Bible from us, and the moment he becomes convinced that these deeds of his are producing the desired results to his country and people, he gets to work and attempts to restore some of those rights and to allow for some of those wrongs. I think it a question of repentance on his part instead of gratitude on ours. What do you think of him should he demand your services and life, for a restoration of your rights and a release from his persecutions? If we are taunted because the suicidal course of the government has been changed, in the name of God, men of the freedom party, go back to your old policy[.] [E]xclude every fugitive from the armies—invalidate the President's Emancipation Proclamation, let your officers be slaves—spies and catchers for Southern rebels, for no negro who has two ideas, one to rub against another, is willing to rest under this new slavery his presumed friends are marking out for him, namely: to keep ever present to the memory that his are a race of slaves and have an eternal tribute to pay to their oppressors. I want to feel as if I had a right to liberty and life, and that if I enjoy it, do not wish it said, that I owe to this one or that one.

It cannot be gainsayed that there is a frightful amount of profanity said to have been learned from the "low whites." Now these "low whites," belong to that race which the Colonel presumes to be the superior race. In what constitutes its superiority if it has a deleterious influence on our actions and character? I think there can be found more instances of barbarism in the whites in this country than in the blacks. Look at the Lawrence massacre, the New York mobs, and the Port Hudson atrocities![18] The fair Southern belle adorns her person with trinkets made from the bones of slaughtered Yankees.[19] Is this not a "polished barbarism?" But the argument of this speech is not logical. It assumes the inferiority of our race, and denies its inferiority by declaring that all that is bad in us has been obtained from the whites which I think very true.

Profanity is a low mean vice, but it is universal in the army. Men are drawn into it almost unconsciously. Those who have been restrained by the associations at home when they get in the army seem to obtain a sort of immoral license. They contract habits and manners there from which they would shrink at home. Our regiment has been peculiarly unfortunate in this manner of spiritual instruction and advice. There have been but a half a dozen lectures delivered to the regiment since it left Readville, 28th last May. But this moral and spiritual void has been filled somewhat by instructive religious tracts and papers contributed by Christian and noble hearted friends in the North—[20] yet while we have so much to regret, there are abundant evidences of a religious revival in our regiment. Are our prayer-meetings a mixture of paganism or barbarism and Christianity? I have witnessed camp-meetings of white Methodists and have seen just as much vehemence and excitement as our meetings are characterized with. It is a characteristic of Methodism in these later days to be exuberant, vehement, and boisterous; and Methodism is almost universal with the American negroes. There are more Methodists, I think statistics say, than every other sect among them unitedly.[21]

The sutler was robbed of his goods by some five or six men in the regiment. The regiment did not rob the sutler. It is utterly impossible to get together any nine hundred or thousand men without some of them being bad enough to do almost anything. All soldiers regard sutlers as regimental Shylocks who demand their money or their lives. They have to pay them fifty cents per pound for rascally butter and twenty-five cents per pound for the blackest kind of sugar; and for everything else they pay equally exorbitant rates. There are few soldiers who think it highly penal to get the best of the sutler. Now this stealing for which the regiment is accused was perpetrated by men whose names are known, and whom Col. Littlefield intends to make pay for the small amount taken. Nor can this be called stealing but a sort of bushwacking raid.

The circumstances are as follows; Mr. De Mortie told the men in the regiment some two or three weeks ago, before he left for his home, that if they would not take the money the paymaster offered them, he would trust them. He went home, and his partners or agents refused to trust the men. The soldiers of other regiments who had been paid off came and bought the sutler's stock out, and he replenished and sold out again, and any one of the 54th could with difficulty get accommodated. This incensed the men and five or six of the most violent tore down his tent. The sutler ran to the Colonel and he reported the circumstance and instantly sent the men off and put a guard over his tent. It was more a riot and a little spitefulness than robbery. The Colonel (Littlefield) had the whole affair quelled in less time than has been occupied in writing this account of it. How unjust to cast odium on the regiment for this act of half a dozen men. Raiding on sutlers is a most common thing in every camp. I have been the witness of many such catastrophes. I don't dispute that the sutler is a very nice man and as just as sutlers generally can be, but I do say this, if his treatment of the men had been more conciliatory this would not have happened. His agent seems to have forgotten that he is a sutler of the 54th and should be prepared to fully accommodate *their* wants, as well as to make his fortune. The sutler trusted the men to two dollar checks, and compelled them to take the entire two dollars worth or nothing. He had no checks of smaller denomination than two dollars thus taking away the chance to economize. Two dollars is enough to answer the wants of a soldier from one to two months. Are we to be denounced as thieves for this?

As to yellow faces I don't indulge in any controversy about color. I think "'tis the mind that makes the man,"[22] not the color of his skin or any peculiarity of his hair. All I wish to know is the man just, is he humane and generous—noble-spirited—if yes, he is a man, if no, he is a slave to passion and iniquity.

I must not forget to tell you that Gov. Andrew has presented us with a new flag (State flag). In the charge on Fort Wagner, the old flag was torn asunder.[23] In his speech to our regiment, Gov. A. told us that the State flag had never fallen into the hands of the enemy and urged if we could not save the flag, save the shreds—if we could not save the shreds save the staff, and his appeal has been heeded to the letter. When on the parapet of Fort Wagner, Corporal Peal,[24] Co. F, who has had the honor to bear the State colors, inadvertently let the flag lean over the crest of the work, a rebel seized it, then commenced a desperate struggle between the corporal and the rebel for its possession. Unfortunately the color parted from the staff and thus by accident the flag was lost. The corporal said, "Ah you dirty rascal you did not get the staff any way," and he brought the staff away with the spear. This flag is a fac simile of the old one, and when Col. Littlefield unfurled it the boys gave it three rousing cheers.

Trusting that health and prosperity are with you, I remain truly yours,

G. E. Stephens.

WAA, 24 October 1863.

1. Because Robert Hamilton reestablished the *Anglo-African*, GES had not addressed any of his correspondence to Thomas.

2. Although the United States and Great Britain had ended the legal slave trade by 1808, the illegal trade continued until the Civil War, largely under American-flagged ships. Denmark halted the traffic in its possessions after 1802. W. E. F. Ward, *The Royal Navy and the Slavers: The Suppression of the Atlantic Slave Trade* (London: Allen and Unwin, 1969), 121, 126, 138–39, 141; W. E. B. Du Bois, *The Suppression of the African Slave Trade to the United States of America, 1638–1870* (1896, reprint, Baton Rouge: Louisiana State University Press, 1969), 131.

3. GES refers to Charles Maurice de Talleyrand (1754–1838), the legendary French statesman, and probably to his 1821 speech in the French Chamber of Peers: "There is more wisdom in public opinion than is to be found in Napoleon, Voltaire, or all the ministers of State, present or to come." J. O. Thorne and T. C. Collocott, eds., *Chambers Biographical Dictionary* (Cambridge: Cambridge University Press, 1984), 1299.

4. Shaw learned of a proposal to replace the Fifty-fourth's rifles with pikes near the end of June 1863. He denounced it and advised his influential father that "pikes against Minie balls is not fair play—especially in the hands of negroes whose great pride lies in being a soldier like white men." Shaw also reacted swiftly to Stanton's 4 June 1863 rejection of equal pay and advised Governor Andrew to disband the regiment if the government refused to uphold its original promise. Duncan, *Blue-Eyed Child of Fortune*, 366–67; Robert Gould Shaw to Gov. John A. Andrew, 2 July 1863, Executive Department Letters, vol. 59, MSA.

5. General Gillmore renamed the fortifications on Morris Island. Works at Cummings Point became Fort Putnam; Fort Gregg became Battery Chatfield; and Battery Wagner became Fort Strong. At the south end of Morris Island Union forces established Fort Shaw; Oyster Point became Battery Purviance; and at the north end of Folly Island they established Fort Green. Order of Maj. Gen. Quincy A. Gillmore, 28 October 1863, Fifty-fourth Regiment Papers, vol. 4, MHS.

6. Montgomery, like Lane, was a strong advocate of black enlistment. In 1862, he had recruited some black troops in Kansas and early in 1863 took his Second South Carolina Volunteers into action. Dudley Taylor Cornish, *The Sable Arm: Negro Troops in the Union Army, 1861–1865* (New York: W. W. Norton, 1966), 73–74, 103–5.

7. James Buchanan (1791–1868), fifteenth president of the United States, earned the enmity of abolitionists for his support of proslavery forces in Kansas during the late 1850s.

8. Both Andrew and Douglass rejected unequal pay. Although Douglass believed that the Lincoln administration eventually would treat the men equitably, he was outraged that Montgomery had used his name to induce the men to accept the lower pay and condemned the insulting speech. Frederick Douglass to Robert Hamilton, 27 October 1863, *WAA*, 31 October 1863.

9. Sometime in August 1863, Douglass and Senator Pomeroy visited Secretary of War Stanton to press for equal pay. During their chilly interview, Stanton admitted that he had pledged to offer black troops equal pay and also

to commissioning black officers eventually. William S. McFeely, *Frederick Douglass* (New York: W. W. Norton, 1991), 228–29.

10. Samuel Clarke Pomeroy (1816–91), an abolitionist and Free State advocate, was Kansas's first U.S. senator.

11. Mark R. De Mortié, the Fifty-fourth's black sutler, received his job at the insistence of Boston's black community and with Andrew's approval. De Mortié supported the regiment's stand on equal pay and extended a $2 line of credit to the men. His actions may have been, as GES suggests, self-interested, and he placed himself in further jeopardy by failing to extend credit to the regiment's officers, who also had not been paid. Robert Gould Shaw to John A. Andrew, 18 April 1863 and R. De Mortié to John A. Andrew, 17 August 1863, Executive Department Letters, vols. 21b, 59, MSA.

12. GES checked the text of Montgomery's speech with Colonel Littlefield before publishing it in the *WAA*. GES to Luis F. Emilio, 8 June 1886, Fifty-fourth Regiment Papers, 1:264, MHS.

13. The regiment and former Sea Island slaves pooled their resources along with donations from Northern blacks to erect a monument in Shaw's honor. By October 1864, they had collected $2,832. Fearing that no monument would survive Morris Island's shifting sands or vandals, organizers instead established the Shaw School for Charleston's black children. Gen. Rufus Saxton (1824–1908), Union commander at Beaufort, South Carolina, from 1862 to 1864, was the first to win War Department permission to raise a regiment of black troops and organized the First South Carolina Volunteers. He also may have originated the idea for the monument, proposing a shaft of Massachusetts granite tall enough to be seen from anywhere on Morris Island. Emilio, *A Brave Black Regiment*, 228–30; *HTIECW*, 659; Michael S. Haynes to John A. Andrew, 13 August 1863, Executive Department Letters, vol. 59, MSA; Edward W. Hooper to Robert W. Hooper, 23 September 1863, Edward W. Hooper Papers, HLHU; Col. Edward N. Hallowell to Gen. Rufus Saxton, 7 October 1864, Fifty-fourth Massachusetts Regiment Records, Letter Books, RG 94, National Archives; Gen. Rufus Saxton "To the Colored Soldiers and Freedmen," 27 July 1863, Broadside Collection, Rare Book Room, Duke University.

14. Enlisted men's pay was raised to $13 a month; Congress increased it to $16 on 1 May 1864. Bell Irvin Wiley, *The Life of Billy Yank: The Common Soldier of the Union* (Indianapolis: Bobbs-Merrill, 1952), 49.

15. Most of the Fifty-fourth's soldiers were free Northern blacks from Pennsylvania, New York, Ohio, and Massachusetts. The literacy rate was very high, and even in the Fifty-fifth Massachusetts, where 247 of the 980 men had been slaves, at least 477 could read. Emilio, *A Brave Black Regiment*, 21; undated memo, Burt G. Wilder Papers, box 4, Cornell University; [Charles B. Fox], *Record of the Fifty-fifth Regiment of Massachusetts Volunteer Infantry* (Cambridge: John Wilson and Son, 1868), 110.

16. The federal government earned substantial profits from the labors of ex-slaves who were compelled to work for their former owners or on plantations administered by government-assigned superintendents. At Port Royal,

South Carolina, ex-slaves were advised that they owned the property they worked. Despite their successful cotton farms, the federal government dispossessed them in October 1865 and returned the land to white control. Willie Lee Rose, *Rehearsal for Reconstruction: The Port Royal Experiment* (New York: Random House, 1964); *WAA*, 4 January 1862.

17. By taking an oath of allegiance to the United States, Southern whites could receive rations, protect their property from seizure, and conduct business. After the war, needy whites received army ration tickets, but Union commanders would only dispense them to aged or disabled blacks. John T. O'Brien, "Reconstruction in Richmond: White Restoration and Black Protest, April-June 1865," *Virginia Magazine of History and Biography* 89 (July 1981): 269.

18. GES refers to the 21 August 1863 sacking of Lawrence, Kansas, by William Quantrill's Confederate raiders, the New York City draft riots of 13–17 July 1863, and the execution of black prisoners after the 27 May 1863 battle at Port Hudson, Louisiana, and at Milliken's Bend, Louisiana. James M. McPherson, *Battle Cry of Freedom: The Civil War Era* (New York: Oxford University Press, 1988), 786; Cornish, *The Sable Arm*, 163–64.

19. Atrocity stories circulated widely throughout the war. Yankees believed stories of savage rebel misdeeds: murder of wounded soldiers, use of poison bullets, desecration of the dead, and skulls used as soap dishes or soup bowels. *Harper's Weekly* printed inflammatory images of Southern women wearing necklaces of "Yankee teeth." Similarly, rebels accused their Northern enemies of slashing the throats or cutting the tongues out of prisoners. Wiley, *The Life of Billy Yank*, 346–48; Bell Irvin Wiley, *The Life of Johnny Reb: The Common Soldier of the Confederacy* (Indianapolis: Bobbs-Merrill, 1943), 311–12; Reid Mitchell, *The Vacant Chair: The Northern Soldier Leaves Home* (New York: Oxford University Press, 1993), 94.

20. Northern liberal and evangelical Bible and tract societies sent millions of their publications to Union troops during the war. Even Confederate soldiers received hundreds of thousands of Bibles from these Northern organizations. Phillip Shaw Paludan, *"A People's Contest": The Union and Civil War, 1861–1865* (New York: Harper and Row, 1988), 349–50.

21. By 1865, membership in the various African-American Methodist churches totaled more than fifty-four thousand. The African Methodist Episcopal Church was by far the largest and most influential, with a foreign missions project and a thriving publications program. Edwin Scott Gaustad, ed., *Historical Atlas of Religion in America* (New York: Harper and Row, 1976), 77, 79; *BAP*, 4:197n.1.

22. The quotation is probably from Isaac Watts (1674–1748), "The mind's the standard of the man," in *Horae Lyricae* (London, 1706), bk 2.

23. Governor Andrew replaced the state flag lost at Wagner; the new banner arrived on 2 October 1863. Emilio, *A Brave Black Regiment*, 84, 131.

24. Cpl. Henry F. Peal (1837–64), an unmarried shoemaker from Oberlin, Ohio, carried the state colors on 18 July. General Gillmore awarded him the Gillmore Medal, one of four members of the regiment who received the

award for heroism at Battery Wagner. Peal carried the state colors again at the Battle of Olustee, where he fell mortally wounded. Ibid., 90, 164, 168, 366; George Washington Williams, *A History of the Negro Troops in the War of the Rebellion, 1861–65* (1888, reprint, New York: Bergman Publishers, 1968), 199.

[November 28, 1863.]

Mr. Editor: In your issue of to-day I notice the article headed "A Defense of Col. Montgomery," and over the signature of S. M. Markley,[1] which, so resembles the speech of Col. Montgomery of the 30th of September, that I think it deserves a passing kick. I should not turn aside to administer this contemptuous rebuke had Mr. Markley not referred to the letter of Oct. 24th [October 3] in an imperious, threatening and insulting manner. Does Mr. Markley deny any word of that speech of Col. Montgomery? Has that speech been falsely reported? Certainly not. The truth is this: S. M. M. endorses the sentiments of that speech. He, like Col. M. has so little regard for our sentiments and feelings that he even forgets to refer to or consult them.

Mr. M. do you think colored men so debased, cowardly and ignorant, that they can brook any and every insult? Would you or Col. M. have addressed a white regiment thus? I think not. But who has made an attack on Col. M? What have I said against his Christianity, or his anti-slavery sentiments, his accomplishments or his achievements? The time has come when words are important. They are things that are weighed and balanced. A man that speaks in times like these, should speak advisedly.

That speech coming from the source it did, ought to have been circulated all over the country. It is another evidence of the folly of manworship and the time has fully come when that should cease. Build a shrine of our principles and if need be, lay upon it life, services and wealth. In my letter giving a synopsis of the speech, I said nothing against Col. M. I simply rebutted the speech as well as I could. When I stood by the side of Col. M., and heard him declaim those sentiments with so much earnestness and vehemence I was filled with amazement and regret, but I consoled myself with the fact that no one or two men can avail against our cause. It rests on the rock of immutability—that rock is *"Justice To All Men,"* without regard to color. Our destiny is united with that of the country—with its triumph we rise, with its defeat we fall.

Contrast the speech of Col. Montgomery and the sentiments of S. M. Markley with the noble course of His Excellency, Gov. Andrew, and the Massachusetts Legislative Council—the one giving us good cheer,[2] extending aid and the right hand of fellowship, the other hewing out a chasm and an impassable gulf between us and our rights and justice. Noble Massachusetts! patroness and protectress of equal rights and the principals of justice! When time-servers, and prejudiced quibblers are buried far down in the grave of oblivion, your escutcheon, glowing with the flaming record of your trials and triumphs, will be regarded by coming generations as an emblem of union, liberty, and equality. Mr. S. M. M. you are impressed with a notion that all the measures and policies adopted by the Administration were adopted especially to benefit the African race—that this is, plainly speaking, "a war for the negro." This is the old Copperhead lie. It fomented riots and mobs by exciting all the baser passions against the African. His features, his hair, the color of his skin, and the fact that his having been a race of slaves, are ridiculed and discanted upon as if to make prejudice of race a passion, abiding and eternal. Ignorant men were made to believe that the white man was not to be benefited by the struggle; that the African was to receive and were receiving all the benefits of this war for the Union. Do you claim allegiance with the great freedom party and yet so unconscious of the grandeur of its principles and policy: *Free Soil, Free Press, Free Speech, Free Men*, not free Africans or free white men. In the providences of Almighty God you cannot imperil the liberty of any individual without detriment to the liberties of the whole body politic. The political system has its laws like that of the physical, which if violated, produce the sufferings that we to-day are living witnesses of, such as riots, tumult, and civil war with all its attendant miseries and calamities. Slavery is as much a curse to the white man as to the black, and emancipation if secured, will be to him as much a blessing. Hence it is a war for the liberty of the human race. We Africans, if justice is accorded to us, cannot say truthfully that it is a war for the white man. I would consider it a curse second only to slavery itself to owe the emancipation of our race purely and solely to the American people. If they had voluntarily and from philanthropic motives and not from military necessity adopted the policy of emancipation, for ages yet to come it would be made the pretext to deny us some right or withhold some benefit. We would stand in the attitude of supplicants and dependents instead of equals, not having by earnest efforts, and co-labor won manly independence.

290 A VOICE OF THUNDER

Mr. S. M. M. says: "The colored people should be very careful of the way in which they assail such men as Col. Montgomery." This may be a warning or a threat; I don't know or care which, as Mr. S. M. M. has not yet been invested with the power of life and death over the colored people. Threats nor insults shall not deter them from rebutting error; nor can an army of Markleys restore Col. Montgomery to the confidence of the colored soldiers in the Department of the South. His sentiments and opinions of the race are so indifferent that I, for one, do not feel that confidence that should always exist between comrades in battle. Unless some sort of explanation is attached to that speech by S. M. M. or somebody else, it must remain on record. I have no desire to be drawn into controversy any farther. The epitaph I offer is, Rest in Peace.

Geo. E. Stephens.

WAA, 12 December 1863.

1. Markley, an unidentified correspondent, accused Stephens of smearing Montgomery's reputation. He defended Montgomery's antislavery record and declared that the colonel supported equal pay, but he did not comment on the controversial speech. The well-to-do black abolitionist William Whipper ridiculed Stephens's letter and claimed that Montgomery's antislavery work far outweighed whatever statements he may have made. Parker T. Smith, "The Speech of Col. James Montgomery," *WAA,* 31 October 1863; S. M. Markley to Robert Hamilton, 6 November 1863, in *WAA,* 28 November 1863; William Whipper to Robert Hamilton, 9 November 1863, in *WAA,* 21 November 1863.

2. Governor Andrew and the state legislature gave the Fifty-fourth unwavering support. On 16–17 November, the legislature approved a bill authorizing the governor to pay the state's black regiments the difference between black and white pay rates. Although the men turned the offer down, they appreciated the sentiment. "Statutes Enacted at a Special Session of the General Court of Massachusetts, 11 Nov. 1863," Fifty-fourth Regiment Papers, vol. 4, MHS.

Morris Island, S.C.,
Jan. 5, 1864.

Mr. Editor: Affairs in this department, from all appearances, remain unchanged, and the reduction of the city of Charleston, seems, to the limited ken of a common soldier, to be a problem for solution in the somewhat distant future.

Since the issuance of Gen. Gillmore's second order against the unequal distribution of labor among the soldiers here, there has been the greatest improvement imaginable.[1] The colored troops here are subject to the most rigorous drill and discipline. This is most desirable; for the bravest troops would be ineffective for almost any service without perfect military training.

The weather here, for the past four or five days has been intensely cold. The water around the marshes, which flows in from the sea, has been frozen hard enough for the drummer boys to slide upon. Our having to depend upon Folly Island for fuel, and the difficulty of keeping on hand a sufficient supply for the large force here, has caused us no little suffering. I have not felt colder weather in New-England.

The disasters which the New York *World*[2] made so much fuss about, are exploded lies. That staunch little craft, the "Planter" still performs regular daily trips around Stony Inlet in defiance of the fussing, sputtering rebels on James Island, and Capt. Robert Smalls still commands.[3]

The noble new Ironsides and all the monitors except the ill-fated Weehawken, ride at anchor in the bay, and grim monsters they are that bode no good to the rebels. No wonder they grinned with demonic joy at the unfounded story that they had been sent to Davy Jones's locker.[4]

First of January in the Camp of the 54th.

The first day of January was duly commemorated by the colored soldiers here. It was the desire of the managers of the affair to make it a brilliant and immense one; but the officers here, for very good reasons, did not take an active part in the ceremonies. Speeches, ceremonies, and demonstrations other than refer to duty and service in the field, are detrimental to good order and military discipline.

The day, however, was celebrated with speeches and the beating of drums. Sergeant Barquet of the 54th was the orator of the day. Sergt. Jones[5] of the 2d S. C. Vols., Corp. Jones and Sergt. Wm. H. C. Gray[6] of Co. C. 54th Mass. Vols., delivered brief addresses. The assembly was organized by the appointment of Sergt. Gray, Chairman, and Sergt. Lee,[7] Secretary. In assuming his position Sergt. Gray said: He esteemed it a high honor to preside at the first jubilee meeting held in the territory, late State of South Carolina. Referring to the day, he

292   A VOICE OF THUNDER

asked: What are we here for? For money? No! but to strive by deeds of valor to add still more to the accumulated testimony of negro patriotism and courage, and to contend even against overwhelming odds for our just and rightful dues. We should not have it said that knowing our rights we did not stand up for them. Let us vindicate our manhood by our conduct. Put away from among us vulgarity and profanity. Do this, and our children will refer with pride to their fathers, who, for the sake of liberty of the human race, suffered the baptism of fire. Corp. Jones spoke well and at length.

At the end of the meeting, three cheers were given for the commander of the Post, Gen. Terry; three for Col. Hallowell; three for the officers of our regiment; and three times three, I think, for Abraham Lincoln.

G. E. S.

WAA, 23 January 1864.

1. Since the 18 July attack the Fifty-fourth and the other black regiments in the Department of the South had been relegated to fatigue duty. Even the New York *Evening Post* complained of the army's exploitation of black troops: "They are treated as menials rather than as soldiers." On 18 September 1863, Gillmore ordered a halt to such discrimination and repeated the order at the end of November. *Evening Post,* in *WAA,* 5 December 1863; [Charles P. Bowditch], "War Letters of Charles P. Bowditch," *Proceedings of the Massachusetts Historical Society* 57 (May 1924): 446; Emilio, *A Brave Black Regiment,* 125–26, 138, 142, 148.

2. The New York *World,* founded in 1860, had been a Republican party organ until bought by Democratic investors who hired the antiwar (Copperhead) Manton Marble as editor. The paper's bitter denunciation of Lincoln compelled the city's provost marshal to suspend its publication temporarily. Frank Luther Mott, *American Journalism: A History of Newspapers in the United States through 250 Years, 1690–1940* (New York: Macmillan, 1941), 350–51.

3. Robert Smalls (1839–1915), a Charleston, South Carolina, slave and a skilled harbor pilot, operated the *Planter,* a Confederate dispatch boat. On 13 May 1862, he steamed the ship through rebel defenses to the Union blockading squadron. The "abduction" of the *Planter* made Smalls a hero, and the story of his daring act was published throughout the North. His bravery and initiative refuted proslavery charges of black inferiority. "What a painful instance we have here of the Negro's inability to take care of himself," one Northern paper sarcastically remarked. The disasters that Stephens mentions may refer to the sinking of the *Keokuk,* a double-turreted Union *Monitor*-class ship that Smalls helped pilot and that sunk after ninety-six hits by Confederate artillery. Because of Smalls's heroics, he and several crewmen survived the sinking. Okon Edet Uya, *From Slavery to Public Service: Robert Smalls, 1839–1915* (New York: Oxford University Press, 1971).

4. The USS *Weehawken*, also of the *Monitor* class, was commissioned on 18 January 1863 and carried a crew of about sixty-seven. On 6 December 1863, the ill-fated ship foundered off Morris Island during a storm, losing about thirty-one men. The Confederate submarine *David* attacked the *New Ironsides* on 5 October, detonating a charge against its hull but failing to sink it. Paul H. Silverstone, *Warships of the Civil War Navies* (Annapolis: United States Naval Institute Press, 1989), 8–10; Emilio, *A Brave Black Regiment*, 140; *OR*, ser. 1, 28:732–33.

5. Jacob E. Jones, born in Holmes, Mississippi, joined the Second South Carolina Volunteers [Thirty-fourth USCT] on 22 May 1863 at Beaufort. He was promoted to first sergeant on 1 June 1863, reduced to private on 9 October 1865, and mustered out of service on 28 February 1866. Compiled Service Records, RG 94, National Archives.

6. Cpl. Alexander Jones (1840–64), an unmarried waiter from Pittsburgh, enlisted on 16 March 1863 and succumbed to disease on 7 July 1864. Emilio, *A Brave Black Regiment*, 356.

7. Sgt. George H. Lee (1842–?), an unmarried hostler also from New Bedford, served from 26 February 1863 to 20 August 1865. Ibid., 352.

[February–March?] 1864.

I shall take this opportunity to refer to the labors and kind benevolence of the Ladies' Soldier's Aid Society of Bridgeport, Ct., towards and in behalf of the members of the 54th Mass. Regt.[1]

Some time last November these ladies made up a box of goods and delicacies for our regiment, valued at about $250, which was forwarded to the care of your humble servant for distribution. At the time the box reached Hilton Head I was home on furlough,[2] and returned to camp in the latter part of December, and did not receive any tidings of it until the latter part of January, when the list of articles which it contained came to hand. Just previous to this, however, I received a letter from Mrs. Jane Johnson, the Corresponding Secretary of the Society, inquiring about it; to which I penned an answer necessarily brief, being just then on the point of departure on the present expedition.

The causes of the delay must have been its misdirection; for it went to Beaufort instead of to Morris Island, where our regiment was then encamped. The box reached Jacksonville on the 23d of February, the day of our return in retreat from Alicia.[3] At what a happy moment did it reach us. We were foot sore, weary, and hungry. All our clothing and equipage left on the field; no blankets; nothing but our arms and equipments left.[4] The box was put in the hands of the sutler of 2d S.C. Vols.

Next morning I sent a half-dozen men down to bring it up, when, lo, a regiment, the 47th N. Y. Vols.,⁵ had broken the box open, robbed the 2d S. C. sutler, and robbed it of its contents. Poor 54th! You seem doomed to misfortune. The case has been laid before Col. Hallowell, and if redress can be obtained, our gallant Colonel will obtain it.

I know the ladies of Bridgeport will be furious in their indignation and regret. But God will reward you. We are fit subjects for your pity and benevolence. This regiment wronged us; and at a time, when the meanest dog of a thief, would have forborne. There are things in human shape which will perpetrate that that dogs will not.

Many a poor fellow's sufferings might have been alleviated with the brandy peaches, jellies, and fruits, which your box contained. Your box contained a large amount of wearing apparel. Large numbers of the wounded are without a change of clothing and what a pity their comrades should thus rob them. They had not been in any danger and had plenty to eat and to wear. That regiment must be somewhat related to the "dead rabbits."⁶ 47th, don't forget the name.

[G. E. S.]

WAA, 19 March 1864.

1. African-American women in Bridgeport, New Haven, and Hartford, Connecticut, had organized aid societies for black troops before October 1863. Black women in Norwich formed at least one other society during the war. John Niven, *Connecticut for the Union: The Role of the State in the Civil War* (New Haven: Yale University Press, 1965), 96; Benjamin Quarles, *The Negro in the Civil War* (1953, reprint, New York: Da Capo Press, 1989), 246.

2. GES went on furlough from 16 November to 31 December 1863. George E. Stephens Pension File, RG 15, National Archives.

3. GES refers to the Battle of Olustee—also known as Ocean Pond—which took place on 20 February 1864.

4. The regiment left much of its equipment at Baldwin and Sanderson and abandoned its remaining knapsacks, coats, and blankets when it moved to the front. During the retreat, Union troops burned the regiment's gear, leaving many soldiers only with what they carried off the field. Emilio, *A Brave Black Regiment*, 158, 162, 170; "Certified Statement of Losses," 29 May 1864, Fifty-fourth Regiment Papers, vol. 4, MHS; unidentified letter extract, 8 April 1864, Executive Department Letters, vol. 59, MSA.

5. The Forty-seventh New York (the "Washington Greys"), organized in September 1861, arrived in the Department of the South in April 1862. It lost 237 men before disbanding on 30 August 1865. Dyer, *Compendium*, 3:1421–22.

6. GES compares the plundering activities of the Forty-seventh New York to one gang of New York City thugs that participated in the July 1863 draft

riots. William C. Davis, *The Imperiled Union, 1861–1865*, vol. 2: *Stand in the Day of Battle* (Garden City: Doubleday, 1983–), 2:200.

Outpost or Camp, in the Field,
Near Jacksonville, Fla.,
March 6, 1864.[1]

Mr. Editor: Action and arduous duties since the 5th ult., the time of the sailing of the present expedition from Hilton Head, have caused the apparently studied silence on the part of your correspondent.[2] A man who has very little to eat and very hard work, and who has for nearly twelve long months labored for nothing, nine of which have been in the very midst of the perils of war and disease, is in no condition to write letters for papers or anything else. The first thing in order is the battle of Alicia, Fla., Feb. 20th, which, to say the least, was a stupendous ambuscade, into which the wily rebels drew our entire force, and routed it with a loss of seven pieces of artillery and upward of 1,300 killed, wounded and missing.[3] The colored regiments particularly suffered severely.[4] And what is still more unfortunate, the greater part of the wounded and all the killed were left on the field.

The circumstances preliminary to the fight are briefly these: Our forces had for several days previous to the battle been concentrating at a place called Barbour, near St. Mary's Creek, for the grand march on Tallahassee, and everything had the appearance of complete preparation, and the men seemed in fine spirits and our success since the landing of Feb. 7th had been marked, though more from good luck than good management. The 40th Massachusetts mounted infantry and the Massachusetts cavalry, under command of Col. Henry,[5] had inflicted considerable damage on the enemy's property, and we anticipated nothing but victory. Our outpost had been established a little above Sanderson, a station on the line of the Jacksonville and Tallahassee Railroad,[6] about six miles westward from and in advance of Barbour. The order was to march at 9 o'clock on the morning of the 20th. The day was a most delightful one. The springs and rivulets along the line of march reminded us of the cool, refreshing waters at home. What a change from the brackish, feverish waters of the Sea Islands! The scenes are not here, however. You can see nothing but pine woods, marsh, and every five or ten miles a cluster of dilapidated, deserted huts, with no sign of agricultural thriftiness. But immense tracts of this pine-woods land are prepared for the collection of pitch. The trees are tapped, and near the roots cavities are hewn out, into which the pitch collects. Barbour is the only spot from Jacksonville to Alicia which possesses any beauty or rural charm. At about 9 o'clock on the 20th of February we took up the line of march, and by 1 o'clock had passed beyond Sanderson.

The advance consisted of the 7th New Hampshire, 7th Connecticut and 8th United States Colored Troops, Col. Hawley's Brigade, and Battery M, 3d United States Artillery.[7] The rear consisted of the 54th Massachusetts and 1st North Carolina (colored).[8] The advance encountered the rebel line of skirmishers about three miles beyond Sanderson, and they fell rapidly back to their entrenchments at Alicia. In such a pursuit lines are deranged, distances loose, so that by the time our troops reached Alicia there was considerable confusion amongst them, and the rebels, who thus planned their defeat, were duly prepared for battle. Our men fought well, but could not withstand, in their disorganized condition, the shock of battle.

The 7th New Hampshire was the first regiment to retreat. The 8th United States was the next having their gallant Colonel (Fribley)[9] and nearly all the rest of their officers killed, and wounded. They are reported to have lost upward of five hundred, killed, wounded and missing, the greater portion of which are prisoners in the hands of the enemy.[10] This was their first battle, and they had been but two or three months from home. They are spoken of in the highest terms. When within about three miles of the field of battle, an aid came riding up to the Colonel of the 54th Massachusetts, saying, "For God's sake Colonel, double quick, or the day is lost."

The 1st North Carolina were in light marching order, the 54th Massachusetts was in heavy marching order, with knapsacks, haversacks, canteens, and every other appurtenance of the soldier. But off went everything, and they double-quicked on to the field. At the most critical juncture, just as the rebels were preparing for a simultaneous charge along the whole line, and they had captured our artillery and turned it upon us, Col. Jas. Montgomery, Col. Hallowell and Lieut.-Col. Hooper[11] formed our line of battle on right by file into line. As the men came into line they opened fire. The 1st North Carolina came into line handsomely, and did splendid execution. They lost their Lieutenant Colonel,[12] who was in command, and a great many other officers. They were under a much heavier fire, I think, than the 54th Massachusetts. Johnny

Reb could not stand. He gave way, leaving his colors and guns on the field. But we did not have sufficient force to attempt to storm their works, so the order to retreat came. And it was a sorrowing spectacle to see our little army, so hopeful and so gallant, in such precipitate retreat after a battle of four short hours. We can learn of nothing in regard to the prisoners of war. We reached the vicinity of Jacksonville on the 23d ult., having marched over one hundred miles in about five and a half days. We brought off the greater part of our provisions and munitions of war, and are now awaiting an attack on the part of the rebels. The 54th Massachusetts lost some one hundred killed, wounded and missing, the greater part wounded.[13] Gen. Seymour[14] says that the Fifty-fourth "is the only colored regiment that is worth a d—n." The other regiments are just as good as the Fifty-fourth, but they are yet unbaptized with the fiery flood of battle. The Fifty-fourth received its baptism at the siege of Charleston, and it was no delicate, fastidious sprinkling, but an old genuine immersion. When the colored regiments here are accustomed to the business of war (and it is certainly a business), they will be able to stand up in the face of death with strong nerves. But everybody knows this.

I heard an artillery officer say to Col. Hallowell, as our regiment was running into the fight, "Colonel, you will have to do your best to keep your men from running to-day. Your men (meaning the colored soldiers) all ran to-day."[15] Now, there was but one colored regiment, at the time he said this, in the fight—the 8th U.S. Colored Troops, which had its Colonel killed; while the 7th New Hampshire, 7th Connecticut, 115th New York,[16] 40th Massachusetts, Battery, M. 3d U.S. Artillery and Cavalry, all white, were with them—and this their initiatory fight at that—almost raw recruits.

Will somebody ask who guarded the rear in the retreat from Alicia to Jacksonville, over a distance of nearly fifty miles, thus saving our army, perhaps from complete annihilation? Until he answers, I will say *the negro troops.* The blame, if there be any, of the failure of the attempt to penetrate into the interior of Florida must fall on the head of the General in immediate command of the forces engaged.

Had Col. Hallowell not seen at a glance the situation of affairs, the 54th Massachusetts volunteers would have been killed or captured. When they entered the field with the 1st North Carolina, which is a brave regiment, they (the 1st N.C.) fired well while they remained, but they gave way, thus exposing the right. On the left the rebel cavalry were posted, and as the enemy's left advanced on our right, their cavalry pressed the left. Both flanks were thus being folded up, and slaughter or capture would have been the inevitable result. We fell back in good order, and established new lines of battle until we reached Sanderson. Here a scene that beggars description was presented. Wounded men lined the railroad station, and the roads were filled with artillery, caissons, ammunition and baggage wagons, infantry, cavalry and ambulances. The only organized bodies ready to repel attack were a portion of the 40th Massachusetts mounted infantry, armed with the Spencer Repeating rifle,[17] and the 54th Massachusetts volunteers.

I cannot account for the rebels failing to harass our retreat, the 54th Regiment being the last to leave the field, and leaving it in such good order led them to suppose that we intended to renew the attack. Had our utter helplessness been known, few of the officers or men of this army would have been able to have returned to Jacksonville. We reached Barbour on the retreat about 3½ o'clock on the morning of the 21st, and at daylight again marched in retreat to Baldwin. Just as we were about to start for the latter place, the 55th Massachusetts volunteers[18] came up to re-enforce us, but they were twelve hours too late. This regiment, with the 3d U.S. Colored Troops and 2d and 3d South Carolina volunteers (colored),[19] were not engaged. The only colored soldiers engaged were the three colored regiments above mentioned, and two of these were never under fire before. I am thus explicit because it has been industriously circulated by those high in authority that the colored regiments caused the defeat by failing to support the white regiments, and running away.

There are, by some strange means, a great many soldiers shot under the military law. I mean colored soldiers.[20] I know of but one such execution since my advent here. Two colored soldiers were shot at St. Simons by some of the officers of 2d South Carolina,[21] and another was shot on St. Helena. I always feel when I refer to the poor fellow shot on St. Helena that I am a partner in the guilt of his execution, for I am the man who brought him to justice or injustice. It was by my hand that he was arrested. I arrested him on Saturday morning and on Sunday morning the poor fellow was shot, by the order of some superior officer.[22] Another has since been executed, I think, at Beaufort, and since the arrival of our expedition there have been four colored men executed: one, a sergeant[23] in the 3d. South Carolina

Vols., Col. M. S. Littlefield, and three privates in the 55th Massachusetts Vols.[24] This Sergeant is charged, so far as I can learn, with having induced some of the men in his regiment to stack arms and refuse to do duty on account of the government refusing to pay them their wages. I suppose it required a victim to show the colored soldiers in the department what they must expect if they don't take the money [the] government offers them, however paltry. The other three men were hung for the base crime of rape, second, in its heinousness to willful murder. They were executed at Camp Finegan on the 19th Feb. I refer to this matter because I do not think a black man should be hung for a crime if a white man is not treated with the same punishment for a like crime.[25] I know in the South the negro is hung sometimes for mere pastime to his bloody executioners, and it may be that we are so far South that its Southern atmosphere has so far tainted our moral sensibility—our regard for the man's life and our respect for the rights of even the basest criminal; for if men are to be shot or hung without a legitimate trial under the civil or military law, the life of no man is protected or safe, and we are living under a tyranny inexorable as slavery itself, more absolute and fearful than the inquisition, which knew no law except its own behests and the perpetuation of its power.

I can feel the utter hopelessness of the condition of slavery though never a slave. I can imagine with what ecstatic joy the slave receives his manumission, and becomes a free man. I know now how gnawing to the feelings slavery in any form must be. We have served in the United States navy several terms, and was there treated like our white mess-mates; but in the army every pledge made on our enlistment has been broken—every promise remains unfulfilled. We are unprotected and there is no refuge—no appeal. Those to whom we looked for the fulfillment of these promises, the maintenance of those pledges, and for that protection secured by every nation for its defenders, have proved to be, in the hour of trial, foes to our every interest. We cannot any longer indulge in any false hope. We may as well look at facts which cannot admit of but one solution, viz.: the fixed determination of the people of the United States to maintain a line of demarkation between the white and black race, and to deny to the black equal rights and justice as enjoyed by the white. Late news from the North show already that there will be a division in the ranks of the party in power.[26] If this be true, we are on the threshold of a pro-slavery reac-

tion. In that event the world will witness the deep perfidy and criminal meanness of a nation which is so lost to duty, dignity, and a sense
of national greatness as to call to its defense the victims of its own
cruel oppression, and then spurn and spit upon them. One year in the
service of the United States has purged me of the major part of my
patriotism.

In conclusion I would call the attention of the friends to the fact
that we have little or no reading matter and no money to pay for it.
Your paper is the only journal which furnishes a complete summary
of current events, especially those which directly interest us. Will they
not send us copies of *The Anglo*? There are a great many colored soldiers here and they all desire to have *The Anglo-African*. Your humble servant gets a copy pretty regularly, but it is worn into pieces
before a hundredth part of the boys get through reading it.

G. E. S.

WAA, 26 March 1864.

1. GES published a brief account of the Olustee campaign, written four days
after this one, in the *Christian Recorder*, 9 April 1864; see Edwin S. Redkey,
ed., *A Grand Army of Black Men: Letters from African-American Soldiers
in the Union Army, 1861–1865* (New York: Cambridge University Press,
1992), 43–47.

2. On 29 January 1864, the Fifty-fourth left for Hilton Head and on 5 February embarked for Jacksonville, Florida. Stephens's Company B, transported with General Seymour on the *Maple Leaf*, arrived two days later. On 9
February the regiment marched to Baldwin, briefly engaged enemy troops at
St. Mary's River, and halted at Sanderson on 11 February. Seymour did not
renew his drive west until the morning of 20 February. Emilio, *A Brave Black
Regiment*, 148–59.

3. Total casualties were 1,828. Ibid., 172.

4. GES refers to the Eighth USCT, organized on 4 December 1863. It arrived at Hilton Head on 16 January 1864 and fought its first battle at Olustee. It remained in Florida until August, when it transferred to Virginia. It
also fought at Deep Bottom, New Market Heights, and Petersburg, witnessed
Lee's surrender at Appomattox, and served on the Texas border until November 1865. It lost 251 men in the war before disbanding on 12 December
1865. Dyer, *Compendium*, 3:1725.

5. Col. Guy V. Henry (1839–99), commander of the Fortieth Massachusetts
Regiment, won the Congressional Medal of Honor for heroism at Cold Har-
bor. The Fortieth Massachusetts, organized in August 1862, arrived in the
Department of the South in August 1863, lost 197 men in the war, and mus-
tered out on 30 June 1865. Henry's command included four companies of the
Independent Massachusetts Cavalry Battalion led by Maj. Atherton H.

Stevens, Jr. (1825–?). Originally part of the First Massachusetts Cavalry, this small unit was assigned to the Fourth Massachusetts Cavalry on 12 February 1864. Dyer, *Compendium*, 3:1263; *Massachusetts Soldiers, Sailors*, 4:106–8, 6:129–31, 161, 421–23; *WWWCW*, 303–4.

6. The Tallahassee-Jacksonville railroad, the most important rail link in the state, proved an important supply line for the Confederate army in the deep South. It also joined a rail line at Baldwin that ran south to Cedar Key. Redkey, ed., *A Grand Army of Black Men*, 40.

7. The Seventh New Hampshire, organized on 13 December 1861, had served in Florida since 12 February 1861. It lost 426 men in the war and disbanded on 17 July 1865. Col. J. R. Hawley of the Seventh Connecticut commanded the short-term brigade from 16 to 29 February 1864. Formed on 13 September 1861, the Seventh Connecticut had been in the Department of the South since October 1861, took part in the first attack on Wagner, and lost 364 men before mustering out on 20 July 1865. Battery C—not M—of the Third Rhode Island Artillery was under the command of Lt. Henry Metcalf. Dyer, *Compendium*, 2:371, 3:1009–10, 1349–50, 1702–3; Emilio, *A Brave Black Regiment*, 161.

8. The First North Carolina Volunteers, organized at New Bern, North Carolina, and Portsmouth, Virginia, in June 1863, never attracted white officers with strong antislavery convictions. The army poorly equipped the unit and issued it, like many other black regiments, outdated or malfunctioning weapons. Many exploded during use. The First arrived in the Department of the South in July 1863 and went to Jacksonville in February 1864, where it was redesignated the Thirty-fifth USCT. In November it fought at Honey Hill, South Carolina. The Thirty-fifth lost 205 men and disbanded on 1 June 1866. Dyer, *Compendium*, 3:1472, 1729; Richard Reid, "Raising the African Brigade: Early Black Recruitment in Civil War North Carolina," *North Carolina Historical Review* 70 (July 1993): 266–97.

9. Col. Charles W. Fribley (?-1864), who took command of the Eighth USCT on 24 November 1863, was shot in the heart at Olustee. Fribley's men placed his corpse on a caisson during the retreat, but white troops commandeered the vehicle and threw the body off. Rebels refused to return any Union dead and buried Fribley on the field. John Whittier Messer Appleton Letterbook, 20 February 1864, 177, WVUL; Pension Files, RG 15, National Archives; Bates, *Pennsylvania Volunteers*, 2:1325, 5:968.

10. The Eighth USCT suffered 300 casualties out of 554 men. The Eighth, Thirty-fifth USCT, and the Fifty-fourth together suffered 626 casualties and abandoned many in the hasty retreat. David James Coles, "'A Fight, a Licking, and a Footrace': The 1864 Florida Campaign and the Battle of Olustee," M.A. thesis, Florida State University, 1985, 118–22, 139, 145.

11. Lt. Col. Henry Northey Hooper (1834–1902?), a Boston merchant, joined the Fifty-fourth on 25 August 1863 but did not arrive in the Department of the South until 16 October. Emilio, *A Brave Black Regiment*, 132, 329; Luis F. Emilio biographical notes, Philip and Betty Emilio Family Collection.

12. Col. James C. Beecher, Harriet Beecher Stowe's brother, on leave at the time of the engagement, left command to Lt. Col. William N. Reed (?–1864), a New York abolitionist. Reed vigorously defended black troops and gained the devotion of his men, sparking charges from white subordinates that he was a mulatto passing for white. Mortally wounded at Olustee, he died at Beaufort on 22 February. Coles, "'A Fight, a Licking, and a Footrace,'" 87–88; *OR*, ser. 1, pt. 1, 35:289; Reid, "Raising the African Brigade," 277; Pension Files, RG 15, National Archives.

13. Estimates of the Fifty-fourth's losses vary. Emilio listed 13 killed, 66 wounded, and 8 missing. Hallowell reported 14 killed and 76 wounded. Official records list 16 killed, 62 wounded, 8 missing. Emilio, *A Brave Black Regiment*, 173; Col. Edward N. Hallowell to John A. Andrew, 24 February 1864, Fifty-fourth Massachusetts Records, Letterbooks, RG 94, National Archives; *OR*, ser. 1, pt. 1, 35:298.

14. Gen. Truman Seymour (1824–91) arrived in the Department of the South in December 1862. Nearly his entire command held him responsible for the needless defeat at Olustee. Relieved in March 1864, Seymour was sent to Virginia, captured in battle, and then sent to Charleston, South Carolina, for imprisonment, where, ironically, he came under fire from the men he previously led. Emilio, *A Brave Black Regiment*, 155–57; *WWWCW*, 582.

15. Stephens and other Fifty-fourth soldiers repudiated false accusations, such as those in the Philadelphia *Ledger* by a white officer in the Third Rhode Island Heavy Artillery, that black cowardice was responsible for the Union defeat. In fact, the Seventh New Hampshire, a white unit, broke under fire. The Fifty-fourth, as Union commanders later acknowledged, saved Seymour's force from annihilation. Frederick M. Binder, "Pennsylvania Negro Regiments in the Civil War," *Journal of Negro History* 37 (October 1952): 407–9; Coles, "'A Fight, a Licking, and a Footrace,'" 118–22.

16. The 115th New York Regiment (the "Iron Hearted Regiment"), organized on 26 August 1862, joined the Department of the South in January 1863. It lost 323 men before mustering out on 17 June 1865. Dyer, *Compendium*, 3:1449–50.

17. The Spencer carbine (and rifle), patented in 1860 by Christopher M. Spencer, made the standard muzzle-loading weapon obsolete. Only the conservatism of Union generals, who thought soldiers would waste ammunition, prevented widespread use of the gun. *HTIECW*, 708–9.

18. The Fifty-fifth Massachusetts Regiment, the state's second black unit, organized in May and June 1863, was led by Norwood P. Hallowell. It briefly served at New Bern, North Carolina, before arriving in the Department of the South in August 1863. Hampered by wounds received at Antietam, Hallowell resigned in November and was replaced by Alfred S. Hartwell. The regiment's fiercest fight took place at Honey Hill, South Carolina, where it suffered 139 casualties. It lost 175 men in the war and disbanded on 25 September 1865. *Massachusetts Soldiers, Sailors*, 4:715–16; [Charles B. Fox], *Record of the Fifty-fifth Regiment of Massachusetts Volunteer Infantry* (Cambridge: John Wilson and Son, 1868).

19. The Third South Carolina Volunteers, organized at Hilton Head in June 1863, saw little action. Combined with the Fourth and Fifth South Carolina Regiments, the Third was redesignated the Twenty-first USCT on 14 March 1864. It primarily performed garrison duty in Charleston and elsewhere in South Carolina and Georgia until mustering out on 7 October 1866. Dyer, *Compendium*, 3:1636, 1727.

20. No thorough study of the black experience with military justice exists, but available evidence shows that most whites displayed little sensitivity to the unique circumstances of black service. Sadistic punishments, "drum-head," or even summary executions of blacks occurred with distressing regularity. Because death sentences inflicted on blacks infrequently underwent a full and proper review, court-martial records cannot be relied upon for an accurate view of the treatment they received. Berlin, *The Black Military Experience*, 433–42; Robert I. Alotta, *Civil War Justice: Union Army Executions under Lincoln* (Shippensburg: White Mane Publishing, 1989), 26–27; Joseph T. Glatthaar, *Forged in Battle: The Civil War Alliance of Black Soldiers and White Officers* (New York: Free Press, 1990), 117–20.

21. GES probably refers to two men from Montgomery's Second South Carolina Volunteers who were shot for desertion. *Christian Recorder*, 30 January 1864.

22. GES arrested a deserter from Montgomery's Second South Carolina Volunteers on the morning of 28 June 1863. While camped at St. Helena—the home of many enlisted men—several soldiers took the opportunity to "visit" their families. Montgomery circulated word that those who refused to return voluntarily would be executed upon arrest. The soldier Stephens captured was taken to Montgomery's tent, where the colonel asked him if there was any good reason why he should not be shot. When the man said no, Montgomery replied, "Very well; you die at half past nine o'clock this morning." Montgomery kept his word. GES to Luis F. Emilio, 27 December 1885, Fifty-fourth Regiment Papers, 1:132–33, MHS; Duncan, *Blue-Eyed Child of Fortune*, 362–63.

23. Sgt. William Walker (1840–64), a former slave from Port Royal, South Carolina, in the Third South Carolina Volunteers, on 19 November 1863, convinced fellow soldiers in his company to stack their weapons to protest unequal pay. On 9 January 1864, a court-martial found Walker guilty of mutiny and set his execution for 1 March. The firing squad clearly sympathized with Walker. Only one out of eleven shots struck the prisoner; a reserve squad finished the grisly task. Black troops and their antislavery allies reacted with horror and indignation. James A. Dix, editor of the *Boston Journal*, scarcely knew "whether the policy pursued by the government in regard to colored volunteers can be best characterized as mean or stupid. It is disgraceful to all who have thus proved themselves insensible to the claims of justice and fair dealing." Howard C. Westwood, "The Cause and Consequence of a Union Black Soldier's Mutiny and Execution," *Civil War History* 31 (September 1985): 222–36; *WAA*, 16 April 1864; James A. Dix to John A. Andrew, 20 April 1864, John A. Andrew Papers, MHS.

24. John M. Smith of Company A, Spencer Lloyd of Company B, and John W. Cork of Company B, Fifty-fifth Massachusetts Regiment, were executed near Jacksonville on 18 February 1864 for rape. Emilio noted that a fourth soldier from another regiment was also hanged. On 19 November 1863, Henry Lawson of the Fifty-fifth was shot, although his name does not appear in the regimental roster. The executions proceeded swiftly, one officer explained, to ensure the regiment's good name. Contrary to official records, one man was marched through Jacksonville to a drum beat and shot by moonlight in the town square. Emilio Notes, 17 February 1864, Fifty-fourth Regiment Papers, vol. 2, MHS; Fifty-fifth Massachusetts Regiment, Descriptive Books, Orderly Books, RG 94, National Archives; Alotta, *Civil War Justice*, 205; [Fox], *Record of the Service of the Fifty-fifth Regiment*, 116, 118–19; Charles B. Fox letter extract, 18–19 February 1864, Charles B. Fox Papers, MHS.

25. According to official records, blacks committed 50 percent of all rapes by Union troops. Because blacks made up about 10 percent of the army, their participation in that crime appears disproportionately high. But the accuracy of those records cannot be accepted because they record no case of a white soldier raping a black woman, which, in fact, occurred with appalling frequency. Alotta, *Civil War Justice*, 32.

26. GES alludes to the dissatisfaction among abolitionists and some War Democrats for Lincoln. Many black leaders and some black troops found Lincoln a complete disappointment and backed John C. Frémont. On 31 May 1864, four hundred delegates met in Cleveland to name Frémont as their presidential candidate. *BAP*, 5:226, 276–78; James M. McPherson, *The Struggle for Equality: Abolitionists and the Negro in the Civil War and Reconstruction* (Princeton: Princeton University Press, 1964), 264–77, 279–81.

Folly Island, S.C.,
May 26th, 1864.

Mr. Editor: The good news has reached here that Gen. Grant is victorious,[1] and that Congress has reluctantly passed a bill equalizing the pay of United States troops.[2] It makes one regret that he is not a participant in the stupendous struggle, but there are those of the proscribed race that are filling up the record with brilliant deeds. But it matters not where you place colored troops, you will find them brave, faithful and cheerful, and under the most discouraging and untoward circumstances. They are not any more or less brave than white troops, but are just like white troops for all the world. They require the same discipline, the same punishment, and the same treatment. A great many people have a notion that colored men must be treated, in social, civil, and military life, different from other men, this I think the grossest of errors.

In this matter of pay, the authorities find that a thousand and one heart burnings and sickenings, distrusts and sufferings, would have been avoided if their policy had been just and equitable. They, no doubt, have come to this conclusion. Mr. Frederick Douglass makes a point when he says, "The Administration has crushed us with its legislation. We want to be (like the rebels) let alone."[3] True, true, indeed is this. Now we cannot ride in the city passenger cars unless they legislate to that effect; we cannot even buy public lands, unless some act or order is promulgated, extending the privilege; we could not be employed upon the public works, unless some provisional law or order was appended to it, and when our so-called masters ran away from us, and went to the war to "break the glorious Union," we could not go out into the world, free, without meeting at every footstep legislative obstructions—laws and rules for the government of not, men, but contrabands; and when we volunteered in the army to fight for the country, after serving a year, we must accept the insulting, starving pay which, it is presumed, legislation had imposed; and legislation must step forward and award us full pay. Is this not a triumphant argument that the policy of the Administration is based on the Dred Scott decision—that "black men had no rights that white men are bound to respect"?

We knew, of course, that the President of the United States distinctly said that his proclamation of Emancipation was issued purely and solely on the grounds of military necessity, hence, the exception of part of Kentucky, Tennessee, Virginia, and Louisiana, and so forth, from its provisions.[4] Another prominent Republican "only wanted to use the colored man against the rebellion," that "he would rather see the waves of the broad Atlantic roll between the races," etc. Such we knew to be the drift of sentiment in high quarters. But why, if military necessity could wring this proclamation, was there not accompanying it a policy that would make it available against the rebellion? If there was a necessity for the first, it follows there was for the second. Why did not the Administration, when it was compelled to substitute the military for the civil law, ignore that accursed dictum of Taney?

Military necessity has proclaimed martial law from the St. Lawrence to the Dry Tortugas, yet the cardinal precept of the slave-driver is held sacred and inviolate. These Copperheads are the silliest fellows imaginable. They want slavery and the slave trade, mobbing and murder, and Congress has not passed any law against the pursuit of their avocations. The colored man can be kicked, cuffed, held to service, and even made a slave of, until Congress passes some law against it. No wonder the free colored men of New Orleans believe that in the change from Southern to Yankee rule they have "traded the devil for a witch."[5]

Yes we want to be let alone, and treated just like other men. If we work, we want our wages. If we want to fight for Uncle Sam, we want to be praised and rewarded, just like other men. If we do not perform our duties, we want to be disgraced and punished. If other men enjoy life, liberty and the pursuit of happiness, we don't want to hold our breath, serve our masters, or bury ourselves in sackcloth and ashes, until Congress drags through its lazy, torturous length some measure ratifying these rights which God has given to all men before congresses or conventions were ever assembled.

The Administration has so compromised itself with the Border slave-States interest that it threatens to maintain the system in every region not affected by the proclamation. One of the most fatal mistakes of this war has been the false and indefinite policy of the Administration. The Emancipation proclamation should have been based as much on the righteousness of emancipation as on the great need of the measure, and then let the people see that the war for slavery and secession could be vigorously met only by war for the Union against slavery.

I shall not forget the stirring words of Mr. Stanton in [the] Cooper Institute,[6] a few weeks before our regiment was mustered into the service. He advocated this idea, and called on the black man to "shoulder his musket and fight for the liberty of the human race," the enfranchisement of the barbarous, lecherous, master, as well as the benighted slaves. This was a soul-stirring appeal, which had it been founded in fact would have met a full response.

Oh, no! this would not do. Mr. Lincoln and Mr. Blair must tell the poor negro, "You had better leave the country—the races cannot exist together." "If there had been no colored people, there would have been no war."[7] He turned to the traitors South, who hate him with a vengeance that every drop of blood in his body could not satiate, "If you do not lay down your arms I will issue a proclamation." They, of course, did not lay down their arms. They knew that the back-bone of their antagonist was too weak, and was too full of conciliation to make emancipation so plain and positive that the black millions could know it of a truth. The heart of the Administration is bent on recon- struction, but I fear there will never be any reconstruction under Pres- ident Lincoln, and his satellites mean another lease to slavery. The enlightened loyalist will never submit to this. The Southerners know this, and know too, though a minority, that they are "thrice armed, having their quarrel just."[8] Why, sir, we can take the whole of Wash- ington, including executive, McClellan, and all, excepting Wilson, Sumner, Stevens,[9] and a few others, put them on board of two or three big ships, and let them emigrate to some foreign part, and let old Ben Butler, Fremont, Hooker, McDowell,[10] and many others we know of, take their places, and can whip the rebellion down South and the sedition up North. Why? Because those men will have but one poli- cy, to wit the destruction of slavery—the beacon by which the old ship of Rebellion hopes to reach the haven of peace and security.

If it be true that Gens. Grant and Butler are bidding fair to kill or capture Lee and his army,[11] we are on the eve of the period that will test the earnestness and the faithfulness of those who represent the North. There is one man whom I know will come out right—Charles Sumner. I trust, those noble men who have risen superior to their prejudices—who have proclaimed for justice and duty, will stand firm in this great crisis of reform. It is full of point and instruction to refer to that great crisis of the Reformation (see D'Aubigne, p. 234).[12] The Council of Augsburg, under the hesitating, indefinite spirit of Con- servatism—the head and power of the Reformation—trembled in the presence of the Papist party, and threatened to surrender all. The re- form was drifting away—still a few more fathoms and it would be lost; already, disunion, trouble, and affright were spreading among its ranks. Melanchthon, Brentz, Keller[13] and others, had conceded so much that there was but one step between the reform and absolute Romanism. Said Melanchthon to Campeggio,[14] the Pope's represen- tative, "There is no doctrine in which we differ from the Roman Church. We venerate the universal authority of the Roman Pontiff, and we are ready to obey him, provided he does not reject us, and that, of his clemency, which he is accustomed to show to our nation, he will pardon or approve certain little things that it is no longer possi- ble for us to change. . . .[15] Now, then, will you reject those who ap- pear as suppliants before you? Will you pursue them with fire and sword?"[16] Thus spoke Melancthon, the great reform chieftain, in the

council of Augsberg. There he stood, ready to surrender every interest, every doctrine, every achievement, to the Roman hierarchy. One
man stood firm—Martin Luther.[17] He, rather than surrender religion,
liberty, or tear down that noble edifice of religious reform which he
had so largely assisted in building up, would suffer all the tortures
which Popish fanaticism could inflict upon him. Said he, "The plan
of Compeggio and the Pope has been to try us first by threats, and
then, if these do not succeed, by stratagems. You have triumphed over
the first attack, and sustained the terrible coming of Caesar; now,
then, for the second. Act with courage, and yield nothing." And again:
"I will not yield a hairs breadth."[18]

Thither we can point those noble men who have made this great
war worthy of the blood and treasure it has wasted.

There are Melancthons, and Kellers, and Brentzes of the present day.
They, for the sake of union and peace, would yield liberty, honor and
country. They would say to the slave god: "We do not differ. There is
no doctrine in which we differ from the slave-driver. Do we not save
slavery wherever it can be saved? and do we not adhere to the Dred
Scott decision?" Did not President Lincoln offer the bait to the Southerners, "If you want to save your slaves, lay down your arms"? If this
war is maintained by the North with a view to the restoration of the
system, God, being just, will never prosper its stupendous villainy,
and its criminality would make the North a bye-word and a disgrace;
for it would then be a war for power and for conquest. Make it a war
for the liberty of the human race, not liberty only for the slave, but
liberty for the master and for every proscribed man; and for breaking
every image of the slave-masters fetish.

I see by your paper that the movement has been made for a national convention.[19] This is good. It will have a significance. We can judge
by the impression it makes on the public mind of its influence, and
it will be representative in its character. I hope our best men will form
it, and carefully, boldly, and skillfully deliberate on the important
issues which will be brought before it. Let it come, it will be the first
step toward a coalition of our forces.

I notice, in your issue of the 12th inst., an article signed, "Wolverine,"[20] which I think a covert stab, directed to the 55th Massachusetts,
and a bid for official favor. The paragraph that contains the whole gist
of its two-thirds of a column reads thus:

"They (the officers) do for the men what others refused to do one year ago. They fill the places for no other object than the elevation of the colored race. . . .[21] Let us look to what constitutes military discipline. What fault can we find there? The officers are bound by a solemn oath to perform their duty, I will do all in my power to sustain them in it. I have been sworn in the service thirteen months, and will be willing to serve twice as long if the government do according to agreement. When I look back to '61 and '62, it makes me strong in my belief that time brings all things right. If I would stop and allow my feelings to govern, I would soon be void of reason. The harder my duties, the more cheerful I try to be. What is thirteen months in the army? To stop at that short period, because I am not made a man from the word go. . . ."[22]

"Wolverine" looked at military discipline, but there he ended. He either smoked it away in his pipe or left it somewhere. It is strictly against military discipline to censure or praise the acts of one's superior officers, yet in the article he writes them down as paragons of virtue and disinterestedness, doing for colored men what others would not do one year ago. I have no word of censure for any of the officers, except those later installments, in some instances. The officers of both the 54th and 55th are true and tried men—men of education and military acquirements. They are every one men of honor and moral worth; but to say they did for us what others would not, and that they hold their position for no other object than the elevation of the colored race, is utterly and positively false. The applications for positions in colored regiments had exceeded the demand long before the organization of the 54th was completed. Is not a colonel or captain of a colored regiment as much a colonel and captain as of a white? and has not the conduct of some of the colored regiments made its officers more distinguished than some others are? There are many staff officers who have good cause to envy both Cols. Hallowell and Hartwell.[23] Their commands are faithful and can be depended upon in every hour of trial and need. They have joined these regiments just as other men accepted offices, for the country, for honor, and for emolument. Colored regiments are grown to be big things.

The men to whom honor belongs are those that made the 54th a success—the Cols. Hallowell, Capts. Walton and Carson, and Major Appleton.[24] When men who were enlisted into the interior of Pennsylvania had to be smuggled in covered furniture carts to the depots,[25] and then when the regiment was completed, with the noble Shaw led it heroically into the deadly breach. But few of those men remain now, and youthful officers have filed the places of most of our comrades in battle. That sacred veneration we used to have has but few objects for its contemplation. All that we have to do, is to be drilled and worked by men whose antecedents or sentiments we know nothing of.

I think both regiments have done their duty. Officers and men all say this, although there is some dissatisfaction about pay. What else must be expected? White regiments would have risen up under the circumstances in open rebellion. Why shall we do less? But the men of the 54th and the 55th know what Herculean efforts their friends are using to have justice done to them, and for their sake they keep in remembrance those lessons of discipline, which are as necessary to the welfare of the regiment as the vital breath is to the system.

Oh, Messrs. Blair and Fessenden,[26] on your heads has the *onus* of blame fallen. There never was any necessity for passing a law to pay us. All laws for paying volunteer militia apply to us as much as to the whitest of men. But "Wolverine" says he is willing to serve thrice thirteen months if the government do according to agreement. Now here is mutiny right square up and down. Suppose Uncle Sam don't pay you, what are you going to do? How dare you set yourself up for a physician? "Heal thyself." After daring to say what you will do under certain circumstances, you say: "When I look back to the years '61 and '62 it makes me stronger in my belief that time brings all things right." So you are one of those time-servers, are you? You would not join the 54th, but time brought you into the 55th. It was time which rolled on and saw American slavery grow from a shipload of slaves to four and a half million of toiling bondmen. It was time that gave South Carolina the opportunity to sow broadcast over this country the seeds of disunion against which you and I have placed ourselves in the balance.

But only two short years have elapsed since stern, hard necessity, and the loyalty of the colored man, have led hundreds of thousands to strike hands with us, and bid us God-speed. What is it to-day that keeps back the secession hordes? "Wolverine" would say, "Rest in peace, time brings all things right." I pity the poor, miserable time server. Again: "What is thirteen months in the army, to stop at that short period because I am not made a man from the word go?" Well, this has not a great deal of sense or point, except the inference that Wolverine is not made a man of. This is a gross insult to those in the 54th and 55th who are men. They speak, stand erect, shoulder a musket, read and write the English language, worship God according to the dictates of their conscience, love, hate, and are patriotic. Perhaps "Wolverine" has not yet attained that state called manhood. Oh, no, "Wolverine!" you and all of us are men, and have all the faculties of the human race, but in this country the practice is to degrade and humiliate the colored man. This spirit is manifested in your regiment and in mine—has insinuated a superiority I don't, nor ever will acknowledge, save only in strict and implicit obedience to every lawful command, or duty to superior officers.

The soldiers of the 54th and 55th are as good as any you usually find, and if they had proper incentives, the non-commissioned officers would be as good as you usually find in other regiments. An officer told me to my face that non-commissioned officers were not as good as they are in white regiments. I suppose he thought that could be no insult to me. The question of pay has caused some little trouble, but the regiments are just as efficient as they ever were if there is any fighting to do. As an evidence of this, on the 22d inst., Gen. Schimmelfennig[27] sent out an expedition to James Island, just opposite Long Island, to take a rebel battery which could be seen from the distance. Its appearance was formidable. It had a towering magazine, brazen guns, and bristling abatis.[28] The expedition consisted of detachments from the 54th N. Y., 74th Pa., 103d N. Y., and nearly the whole of 55th Massachusetts Vols., who were the storming party.[29] They thought of deadly assault, of gaping wounds and of victory in the midst of death. The landing was effected just at day at two points, one above and the other below the battery. They had to pass through a marsh waist deep. Col. Hartwell led the storming party, and forbade any man to discharge his piece, until ordered. As soon as they landed the rebels opened fire. On they steadily advanced, until they reached terra firma, which, as soon as they did, they opened with cheers, the rebels turned and ran, and did not make any stand whatever, and what was their astonishment when they reached this famous work they found it empty—not a rebel to be seen. The magazine contained sticks and stones, the brazen guns were made of wood, and the bristling abatis was rotten, a mere sham. Gen. Schimmelfennig demolished it in very short order. There is no doubt the 55th would have acquitted them-

selves nobly had they met "foemen worthy of their steel." Col. Von
Gilsa[30] complimented them for their promptitude and anxiety to be
led into action. Col. Hartwell told them they did all that could be
expected from men. Said he, "not a man has flinched from duty." This
was different from some of the men from one of the New York regiments. Capt. Nutt[31] of the 55th and some of his men found one of its
Captains hid in the bushes. His excuse was, that he gave out, and
could not keep up with his company.

Before the 55th left the dock Col. H. told them they were about to
take part in what might result in a serious affair, but every man was
ready and even anxious to follow their leader. What say you to this
Mr. Wolferine, or "Wolverine," are these the men you assail, or are
they the things that have not been made men of. Since the return of
the 54th from Olustee they have been engaged in several reconnais-
sances, and some portion of them stands the rebel fire every night. Is
this the conduct you speak of that is going to ruin the African race?
If half a dozen men shrink from duty and have to be punished, don't
for the sake of justice and right, don't assail a body of men who are
proving, each day they live, their manhood. Although "Wolferine"
still owns allegiance to his canine brotherhood, if a dozen men shrink
from duty bring them to a strict and if need be, a bloody account, but
give honor to whom honor is due.[32]

G. E. S.

WAA, 18 June 1864...

1. Ulysses Simpson Grant (1822–85) received command of all Union armies
in the winter of 1863. Stephens refers to erroneous press reports of Lee's defeat in The Wilderness Campaign and at Spottsylvania, Virginia. The horrific
fighting between 5 and 12 May 1864 cost Grant about thirty-two thousand men
and Lee eighteen thousand. James M. McPherson, *Battle Cry of Freedom: The
Civil War Era* (New York: Oxford University Press, 1988), 729–33.

2. In February 1864, Sen. Henry Wilson introduced a joint congressional
resolution to equalize pay. The day before Stephens wrote this letter, a congressional committee finally approved Wilson's bill. Because it excluded soldiers who had been slaves, the House rejected it. Colonels Hallowell and
Hartwell, Governor Andrew, Senators Sumner and Wilson, and others continued the fight, and in mid-June Congress adopted legislation that equalized
pay to 1 January 1864. Unsatisfied, supporters of black troops continued the
battle, and, in July, Attorney General Bates reversed an earlier decision and
made the 1862 Confiscation Act—which did not specify pay rates—the legal
basis for black enlistment. Thus, anyone free on 19 April 1861 was entitled
to equal pay from the beginning of their service. Herman Belz, "Law, Poli-

tics, and Race in the Struggle for Equal Pay during the Civil War," *Civil War History* 22 (September 1976): 197–201; Berlin, *The Black Military Experience,* 362–68.

3. GES emphasizes a theme that Douglass used in his wartime speeches. When whites asked, "What shall be done with the negro?" Douglass answered, "Your *doing* with them is their greatest misfortune. They have been undone by your doings," Douglass declared, "and all they now ask and really have need of at your hands, is to let them alone." James M. McPherson, *The Struggle for Equality: Abolitionists and the Negro in the Civil War and Reconstruction* (Princeton: Princeton University Press, 1964), quotation on 187; David W. Blight, *Frederick Douglass' Civil War: Keeping Faith in Jubilee* (Baton Rouge: Louisiana State University Press, 1989), 177–82.

4. In his often-quoted 22 August 1862 letter to Horace Greeley, Lincoln clearly stated his position on emancipation: "My paramount object in this struggle is to save the Union, and is not either to save or to destroy slavery. If I could save the Union without freeing any slave, I would do it; and if I could save it by freeing some and leaving others alone, I would also do that." The Emancipation Proclamation of 1 January 1863 did not free slaves in the border states. Nicholay and Hay, *Abraham Lincoln,* 6:152–53; *WAA,* 1 January 1863.

5. Since the federal occupation of New Orleans in 1862, blacks observed federal Reconstruction polices in action. Despite Louisiana's well-educated and wealthy free creole elite, the Lincoln administration sided with white planters, enforced harsh labor contracts on the former slaves, and rejected black suffrage. The experience provided blacks with a chilling example of what to expect at the hands of Northern white politicians. C. Peter Ripley, *Slaves and Freedmen in Civil War Louisiana* (Baton Rouge: Louisiana State University Press, 1976).

6. GES refers to impromptu remarks by the political abolitionist Henry B. Stanton (1805–87) at a meeting of the American Anti-Slavery Society in New York City's Cooper Institute (Union). Founded in 1857, the institute offered working citizens a free education, and its auditorium was the setting for Lincoln's famous 27 February 1860 address outlining the Republican party's views on slavery. Walter M. Merrill and Louis Ruchames, eds., *The Letters of William Lloyd Garrison,* 6 vols. (Cambridge: Harvard University Press, 1971–81), 5:18n.3, 156n.11; Richard N. Current, ed., *The Political Thought of Abraham Lincoln* (Indianapolis: Bobbs-Merrill, 1967), 139–62.

7. Although Lincoln abandoned colonization in 1863, blacks remained suspicious of him and resented his opinion, voiced during a White House meeting with Edward M. Thomas and four other black leaders on 14 August 1862, that "but for your race among us there could not be war." In this widely publicized encounter, Lincoln also claimed that racial equality was both impossible and undesirable. He hoped blacks would accept colonization as the only solution to the nation's racial conflicts. Blight, *Frederick Douglass' Civil War,* 137–38; *WAA,* 3 January 1863.

8. GES quotes Shapespeare's *King Henry VI,* part 2.

9. In addition to Sumner, GES mentions two of Congress's most important Radical Republican leaders: Henry Wilson (1812–75), a U.S. senator and abolitionist from Massachusetts; and Thaddeus Stevens (1792–1868), the powerful antislavery Pennsylvania congressman whose commitment to racial equality helped secure civil rights and Freedmen's Bureau legislation. *HTIECW*, 718, 832.

10. Gen. Irwin McDowell (1818–85) participated in both Union defeats at Bull Run. *HTIECW*, 459–60.

11. Robert E. Lee (1807–70) received command of the hundred-thousand-man Army of Northern Virginia on 31 May 1862. He miraculously resisted Grant's onslaughts and bottled up General Butler south of Richmond in The Wilderness and Spottsylvania Campaigns. *HTIECW*, 429–31; McPherson, *Battle Cry of Freedom*, 731–32.

12. Jean Henri Merle d'Aubigne (1794–1872) wrote the *History of the Great Reformation of the Sixteenth Century, in Germany, Switzerland. . . .* The book was available in various English editions beginning in 1838.

13. GES mentions two of Germany's most important Lutheran reformers. Philip Melanchthon (1497–1560), Luther's colleague, assumed leadership of the German Reformation after Luther's death, and Johann Brenz (1499–1570) was coauthor of the Württemberg Confession of Faith and a popular Protestant catechism. Andreas Keller was an obscure Lutheran pamphleteer. Magnus Magnusson and Rosemary Goring, eds., *Cambridge Biographical Dictionary* (Cambridge: Cambridge University Press, 1990), 204, 999; Steven Ozment, *Protestants: The Birth of a Revolution* (New York: Doubleday, 1992), 232.

14. Lorenzo Campeggio (1472–1539) was a Roman Catholic cardinal who represented Rome at the 1530 Diet of Augsburg. *New Catholic Encyclopedia*, 18 vols. (New York: McGraw Hill, 1967), 2:1113.

15. Ellipsis in original.

16. d'Aubigne, *History of the Great Reformation*, 572.

17. Martin Luther (1483–1546) was the German founder of the Reformation. The 1530 Diet of Augsburg, called by German Emperor Charles V, met to unify dissenting Protestant sects, Lutherans, and Catholics against the Turks and French. Melanchthon hoped to prove that Lutherans had introduced no doctrine or ceremony "that is contrary to Holy Scripture or the universal Catholic Church." His concessions to Catholic authorities led to fierce opposition by strident Lutherans. Magnussan and Goring, eds., *Cambridge Biographical Dictionary*, 926; Lewis W. Spitz, *The Protestant Reformation, 1517–1559* (New York: Harper and Row, 1985), 113–15.

18. d'Aubigne, *History of the Great Reformation*, 573.

19. GES refers to the black national convention that met at Syracuse, New York, on 4–7 October 1864.

20. "Wolverine" defended his regiment's white officers as the most "generous, open-hearted and faultless set of men" that could "be found on the continent of America." He opposed the protests over unequal pay, asserting that the controversy would damage the reputations of the regiments and harm

the long-term interests of the men. Justice eventually will come, he asserted: "Let our motto be Patience and Perseverance." *WAA,* 14 May 1864.

21. Ellipsis in original.

22. Ellipsis in original.

23. Col. Alfred S. Hartwell (1836–1912) assumed command of the Fifty-fifth
Massachusetts in November 1863. Although committed to equal pay and
commissions for black troops, Hartwell never enjoyed the level of respect the
unit had accorded to Norwood P. Hallowell. A distinguished jurist, he served
as chief justice of the Hawaii Supreme Court from 1907 to 1911. Service
Records, Alfred S. Hartwell Papers, Hawaii State Archives; [Charles B. Fox],
*Record of the Service of the Fifty-fifth Regiment of Massachusetts Volunteer
Infantry* (Cambridge: John Wilson and Son, 1866), 98; "Judge Alfred Stedman
Hartwell," *Hawaiian Historical Society Annual Report* (1945): 7–8.

24. John Whittier Messer Appleton (1832–1913), a Boston clerk with firm
antislavery convictions, was the first officer selected for the Fifty-fourth and
served as its Boston recruitment officer. "Carson" is a misprint. Emilio, *A
Brave Black Regiment,* 8, 9, 133, 329; John Whittier Messer Appleton to ?,
19 February 1879, 31 March 1882, Appleton Family Papers, MHS; John Whittier Messer Appleton Letterbook, 13 December 1863, 1, 127, WVUL.

25. Racist opposition to black recruitment in Philadelphia, especially during the first months of 1863, was intense. Robert R. Corson, a white recruiter and philanthropist, bought rail tickets for the men he sent to Boston and
placed them on the trains at night, one at a time, "to avoid creating excitement." Misc. notes, Fifty-fourth Regiment Papers, 1:13, MHS.

26. William P. Fessenden (1806–69), moderate antislavery U.S. senator from
Maine, became Lincoln's secretary of the treasury in July 1864. Blair's relentless commitment to colonization and Fessenden's opposition to equal pay
enraged black troops. *HTIECW,* 257–58; Belz, "Law, Politics, and Race," 204;
McPherson, *The Struggle for Equality,* 216.

27. Gen. Alexander Schimmelfennig (1824–65), a former Prussian engineering officer, commanded the Northern District in May 1864. The 22 May 1864
strike against James Island mentioned by GES was a diversionary action designed to test rebel troop strength. *WWWCW,* 572; [Charles P. Bowditch],
"War Letters of Charles P. Bowditch," *Proceedings of the Massachusetts
Historical Society* 57 (May 1924): 470; E. Milby Burton, *The Siege of Charleston, 1861–1865* (Columbia: University of South Carolina Press, 1970), 283;
OR, ser. 1, pt. 2, 35:98.

28. Abatis, an ancient defense measure, are structures made from felled
trees and sharpened limbs that have been placed outward from a defensive
work to obstruct an enemy's advance. *HTIECW,* 1.

29. Neither the Seventy-fourth Pennsylvania nor the Fifty-fourth New
York took part in this minor skirmish. The 21–22 May 1864 action included
250 men from the Fifty-fifth Massachusetts and the 103d New York Regiment. The Fifty-fourth New York Regiment, organized in October 1861, arrived in the Department of the South in August 1863. It mustered out on 14
April 1866 after losing 142 men in the war. The 103d (the "Seward Infantry"),

316 A VOICE OF THUNDER

organized in March 1862, arrived in the Department of the South in July 1863, lost 168 men in the war, and mustered out on 7 December 1865. On 22 May the two regiments crossed over to James Island at dawn and drove off rebel pickets. The action resulted in nine Union losses and gave the Fifty-fifth its first combat experience. Dyer, *Compendium*, 3:1424–25, 1445–46; [Fox], *Record of the Service of the Fifty-fifth Regiment*, 27; *OR*, ser. 1, pt. 1, 35:76–77.

30. GES mentions Leopold von Gilsa, former colonel of the Forty-first New York Regiment, who commanded Folly Island, Northern District, until 26 October 1864. *WWWCW*, 678.

31. William Nutt (1836–?) joined the Fifty-fifth Massachusetts as captain in May 1863. Promoted to major in November 1864, he mustered out on 29 August 1865. After the war, Nutt worked for the Freedmen's Bureau. [Fox], *Record of the Service of the Fifty-fifth Regiment*, 99.

32. Other members of the Fifty-fifth Massachusetts reacted with anger to Stephens's letter. "Picket" rejected his account of the James Island attack, correctly stating that rebels made a brief stand and retreated when outflanked. "Picket" acknowledged Stephens as the spokesman for the black regiments but admonished him to provide more accurate accounts of action by other black regiments. *WAA*, 30 July 1864.

Folly Island, S.C.,
June 18th, 1864.

Mr. Editor: The mail continues to advise us of the steady advance of Gen. Grant toward Richmond. The news by this (to-day's) mail is of a more cheering character to those who are loyal, than usual. The capture of Petersburg is certainly tremendous.[1]

We have been anticipating good news for three or four days, because we have had late advices through Rebel sources.

The Rebels had the impudence to present a flag of truce to make the following modest request—"That as the Confederate authorities had sent thirty of forty staff and ten or fifteen general officers for safe keeping to Charleston, that the General Commanding will please not fire on the city."[2]

Gen. Schimmelfennig, who commands the District, sent orders immediately to the Morris Island Batteries to fire forty shells into Charleston.[3] It is said that they positively refused to communicate with any officer commanding colored troops. The truce party presented itself at the picket line of Cole Island, and it happened that the 55th Massachusetts Volunteers were on picket (on this line the pickets approach each other as near as one hundred yards, but are not allowed to fire upon each other). The rebel officer said that he did not wish to insult the officer who commanded the 55th picket, but his instructions were "To not recognize, officers of colored troops."

The officer of the picket sent word to Gen. Schimmelfennig, who sent Capt. Quintin[4] of the 103d N. Y. Vols. They were not very communicative, but furnished files of Richmond papers, which announce that Gen. Grant, has again changed his base, which is significant of some movement which bodes no good to their cause. Gen. S. also told them that if any harm should befall our prisoners in Charleston he would tie their prisoners to trees in front of our batteries.

Private Wallace Baker,[5] Co. I, 55th Regt. Mass. Vols. was shot to death with musketry this morning at 10½ A.M. for striking his superior officer, Lieut. Ellsworth,[6] 55th Mass. Vols. Baker is one of those men who had become insubordinate from the unjust treatment to which the colored Massachusetts soldiers had been subjected.

Lieut. Ellsworth is one of the new batch of Lieutenants promoted from some white regiment to a lieutenancy in the 55th. This man Baker, was insolent and insubordinate, and for not promptly obeying him, Lieut. Ellsworth struck or attempted to strike him with his sword. Baker caught the Lieutenant's sword and struck him several violent blows in the face, and said, "You damned officers, do you think you can strike me and I not strike you back again? I'll strike you! I'll be damned if I don't." For this he was arraigned, tried, and sentenced to be shot, by a court martial convened at this post. He suffered the extreme penalty of the military law, and died like a soldier—in the presence of the troops posted on this island. The Rev. Mr. Bowles,[7] Chaplain of the 55th, paid every attention to the unfortunate soldier, being continually with him, from daylight to the moment the rattling rifles told us that another victim had been offered up on the altar. . . .[8] No man ever met his death with less trepidation than Wallace Baker. On his way to the place of execution, strongly guarded by a strong guard from the 54th New York Volunteers, he bade the boys a hearty "good-bye." To one, he remarked, "They have me in a pretty tight place to-day, boy," and just before he was shot he called a friend to his side and requested him to write to his folks and tell them what had become of him, and what it was for. He then seated himself on his coffin, his hands were pinioned, his eyes blindfolded, and a party of his comrades gave him a sudden and consequently easy death. He never struggled a second after the first volley, every ball taking a fa-

tal effect. During all the ceremonials of the execution, such as reading the sentence and its confirmation, and the order appointing the
time and place of execution, he remained firm, and when he spoke
no tremor could be detected in his voice.

By the way, the paymaster has just paid the 55th boys a visit, offer-
ing them seven dollars per month. He offered the Chaplain, Rev. Mr.
Bowles, seven dollars too,[9] and he told the paymaster if he, the paymaster, thought it was according to the law for him to be paid on his
commission that paltry sum he would take it, but Mr. Paymaster
backed down and said he would await instructions. We are waiting
patiently for the return of Col. Hallowell,[10] for we are anxious to know
what our fate is to be.

G. E. S.

WAA, 9 July 1864.

1. The Petersburg Campaign, the longest sustained operation of the war,
began on 15 June 1864 and concluded on 3 April 1865. At this point, Grant
did not capture Petersburg but successfully removed his forces from Cold
Harbor without Lee's knowledge and then began the historic siege that resulted in forty-two thousand Union and twenty-eight thousand Confederate
casualties and a Union victory. *HTIECW,* 577–79.
2. On 13 June, Union troops learned that Confederates had moved fifty
Union officers into Charleston to halt the Union bombardment. Federal commanders threatened to place an equal number of rebel officers in the line of
fire, which led to an exchange of prisoners on 3 August. Because rebels persisted in confining Union soldiers in Charleston, several hundred rebel officers were placed in a stockade beside Battery Wagner, in the line of fire. Emilio, *A Brave Black Regiment,* 195–96, 218, 222, 226; *OR,* ser. 1, pt. 2,
35:131–32.
3. Because Charleston remained a place "of arms," Union commanders
refused to halt the shelling. *OR,* ser. 1, pt. 2, 35:131.
4. "Capt. Quintin" is probably a misprint; no one by that name served in
the 103d.
5. Pvt. Wallace Baker (1844–64), a "farmer" from Hopkinsville, Kentucky,
joined the Fifty-fifth on 19 June 1863 and was shot almost exactly one year
later. Fifty-fifth Massachusetts Regiment, Descriptive Book, Company I, RG
94, National Archives.
6. Thomas F. Ellsworth (1840–?), commissioned a second lieutenant on 24
October 1863, received the Congressional Medal of Honor "for gallantry" at
Honey Hill, South Carolina. After contracting typhoid fever, he mustered out
on 19 June 1865. Compiled Service Records, RG 94, National Archives;
[Charles B. Fox], *Record of the Service of the Fifty-fifth Regiment of Massachusetts Volunteer Infantry* (Cambridge: John Wilson and Son, 1868), 103.

7. John R. Bowles (1826–?), a Baptist clergyman born in Lynchburg, Virginia, became chaplain of the Fifty-fifth on 18 February 1864. On 18 June, Bowles was ordered to "offer whatever of Spiritual Aid & comfort in his power to Private Wallace Baker." He resigned his commission on 12 June 1865. Compiled Service Records, RG 94, National Archives; [Fox], *Record of the Service of the Fifty-fifth Regiment*, 101.

8. Ellipsis in original.

9. The fourteen African-American chaplains in the U.S Army suffered the same discrimination as other black troops. Governor Andrew had commissioned Bowles and Samuel Harrison of the Fifty-fourth with the understanding that they would receive full officer's pay. White officers in both regiments supported the chaplains' claims, and Andrew appealed directly to President Lincoln for justice. Attorney General Bates authorized the president in April to provide Harrison—and, presumably, Bowles—with full pay. Edwin S. Redkey, "Black Chaplains in the Union Army," *Civil War History* 33 (December 1987): 331–32; Samuel Harrison to John A. Andrew, 15 September 1863, 2 May 1864, Executive Department Letters, vol. 59, MSA; Alfred S. Hartwell to Abraham Lincoln, 13 May 1864, Alfred S. Hartwell Papers, box 1, MSL; John A. Andrew to President Abraham Lincoln, 22 March 1864, Executive Department Letters, vol. 59, MSA; John A. Andrew to President of the United States, 13 May 1864, Fifty-fourth Regiment Papers, vol. 4, MHS; *Liberator*, 13 May 1864.

10. In March 1864, the Fifty-fourth's officers urged Hallowell to lobby government officials in Washington. Ironically, he delayed his travel because of mutinous conditions in the unit over the pay issue. He finally left Morris Island on 6 June and returned on 16 July with assurances that the men would soon receive their pay. Emilio, *A Brave Black Regiment*, 195, 217; John Whittier Messer Appleton Papers, 20 March, 7 June 1864, Diary of John Ritchie, 27 April 1864, Fifty-fourth Regiment Papers, vol. 2, MHS; New York *Herald*, 19 June 1864.

Morris Island, S.C.,
Aug. 1, 1864.

Mr. Editor: Two or three months ago, it was announced that Congress had passed a law equalizing the pay of colored troops. This was at the closing period of the session. The colored troops which had been enlisted under the law of 1862, were unpaid. This was known, of course, at Washington. The noble Major Stearns[1] was compelled to resign, because the pledges he had been authorized by Sec. Stanton to make to the colored man, were broken by the War Department, who refused to pay soldiers who had black skins more than seven dollars per month.

Thus free men were reduced to servitude. No matter what services he might render—no matter how nobly he might acquit himself—he must carry with him the degradation of not being considered a man, but a thing. The foreigner, the alien of whatever color, or race, or country, are enrolled and paid like native Americans; but the latest refinement of cruelty has been brought to bear on us.

In the Revolutionary War, and in the War of 1812, colored men fought, and were enrolled, and paid, the same as the whites;[2] and not only this, were drilled and enlisted indiscriminately in the same companies and regiments. Little did our forefathers think that they were forging chains for the limbs of their own race. Look how nobly Forten, Bowers, and Cassey,[3] and those colored patriots of the last war, rallied to the defence of Philadelphia; yet how were the colored people repaid? By stripping them in '36 of their right of franchise.[4] Now the plan is to inveigle the black man into the service by false pretences, and then make him take half pay. If he don't take half pay and behave himself, as a vender of religious tracts down here said, "Shoot 'em." Why, sir, the rebels have not reached the daring extreme of reducing free men to slaves. Does the Lincoln despotism think it can succeed? There are those who say, you should not talk so—"you hurt yourself." Let me say to those men, we cannot be injured more. There is no insult—there is no cruelty—there is no wrong, which we have not suffered. Torture, massacre, mobs and slavery. Do you think that we will tamely submit like spaniels to every indignity?

I shall speak hereafter [of] my wrongs, and nothing shall prevent me but double irons or a pistol-ball that shall take me out of the hell I am now suffering: Nearly eighteen months of service—of labor—of humiliation—of danger, and not one dollar. An estimable wife reduced to beggary, and dependent upon another man[5]—what can wipe out the wrong and insult this Lincoln despotism has put upon us? Loyal men everywhere hurl it from power—dismember it—grind it to atoms? Who would have believed that all the newspaper talk of the pay of colored soldiers having been settled by Congress was a base falsehood. There is not the least sign of pay, and there are hints from those in authority that we will not get paid, and will be held to service by the terrors of our own bullets. Seventeen months and upwards! Suppose we had been white? Massachusetts would have inaugurated a rebellion in the East, and we would have been paid. But—Oh, how insulting!—because I am black, they tamper with my rights. How dare I be offered half the pay of any man, be he white or red.

This matter of pay seems to some of those having slaveholding tendencies a small thing, but it belongs to that system which has stripped the country of the flower of its youth. It has rendered every hamlet and fireside in this wide country desolate, and brought the country itself to bankruptcy and shame. It is a concomitant of the system. Like as the foaming waves point the mariner to the hidden rocks on which his storm-driven ship will soon be lost, this gross injustice reveals to us the hidden insidious principles on which the best hopes of the true patriot will be dashed.

G. E. S.

WAA, 27 August 1864.

1. George Luther Stearns (1809–67), a zealous supporter of John Brown in the 1850s, received a major's commission in 1863 to direct the government's recruitment of black troops. He resigned in March 1864, disappointed by Stanton's lack of support and in protest over the issue of unequal pay. Henry Greenleaf Pearson, *Life of John A. Andrew: Governor of Massachusetts, 1861–1865*, 2 vols. (Boston: Houghton, Mifflin, 1904), 2:81–84; *WAA*, 16 April 1864.

2. Blacks fought in many battles during the Revolution, including Bunker Hill, Monmouth and Trenton, New Jersey, and Yorktown. During the War of 1812 they made up nearly a quarter of Oliver Hazard Perry's Lake Erie fleet. As Andrew Jackson freely acknowledged, blacks played an important role in his victory at New Orleans and received the same pay and bounties given to whites. *BAP*, 5:79n.11.

3. GES mentions James Forten, Sr. (1766–1839), John C. Bowers, Sr., and Joseph Cassey (1789–1848), who helped assemble a force of 360 Philadelphia blacks in September 1814 to construct bulwarks along the Schuylkill River. Forten, patriarch of the important black antislavery family, turned his home into a meeting place for American and British abolitionists. Bowers became an influential foe of the American Colonization Society and attended the first black national convention. Cassey, a French West Indies native, made a fortune in real estate and lending, became an outspoken abolitionist, and contributed heavily to William Lloyd Garrison's *Liberator*. Julie Winch, *Philadelphia's Black Elite: Activism, Accommodation, and the Struggle for Autonomy, 1787–1848* (Philadelphia: Temple University Press, 1988), 20–21, 38, 44, 46–47, 94; *BAP*, 3:88–89n.4, 89–90n.5.

4. Despite Robert Purvis's eloquent *Appeal of Forty Thousand* (1838) and the mass mobilization of state blacks, white voters approved a new state constitution in October 1838 that denied African Americans the right to vote. *BAP*, 3:252–55.

5. Susan Stephens and her children may have relied on Andrew F. Stevens (1840–98), a well-known caterer and restaurateur, who had lived at Stephens's father's house since at least 1850. Stevens, of uncertain relationship to the Stephens family, had been a member of the Banneker Institute and attended the same Baptist church. After the war, he was named president of the city's Caterer's Association, won a seat on the common council, and in 1884 helped found the Citizen's Republican Club. Philadelphia city directory; 1850 U.S. Census; Banneker Institute membership records, LGC, HSP; *WAA*, 14 November 1863; Roger Lane, *William Dorsey's Philadelphia and Ours: On the Past and Future of the Black City in America* (New York: Oxford University Press, 1991), 113, 206, 418.

[August] 1864.

We have had quite recently a delicate *morveau*[1] for Copperhead eulogy or denunciation, as they may elect: 2d Lieut John S. Marcy, 52d Penn. Vols.,[2] refused to do duty with colored troops (part of the 54th Mass. Vols.). He was placed under arrest by Capt. Gurney, of the 127th New York Vols.,[3] for disobedience of orders, and Lieut. Col. H. N. Hooper, 54th Mass. Vols. General Officer, at the time, of the post, preferred charges against him; and there is a chance that this victim of his own folly will be tried on the square merits of this great question of prejudice.

Another officer, high in authority here, has been terribly exercised about the employment of colored clerks around the different headquarters. Quite a number of the officers of the 54th have been called to staff duty; there are so few in the white regiments that are so well qualified, educationally, for the position. These officers prefer to have their clerks from their own regiment. This high officer in rank squirms at this, they say, and chews the vexatious cud of discontent. I hope he may chew the cud till he dies.

G. E. S.

WAA, 3 September 1864.

1. The word means snotty or bratlike.
2. Lt. John S. Marcy, who mustered into the Fifty-second Pennsylvania on 12 February 1862, refused orders to work with soldiers of the Fifty-fourth on 15 July 1864, declaring, "I will not do duty with colored troops." His court-martial led to a dishonorable discharge on 21 September 1864. The Fifty-second, organized on 5 November 1861, joined the Department of the South in January 1863, remained in the Charleston region until April 1865, and disbanded on 12 July 1865. Compiled Service Records, RG 94, National Ar-

chives; Dyer, *Compendium*, 3:1591–92; Emilio, *A Brave Black Regiment*, 196, 217; Bates, *History*, 2:47–91.

3. Capt. James W. Gurney joined the 127th New York Regiment on 27 August 1862. "Habitually intemperant," he was arrested on 30 June 1864 for "drunkenness on duty" and later resigned rather than face a court-martial. The 127th (the "National Volunteers") organized on 8 September 1862, arrived in the Department of the South in August 1863, and remained until mustering out on 30 June 1865. Compiled Service Records, RG 94, National Archives; Dyer, *Compendium*, 2:196.

Morris Island, S.C.,
Aug. 1st, 1864.

Mr. Editor: Writing to-day, our mind is carried back to Aug. 1st, 1832, made memorable by the emancipation of all the slaves in the British dominions. The history of that struggle and triumph has been our theme down to the present day, and will continue to be a landmark of liberty as long as tyranny tampers with men's rights, and proscription and slavery finds defenders.

British West India Emancipation was peaceful, immediate and unconditional, and so certain, so complete, so positive, that "slaves cannot breathe in England." It was the creature of national penitence, a symbol of a national magnanimity, and the fruition of high moral convictions.

Clarkson, Wilberforce[1] and those other great reformers, acted on the principle that the end and aim of all governments should be to secure the liberty and happiness and peace of all; they believed that man a true benefactor of the race who contributed his talents and energies to these ends; to them, "Property in man was a monstrosity, and therefore slavery had but one right—to die."

It is a relief to look back upon the history, the scenes and incidents of this great event, surrounded as we are by doubts and fears, by death and disaster, and with our future so dark and hopeless. Oh that this nation could learn wisdom by the lessons of the past! How earnestly have our champions of human liberty warned her of the rocks that lay in the path of human slavery! It seems that Divine Providence has lavished blessings on the British nation. In point of wealth and in the extent of her dominions she is the mistress of the world. Her influence is felt and acknowledged by every nation on the face of the earth; her flag is the emblem of liberty, and to her belongs the honor of having founded anti-slavery literature. No nation is so free as England from popular dissensions. She is (to use the words of one of her ablest statesmen) "the protectress and patroness of weak and progressive nations," and her boundaries afford ample protection and refuge for the oppressed of whatever country or condition.

We cannot fail to contrast the United States Emancipation with British West India Emancipation. United States Emancipation is a nondescript. It is prospective and walled around with conditions—a creature—an abortion wrung from the Executive womb by necessity—"brought into this world not half made up"—the dogs laugh at it as they pass. It being no purpose of the Administration to touch the Divine (!!) Institution, and its heart so tender and sensitive of the slaveholders' interests it would not think of such a thing; but Doctor Necessity gave the executive *lady* a sudden visitation. United States Emancipation is the fulmination of one man, by virtue of his military authority, who proposes to free the slaves of that portion of territory over which he has no control, while those portions of slave territory under control of the Union armies is exempted, and slavery receives as much protection as it ever did. United States officers and soldiers are yet employed hunting fugitive slaves. In those exempted slave regions, the slaveholder possesses rights that have never been accorded to the freedman. He can whip his slave and sell him; if he has imbued his hands with loyal blood, and trampled the boasted flag under foot, he can wipe out those stains and atone for that dishonor by complying with certain conditions. Has slavery rightful immunity from just and merited punishment? United States Emancipation fails to accuse the Giant Criminal of any of its manifold crimes—its atrocious guilt—from the shambles on the Coast to the plantations in the South, including the fearful sufferings of the middle passage; its piracy, its murder, its lust, its cruelty, its moral debasement, and finally, its encroachment, its insolence, and its rebellion and warfare against the nation that has so tenderly nursed it and still feeds it with the pap of indulgence. Verily, United States Emancipation is a symbol of national selfishness, an indice of a blind infatuation, and a fulmination of Executive folly and indecision.

G. E. S.

WAA, 3 September 1864.

1. Thomas Clarkson (1760–1846) and William Wilberforce (1759–1833) were England's most famous antislavery leaders. Clarkson's writings and

organizing abilities led to the West Indian Emancipation Act of 1833. Wilberforce sat in Commons from 1780 to 1825 and introduced the first bill to end slavery in the West Indies. Black abolitionists honored both men, often naming antislavery societies after them. Leslie Stephen and Sidney Lee, eds., *Dictionary of National Biography*, 30 vols. (Oxford: Oxford University Press, 1917–), 4:454–57, 21:208–17; Benjamin Quarles, *Black Abolitionists* (New York: Oxford University Press, 1969), 118–19, 129–30, 136, 142.

Camp of the 54th Mass. Vols.,
Morris Island, S.C.,
Aug. 20, 1864.

Mr. Editor: The Massachusetts soldiers here have not been paid yet. The Paymaster gave our officers a flying visit, and I understand left quite an installment of the needful amongst them; but the soldiers did not get so much as the sight of a dollar. It strikes me that some enterprising fellow, who has the interest of Uncle Sam's hero martyrs at heart—who desires to improve their minds—one who exulteth in the distribution of Bibles, newspapers and religious tracts—would do well to send along a few photographic albums, filled with types of the various denominations of our shinplaster currency. We have got greenbacks on the brain and ought to be amused with the shadow if we don't get the substance.

"Is this a greenback which I see before me? Come, let me clutch thee!—I have thee not—yet I see thee still!" "Yes," says a rough-and-tumble fellow, "you do see it—by the eye of faith."

Eighteen months in the army and not one dollar of pay! Eighteen months of unrequited service for a country that believes the liberty of colored men a matter of secondary importance; one that founded that school of morals and theory of social economy which teaches that human Slavery is a Divine institution, full of beauty and beneficence; one that has created great volumes of pro-slavery literature, which remain firm as monuments to disgrace it in future years. Eighteen months of unrequited service for a country—the one only of the nations of the earth that has proclaimed a deed of universal outlawry against the African race, and in every individual citizen of which the colored man finds a petty tyrant, ready to degrade and humiliate him on the flimsiest pretext. It were better far to be subject to the tyranny of all the despots of the old world than to be, as we are, subject to the tyrannies of these hundreds of thousands of petty tyrants, backed by the civil law and military power.

Says some cow-hearted slave, "What's your remedy? Had you not better endure the ills you have than fly to others you know not of?" "No, dog!"—anything is better than slavery, massacre and universal scorn, and the remedy is sturdy resistance and an aroused and purified public sentiment. Do you not know that the more manhood you exhibit, the more brave men will respect you?—cowards will not—and there are plenty of brave men in America. The more unwilling you are to bow your head and bend your knee, the less men will require it of you. And again, if you do not possess the physical courage to resist every insult and indignity, and manifest a readiness to sacrifice every interest, and even life itself, for your rights, you do not deserve to be a free man. And if you were made a freeman, you would soon become a slave again.

"Whatsoever ye would that men should do to you, even so do to them" is an embodiment of Christ's teachings for Christian conduct. "Better die free than live slaves" is an embodiment of the teachings of that great charter of freedom, Natural Rights, which God gives to every man. Base men will rob you of the glorious heritage, and if you are so base, so servile, as to disregard it, and suffer it to be torn from you, you deserve the coffle and the lash as a merited punishment; and your children, and your children's children, should curse you in your grave for your monstrous and atrocious bequest of shame and ignominy.

G. E. S.

WAA, 10 September 1864.

Camp of the 54th Mass. Vols.,
Morris Island, S.C.,
Aug. 20, 1864.

Mr. Editor: Whose heart does not burn with indignation while reading the bitter, hate-inspired accounts of the recent disaster before Petersburg?[1] Have soldiers ever before been thus assailed? Even before the corpses of their dead comrades were cold, long, leaders tell us that the feeling against the colored soldiers amongst the white soldiers is very bitter; our authorities are denounced for putting such men under the command of the marvelous Grant, who, I suppose would have captured Richmond, Lee, and his army, and Jeff. Davis to boot, if it had not been for the denounced colored division. And these are the men who have so nobly upheld the flag and sustained the honor and prowess of the race in the terrible battles in the recent march of the Potomac Army from Spottsylvania Court House to the banks of the Appomattox, and raw recruits side by side with veterans of that army.

I think I can see J. G. B.'s[2] demonical grin as he listens to the long hoped for story of a repulse of the colored division, the first text he has had, to weave a leader on the favorite theme, and the imps that attend his Satanic Majesty are hoarse with screeches of "nigger!" "nigger!" Cursed depravity! base villainy! You have preached negro inferiority all your lives, and you cherished dogma has come to grief. These men, some of whom were a few days ago slaves, have braved the ordeal, and come from the fiery flood purged of the dross which mean prejudice attaches to him; and glowing with the attributes of true manhood, side by side with the white veteran soldier, he is able to seize and bear off trophies of victory. Your theory is scattered to the four winds. You are enraged and discomfited. Your aim to fix on the colored soldier the alternatives of never varying success or inferiority.

Suppose you subject the other soldier to this same test. Take the record from the first Bull Run to the recent assault before Petersburg. Have you ever told the white soldiers they were inferior? I happened to be in Washington at the time of the first battle of Bull Run. I suppose both sides were inferior, if a relative term can be used here. I saw the fugitives rushing into the city without arms and accoutrements and hats, and some actually ran out of their shoes, and all were more scared than hurt. Some of the fearful Zouaves did not stop retreating until they reached New York, and the joke of the matter is, that the rebels were scared equally as bad as our men, and ran like very dogs; but, unfortunately, they discovered the joke first, and took advantage of it. Gen. Hooker's division, one of the best in the Potomac Army, gave way before the enemy in panic at the second Bull Run battle, and the brave McDowell in vain, with drawn sword, endeavored to stem the fugitive torrent. But it is needless to refer to the many facts in every war which proves that the bravest soldiers will meet reverses. Would you denounce the veterans of the Army of the Cumberland for the disaster at Chattanooga,[3] and call them inferior? How would they feel? Would that cheer them for future victory? Would it sooth the grief of the bereaved? Would it atone for the sacrifices, the discomforts and the perils of the soldier in the field? All to be asked is, subject to the colored soldier to the same tests that you do to the other—not greater, not lesser.

The Late Disastrous Raid on James Island.

The last expedition against Charleston, when the facts became known, would reveal one of the most skillfully planned expeditions of the war, and failed through the cowardice or incompetence of subordinates. A Court of Inquiry is about to assemble, it is said, to ferret out the guilty parties. The only redeeming feature of the whole affair was the splendid charge of the 55th Mass. Vols., upon a rebel battery and the capture of two twelve pounder howitzers. One thing that goes far to prove that grave error lies somewhere is, that the expedition was a complete surprise to the enemy, and they were found totally unguarded at the main point of attack.[4]

G. E. S.

WAA, 17 September 1864.

1. The disastrous 30 July 1864 Battle of the Crater at Petersburg, Virginia, began with the detonation of eight thousand pounds of gunpowder that had been placed at the end of a tunnel dug under Confederate lines. Union troops became disorganized in the attack, allowing rebels time to regroup and pour withering fire into the men trapped in the blast's crater. Despite the obvious failure of Union leadership, the Northern press blamed black soldiers for the disaster. A subsequent court of inquiry fully exonerated them. The battle cost 3,798 Union and 1,500 rebel casualties. *HTIECW,* 19; Dudley Taylor Cornish, *The Sable Arm: Negro Troops in the Union Army, 1861–1865* (New York: W. W. Norton, 1966), 273–78.

2. James Gordon Bennett (1795–1872), flinty New York editor and founder of the *Herald,* approved of slavery and opposed the war. His paper became well known for its scurrilous caricatures of blacks. Benjamin Quarles, *The Negro in the Civil War* (1953, reprint, New York: Da Capo Press, 1989), 166.

3. The Union Army of the Cumberland, commanded by Gen. William S. Rosecrans, fled to Chattanooga after its defeat at Chickamauga (19–20 September 1863), where Confederate Gen. Braxton Bragg immobilized it. Not until the costly battles at Lookout Mountain and Missionary Ridge at the end of November 1863 did Union forces turn a frustrating trap into an unqualified success. *HTIECW,* 133–35, 196; James M. McPherson, *Battle Cry of Freedom: The Civil War Era* (New York: Oxford University Press, 1988), 678–81, 858.

4. The Union attack on James Island took place on 2–9 July 1864. The Fifty-fifth Massachusetts, Thirty-third USCT, and the 103d New York Regiment led the Union assault, with the Fifty-fourth Massachusetts and other units held in reserve. The Fifty-fifth's capture of two cannon comprised the Union assault's only success. Had the attack broken rebel lines, Charleston might have fallen. Instead, Union forces sustained 300 casualties and lost 140 as prisoners. An inquiry concluded that the "chief cause of failure was the

want of dash, energy, and authority on the part of the subordinate officers." Real blame lay with the Union generals who ordered the attack without sufficient planning. Emilio, *A Brave Black Regiment,* 199–216; [Charles B. Fox], *Record of the Service of the Fifty-fifth Regiment of Massachusetts Volunteer Infantry* (Cambridge: John Wilson and Son, 1868), 28–32; Alfred S. Hartwell to Edward W. Kinsley, 9 July 1864, Edward W. Kinsley Papers, MHS; *OR,* ser. 1, pt. 1, 35:36, 40–41.

Index

DONALD YACOVONE is associate editor of publications at the Massachusetts Historical Society. An assistant editor of the *Black Abolitionist Papers,* he is also author of *Samuel Joseph May and the Dilemmas of the Liberal Persuasion, 1797–1871.* He holds a Ph.D. from the Claremont Graduate School.

Books in the Series Blacks in the New World